THANK GOD THEY'RE ON OUR SIDE

THE
UNITED STATES
AND RIGHT-WING
DICTATORSHIPS,
1921–1965

THANK GOD THEY'RE ON OUR SIDE

DAVID F. SCHMITZ

The University of North Carolina Press

Chapel Hill and London

Library of Congress Cataloging-in-Publication Data
Schmitz, David F.
Thank God they're on our side : the United States and
right-wing dictatorships, 1921–1965 / by David F. Schmitz.
    p. cm.
Includes bibliographical references (p.   ) and index.
ISBN 978-0-8078-2472-6 (cloth: alk. paper)
ISBN 978-0-8078-4773-2 (pbk. : alk. paper)
    1. United States — Foreign relations — 20th century.
2. Totalitarianism — History — 20th century. 3. Right-wing
extremists — History — 20th century. I. Title.
E744S396   1999
327.73 — dc21   98-35054
                     CIP

09 08 07   7   6   5   4

TO SARAH

Contents

Acknowledgments

I thank all of the archivists and librarians at the various presidential libraries and archives with whom I worked to complete this book for their professional assistance, aid, and advice. The staff at Penrose Library at Whitman College warrants a special thanks for their assistance.

Once again, Lewis Bateman, Executive Editor at the University of North Carolina Press, proved to be an ideal editor, providing expert advice and support throughout the process. I also thank Ron Maner and Trudie Calvert for their editorial assistance.

Whitman College provided generous travel grants to presidential libraries and archives, Abshire Awards for student research assistance, and a sabbatical leave to complete the writing of the book. The Abshire Awards provided me with three excellent student assistants, Aaron Forsberg, Jeff Holifield, and Rob Neal. Aaron, who is now an excellent young scholar of American economic diplomacy, also read Chapter 5 and provided valuable comments on Eisenhower's policy. Other students who served expertly as research assistants were Doug Elliot, Natalie Fousekis, Stephen McHale, and Kristin Relyea. Chris Lenhart and Alex Rolfe assisted me with the bibliography. Amy Portwood deserves special mention. She provided invaluable last-minute assistance as a research intern during the summer of 1997. Moreover, she read the entire manuscript and made editorial and substantive recommendations that improved the book.

Rich and Carla Scudellari opened their home in Saratoga, California, to me numerous times on research trips to Stanford University and have always willingly listened to me discuss my work. My former students David Wickwire and Melissa Mehlhoff Wickwire were gracious hosts in Austin during my visits to the Johnson Library, as were Mark Burles and Jessica Harris Burles in Washington, D.C., during a visit to the National Archives.

At Whitman, my colleagues provide as rewarding an environment as a teacher and scholar could want. I particularly thank David Deal and Tom Edwards for their consistent encouragement of my work and Fred Breit and Tim Kaufman-Osborn for their friendship, advice, and criticisms. Shannon Callister provided enormous last-minute assistance with the computer that saved me from numerous problems.

I was fortunate to spend the 1997–98 academic year at St. Lawrence University as the Vilas Professor of American History. I thank Dean Thomas Coburn and David Lloyd for their support. My colleague in American history Liz Regosin read the conclusion and provided excellent overall advice. She and Jean Williams made my year in Canton, New York, memorable, and they are the best of friends. I also thank the "inner sanctum" of students at St. Lawrence, particularly Matt Fero, Jonas Hart, Caitlin McAndrews, and Tom O'Neil.

Students in my spring 1995 Seminar in American Foreign Policy were the first to read a draft of the final manuscript. Amy Alger, Audrey Anderson, Thomas Armitage, Christopher Lenhart, Ryan McFarland, Kelly Meagher, Richard Mullen, Robert Neal, Huy Nguyen, Chris Phillippi, Tami Shallbetter, and Robert Simison thoughtfully read the book, listened to me work out my ideas, and stimulated new ideas with their valuable feedback. Danielle Garbe contributed valuable help by proofreading a next-to-final draft.

Many scholars provided generous assistance throughout the writing of this book. David Broscious provided me with a citation for the Truman administration's evolving Cold War policy that I could not locate. Joel Blatt's and Robert McMahon's comments on two different papers I delivered early in this project helped me immensely at that critical stage. Bob McMahon's continued interest in the project, encouragement, and advice helped make this a better book. Michael Hunt read an early draft of the manuscript and provided excellent comments and suggestions for expanding the scope of the work. His encouragement made this a more ambitious project than I originally intended, and for that I am grateful. Carolyn Eisenberg, Tom Knock, and Doug Little all spent much time discussing my ideas with me, providing useful criticisms, ideas, and support along the way. In addition, Tom Knock and Doug Little read an earlier draft of the manuscript. Chris Jespersen, Bill Walker, and Paul Hoornbeek read the final manuscript and provided excellent suggestions for revisions, additions, and deletions. Michael Krenn was generous to a fault. He did double duty, reading some early chapters and then the completed manuscript. In addition, he directed me to some critical documents on the Truman administration. They are all true friends. A special thanks, as always, goes to Lloyd Gardner for his support and advice over the years and on this project. He continues to provide a model for scholarship, professionalism, and friendship.

The support of my family, and especially my mother, is immeasurable. I have not asked them to read, yet, any of this work, but they have all contributed to it in numerous ways. I especially thank my sister Terry and my brother-in-law Kevin for their hospitality every time I visit "home." My wonderful children, Nicole and Kincaid, are a constant source of joy, inspiration, and love. Most of all, I thank Sarah Blattler. She made numerous sacrifices to make this book possible and provided encouragement and support throughout. For all that was and, more important, for all still to come, I dedicate this book to her.

THANK GOD THEY'RE ON OUR SIDE

So we beat on, boats against the current, borne back ceaselessly into the past.

—F. SCOTT FITZGERALD, The Great Gatsby

INTRODUCTION
Our Sons of Bitches

Neither the makers nor the critics of American foreign policy in the twentieth century have resolved the conflict between the desire to encourage democracy abroad and the need to protect American interests. Promoting human rights and democracy demands a toleration of instability and change in regions considered crucial to American business or defense, often leaving no clear choice between conscience and self-interest and making strong, stable right-wing dictators attractive to policymakers. This book examines American policy toward right-wing dictators and why the United States has supported such regimes despite its avowed commitment to liberalism and democracy internationally. Patience with the world is a quality that is in short supply in the White House and State Department, and the demand for order and stability underlies the drive for quick solutions to problems. Although the United States is philosophically dedicated to supporting democracies and human rights abroad, makers of foreign policy have often chosen instead to support right-wing autocracies as a defense against democratic or left-wing movements that appeared either unstable or prone to communist ideology. The often quoted apocryphal statement by Franklin D. Roosevelt concerning Anastasio Somoza García of Nicaragua, "he may be a son-of-a-bitch, but he is our son-of-a-bitch," captures the ambivalence of American attitudes and policy toward right-wing dictatorships.[1]

Beginning in the 1920s, American policymakers developed and institutionalized the logic, rationale, and ideological justifications for U.S. support of right-wing dictatorships that have influenced American policy ever since. Although scholars have examined specific presidents and U.S. policy toward specific nations, no systematic analysis of the origins and development of American foreign policy toward and support of right-wing dictatorships exists.[2] In response to the broad revolutionary challenges of the 1910s, particularly the Bolshevik Revolution in Russia and the Great War, American officials developed a persistent concern with order and stability. The economic and political dislocation that had occurred during the last decade could easily lead to the spread of the revolutions in Mexico, China, and Russia. Policymakers, therefore, came to support authoritarian governments that promised stability, anti-Bolshevism, and trade with the United States. From Warren Harding and Herbert Hoover to Dwight Eisenhower and Lyndon Johnson, similar ideas about the world continued to be echoed as fresh arguments to explain why the "national interest" demanded that the nation side with dictatorial rulers and regimes rather than with incipient democracies such as the Spanish Republic or Guatemala after the 1944 revolution. These latter governments, though theoretically more aligned with the stated principles of the United States, never received the support that might have allowed their experiments in democracy to bear fruit.

This lesser-of-two-evils approach to foreign policy, supported by oversimplified bipolar worldviews and influenced by racism and at times by irrational fears of one political system creating blindness to the shortcomings of another, led the United States to support and align itself with many of the most brutal regimes in the world. John F. Kennedy provided an excellent example of this thinking in 1961 when discussing the Dominican Republic. "There are three possibilities," he said, "in descending order of preference: a decent democratic regime, a continuation of the Trujillo regime or a Castro regime. We ought to aim at the first, but we really can't renounce the second until we are sure that we can avoid the third."[3]

Rationalizations for supporting right-wing dictatorships had to be developed to justify American actions. Much like southerners in the 1830s who were forced by abolitionists' attacks to defend slavery, State Department officials, pressed by nascent twentieth-century nationalism and communism, needed to justify supporting right-wing dictators while placing such a policy in the context of protecting liberalism. In conjunction with an increasingly rigid anti-Bolshevism that became the framework for analyzing and understanding all political unrest, these reasons allowed American policymakers to support right-wing regimes in the defense of freedom.[4] Following the broad definition used by American policymakers, right-wing dictatorships are defined here as any anti-democratic regime that is not socialist or communist. Although this description covers different types of governments, United States officials, as I will demonstrate, grouped all of these regimes together whenever they addressed the question of American policy toward what the Truman administration termed "disreputable governments."

Although the policy of supporting right-wing dictators violated stated American ideals, policymakers believed it would serve the national interest of the United States and promote development in other nations. The policy was not simply a cynical realism or a cold disregard for the peoples of other countries. Based on a paternalistic racism that categorized non–Western European peoples as inferior, vulnerable to radical ideas and solutions, and, therefore, in need of a firm government to maintain order, authoritarian regimes were viewed as the only way nations such as Nicaragua or Iran could undergo economic improvements that would allow the development of more "mature" populations. Although this attitude undermined the avowed rectitude of American leaders, democracy was not seen as a viable option for newly independent nations or many countries in Latin America. Strong dictators, therefore, were believed to be necessary antidotes for the ills of political and social disorder and conduits for modernization. Hence policymakers believed that support for authoritarian regimes protected liberalism internationally by preventing unstable areas from falling prey to Bolshevism while allowing time for nations to develop a middle class and democratic political institutions. Expediency overcame a commitment to the ideology of democracy because the policy appeared to provide immediate benefits. The United States gained friendly if brutal and corrupt allies who provided stability, support for American policies, and a favorable atmosphere for American business.

Before World War I, the problems of unrest and disorder were seen as the manifestations of politically immature people, irresponsible individuals, or bandits. The postwar threats of nationalism and communism, unlike these previous disruptions, served to threaten the entire international system within which the Western nations operated. U.S. support for right-wing dictatorships after World War I, therefore, represented a new development and a departure from both Woodrow Wilson's policy of promoting self-determination and political democracy internationally and earlier support for or tolerance of military and authoritarian regimes, particularly in Latin America. American leaders became preoccupied by international order in the wake of the disruption of World War I, the rise of radical nationalism combined with a decline of Western power, a questioning of traditional authority in nations, and greater demands for self-determination. This emphasis on order came to permeate policy-making in Washington, and the United States found strong-arm rule, the maintenance of stability, anticommunism, and protection of investments sufficient reasons to support nondemocratic rulers. On the other side of the ideological coin, Wilson and his successors would go so far as to adopt a policy of nonrecognition of different communist governments, reversing the traditional policy of support for any government that could maintain itself in power.[5]

This policy was not without its problems and detractors, nor did it remain static. Critics charged that in addition to the questionable morality of supporting right-wing dictators, the policy, though providing short-term benefits, usually led to larger problems for the United States in the long run, mainly long-term instability. Many supporters of the policy realized this danger, yet they saw no other way to protect more pressing U.S. interests. Dictatorships created political polarization, blocked any effective means for reforms, destroyed the center, and created a backlash of anti-American sentiment that opened the door to radical nationalist movements that brought to power the exact forms of governments the United States most opposed and originally sought to prevent. From Cuba to Iran to Nicaragua, and most tragically in Vietnam, the limits of this policy were discovered. Pendulum swings in policy appeared after times of crisis and failures. Most notably, the rise of Adolf Hitler and World War II provided a fundamental challenge to the ideas that supporting right-wing dictators enhanced American interests and brought the debate over support of authoritarian governments to the fore. Roosevelt confronted the problem of Nazi Germany at first by efforts to appease Hitler, a strategy he abandoned when it became clear that Germany was intent on war. The wartime opposition to fascism and the triumph of the Allies made the promotion of democracy and change paramount concerns, and the opposition to authoritarian governments, such as Juan Perón's in Argentina and Francisco Franco's in Spain, became American policy.

Ultimately, however, the logic and policy developed during the inter-war years would be carried over into the post–World War II period. The success of establishing democratic governments in Germany and Japan notwithstanding, the emerging Cold War with the Soviet Union caused the policy pendulum to swing back to the right. Washington came again to prefer "stable" right-wing regimes in the Third World over in-digenous radicalism and dangerously unstable democratic governments. The Truman and, especially, Eisenhower administrations chose to work with authoritarian rulers or the local military in nations such as Greece, Spain, Iran, and Guatemala rather than nationalist leaders or democratic forces that appeared vulnerable to communist takeovers. In addition, af-ter World War II a new variable was added to the justifications for sup-porting dictators that would have tragic results. Authoritarian regimes now provided more than stability and the protection of American inter-ests. They were part of the "free world" and through nation building would be the instruments for the creation of strong and free societies. Equating dictators with freedom blinded American leaders to the con-tradictions and failures of their policy.

In the wake of the 1959 Cuban revolution and Fidel Castro's coming to power, the United States reevaluated its policies toward Latin America and support for such regimes as Fulgencio Batista's and briefly changed its emphasis to the promotion of reform in the Third World as a better insurance against revolution. Kennedy's 1961 Alliance for Progress was the centerpiece of this vision, and the overthrow of Rafael Trujillo in the Dominican Republic signaled change. Yet by the mid-1960s, the pendu-lum had swung back away from reform to the position of supporting dic-tators. With the 1963 overthrow of Ngo Dinh Diem, the crisis in Viet-nam came to dominate the making of American foreign policy. Unrest and potentially unreliable governments were seen as dangerous invita-tions to Soviet advances. The Johnson administration supported the mil-itary overthrow of the government in Brazil in 1964, and in 1965, when authoritarian rulers failed to provide the stability and bulwarks against communism Washington demanded, decided to intervene militarily in the Dominican Republic and Vietnam to ensure the proper order in those nations.

Johnson's military interventions in 1965 mark the appropriate end point of this work for three reasons. First, the American military inter-vention in the Dominican Republic and Vietnam marked the culmina-tion of the policy analyzed here. The Johnson administration's determi-nation to establish stability and order acceptable to Washington, which had provided the basis for working with repressive dictators, forced the president to pursue the policy to its logical conclusion of a U.S. intervention to salvage the discredited regimes. Second, the Vietnam War served to undercut much of that logic and support and brought multiple challenges to the foreign policy consensus of containment and support of right-wing dictators. Support of authoritarian regimes was not completely abandoned by any means, as Richard Nixon's policy in Chile and the continued good relations with leaders such as the Shah of Iran demonstrate. Indeed, many of the arguments about credibility and the need to keep on fighting in Vietnam were determined by the desire to assure such governments of continued American support. But the political climate and debates changed enough during the war to demand an extended examination that does not fall within the scope of this work. Those developments and questions deserve separate treatment. Third, access to the primary sources necessary for a careful examination of the period after 1965 is limited. Only a partial and fragmented portrait of policy is available. The epilogue outlines the debates that emerged during the 1970s concerning American support of right-wing dictatorships and demonstrates the differences between the post–Vietnam War period and the years examined in this book.

1 PEACE MUST FIRST BE RIVETED
The Republican Response to Revolution and Dictatorship

he Republicans came to power in 1921 at a time of great apprehension concerning American relations with the rest of the
world. Economic and political readjustment from the Great
War was their primary concern, and these problems were compounded by the postwar depression and unrest in Eastern Europe and
elsewhere. Casting two large shadows over these problems were the unsure relationship with former allies and enemies caused by the rejection
of the Versailles Treaty and the new challenge posed by Bolshevism in
Russia. Wilson had placed his faith in the League of Nations as the mechanism that would allow peaceful, nonrevolutionary change to occur in
Europe and provide collective security to prevent another war and concomitant revolutions.

Wilson's political program for peace was, however, rejected by Republican leaders. While they shared with Wilson a concern for American
interests in Europe, particularly economic, and an abhorrence and fear
of Bolshevism, Republican officials such as Secretary of State Charles
Evans Hughes had little faith in the League. He did not believe that it
could deter a great power from aggression and held steadfastly to the position that the only means to peace was through stability and economic

prosperity. This would allow the powers to cooperate with each other and recognize their common goals. For Hughes, this would mean the codification of shared principles into international law to serve as a guide for the conduct of nations.[1] Of primary importance was the economic stabilization of Europe. This, in turn, placed a premium on the return of political order.[2]

But without the active involvement of the United States in the League of Nations and considering the political problems of Europe, how could there be a guarantee of political stability and, therefore, gradual change? The policy rested on the equation that economic recovery would end social unrest, bring American trade and credits, and halt the threat of revolution. Seeking a way out of this dilemma led Hughes to reverse the Wilsonian commitment to supporting self-determination and democracy internationally. Order and stability had to be the primary considerations. Republican policymakers backed those groups which they thought could ensure the necessary requirements for American support—political stability, anti-Bolshevism, and receptiveness to increased trade and friendly relations with the United States—and came to favor and actively support "stable" right-wing regimes over what they perceived to be unstable democratic or radically nationalist governments.

Economic stability was also considered to be vital for American prosperity as well as a means to avoid unrest and contain revolution. That the United States was now, for the first time, a creditor nation as well as the world's leading industrial producer made the problems of Europe and the United States directly interrelated. As Hughes stated in 1921, "The prosperity of the United States largely depends upon the economic settlements which may be made in Europe."[3] He returned to the same point the next year in a major foreign policy address. Discussing European economic difficulties Hughes argued: "The economic conditions in Europe give us the greatest concern. . . . It is idle to say that we are not interested in these problems, for we are deeply interested from an economic standpoint, as our credits and markets are involved, and from a humanitarian standpoint. . . . We cannot dispose of these problems by calling them European, for they are world problems and we cannot escape the injurious consequences of a failure to settle them."[4]

Economic recovery would, in theory, guarantee political stability and overcome the rivalries among nations. Political stability was, however, necessary for economic recovery to begin. As Hughes noted in 1922, he desired to aid "in the re-establishment of stable conditions and thus . . . contribut[e] to the welfare of other peoples, upon which our own prosperity must ultimately depend."[5] Republican efforts to escape this Catch-22 led them to favor right-wing dictatorships. While President Warren G. Harding set the tone for the New Era diplomacy through his views on reconstruction and radicalism, Hughes had the major responsibility for developing, formulating, defining, and, in conjunction with Secretary of Commerce Herbert Hoover, implementing American policy during the 1920s.

American officials first articulated their emerging rationale for supporting right-wing dictatorships in response to the post–World War I events in Italy. American support of Benito Mussolini was based on a view of events in Italy that served American purposes and interests. Two ideas were central to this view: that there was a threat of Bolshevism in Italy and that Italy was not prepared for democratic government. This unpreparedness and inability at self-government created the instability that bred Bolshevism. These beliefs served to legitimize U.S. support of Mussolini in the name of defending liberalism. To justify this new perspective, State Department officials reclassified Italy and ignored Mussolini's destruction of a liberal constitutional government. A nation that had been an ally during the war was now treated as if it were an ungovernable developing nation in need of a firm hand to guide it.

Thus American policymakers welcomed the coming to power of fascism in Italy. They saw the fascists as strong anti-Bolsheviks and ignored the antidemocratic nature of the regime. The fascists, officials believed, would bring the stability that would prevent Bolshevism and that was a precondition for economic recovery. This position led American policymakers to embrace Mussolini and actively support the fascist government in Rome. Italian fascism was perceived as meeting all the qualifications for U.S. support: promise of political stability, anti-Bolshevism, and increased trade with the United States.

Choosing Autocracy

Woodrow Wilson confronted the greatest revolutionary challenges liberalism had faced to date. Wilson had long distrusted radicalism and revolution. In 1904, for example, he had labeled the Populists as dangerous "radicals" who were "contemptuous alike of principle and experience." The United States, he declared, "will tolerate no party of discontent or radical experiment."[6] When Wilson became president in 1913, there had grown, according to Secretary of the Navy Josephus Daniels, a "feeling in some countries that a Democratic victory would be hailed by those seeking to foment revolution as an encouragement." A two-hour-long cabinet meeting was held on 11 March 1913 to discuss the "importance of making known this country's attitude as encouraging stable government." The next day Wilson issued a general message to all of Latin America which stressed the importance of order and the rule of law.[7]

In his message to America's neighbors, Wilson wrote that "cooperation is possible only when supported at every turn by the orderly processes of just government based upon law, not upon arbitrary or irregular force." Striking the same theme in a more ominous tone, Wilson stated that "there can be no freedom without order" and that the United States "can have no sympathy with those who seek to seize the power of government to advance their own personal interests. . . . We shall prefer those who act in the interest of peace and honor, who protect private rights and respect the restraints of constitutional provisions." The president concluded by noting that "from these principles may be read so much of the future policy of this Government."[8] The signs that Wilson saw revolutions as unnecessary and wasteful and that he would intervene in other nations in the hemisphere were unmistakable. Even with Wilson, who gave much thought to the problems in Mexico and Russia and demonstrated an understanding of change, a tendency to ignore local conditions that gave rise to revolutions became inherent in the American response.

In his efforts to "teach the South American Republics to elect good men," Wilson dispatched American troops to Mexico, Haiti, Cuba, and the Dominican Republic. Secretary of State Robert Lansing elaborated on the administration's concern with revolution in a November 1915 memorandum to the president. Fearing the growing influence of Europeans in fomenting revolution, Lansing wrote that "stability and honesty in government depend upon sufficient force to resist revolution and on sufficient control over the revenues and over the development of the resources to prevent official graft." Preventing the "small republics of America" from continuing to fall prey to revolutions "requires that the United States should intervene and aid in the establishment and maintenance of a stable and honest government." Such intervention, which conflicted with ideals of equality among states, was necessary to protect the national interest. "The integrity of other American nations," Lansing declared, "is an incident, not an end."[9]

Justifying his intervention in Mexico, Wilson believed that he was protecting the Mexicans from outside interference and the special interests of imperial nations that had originally caused the Mexican Revolution. As Lloyd Gardner has noted, what Mexico needed, Wilson thought, "was an *American* revolution, if it was to break free from foreign economic dominion, avoid a violent lurching back and forth between reaction and anarchy, and, most important, not set the wrong precedent as the world moved out from under the shadow of the dying imperial order."[10] Mexico could not do this unaided, and Wilson was determined to guide it. Mexico would have to learn to "take help when help is needed."[11] As Wilson explained in a 1918 address to Mexican newspaper editors, "When we sent troops into Mexico, our sincere desire was nothing else than to assist you to get rid of a man who was making the settlement of your affairs for the time being impossible."[12] Wilson believed that though the European nations might be ready for self-government, the inequality of peoples did not make this a universal principle.

The Bolshevik Revolution in Russia made Wilson "sweat blood" and provided the greatest challenge to his vision of liberalism.[13] Wilson led the United States into World War I to destroy autocratic rule and militarism in Europe. He hoped that by promoting liberal, democratic forces in Europe, he could, in conjunction with the guarantees of the League of Nations for collective security, solve the dual problem of war and revolution. The Bolshevik Revolution shifted the president's attention from his battle to eliminate autarky to the concern with revolution and containing Bolshevism.

The dilemma Wilson faced, of maintaining order to prevent revolution without relying on the old order in Europe, was one that he could not resolve. Still, Wilson resisted as best he could so that the Great War would not have been fought in vain and that the conditions that bred revolutionary upheaval would be eliminated. As Wilson said of World War I while in Europe in early 1919, "This has indeed been a people's war. It has been waged against absolutism and militarism, and these enemies of liberty must from this time forth be shut out from the possibility of working their cruel will upon mankind." During the war he told his advisers that "the conservatives do not realize what forces are loose in the world at the present time. Liberalism is the only thing that can save civilization from chaos—from a flood of ultra-radicalism that will swamp the world."[14]

Initially, Wilson thought the Bolshevik regime would collapse on its own because it was the antithesis of civilization. When it survived its first weeks and took Russia out of the war, Wilson turned to nonrecognition and containment. If it could not expand, the president was sure that Bolshevism would burn itself out and a more moderate political force would emerge from the chaos of Russia. The Allies and Secretary of State Robert Lansing wanted to help accelerate that process and advocated a direct military intervention in Russia. Lansing wrote Wilson that "nothing is to be gained by inaction, that it is simply playing into the Bolsheviki's hands." He believed that for the immediate future the only "hope for a stable Russian Government lies . . . in a military dictatorship backed by loyal disciplined troops."[15]

Debate continues concerning Wilson's decision to send troops to Russia in July 1918. Wilson often stated his belief that intervention would only add to the turmoil in Russia "rather than cure it" and justified his action as assisting the war effort against Germany and aiding the Czech Legion. He also noted that such action would strengthen the opposition forces in Russia to fight the Bolsheviks and allow the Czechs to "consolidate their forces and get into successful cooperation with their Slavic kinsmen and to steady any efforts at self-government." The intervention had both anti-German and anti-Bolshevik objectives. Indirect as it may have been, the United States had intervened in Russia to contain the Bolshevik fire and possibly extinguish it.[16]

The president did, however, reject any expansion of the Allied military efforts. He compared military interventions to check revolutions to using a broom to sweep back the tide. In March 1919, for example, he told the other Allied leaders that the West should "let the Russians stew in their own juice until circumstances have made them wiser, and let us confine our efforts to keeping Bolshevism out of the rest of Europe." Wilson held steadfast to his belief that if left to themselves free of outside interference, moderate Russians would topple the Bolshevik regime. "I do not fear Bolshevism," Wilson stated in 1920, "but it must be resisted. Bolshevism is a mistake and must be resisted as all mistakes must be resisted. If left alone, it will destroy itself. It cannot survive because it is wrong."[17]

Secretary of State Bainbridge Colby made much the same point when he outlined the official policy of the United States toward the Bolshevik regime on 10 August 1920, a policy that would remain in place until 1933. Colby wrote that American policy was based on the premise that the "present rulers of Russia do not rule by the will or the consent of any considerable portion of the Russian people." Moreover, the "existing regime in Russia is based upon the negation of every principle of honor and good faith, and every usage and convention, underlying the whole structure of international law." Disclaiming that U.S. nonrecognition had anything "to do with any particular political or social structure which the Russian people themselves may see fit to embrace," Colby asserted that the "United States maintains unimpaired its faith in the Russian people. . . . That they will overthrow the existing anarchy, suffering and destitution we do not entertain the slightest doubt."[18]

Wilson, trying to balance peacemaking and encouraging liberalism in Europe while responding to V. I. Lenin, began to compare autocratic rule favorably to Bolshevism. Campaigning for the ratification of the Versailles Treaty, Wilson spoke of the danger of postwar disorder and of power passing from the old order, one group of "old and distinguished and skillful" autocrats to new "amateur and cruel" dictators as a result of continued unrest.[19] Order was needed to halt the progress of Bolshevik influence.

The revolution in Russia led to the establishment of "a closer monopoly of power in Petrograd and Moscow than there ever was in Berlin, and the thing that is intolerable is not that the Russian people are having their way but that another group of men more cruel than the Czar himself is controlling the destinies of that great people." The mere presence of this government, which rules by "terror," and the "poison of disorder, the poison of revolt, the poison of chaos" it spreads, must be checked. Appealing to the rising domestic fears of radicalism, Wilson proclaimed that the Bolshevik Revolution meant "government by terror, government by force, not government by vote." It was, therefore, the "negation of everything that is American."[20] By making such a comparison, Wilson opened a wedge for criticism of his own policy.

Republican leaders eagerly stepped into this opening. The Red Scare, too long seen as merely a sad closing to World War I or a prelude to McCarthyism, had an immediate impact on the politics of the 1920s as the fear of revolution and radical thought became a fixture in American thinking. Hughes began to develop his opposition to Wilson's position as early as 1919. He argued that the greatest danger in the postwar world was "not in the menace of force employed to further imperial designs, but in the disorder due to the breakup and the removal of traditional restraints and the tendency toward revolution within States."[21] Though Germany had been defeated, revolutions in Russia, Bavaria, and Hungary threatened American interests. Hughes feared that there "has never been a time so pregnant with opportunities for future discord." He blamed Wilson for this development. "New territorial adjustments, the establishment of new States and new international agreements, although intended to secure peace, will undoubtedly carry with them the seeds of dissension." "It should be recognized," Hughes continued, "that the occasions for strife have not been removed as a result of the war, but may have been multiplied." Summarizing his criticism and worries, Hughes stated that "again, governments heretofore stable have been overthrown, and vast populations in Russia and in what were formerly the Central Powers are unrepresented by governments with which other nations can deal with complete assurance."[22]

Protection against future war and unrest could come only from favorable "economic conditions which are an assurance that for a considerable time at least we shall not have a recurrence of world strife."[23] Again criticizing Wilson, Hughes stated in 1920 that "it was a highly dangerous role for an American President virtually to appeal to foreign peoples against their Governments. It was still more dangerous to excite hopes which could not be satisfied."[24] The decline of old forms of authority and demands for self-determination were the new and more difficult problems that had to be faced. Hughes believed that "it is self-determination which makes for wars and places obstacles in the way of plans for keeping the peace."[25]

For order to be restored, Hughes believed, the Western European states and the United States needed to cooperate actively against the menace of Bolshevism. The codification of international law, which Hughes believed to be possible because of the shared logic and agreement on "the essentials of public justice" among the powers, would "give formal definiteness to accepted principles."[26] Progress, therefore, depended on rational change and patience. "This is the hardest lesson for democracy to learn," according to Hughes. "It does not mean weakness or paltering; it simply means a desire to bring about good order by orderly processes; it means recognition of our mutual dependence." This position was his reason for opposition to revolution. Hughes believed that "no remedy is possible which does not have its roots in general sentiment." Believing revolutions to be the acts of minority extremists, Hughes thought lasting reforms were possible only with the adoption of the "virtues of sobriety, industry, thrift and moderation, upon the realization of our mutual dependence, and upon the gradual supplanting of motives of mere self-interest by those inspired by the appeals of brotherhood."[27] As a progressive Republican, Hughes "was convinced that order was fundamental to progress."[28]

Applying these views in practice, Hughes continued the nonrecognition policy toward the Soviet Union. Echoing Theodore Roosevelt's famous corollary to the Monroe Doctrine, he argued that the "most important principle to be maintained at this time with respect to international relations is that no State is entitled to a place within the family of nations if it destroys the foundation of honorable intercourse by resort to confiscation and repudiation." In addition, a nation must "maintain an adequate system of government through which valid rights and valid engagements are recognized and enforced."[29]

The containment of the Soviet Union was crucial in Hughes's view. European nations and the United States had to cooperate to bring about stability and prevent the spread of Bolshevism. Hughes considered Mexico an obvious example of a nation to which Bolshevism could spread. Mexico was, Hughes wrote Harding, watching the Soviet Union and would be willing to follow the Soviet example if it was successful.[30] Reflecting back in 1927 on his time in office, Hughes observed that "it is easy to point to places of chronic unrest among the smaller nations." But as long as the great powers maintained peace among themselves, they could isolate the problems.[31]

President Harding and Secretary of Commerce Hoover both agreed with the secretary of state that the promotion of stability and the combating of revolution were primary concerns for American foreign policy making. Harding saw Bolshevism and the danger of revolution as the main threats to the postwar world. In addition, like Hughes, the president believed that political and economic stability were vital to American prosperity and did not see the old political order in Europe or right-wing dictatorships as a threat to peace or the interests of the United States.

As a senator from Ohio, Harding was outspoken in his opposition to Wilson's war aims. In voting for war in April 1917, Harding provided the caveat that he was "not voting for war in the name of democracy" because it was "none of our business what type of government any nation on this earth may choose to have." Harding would, of course, change this position after the Bolshevik Revolution in Russia. In July, he worried that Wilson was being "encouraged in a pitiable endeavor to instigate revolt against governmental authority." In an interview with the *New York Times*, Harding stated that the United States needed "a supreme dictator" if it was to win the war. When asked if this meant the complete abandonment of democracy, Harding responded: "Call it what you will, it is the only way to win the war. However, it means that we abandon nothing except the incapacity of all legislative bodies in war time." In the most illuminating comment in the interview, Harding defended such measures as necessary for saving democracy. "We would put on autocracy as a garment only for the period of the war." Later he again noted, "We have a republic to save. We can't do it with the processes of a republic."[32]

Harding's profoundly undemocratic attitudes shaped his view of the postwar world and Wilson's efforts at peace. After the war, Harding argued that the Wilson administration had "preached the gospel of revolution in the central Empires of Europe" and that the "menace of Bolshevism" threatening Europe "owes a very large part . . . to the policies and utterances of the Chief Executive of the United States." Wilson's war for democracy was "a lie," Harding declared. He found Wilson "so eager to make war on constituted authority that we proclaimed revolution as one of the greatest essentials to bringing about peace and tranquility in the world." Harding completely ignored the actions and desires of the people of Europe and claimed that Wilson had "lighted a fire there that is difficult to put out now." Given the choice between "hateful autocracy" or "destroying anarchy," Harding declared, "I choose autocracy." Bolshevism, he believed, had to be destroyed wherever it was found. The reestablishment of constituted traditional authority, what Harding termed a "return to normalcy," must be American policy. "Peace must first be riveted and the Bolshevist beast slain," Harding told the Senate on 15 January 1919, if Western society were to survive. "Bolshevism is a menace that must be destroyed, lest it destroy."[33]

Hoover's views complemented those of the president and secretary of state. He too stressed cooperation among the great powers and political and economic stabilization along with an expansion of American trade. The restoration of order in Europe was essential for both American prosperity and the containment of Bolshevism.[34] As a progressive and an engineer, Hoover had a low tolerance for politics and its imprecision. Hoover was frustrated after the war by political squabbling and politicians who allowed emotions and special interests to interfere with an observance of the facts and solutions based on them.[35]

Hoover was acutely aware of the instability in Europe from 1918 to 1920 and the danger of revolution, and he worked hard to isolate the Bolshevik menace in Russia. He described "the whole of American policies" in postwar Europe as being developed "to prevent Europe from going Bolshevik."[36] On recognition of the Soviet Union and Bolshevism, Hoover wrote President Wilson in March 1919 that "we cannot even remotely recognize this murderous tyranny without stimulating actionist radicalism in every country in Europe and without transgressing on every National ideal of our own." He argued that "the Bolsheviki most certainly represent a minority in every country where they are in control." He continued by comparing them with dictatorships in the past: "As a tyranny, the Bolshevik has resorted to terror, bloodshed and murder to a degree long since abandoned even amongst reactionary tyrannies."[37]

As head of the American Relief Administration (ARA) after World War I, Hoover was deeply involved in the quest to establish the right type of order and stability in postwar Europe. Hoover's ARA fought both hunger and revolution in Eastern Europe.[38] The case of Hungary is instructive on the development of Hoover's ideas on revolution and dictatorships and how he shifted his position in response to his inability to control the situation. Moreover, Hoover became less concerned with the problems of autocracy while remaining fixated on the danger of revolution and Bolshevism.

Hoover, writing about revolution in Europe, noted that "it simply cannot be denied that this swinging of the social pendulum from the tyranny of the extreme right to the tyranny of the extreme left is based on a foundation of real social grievance." But "if former revolutions in ignorant masses are any guide, the pendulum will yet swing back to some moderate position when bitter experience has taught the economic and social follies of present obsessions." Initially, therefore, Hoover argued against military intervention to topple Bela Kun's Bolshevik regime in Hungary. Such an action would involve the United States in "years of police duty, and . . . make us party to re-establish[ing] the reactionary classes in their economic domination over the lower classes."[39] This was not only unpopular but expensive and a strategic nightmare, and as the intervention in Russia was demonstrating, it allowed the radicals to adopt the nationalist banner. It was necessary, Hoover believed, to use food relief and moral force to allow the pendulum to swing back. As Hoover wrote to Wilson in April 1919, "If the disturbing elements . . . consider that they will be as secure as to food supplies after disturbance [communist revolutions] as before, our present potentiality to maintain the status quo of order is lost."[40] But once the blockade of food failed to bring down Kun's government, Hoover began to advocate his removal by force. In August, Bela Kun fled Hungary and a right-wing dictatorship was established which attacked both liberals and radicals alike. Although Hoover expressed concern that the "Bolsheviks were . . . claiming that the allies were . . . re-establish[ing] a reactionary government" in Hungary, no actions were taken against the new regime and ARA aid was delivered.[41]

Economic organization was for Hoover the key to civilization, and he believed the system in the United States was the most efficient and developed form. "We must all agree," Hoover wrote Wilson in a lengthy letter concerning the danger of Bolshevism, "that our processes of production and distribution, the outgrowth of a hundred generations, in the stimulation of individual initiative, the large equality of opportunity and infinite development of mind and body, while not perfect, come about as near perfection as is possible." In comparison, "the Bolshevik's land of illusion is that he can perfect these human qualities by destroying the basic processes of production and distribution instead of devoting himself to securing a better application of the collective surplus."[42] Economic systems, he was suggesting, determine the political system. The development of the free market was, therefore, much more important than the type of government a nation had, for free markets would lead to democratic institutions.

The danger of Bolshevism in the United States that was fueling the Red Scare at home did not concern Hoover. Because of its economic advances, he did not think Bolshevism could infect the United States. Bolshevik propaganda, he asserted, found fertile soil only where order had been destroyed by the war and "where the gulf between the middle classes and the lower classes is large, and where the lower classes have been kept in ignorance and distress." The solution, according to Hoover, was in a return to order and stability, not the promotion of democracy. In a criticism of Wilson, Hoover wrote that the "American people cannot say that we are going to insist that any given population must work out its internal social problems according to our particular conception of democracy." Instead, we had to realize that "in the swing of the social pendulum from the extreme left back toward the right, it will find the point of stabilization based on *racial instincts* that could never be established by outside interference."[43]

When Hoover returned from Europe, he expressed his opposition to revolutions in dramatic words. In his widely read book *American Individualism*, first published in 1922, Hoover discussed the problem of revolution that beset the world. He turned around Thomas Jefferson's well-known analogy of revolutions to summer thunderstorms that were periodically necessary to clear the stagnant air of political tyranny. Jefferson's construction made revolutions necessary and positive events. To Hoover this was very dangerous thinking. He characterized modern revolutions as "no summer thunderstorm clearing the atmosphere. In modern society it is a tornado leaving in its path the destroyed homes of millions with their dead women and children."[44] *American Individualism* was Hoover's reaffirmation of the values and political structure which he believed had brought the United States greatness, as well as his solution for the revolutions that were threatening the world.

The American people had witnessed "in the last eight years the spread of revolution over one-third of the world." Thus Hoover was prompted to examine and reassert the social philosophy of individualism as he understood it. With repeated references to the "ghastly failure of Russia," Hoover argued that only economic prosperity could bring order and was a necessary precondition for the development of political freedoms. Moreover, prosperity was possible only through a system that respected the individual and the "primary self-interest impulse of the individual to production." Returning to his comparisons with the Soviet Union, Hoover, again playing off of Jefferson's depiction of revolutions, particularly his notion that the Tree of Liberty needs to be nourished by the blood of tyrants, sought to destroy any romantic image of revolution. "Socialism in a nationwide application," Hoover wrote, "has now proved itself with rivers of blood and inconceivable misery to be an economic and spiritual fallacy and has wrecked itself finally upon the rocks of destroyed production and moral degeneracy." In conclusion, he sadly noted that "I believe it to have been necessary for the world to have had this demonstration." For Hoover it proved that there was only one road to prosperity.[45]

"We have long since realized," Hoover concluded, "that the basis of an advancing civilization must be a high and growing standard of living." As for politics, "democracy is merely a mechanism which individualism invented as a device that would carry on the necessary political work of its social organization. Democracy arises out of individualism and prospers through it alone." It is no wonder that Hoover could so confidently assert that the "failures and unsolved problems of economic and social life can be corrected; they can be solved within our social theme and *under no other system*."[46]

Racial Hierarchy

Along with the demand for stability and anti-Bolshevism, questions of race continued to play a large role in the considerations of the makers of American foreign policy after World War I. Racism has been a central issue in the United States since its colonial days. By the middle of the nineteenth century, white Americans' views on race had been codified into "scientific" explanations of an identifiable hierarchy of races. Anglo-Saxons saw themselves as the superior race, marked by the characteristics of industry, high intelligence, commitment to morals and democratic government, and high material achievements. Rising nationalism, the Mexican-American War, increasing sectional tensions, and the new "scientific" studies combined to produce this dogmatic racism of Anglo-Saxon dominance.[47] All other nationalities and races were ranked in descending order based mainly on the color of their skin. Other Western Europeans came first, followed by Latin Europeans and Slavs, Orientals, and blacks.[48]

The widespread appeal of Social Darwinism in the second half of the century, in conjunction with the advances in industrialization and contact with new immigrant groups from Southern and Eastern Europe, served to reinforce the quasi-scientific basis of such beliefs. In foreign policy, as Michael Hunt states, the "idea of racial hierarchy proved particularly attractive because it offered a ready and useful conceptual handle on the world. It was reassuringly hardy and stable in a changing world. Rather than having to spend long hours trying . . . to puzzle out the subtle patterns of other cultures, the elite interested in policy had at hand in the hierarchy of race a key to reducing other peoples and nations to readily comprehensible and familiar terms."[49] In conducting foreign policy, American officials found what they considered to be many examples to support their views. By the 1890s Anglo-Saxonism and white supremacy over the rest of the people of the world were the dominant rationales for American imperialism.[50] The Spanish-American War brought many indications of the impact of race on American policy.

In defending his Philippine policy, President William McKinley argued that it was the United States's duty to save the Filipinos "from savage indolence and habits" and "set them on the pathway of the world's best civilization."[51] He did not believe that the "little brown men" were capable of self-government or would defy the benevolence of the United States.[52] The Schurman Commission, sent to the Philippines by McKinley to gain Filipino approval of U.S. sovereignty over the archipelago, found that the "Philippine people were not capable of independent self-government."[53] The president and Secretary of War Elihu Root likened Filipinos to children who needed protection and guidance. Leaving the islands to themselves would mean anarchy and the "worst evils of semi-civilized misgovernment."[54]

Theodore Roosevelt was the most outspoken political leader to assert Anglo-Saxon superiority and the inferiority of other peoples. Responding to Rudyard Kipling's poem on the Philippines, "White Man's Burden," Roosevelt wrote his good friend Henry Cabot Lodge that it "was very poor poetry but made good sense from the expansion point of view." Roosevelt dismissed political and cultural explanations of differences between nations. He argued, for example, that blacks had "been kept down by lack of intellectual development as by anything else."[55] Roosevelt believed that through a period of long historical development, Anglo-Saxons had developed to a more advanced state than any other group. This allowed, indeed demanded, that they direct the development of others. "Our people are now successfully governing themselves," Roosevelt told Congress in his 1901 State of the Union Message, "because for more than a thousand years they have been slowly fitting themselves . . . toward this end. What has taken us thirty generations to achieve, we cannot expect to see another race accomplish out of hand." Referring specifically to the Philippines, Roosevelt stressed both the size of the problem and the duty of the United States. The people there were starting "very far behind the point which our ancestors had reached even thirty generations ago. In dealing with the Philippine people we must show both patience and strength. . . . We hope to do for them what has never before been done for any people of the tropics—to make them fit for self-government after the fashion of the really free nations."[56]

That this undertaking was part of the historical mission of the United States was self-evident to the president. While the United States was engaged in crushing the Filipino insurgents led by Emilio Aguinaldo, Roosevelt declared that "history may safely be challenged to show a single instance in which a masterful race such as ours, having been forced by the exigencies of war to take possession of an alien land, has behaved to its inhabitants with the disinterested zeal for their progress that our people have shown in the Philippines." Like President McKinley, Roosevelt found it impossible to believe that the Filipinos (or Latin Americans) really objected to the rule and good intentions of the United States. The resistance was obviously led by ignorant men who sought only to promote themselves and their own power. "To leave the islands at this time," Roosevelt told his critics, "would mean that they would fall into a welter of murderous anarchy. Such desertion of duty on our part would be a crime against humanity."[57]

Roosevelt alternated between visions of people who lived outside the Anglo-Saxon world as being savages and bandits, often equating them with the American Indians who had to be moved out of the way for the winning of the West, and children who needed guidance. During his efforts to obtain canal rights on the Panama isthmus, Roosevelt called the leaders of Colombia bandits, "foolish and homicidal corruptionists," and a "lot of jack rabbits" who should not "be allowed to bar one of the future highways of civilization."[58] He agreed with his friend Whitelaw Reid that "if men will not govern themselves with respect for civilization . . . then when they get in the way, they must be governed."[59] Anglo-Saxon expansion over "backward" and "inferior" people was inevitable. As he wrote in his popular history of the United States, *The Winning of the West*, "During the past three centuries, the spread of the English-speaking peoples over the world's waste spaces has been not only the most striking feature in the world's history, but also the event of all others most far-reaching in its effects and importance."[60]

If few American politicians put matters as dramatically as the old Rough Rider, they nonetheless held to many of the same convictions and impulses. Woodrow Wilson, for example, argued in 1901 that to expect Anglo-Saxon behavior from or to impose democratic institutions upon inferior people would be a "curse" because they were still in the "childhood of their political growth." They needed British and American guidance and Anglo-Saxon character.[61] The next year Wilson wrote that the Filipinos "must obey as those who are in tutelage" because they were "children." It would, therefore, be wrong to grant such people self-government without their first having learned the "discipline of law."[62]

Similar attitudes shaped U.S. policy in dealings with Cuba. The initial American reaction to Cuba's revolt was a hope that Spain could restore order. When Madrid proved incapable, the fear of continued instability in Cuba brought about American intervention. As President McKinley's war message to Congress made clear, however, the United States was not entering the war as a co-belligerent of the Cuban rebels. McKinley called for military action that "involved 'hostile constraints' upon both contending parties" in order to "put an end to the barbarities, bloodshed, starvation and horrible miseries" which could not be ended by either the Spanish or the Cubans. It was up to the United States to establish "a stable government, capable of maintaining order and observing its international obligations."[63]

After the war it was inconceivable to American leaders that Cuba could be granted complete independence. General Leonard Wood, head of the American forces in Cuba, expressed the widespread American dislike of Cubans when he noted that the Cuban army was "made up very considerably of black people, only partially civilized."[64] Blocked from annexing Cuba by the Teller Amendment, the McKinley administration sought other means for resolving the question. Secretary of War Root came up with the mechanism of making Cuba a protectorate through the Platt Amendment, which granted the United States the right to intervene in Cuba to maintain order and protect American interests. Rubin F. Weston has noted that the "relationship between the Cubans and the United States was similar to that of the Southern Negroes and the Southern states."[65]

Maintaining order in the Caribbean and Central America was becoming an ever-growing concern of Roosevelt and other American officials. President Roosevelt worried constantly about unrest to the south and sought different means to preserve civilized order through the assertion of police powers over what he once called "these wretched republics."[66] In 1902 Roosevelt informed the Congress that he believed that "more and more the increasing interdependence and complexity of international political and economic relations render it incumbent on all civilized and orderly powers to insist on the proper policing of the world."[67] The United States beat was to be the Western Hemisphere.

On 6 December 1904, Roosevelt provided his rationale for why revolutions were dangerous and justification for American intervention in Latin America. The Roosevelt Corollary to the Monroe Doctrine proclaimed:

> If a nation shows that it knows how to act with reasonable efficiency and decency in social and political matters, if it keeps order and pays its obligations, it need fear no interference from the United States. Chronic wrongdoing, or an impotence which results in a general loosening of the ties of civilized society, may in America, as elsewhere, ultimately require intervention by some civilized nation, and in the Western Hemisphere the adherence of the United States to the Monroe Doctrine may force the United States, however reluctantly, in flagrant cases of such wrongdoing or impotence, to the exercise of an international police power.[68]

Soon after Roosevelt wrote these words, American troops were dispatched to Cuba, Nicaragua, Haiti, the Dominican Republic, and Honduras, and Washington established American financial protectorates in Haiti, Nicaragua, the Dominican Republic, and Cuba. In one of his frequent intemperate moments, this time caused by unrest in Cuba in 1906, Roosevelt blurted out that he was "so angry with that infernal little Cuban republic that I would like to wipe its people off the face of the earth." All he expected of the Cubans, he explained, was that they "behave themselves."[69] Henry Cabot Lodge noted that the "general feeling is that [the Cubans] ought to be taken by the neck and shaken until they behave themselves."[70]

American soldiers in Haiti referred to their opponents in the guerrilla war, the *cacos*, as "bad niggers as we would call them at home." General Smedley Darlington Butler, head of American occupation forces in Nicaragua and then Haiti, characterized the *caco* leaders as "shaved apes, absolutely no intelligence whatsoever, just plain low nigger."[71] Assistant Secretary of State William Phillips summarized the reason for American intervention as stemming from the "complete incompetence" of the Haitians and the "failure of an inferior people to maintain the degree of civilization left them by the French, or to develop any capacity of self government entitling them to international respect and confidence."[72]

In 1908, George W. Crichfield published a popular account on Latin America titled *American Supremacy: The Rise and Progress of the Latin American Republics and Their Relations to the United States under the Monroe Doctrine*, which contained all of the held stereotypes of Latin Americans. It described the population as "usually lazy, insolent, and good-for-nothing" mestizos who had mixed "an infusion of Negro blood into this peon mixture" that "generally brings about a product which is wholly and irretrievably bad." As a rule, they could not be trusted and had to be cared for and led. "A Latin American may profess undying affection for a person, but he may be at the same time planning literally to cut his throat. . . . Bad faith is universal."[73]

The American terms of affection for peasants in Haiti and elsewhere—"docile, happy, idle, irresponsible, kindly, shiftless, pleasure-loving, trustworthy"—echoed the patronizing views used to describe a black who "knew how to keep his loyal, unthreatening place according to white racial norms imported from the United States."[74] American leaders commonly referred to the southern states and race relations in the United States, often drawing a parallel with the period of Reconstruction. For their understanding of this period, officials relied on the work of the so-called Dunning school of Reconstruction history which dominated historical writing during the first half of the twentieth century. Reconstruction was portrayed as the "nadir of national disgrace," an uncivilized experiment in black rule that "pandered to the ignorant negroes." Newly enfranchised freedmen, the interpretation read, in conjunction with corrupt whites and the Radical Republicans in Congress, set out to humiliate the South. The state governments that they established were corrupt and incompetent and led to bankruptcy, chaos, and destruction. Only when decent white southerners organized to drive these governments out of power and restored dignity to the region was the South saved from the disastrous, misplaced idealism of the radical reformers.[75]

James Ford Rhodes, summarizing the prevailing view of the time, wrote that "no large policy in our country has ever been so conspicuous a failure as that of forcing universal negro suffrage upon the South."[76] This interpretation helped to legitimize Jim Crow laws and the prevailing segregation and discrimination against blacks in all parts of the nation.[77] John Burgess directly addressed the relationship between foreign policy and Reconstruction in his 1902 study *Reconstruction and the Constitution*. "Now that the United States has embarked on imperial enterprises," he wrote, "the North is learning every day by valuable experiences that there are vast differences in political capacity between the races, and that it is the white man's mission, his duty . . . to hold the reins of political power in his own hands for the civilization of the world." Burgess concluded that the "Republican party, in its work of imposing the sovereignty of the United States upon eight millions of Asiatics, has changed its views in regard to the political relations of races and has at last virtually accepted the ideas of the South upon that subject."[78]

Theodore Roosevelt blended this historical view of blacks and other "inferior" races with policymaking. Speaking again on the Philippines in 1904, Roosevelt argued that "at present they [Filipinos] are utterly incapable of existing in independence . . . or of building up a civilization of their own." Roosevelt's view reached beyond mere colonial service as befitted a founder of a liberal empire. The United States would instruct the Filipinos to enable them to "rise higher and higher in the scale of civilization and of capacity for self-government."[79] What Roosevelt proposed as the means to achieve this amounted to an expansion of Booker T. Washington's Atlanta Compromise for the Asian archipelago and Latin American nations.

Roosevelt made Washington an informal adviser and created a stir by having him to dinner at the White House. He embraced Washington's idea of black withdrawal from political affairs and concentration on self-improvement as a solution to the problems of race. This meant the voluntary acceptance of an inferior place for the present until African Americans could demonstrate to white America their value and right to equality. The president, and other policymakers who followed him, believed that a similar submissive attitude by "inferior people" to U.S. leadership would prove the most beneficial to both them and the United

States. The ability for self-government was not "yet in sight, and it may be indefinitely postponed if our people are foolish enough to turn the attention of the Filipinos away from the problems of achieving moral and material prosperity, of working for a stable, orderly, and just government, and toward foolish and dangerous intrigues for a complete independence for which they are as yet totally unfit." The prevailing white opinion for acceptable black behavior in the United States was directed outward. As Roosevelt concluded, it was most important that the Filipinos "should remember that their prime needs are moral and industrial, not political."[80]

Because so many "unstable" areas were rich in resources, American officials eagerly offered assistance or intervened to provide order. Praise of the potential of the nations of Central America and the Caribbean was followed by denigrating commentary on their societies. The United States minister to Nicaragua, for example, described it as "one of the most fertile, beautiful countries in tropical America, which would rapidly advance in wealth and population were there security of life and property." Much the same was believed of Santo Domingo. "All that is needed is a stable Government and peace," the United States minister noted in 1903, "so that the capitalists who may desire to invest have no fears" in opening up its riches. Root concurred, noting that "with her phenomenal richness of soil" Santo Domingo "ought to be among the richest and happiest" nations. "But the island has been the scene of almost continual revolution and bloodshed."[81]

In his summary of his 1906 trip to Latin America, Root indicated the concerns of American officials. He explained to a gathering of American business leaders that the United States was emerging not only as the world's leading manufacturer but also as an important creditor nation. This situation was particularly important for relations with Latin America, where American capital was needed. There was, Root assured the audience, a nicely balanced relationship between the U.S. production of manufactured goods and the Central and South American need for such products and markets for their raw materials. The secretary of state characterized the relationship as a perfect match: "Where we accumulate, they spend. While we have less of a cheerful philosophy . . . they have less of the inventive faculty which strives continually to increase the productive power of men."[82]

Root's Republican successors held firmly to these same ideas. Difficulties with the nations of Latin America, Hughes asserted, arose from "differences between us in temperament and manners."[83] His view received support from the rest of the State Department, which held an even dimmer view of Latin America. The chief of the Division of Western European Affairs, William R. Castle, wrote in his diary after a meeting of the department's division chiefs that "Francis White [chief of the Division of Latin American Affairs] spends rather too much time discussing little piffling things but perhaps they seem piffling because the countries about which he talks are so absurd themselves." When a Foreign Service candidate mistakenly pronounced Nicaragua's capital, Managua, as "manure," White remarked to Castle that this "name should be generally adopted."[84] New Foreign Service officers were informed that "professional standards demanded that good diplomats appreciate those subtle distinctions in 'national psychology' which made various countries conduct their affairs differently."[85]

Understanding these distinctions meant acknowledging the backwardness of the people and, therefore, the need for more patience on the part of the diplomat. The State Department "exhibited an uninhibited and unembarrassed paternalism" toward Latin Americans during the interwar years. Francis White told new diplomats that they should not expect modern democracy in Latin America because the "Latin temperament and climate" and the "low racial quality" of the people were barriers to political advancement. Influence could be exerted, however, because Latins were "very easy people to deal with if properly managed." They "responded well to patience" and could, therefore, be protected from their own ignorance. A departmental skepticism concerning self-determination reinforced these views. Career diplomats saw economic conditions as the key basis for promoting international harmony and protecting American interests. As Castle lectured new recruits, many people had been misguided to support self-determination after the war, but diplomats knew that economic considerations were "more vital and more lasting than any others."[86]

Consequently, the rise of nativism and the demands for immigration restriction received support from the State Department. Nelson T. Johnson lectured Foreign Service recruits on the connection between the Reconstruction era and the need for immigration control. His view held that blacks and the newer immigrants from Southern and Eastern Europe were inferior to Anglo-Saxons and shared the characteristics of being lazy, dirty, irresponsible, disposed to criminality, and vulnerable to radical political ideas. Granting citizenship to former slaves, Johnson argued, had been a mistake and demonstrated the folly of giving self-determination to inferior people. Were the United States to do it over again, Johnson believed, "we would not admit Negroes to citizenship. We do not propose at present to grant the right to yellow people." With these examples, he concluded that it was necessary also to restrict the continued immigration of undesirable Europeans.[87]

Such positions led to limited tolerance of radical or nationalist revolutionary movements and a disposition to impose order to create American-style economic institutions. It was the duty of the United States to make sure that the most important social institutions of a society were properly established and protected. Opposition to this program indicated ignorance or malicious intention. Only after trade had expanded and economies grew could concern properly turn to political systems. The rationalizations and justifications used by Republican policymakers for supporting right-wing dictatorships were, therefore, already in place when they came to power in 1921. Experience in office would not significantly change these views.

The Man of the Hour

When the Republicans came to power in 1921, Italian-American relations were strained over Wilson's refusal to grant Italy the port city of Fiume.[88] The disagreement over Fiume reached its climax in April 1919, when Wilson appealed directly to the Italian people to give up their nation's claim to the port.[89] Italy's prime minister Vittorio Orlando, who quickly left the Versailles Conference in protest over the president's action, returned to Rome, where he received an overwhelming parliamentary vote of confidence. Orlando, however, did not remain in power past June 1919. Constant domestic unrest created governmental instability, and no ministry was able to maintain itself in power long enough to initiate economic recovery. Between March 1920 and June 1922, Italy had six governing ministries and four prime ministers. Labor strikes were frequent occurrences, and the State Department was concerned about Italy's future. State Department official Gordon Auchincloss noted in his wartime diary that "if we are not careful we will have a second Russia on our hands" in Italy. Expressing a widely held belief among American officials, he wrote that "the Italians are like children. They must be lead [sic] and assisted more than almost any other nation."[90] A department memo in the summer of 1919 summarized the full extent of U.S. fears: "The situation in Italy is very serious. . . . If a revolution broke out in Italy it may easily spread to the rest of Europe and even to the United States. Italy is probably the greatest source of danger in Europe today."[91]

The political crisis in Italy peaked when workers occupied the factories in September 1920. At the same time, nationalist groups and the newly formed fascist organizations continued their agitation for Italian possession of Fiume. Mussolini's followers frequently took the law into their own hands to break up labor demonstrations or strikes. Outbreaks of violence and street fighting between fascist squads and left-wing groups were common, and the government was incapable of preventing them.[92] Although the threat of revolution passed when the factory occupation failed, problems of political instability and economic depression remained.

In the fall of 1920, Italy and Yugoslavia reached an agreement that allowed Italy to control Fiume while Yugoslavia controlled the territory around the city.[93] With the disposition of Fiume seemingly settled, American policymakers and businessmen turned their attention to their overriding concern for a stable political climate favorable to increased American trade and investment. The U.S. government had loaned Italy over $600 million in 1919 for stabilization and reconstruction purposes.[94] In New York, leading businessmen and bankers, headed by Standard Oil's lawyer Charles Evans Hughes and J. P. Morgan's Thomas Lamont, formed the Italy America Society to help increase trade between the two countries. Yet the political and economic situation in Italy did not stabilize as American officials hoped it would. When Hughes took control of American foreign policy in 1921, the Italian government clearly had no plan or means for ending the violence and unrest. In response, private American capital, although very interested in Italy, refused to assist the government's reconstruction program.

Wilson's last ambassador to Italy, Robert Johnson, emphasized the fascist danger to governmental stability. Writing to Hughes in March 1921, Johnson argued that Italy's problems did not stem from the danger of a revolution from the left, but rather from the current government and its reliance on the extreme right. The right appeared to stand for law and order, through its vigilant moves against strikers and demonstrators, and the fascists, not the government, were gaining public approval for their actions.[95] Johnson worried that the government's refusal to control the fascists would bring about its demise. During one series of strikes, the ambassador reported that fascist direct action against the disruptive strikers and socialist deputies "goes to show that public opinion would back government if strong action were taken by latter" to stop the strikes and the "grave disorders" they were causing in Italy. Unfortunately, Johnson noted, "there is no indication that [the government] will act with firmness which was hoped and expected."[96]

Ambassador Johnson, however, was not comfortable with the fascists, their methods, or what they represented. Johnson did not believe Italy was on the verge of social revolution, but he did believe that firm action by the government was necessary to end the disruptions. The embassy's reports consistently pointed out that most of the violence and much of the general disorder were instigated by the fascist squads. Johnson grouped them with the radical left—which to him meant extremism and violence—and saw both as part of the lawlessness he wanted the government in Rome to contain. He reported that the majority of Italy's left was social democratic.[97] As a June 1921 embassy summary of recent events noted, in continuing battles between the fascists and the socialist and communist labor groups, "in general, the fascisti seem to be the aggressors, while the communists . . . have . . . shift[ed] the imputation of lawlessness and violence from the party of 'Red' revolution to the self-constituted party of 'law and order.'"[98]

A week later the embassy reported to Hughes that unless the "fascisti reaction can be checked, the social problem may assume an acute aspect in the near future and the country thus [be] crystallized into class-conscious strata."[99] The fascists' actions were not only disruptive, they were thought to be driving the social-democratic and the communist left together into a stronger opposition to the government. As the embassy reported in July 1921, "The situation in Italy as regards the unending— in fact . . . in-creasing [sic]—struggle between the Fascisti on the one side, and the Socialists, Communists . . . on the other side, is already a very serious one and now threatens to become much worse." Yet "the Government has not done anything to strike at the roots of this evil."[100]

Johnson's views, however, did not influence the Harding administration, which made no effort to aid Italy's beleaguered government. The change of administration and American diplomatic personnel in 1921, along with changes in Italy, began to steer American policymakers' opinions toward a more favorable view of the fascists. With the arrival in Rome of Richard Child, Harding's appointee as ambassador, embassy reports began to reflect a positive view of Mussolini and his followers. Most reports from Rome still told the same basic story: Italy was beset by constant strikes by left-wing workers who were sympathetic to the Bolshevik Revolution in Russia. They were opposed by the nationalists and fascists, who kept up a constant agitation over not receiving all of the territory around Fiume and violently opposed labor strikes. Rome's inability to control events or improve the economy continued to be a main feature of all reports, which portrayed Italian political leaders as weak, indecisive men who were unable to lead their nation during its crisis. But the interpretation of who was responsible for Italy's problems changed: no longer was the blame placed on the government's refusal to make changes and on its reliance on the reactionary right. Child placed the blame on left-wing parties and labor organizations and emphasized the danger of Bolshevism in Italy. Even more important, Child presented a positive interpretation of the Fascist Party.

With Wilson out of office, Italian prime minister Giovanni Giolitti turned to the United States for both economic and political support. Giolitti had long been aware of Italy's need for foreign capital to begin social reconstruction and defuse the explosive political situation. In April 1921, in an effort to overcome past difficulties with the United States at Versailles, Giolitti informed Washington that Italy supported American principles in foreign affairs, particularly the right of self-determination.[101] The prime minister quickly followed up his early contact with the Harding administration by offering to accept American arbitration in the continuing dispute with Yugoslavia over Fiume.[102] Despite his professed respect for self-determination, Giolitti most likely believed that the Republican administration would be more inclined to accept Italy's position and change Wilson's policy. He even proposed an alliance with the United States, a request that Washington immediately rejected.[103]

The reason behind Giolitti's moves was clear. As Ambassador Child explained to Hughes, Italy's recent efforts to obtain American friendship stemmed from "the hope of cooperation of American capital in Italian economic aspirations." "There is a continuous demand for American financial cooperation," Child pointed out, especially American investment in railway and waterpower development. Child understood that "a succession of weak ministries" in Italy had sought American friendship and capital to bolster their images.[104] He remained skeptical, however, that the political instability would end and the investment climate improve. The ambassador included Italian leaders when he wrote Harding that the "present European statesmanship is lacking in men who have a range of vision and square strong jaw," an observation with which the president agreed. "The succession of internal dissensions," Child wrote Harding in October 1921, "is the story of Italy's successive failures to ever reach the place which rightly belongs to her." He added that Italy "nearly went Bolshevik" and that the danger still remained. Harding, who trusted his old friend's judgment and believed that Child had an "active, forward-looking mind," replied that he hoped the "threat of destruction by radicals" and the "activities of Reds" were not making Child's "life miserable."[105] Meanwhile, private capitalists continued to refuse to invest in Italy, and the U.S. government offered no support. All the State Department did was urge the Italian government to take stronger action against labor unions so that reconstruction to ameliorate conditions in Italy would begin, thereby clearing the way for American investment.

By July 1922, Italy appeared to American officials to be in a state of crisis. The fifth coalition in two years fell at the same time the unions were planning a general strike. Child saw the strike as a direct test of the government's ability to maintain order and prevent a revolution. Among the center parties no individual or group appeared to be strong enough to establish an effective government. Child's reports and warnings of impending danger were well received in Washington and discussed by Harding and Hughes.[106] On 23 July, the embassy in Rome reported to Washington that it was not optimistic about Italy's political future. "The socialists are still making trouble" in the effort to form a new government "and are mischievously upsetting all chances of good government by playing party politics for their own personal advantage. . . . No one believes that a strong government can come as long as Parliament is elected by the present system of proportional representation." This meant that there must be a continuation of coalition governments in Italy, which the embassy described as being "all very well in the time of war, but a many headed, cannibalistic monster in the time of peace."[107]

These comments isolated what American policymakers perceived to be the greatest problem in Italy: the lack of a strong government that could put an end to labor unrest and the Bolshevik threat, begin Italy's economic recovery, and return Italian society to "normalcy." In the State Department's view, traditional authority in Italy had been displaced during the war, and it was the Italian government's job to restore it. Until the power of labor and left-wing parties was diminished and the government reformed, policymakers held little hope for Italy and feared that it might yet provide Bolshevism with an inroad into Western Europe.

In August, Child submitted to the State Department a special report on fascism prepared by the embassy's military attaché. Although it offered no evidence, the report began by noting that the fascists now appeared to have enough strength to overthrow the government by force and that "most Italians are now convinced that a thorough reform and reorganization of the government are necessary in order to prevent the impoverishment of the country, to permit commerce and industry to recover from the depression . . . and the wave of socialism which has swept over Italy."[108] To the embassy staff, it was clear that the present rulers of Italy under its constitution could not provide the strong leadership the embassy and the State Department thought was needed. New institutions and leaders were required.

The basic thesis of the report held that the Fascist Party was the upholder of traditional authority in Italy and a force for strong, effective government. Gone was the Wilsonians' fear of the fascists as disrupters of society and worries about their reliance on violence. Rather, Mussolini and the fascists were praised for their pledge to reorganize Italy's government and save the nation from the supposed Bolshevik threat. It did not mention the fascists' responsibility for the violence in postwar Italy or the illegality of their actions. Instead, it portrayed the fascists as a growing, vibrant party that was disciplined, patriotic, and willing to take action against the nation's enemies, among which the report included not only socialists, communists, and anarchists, but republicans. Moreover, the report claimed that the party's popularity extended beyond its own rank and file. "The bulk of the population which is neither Fascista or [sic] Socialist is inclined to lend at least their moral support to the Fascisti, realizing that they have broken up many strikes and probably saved the country from going Bolshevik." The report added that "by appealing to the national spirit of all Italians to assist in saving the country from Bolshevism, the fascisti soon won the favor, if not the enlistment, of all patriotic Italians."[109]

Finally, the report portrayed Mussolini as having full control over his followers, acknowledging that he did not hesitate to command as a dictator. It was too early to tell what Mussolini was going to do, but it was certain that he, and not the second Facta ministry, was in charge of Italy's political future. The celebratory tone of the report, its glossing over of fascist totalitarianism, and its view of popular support for fascism made it clear that if Mussolini did decide to seize power, he would have the embassy's full support. Democracy was seen as dangerous for Italy. As Child again wrote Harding, the old leaders were men who "lack[ed] courage on the one hand and patience on the other."[110]

In October, Child wrote to Hughes that the Fascist Party had made its final break with the weak and ineffective governing coalition in Rome. "The Fascisti no longer dedicates itself to support the government against revolution. For all intents and purposes it now proposes revolution." Child recognized that government by the fascists would mean a dictatorship for Italy, but he justified such a prospect, and the end of constitutional democracy, by claiming that "people like the Italians . . . hunger for strong leadership and enjoy . . . being dramatically governed."[111]

March on Rome

Child's immediate reaction to the "March on Rome," that it was "a fine young revolution," signaled what would become the official attitude of the U.S. government and American business leaders to the new regime.[112] Child reported to Hughes that the fascist revolution had infused Italian national life "with zeal, temporary calm and hopefulness"[113] and that the general tendency in Italy was toward "increased confidence[,] *good nature*[,] normalty [*sic*] of functions" since the fascist takeover.[114] Child's telegram to Hughes, sent while the fascist blackshirts were still entering Rome, recognized the constitutional implications of the takeover: "The essence of events, whatever technical arguments may be used to create an appearance of constitutionality, is the fact that King, Ministry, and Parliament have capitulated with a surrender of constitutional prerogatives to . . . force."[115] Mussolini was described as a "magnetic character" of "stern deportment and convincing oratory" and a strong leader.[116] Harding, referring to Child's analysis of fascism and recent events in Italy, wrote on 2 November to his ambassador that he believed he had the "situation well appraised, and I am very thoroughly in accord with many of the views which you express."[117] The question of whether to recognize this revolutionary takeover of power never arose. The violent, antidemocratic nature of the fascist regime was simply rationalized away as a return to "normalcy." Traditional authority was being restored and a strong government established for a people who could not, the administration believed, govern themselves.

In his first full report on 4 November to the State Department on the fascist revolution, Child succinctly summarized the State Department's thinking about Italy for the four years before Mussolini's accession. Characterizing Il Duce's predecessors as "weak and halting ministers . . . unable to lead," Child noted that "the Italians prefer a determined Mussolini" to their former government. Even if the people did not like his means of gaining power, Mussolini still represented the "aspirations" and "all the hopes of Italians who long for a breathing space of peace and domestic tranquility."[118] As would happen time and again during the years of fascist rule in Italy, an American official justified acceptance of Mussolini's dictatorship by ascribing to the Italian people the sentiments held by American policymakers themselves concerning events in Italy.

Secretary of State Hughes exchanged early greetings with Mussolini. The fascist leader telegraphed Hughes on the day his followers marched into Rome that he anticipated "friendly economic and spiritual collaboration" with the United States.[119] Hughes responded quickly, wiring back on 2 November that he would be "glad to cooperate" and offering Mussolini his "best wishes for the happiness and progress" of Italy.[120] Child wrote Harding on 16 November that Mussolini's quick selection of a new ambassador to the United States, Don Gelasio Caetani, was an index "of the spirit and vigor of the new Italian administration."[121]

At the same time, Italian officials in Washington reported to Rome that the U.S. attitude toward Italy had changed. The Harding administration's reaction to the fascist takeover was very favorable because American officials believed that it had ended the Bolshevik threat to Italy. The first Italian ambassador to the United States under Mussolini noted that American officials had told him that before the March on Rome the U.S. government was convinced "Italy was on the brink of ruin, a prey to Bolshevism, with parties torn to pieces in an everlasting wrangle and without a strong government." Subsequently, policymakers came to view Italy as "the first nation to have the courage to conquer Bolshevism."[122]

Amid the positive notices exchanged between Rome and Washington came two early warnings from the American embassy that would greatly influence policymakers' views and subsequent actions toward Italian fascism. The first one raised State Department fears of an aggressive fascist foreign policy. Ambassador Child informed Washington that Mussolini seemed likely to pursue a "chauvinistic, hazardous foreign policy." The ambassador's reasoning was twofold. Mussolini had taken for himself the position of minister of foreign affairs, which suggested that he would seek to annex Fiume and other territories that his supporters desired for Italy. Child also feared that, having come to power without a clearly defined domestic program beyond anti-Bolshevism and the restoration of order, Mussolini might attempt "to direct attention from his failures at home by supernationalistic foreign policies."[123]

Although Child quickly changed his position on Mussolini and the prospects of an aggressive foreign policy, he introduced an analysis of a split between "extremist" and "moderate" fascists that bothered some in the State Department. On 4 November, Child reported that the "realities of power" would lead to "considerable moderation" by the fascists and that "the sounder elements of the Party" would prevail. A week later Child informed the Department that the "extreme" elements within the Fascist Party were being brought under control by Mussolini. The blackshirts had been demobilized and Mussolini had disciplined unauthorized acts of violence by his supporters.[124]

Child's distinction between the "moderates," of which Mussolini was the leader, and the "extremists" would become central to all State Department thinking on fascism, helping to provide the ideological grounds for the continued support of Mussolini. Republican officials assumed that the moderates represented more traditional conservative elements at the center of the party who could be counted on to keep Italy's policies on a "safe" course, while the extremists were fringe members responsible for the party's unsavory actions.[125] Central to this distinction was the implicit conviction that the fascists were basically sound.

Despite Child's views, the department continued to worry about Italian foreign policy. While accepting Child's analysis of the divisions within the Fascist Party and his view that Mussolini represented the more moderate foreign policy wing, the department worried that deteriorating conditions inside Italy could force Mussolini to seek the support of the extremists by pursuing an aggressive foreign policy. This point was underscored by the second warning sent from Rome regarding Italy's domestic situation.

In the month following Mussolini's triumph, F. M. Gunther, the acting embassy chargé d'affaires, sent three letters to Hughes on the political situation in Italy. The March on Rome had turned the tide against Bolshevism in Italy, Gunther noted, but Italy was not yet secure. "The great danger," Gunther reported, "lies in the possibility of a swing of the pendulum later on in the other direction . . . the limit of which might be difficult to fix." A collapse of Mussolini's power could precipitate such a crisis. "Italy was arrested," Gunther repeated, "on the brink of . . . a grave financial and consequently social crisis by the advent of Mussolini and his followers. Should something happen to break his power," the collapse of the nation would be sudden and chaos would result. Gunther concluded that "the Socialists and others are waiting and watching" for this to happen. For Italy to recover from the war, avoid chaos or Bolshevism, and begin to prosper, Gunther concluded that it was imperative that Mussolini remain in office. He found no alternative.[126]

By the end of Mussolini's first year in power, the main outlines of American policy concerning fascism had been drawn. First and foremost, fascism in Italy was seen as a bulwark against the spread of Bolshevism, an authority guaranteeing the maintenance of social order, and an antidote for the illness of successive weak governments. Second, strong fascist rule ensured that Italy would begin its postwar economic reconstruction free from the challenges of labor; reconstruction would provide economic opportunities for the United States. Third, Mussolini was considered to be very popular and fully in control. This understanding on the one hand made it easier for American officials to ignore the domestic terror and the destruction of democratic institutions under Mussolini; on the other hand, it tended to obscure the view of fascism as a unique social movement. Rather, they tended to equate fascism with Mussolini, who was seen as a moderate and the only reliable implementer of the policies essential to order, economic recovery, and development.

Mussolini's frequent belligerent speeches on foreign affairs left American officials with lingering fears that the fascists might still seek to use territorial gain to aid Italy's economic recovery, rather than working within a cooperative international order. Fascist domestic policy, however, raised hardly a whisper of protest from American diplomats, and, on the foreign front, they remained convinced that U.S. economic power and aid, which Italy needed and desired, would provide enough leverage to curb Italian chauvinism. In addition, by promoting Italian economic recovery, such aid would help to keep Mussolini and the moderates in power.

Other American leaders were quick to note the economic benefits Mussolini's regime could bring to the United States. Secretary of the Treasury Andrew Mellon was among the high government officials who actively supported Mussolini. The secretary praised Mussolini's regime, declaring that he was "making a new nation out of Italy." Under fascism, the United States was seeing "Italy emerge from the chaos of war, straighten out her industrial troubles, cut her expenditures and put her budget in equilibrium, all under the direction of one strong man with sound ideas and the force to make these ideas effective." Such a man, Mellon believed, deserved American support and sympathy. Mellon would later orchestrate a lenient debt settlement for Italy that allowed Rome to borrow money from American banks.[127] Under Secretary of State William Castle noted approvingly in his diary that "Mussolini believes in hierarchy—that the success of government consists in finding everyman his rightful place in the scheme of things, not in leveling us all to a single, indiscriminate status. Horribly undemocratic—but true!"[128]

American businessmen were no less enthusiastic about Mussolini and his government. Thomas Lamont of J. P. Morgan remarked after his first meeting with Mussolini that the Italian dictator was "a very upstanding chap."[129] He wrote later that Italy was "going to be a great country even despite its very limited natural resources."[130] Otto Kahn, of Kuhn, Loeb, praised the recent change of government in Italy at the 1923 meeting of the International Chamber of Commerce. "Parliamentary wrangling and wasteful impotent bureaucracy" had been replaced by an "efficient and energetic . . . government," which had united Italy in "a spirit of order, discipline, hard work, patriotic devotion and faith."[131] Ralph Easley of the National Civic Federation wrote to Thomas Lamont after visiting Italy, "I think, were we in Italy, we would all be with Mussolini."[132] And Judge Elbert Gary of United States Steel remarked while in Rome in 1923 that "we have here a wonderful renaissance of youthful energy and activity. A masterhand has, indeed, strongly grasped the helm of the Italian state." Gary added that he felt "like turning to my American friends and asking them whether they don't think we, too, need a man like Mussolini."[133]

American policymakers were, however, premature in their assessment of Mussolini's control over Italy. Their unbounded optimism about Italy's future was checked in 1924 when Italian opponents of Mussolini attempted to move the political pendulum back toward the center. The Matteotti Affair of June 1924 presented the Mussolini regime with its greatest domestic crisis. On 10 June 1924, a gang of fascist thugs abducted and murdered Giacomo Matteotti, a reformist socialist deputy in Italy's parliament. His disappearance immediately aroused suspicions among his fellow party members who knew he was preparing to make a speech in parliament about financial irregularities by many high fascist officials. Earlier in the month Matteotti had delivered a bitter address attacking the government's conduct of the recent Italian elections and the continuing "decline of liberty in Italy." Many prominent fascists were implicated and arrested in connection with Matteotti's murder, including Cesare Rossi, director of the fascist press bureau, and Filippo Filipelli, a well-known fascist newspaper publisher and government official. Both were considered by American officials to be extreme fascists.[134]

The new American ambassador to Italy, Henry Fletcher, a career diplomat and prominent member of the Republican Party, reported to Washington on 20 June that although many prominent fascists were being implicated in the murder, Mussolini remained untouched by guilt. The ambassador noted with relief that Mussolini would "weather the storm"; there was "no combination strong enough to replace him."[135] In a long letter to the secretary of state on 23 June, Fletcher acknowledged that "the Fascist Party . . . has been dealt a staggering blow." He concluded, however, that he did not believe "the [Italian] people generally wish to return to the parliamentary incompetence and social disorder which brought on the Fascisti revolution."[136] The main problem was whether Mussolini could hold the party together and maintain his power. If he failed to do so, Fletcher feared political unrest would again overtake Italy. The Western European Division of the State Department concluded in October that "Mussolini had a fairly stiff struggle with Farinacci [leader of the extremists] and the wild men" and noted that another crisis could bring the "entire situation into a state not far from political chaos."[137]

The crisis appeared to subside, and William Castle was optimistic when he visited Italy in November 1924. Castle was taken with both the beauty of Rome and the work of Mussolini. "What a place this is," Castle noted in his diary upon arriving in the Italian capital. "I should like to be ambassador here just for the joy of spending four years here and that in spite of the Italians." In his meeting with Mussolini, Castle informed the Italian dictator that "what he had done to bring order in Italy, to set people to work and to make a beginning of settling the grave economic situation had been much appreciated in America by those . . . who had known Italy before." Mussolini responded positively, telling Castle that Italy had known no strikes for two years and that he had put the people hard at work. Discipline was necessary, Il Duce stated, playing to American prejudices, because the "Italians have not the self control . . . of the Anglo-Saxons" and have to learn "to work."[138]

Castle agreed, noting afterward that the "fall of the Government would throw Italy into a state of anarchy worse than that from which it emerged two years ago." He found Mussolini "passionately patriotic and if he is conscious of the fact that he is the man of the hour he is still conscious of the truth." He had "saved Italy," the "one country which had put the war behind it." In an enigmatic reading of recent events in Italy that ignored the numerous murders and arrests of opposition members, Castle claimed that the "socialists are not crushed by the Fascisti" in Italy; "they are at work and are, therefore, not interested in the tirades of the demagogues."[139]

It was not long, however, before the next crisis for Mussolini's regime came and tested American faith. In December, Rossi, who believed he was being made a political scapegoat by Mussolini, published a paper that directly implicated Mussolini in the many assaults carried out by the Fascist Party on members of the opposition. Fletcher immediately telegraphed the State Department that Mussolini's position was "more seriously threatened than at any previous time" by Rossi's charges. Castle briefly worried that these charges "may be the straw that will break Mussolini's back."[140] The embassy's analysis of events reflected Child's old view of the divisions within the Fascist Party, reporting that as a result of Rossi's charges, "the Government is threatened by a split between extremists and moderates." This development, the department feared, could lead to the fall not only of Mussolini but of the whole government.[141]

Subsequent events, however, demonstrated the unity of purpose within the fascist movement. Instead of putting Mussolini on the defensive as the department feared, the "Rossi Memorial" led directly to Mussolini's final crackdown on his political opposition. Even the limited constitutional law and rights that had remained in Italy were now abolished. Mussolini rallied his supporters in a New Year's speech with the promise to bring peace to Italy, "by force if necessary." In the days and weeks that followed, groups of fascists violently repressed all those seen as enemies of Mussolini and fascism and destroyed the few remaining opposition newspapers. The American embassy in Rome, in a February 1925 message to the State Department, indicated that it fully comprehended the totalitarian dimensions of Mussolini's words and actions: "Fascism . . . has seized the neck of the bottle of political control. During the last two months it has effectively stifled hostile elements in restricting the right of free assembly, in abolishing freedom of the press and in having at its command a large military organization."[142]

Mussolini's choke hold on the "neck of the bottle of political control" in Italy and his use of methods supposedly reserved to the extreme fascists should have obliterated any notion of a split among fascists between moderates and extremists. Rossi's admissions made it clear that the Fascist Party was united in its desire to destroy all opposition and its willingness to use force when necessary. Yet no U.S. communications characterized Mussolini's behavior as extreme. The entire analytical basis of American support for Mussolini had proved erroneous, but in the crisis it did not seem to matter. American officials accepted Mussolini's crackdown as another step to prevent Italy from sliding back into a situation that would allow various groups to compete effectively for power. Their first priority was order and anticommunism in Italy. Any democratic alternative to fascism was seen as political chaos, which might bring the socialists to power.

Fletcher's personal letter to the new secretary of state, Frank B. Kellogg, in July 1925, demonstrated the anti-Bolshevik mind-set in which American policy had now become locked. The ambassador belittled the opposition as "old, flabby and discredited" men who had attempted, but had been unable, to "unhorse" Mussolini. Fletcher then summarized the events of the past year as a simple choice which the people of Italy had faced between two stark opposites: "a choice between Mussolini and Fascism and Giolitti and Socialism, between strong methods of internal peace and prosperity and a return to free speech, loose administration and general disorganization. Peace and prosperity were preferred. . . . The country was thankful to have escaped so quickly, under Fascism, from the danger and disorganization of Bolshevism that it had no desire to turn back."[143] "Strong methods of internal peace," Fletcher's euphemism for the violent suppression of the antifascist opposition and democratic rights, were preferred by American policymakers to the danger of free speech and possible domestic instability. Indeed, Fletcher was now laying the blame for Italy's crisis at the feet of the opposition, not the fascists.

Given this understanding of Italian affairs, it is not surprising that American policymakers held firm to their favorable analysis of Mussolini and failed to reevaluate their views on Mussolini and fascism in the wake of the Matteotti crisis. Events in Italy had come to their logical conclusion, and the State Department saw no reason to change its position. Stability, economic recovery, and enlarged economic opportunities for American traders and investors were advantages U.S. policymakers were unwilling to sacrifice to defend political democracy in Italy. When former prime minister Francesco Nitti wrote to Kellogg in 1925 from his refuge in Switzerland criticizing Mussolini's regime and the end of Italian democracy and calling upon the United States to join in protest, he was ignored. William Castle remembered him as the man who "nearly wrecked what was left of Italy after the war" and remarked in a memorandum to Kellogg that "he denies any connection with the Bolsheviks but is undoubtedly very persona grata in Moscow for the fact that he is a troublemaker."[144] The next year Secretary Kellogg labeled all groups opposing Mussolini as "communists, socialists, and anarchists."[145] No attempt was made to discriminate among the opposition groups or to consider seriously their objections to fascism.

But the Matteotti Affair had demonstrated how fragile Mussolini's control might prove to be if another major internal crisis occurred in Italy. American leaders urged the Italians to settle the question of Italy's war debts to the United States so private American capital could again be loaned to Italy. Italy received the most favorable debt settlement of any nation, and American private capital was soon flowing into Italy. Republican officials believed that this capital would not only help stabilize the Mussolini government by aiding economic recovery, and therefore provide for increased American trade, but that it would help to maintain the moderates in power and provide the United States with a lever to influence events in Italy and to curb any national chauvinism in the fascists' foreign policy. After a year of renewed worry about instability and social revolution in Italy, policymakers hoped to have loans in hand through which they could limit future swings of the Italian political pendulum. By 1930 American firms had loaned Italy over $460 million, while direct investments by American companies had reached over $121 million, and portfolio investments accounted for almost $280 million more in American investment.[146]

The Root Doctrine

The American response to Mussolini's seizure of power and to the emergence of fascism marked the first time U.S. policymakers had developed the logic and rationale for actively supporting a right-wing dictatorship in the modern era. Throughout the interwar years and into the Cold War period, both Republican and Democratic administrations would fall back on similar positions when governments were overthrown by right-wing dictators. The perceived threat of Bolshevism was central to the rationalization for supporting right-wing dictators, along with the idea that Italy was not prepared or developed enough for democracy. Just as Mussolini was portrayed as a moderate who represented traditional authority and provided the firm hand needed for the development of both the economy and the political culture, so would future tyrants receive friendly brush strokes that covered over their brutality and undemocratic rule.

American officials could have selected a variety of policies toward fascism in Italy and did not have to provide both economic and political support to Mussolini. They did so because they were genuinely enthusiastic about Il Duce and his program in Italy. Hughes, who met Mussolini in 1926 after he retired as secretary of state, said that "he could not help liking Mussolini and got no suggestion that the man had any thought whatever of himself as distinguished from his country." Furthermore, he found that "Mussolini had not only the obedience but the enthusiastic support of the majority of the people." [147]

As Elihu Root, now the senior foreign policy spokesman of the Republican Party, explained in a 1926 talk to the Council on Foreign Relations in New York, a solution to the persistent problem that had faced American officials since the turn of the century had been found. Speaking on the U.S. obligation to the Philippines, Root declared that "duty calls for the application of whatever we have been able to learn upon a very particular subject, and this is, of the way in which competency for self government may be acquired by man." He reminded the group's business and political leaders that "we have had some lessons. We started the reconstruction of the South at the close of the Civil War upon the theory that if you gave the black men the vote, they would be able to take care of themselves and to govern themselves and the country in which they lived, and it proved to be a most dismal step, a terrible mistake, with the most serious evils following. That same idea," he believed, "has existed with regard to many countries. Poor Mexico is giving an illustration of the difficulty of finding a simple solution of that problem." Root, however, found one nation to praise: "Italy has a revival of prosperity, contentment and happiness under a dictator, who was the man of the hour to seize upon the fact that the Italians had undertaken to govern themselves without quite having learned the hang of it." [148]

2 THE ORIGINS OF THE GOOD NEIGHBOR POLICY
The Quest for Order in Latin America

"Our interests do not lie in controlling peoples," Secretary of State Hughes often stated in explaining his Latin American policy. "Our interest is in having prosperous, peaceful, and law abiding neighbors with whom we can cooperate to mutual advantage."[1] Hughes, therefore, rejected the suggestion that American policy was imperialistic. Responding to the chorus of charges of imperialism by Latin Americans and U.S. critics alike, Hughes argued that imperialism was "a phrase which serves as a substitute for thought and suggests the moral indignation which is so often used to cover a multitude of delinquencies in argument." It was, Hughes believed, the shortcomings of Latin Americans that forced the United States to intervene: "It is revolution, bloodshed and disorder that bring about the very interposition for the protection of lives and property that is the object of so much objurgation."[2] The career officers in the State Department voiced similar feelings and were offended by the notion that the United States was an imperial power. Dana Munro, a longtime fixture in the Latin American Division, dismissed charges of imperialism as being made out of ignorance. It was revolutions and financial crises that prompted

American intervention for the benefit of the Latin Americans, not an American desire for control.[3]

That Hughes and others so often reasserted American innocence of imperialism is telling, but the real significance lies in their narrow view of the proper relationship between the United States and the other nations of the Western Hemisphere. Of particular importance was the Caribbean basin, where American forces had intervened no fewer than twelve times in seven different nations and where the United States maintained financial supervision of three nations, the Dominican Republic, Haiti, and Nicaragua, when the Republicans came to power. Henry L. Stimson, secretary of state from 1929 to 1933, noted that the Caribbean area was "the one spot external to our shores which nature has decreed to be most vital to our national safety, not to mention our prosperity." Unrest and instability in the region, therefore, created a serious problem and made a means for maintaining order necessary. Unfortunately, according to Stimson, Mexico, Central America, and the Caribbean nations were the areas "where the difficulties of race and climate have been greatest."[4] As Stimson lamented at another point, the situation did not improve even after American involvement: "I am getting quite blue over the bad way in which all of Latin America is showing up." Disorder was growing, "yet if we try to take the lead for them, at once is a cry against American domination and imperialism."[5]

The United States had to find a new means to establish order in the region. Military interventions failed to provide a long-term solution and further exacerbated the problem of instability. In addition to being costly, the sending of American forces raised anti-U.S. sentiment in the region. The quest for order in a framework acceptable to Washington but without direct American intervention would lead the United States to support brutal dictatorships in the region, most notably in Nicaragua, El Salvador, and Cuba. Similar to the situation in Italy, the specter of Bolshevism and the argument that the people were not yet ready for democracy underlay the United States policy toward these nations from 1927 to 1936 and the eventual support of right-wing dictators. After striving to establish a democratically elected government in Managua and Havana and to uphold the democratic process for changing governments in San Salvador, the United States reversed its course in the face of growing unrest. The need to secure stability and American interests without direct military action brought about these reversals. Finally, American officials resolved the conflict between self-determination, in the form of radical nationalism, and American interests by opting to support the military dictatorships of Anastasio Somoza García in Nicaragua, Maximiliano Hernández Martínez in El Salvador, and Fulgencio Batista in Cuba, choosing to ignore their bloody roads to power in favor of a political climate that imposed order and combated Bolshevism.

By 1933, dictators ruled at least fifteen of the twenty Latin American republics; many of them had come to power in the last two years.[6] There were no assurances that this upheaval was over or that the momentum might not swing to left-wing or radical nationalist movements. Given these circumstances and concerns, Franklin Roosevelt accepted and extended the policies and ideas of his Republican predecessors in most areas of the world. The tension between the U.S. desire for democratic governments and its quest for stability and nonradical political change was drawn even tighter during the 1930s. There would be no fundamental changes in the ideology and policies toward right-wing dictatorships. The Roosevelt administration endorsed the Republicans' solutions to the problems in Nicaragua and El Salvador and followed those models in formulating its own policy toward the unrest in Cuba in 1933–34.

Nicaragua: The Best Man for the Position

Since the first landing of American marines in Nicaragua in 1912, the United States had sought to impose stability in that nation.[7] But direct military intervention was seen by the State Department in the 1920s as paradoxically part of the problem that created instability as much as part of the solution. In place of military force, Republican leaders searched for methods to maintain stability while ensuring the continued American domination of the region. Order and respect for international law, the primary concerns of Hughes, would ensure protection of American security interests and exports to all the nations of Central America. Hughes sought to remedy this problem through treaties with these nations. In December 1922, he sponsored a conference in Washington to discuss regional stability, guarantees for order and the protection of property, and how to combat revolutions. All the nations agreed that they would not recognize any governments that resulted from coups d'état.

Although the United States did not actually sign the treaty, it agreed to abide by this provision. Hughes hoped that the treaty would remove the necessity for continued United States intervention. He believed that the lack of Washington's recognition and an always implied threat of

American intervention would deter unconstitutional seizures of power, improve the stability of the region, provide stability for existing governments, and thus promote the growth of trade and economic development.[8] That political change could occur in most of these nations only by revolution did not dissuade Hughes. Stability, the rule of law, and increased economic activity were of primary importance. Even though Hughes recognized that the "formal processes of constitutional government are so susceptible of abuse by those holding power that revolution has frequently appeared to be the only remedy," he still believed that the 1923 Washington Treaty would "promote stability" as opposed to "the side of bloodshed and disorder."[9] Stimson also believed the treaty had a positive effect. Many "a contemplated revolution has been abandoned," he argued in 1931, because of "a simple reminder by a minister from this country" that even if successful the new government would not be recognized. "In many more cases . . . the knowledge of the existence of the policy prevented even the preparation for a revolution or *coup d'etat*."[10]

Along with internal upheavals, another potential source of trouble in the region was Mexico. Hughes feared that Mexico was involved in a "socialistic experiment," having claimed the right to confiscate land and subsoil minerals.[11] Relations had broken down between Mexico and the United States during the Wilson administration, and Hughes continued the policy of nonrecognition of the Obregón government. The secretary of state could not understand the Mexican position and why Mexico City refused to follow the leadership of Washington. He saw not "the slightest reason why there should be antagonism between the peoples or the Governments of the United States and Mexico." The nature of a friendly relationship appeared obvious: "Mexico is a land of great resources which need development. Citizens of the United States who are not adventurers, and are not seeking opportunities of exploitation to the disadvantage of Mexico, have capital to invest. But confidence is essential to sound economic relations."[12] The problem was that Mexico's claims threatened American property and undercut any confidence in its government.

The situation only worsened during the administration of Calvin Coolidge. His secretary of state, Frank B. Kellogg, warned that Mexico's "alien land and petroleum laws" created a serious situation which placed that nation "on trial before the world." Coolidge's ambassador to Mexico, James Sheffield, blamed the problems in relations on the Mexicans and their "Latin-Indian mind, filled with hatred of the United States." He believed that the "main factors are greed . . . and an Indian, not Latin, hatred of all people not on the reservation. There is very little white blood in the Cabinet."[13] By 1926, the State Department concluded that Mexico was under Soviet influence and presented a danger to the whole region. In a report titled "Radical and Socialistic Influences in Mexico," the Division of Mexican Affairs concluded that President Plutarco Elias Calles was the "most dangerous man for the future of Mexico" and repeated that "in fact, it has been stated that he is a much redder bolshevist than Lenin ever was."[14] Under Secretary of State Robert Olds claimed in November that Mexico was "seeking to establish a Bolshevik authority in Nicaragua to drive a 'hostile wedge' between the U.S. and the Panama Canal."[15] Effective barriers to this danger needed to be erected in Central America.

The outbreak of civil war in Nicaragua in late 1926 brought forth fears of Mexican influence and a renewed round of American intervention that culminated in the emergence of the Somoza dictatorship. The fighting centered on the contested presidency of Nicaragua. In 1924, a coalition party of Conservatives and Liberals had defeated Emiliano Chamorro, only to be overthrown the next year by Chamorro and his supporters. Chamorro, whom the United States refused to recognize under the 1923 treaty, was himself forced from power in 1926 and replaced by the Conservative Adolfo Diaz. The former vice president from the 1924 election, Liberal Juan Sacasa, with the support of Mexico, claimed that the presidency rightly belonged to him and began a military campaign to oust Diaz.[16]

The United States made its preference known by recognizing Diaz and again dispatching troops to Nicaragua, which had been withdrawn in 1925, to help restore order. Coolidge told the press in December 1926 that American intervention was necessary because "there is a revolution going on there and whenever a condition of that kind exists in Central American countries it means trouble for our citizens that are there and it is almost always necessary for this country to take action for their protection."[17] Olds pointed out the historical reasons for the Coolidge administration's actions in a memorandum prepared on 2 January 1927.

> The Central American area down to and including the Isthmus of Panama constitutes a legitimate sphere of influence for the United States. . . . Our ministers accredited to the five little republics stretching from the Mexican border to Panama . . . have been advisors whose advice has been accepted virtually as law . . . we do control the destinies of Central America and we do so for the simple reason that the

national interest absolutely dictates such a course. . . . At this moment a deliberate attempt to undermine our position and set aside our special relationship in Central America is being made. The action of Mexico in the Nicaraguan crisis is a direct challenge to the United States. . . . We must decide whether we shall tolerate [Mexican interference] or insist upon our own dominant position. . . . Until now Central America has always understood that governments which we recognize and support stay in power, while those which we do not recognize and support fall. Nicaragua has become a test case. It is difficult to see how we can afford to be defeated.[18]

Drawing on Olds's analysis, President Coolidge sent Congress a lengthy message on 10 January explaining his reasons for reintroducing American troops in Nicaragua. The events in Nicaragua, Coolidge claimed, "seriously threaten American lives and property [and] endanger the stability of all Central America." He invoked the obligation of the United States under the 1923 treaties to support the existing government and to oppose the Liberals' efforts to remove Diaz from power: "There is no question that if the revolution continues American investments and business interests in Nicaragua will be seriously affected, if not destroyed." Coolidge concluded, therefore, that "the United States can not . . . fail to view with deep concern any serious threat to stability and constitutional government in Nicaragua tending toward anarchy and jeopardizing American interests, especially if such state of affairs is contributed to or brought about by outside influences or by any foreign power."[19] The American economic interest at the time amounted to almost $10 million in direct investments, although the Commerce Department noted that "these may be in reality worth many times that value at some future date" because many of the landholdings were not yet developed. Its estimates ran as high as $20 million.[20]

Secretary of State Kellogg rounded out the president's analysis when he delivered a report to the Senate on 12 January titled "Bolshevik Aims and Policies in Mexico and Latin America." The "outside influences" and "foreign power" the president referred to were identified as Bolshevism and Mexico. Kellogg argued that through Mexico, Bolshevik leaders had set out "as one of their fundamental tasks the destruction of what they term American Imperialism as a necessary prerequisite to [a] . . . revolutionary movement in the world." Thus support for Diaz was not only support for stability and the protection of American business in Nicaragua but also part of stemming the tide of international communism.[21]

Critics, led by Senator William Borah of Idaho, castigated Kellogg and the administration for drawing the specter of communism into the discussion on Nicaragua. Borah pointed out that the civil war was a product of internal Nicaraguan politics and charged that Kellogg's only purpose in finding Bolsheviks there was to provide cover for the use of marines to protect American investments. Kellogg's analysis still provided the basis for U.S. policy, but the extensive criticism of the use of troops spurred the secretary of state to search for a method to resolve the conflict on terms favorable to the United States without the use of force. Toward that end he sent the former secretary of war Colonel Henry L. Stimson to Nicaragua in April 1927.[22]

Stimson believed he understood the problem the United States faced in finding a resolution to the problem in Nicaragua. According to Stimson, Nicaraguans "were not fitted for the responsibilities that go with independence and still less fitted for popular self-government." This situation remained for the next century, with the result being "a concentration of practically all the powers of government in presidential dictators" and revolution being the only means to change government.[23] On his return from Nicaragua, Stimson would concur with Root's assessment that United States recognition of the independence of the Latin American states had been "premature." The Latin Americans were "admittedly like children and unable to maintain the obligations which go with independence."[24] This simplistic analysis would guide the colonel and American policymakers as the United States established the institutions of modern Nicaragua.

The United States could, of course, simply have used more troops to ensure Diaz's continuation in power, but that "did not get to the root of the evil." Nor did prohibiting revolution by treaty, which merely tended to "perpetuate the power of the party or individual who happened to be in control of the government." The State Department feared that without a negotiated settlement, Diaz would lose unless he was provided with massive American military support, which would only inflame critics at home and raise the cry of American imperialism in Latin America. Stimson, therefore, set out to resolve the present crisis through a new election under American supervision and the establishment of a "new and impartial police force . . . to take the place of the forces which the government was in the habit of using to terrorize and control elections." This, too, would be done under American guidance. Stimson concluded that the American restructuring of the politics and institutions of Nicaragua was "the only road by which a bloody and devastating revolution could be stopped and ballots substituted for bullets."[25]

Stimson quickly set the terms for a settlement after his arrival in Managua. The issue of U.S. recognition of Diaz was not negotiable. He would remain president until American-sponsored elections were held in 1928. Stimson favored the Conservatives, who were willing to follow the American lead. As he recorded in his diary, Stimson found "all conservatives, wealthy, dreadfully frightened of liberal success." They "wanted us not only to give military protection but to run their finances in absolute US control. Were very frank in admitting Nicaraguan incompetence and corruption."[26] He informed Washington that "Diaz has behaved well consistently and is evidently willing to entirely subordinate his own personal interests to a constructive peace program. So far as I can see no other equally intelligent and conciliatory substitute for him could be found or even desired."[27] In addition, both sides had to accept the creation of a U.S.-trained and commanded constabulary and the continued presence of U.S. Marines until the Guardia Nacional (National Guard) was prepared to take over peacekeeping chores. The United States was not conducting negotiations between the two sides; it was imposing a settlement. The Conservatives, for obvious reasons, agreed immediately with all of Stimson's demands, but the Liberals balked at the retention of Diaz as president. It was against Diaz that they had begun the civil war and had been fighting. But in the end, the Liberals had little choice. In his meeting with José Moncada, Sacasa's chief general, Stimson left no doubt about his commitment to Diaz. He told Moncada that "forcible disarmament would be made of those unwilling to lay down their arms." With the direct threat of more American marines entering the fighting, Moncada agreed to the American terms.[28]

It was during these negotiations with Moncada that Stimson first met Anastasio Somoza. Stimson, a New York corporate lawyer, associate of Elihu Root, and close friend of Theodore Roosevelt, was accustomed to deferential behavior from those he thought inferior to him. He immediately liked Somoza, who sought to ingratiate himself with Stimson. The colonel described Somoza as a "very frank, friendly, likeable young liberal" and noted that, because he spoke fluent English, Somoza "impresses me more favorably than almost any other" person.[29] So impressed was Stimson that he had Somoza act as his interpreter for the next few days while he finished the agreement. The contrast with his views on Augusto Sandino could not have been greater.

Stimson cabled Washington on 15 May that "the civil war in Nicaragua is now definitely ended."[30] Yet when the agreement was reached, Sandino, one of Moncada's generals, refused to lay down his arms and vowed to continue to fight until all American troops were withdrawn from Nicaragua. Sandino's promise to continue fighting did not, however, concern Stimson. Sandino was left out of the agreement because Stimson adopted the interpretation that Sandino was "a bandit leader" who employed "plainly unprincipled and brutal activities." He explained to the State Department that his threat to use force if the Liberal forces did not disarm was "a warning to the bandit fringe."[31] To Stimson, "Moncada was an officer and a gentleman" while "Sandino was a man of the people, and therefore nothing better than a bandit."[32] Responding to Sandino's call for social change, Stimson dismissed him as a man who "came back to Nicaragua on the outbreak of the revolution in order to enjoy the opportunities for violence and pillage which it offered."[33] Stimson continued to hold these views when he became secretary of state under Hoover. He saw American policy as an unqualified success, "punctuated only by sporadic outbreaks from the bandit Sandino."[34]

Stimson's views of both men were soon adopted by other American officials. Charles Eberhardt, the American minister in Managua, wrote Kellogg that Sandino "preached communism . . . and death to the Americans until the rabble of the whole North Country joined him in his plan to massacre Americans there and to set up his own government."[35] The State Department denounced Sandino for using the "stealthy and ruthless tactics which characterized the savages who fell upon American settlers in our country 150 years ago."[36] In 1933, the State Department was still referring to Sandino and the movement he led in these same terms. An overview of American policy toward Nicaragua discusses Sandino's "career in banditry" and the "chronic bandit depredations" of his followers.[37] Somoza, in contrast, emerged as a favorite of the Americans in Nicaragua. In 1932, General Calvin Matthews, the commander of the United States training mission in Nicaragua and also the current head of the Guardia Nacional, and Matthew Hanna, the U.S. minister to Nicaragua, backed Somoza for the position of director of the Guardia upon the final withdrawal of the U.S. Marines at the beginning of 1933.

Moncada and the Liberals won the 1928 election, but stability in Nicaragua still rested with the marines and the National Guard, not the electoral process. The central goals of American policy were the elimination of Sandino and the creation of a force that could maintain a friendly government once American forces were withdrawn. A democratically elected government would be good but was not an essential part of this policy. When Brigadier General Frank McCoy, whom Coolidge placed in charge of the American electoral mission in Nicaragua, asked for additional troops and absolute control over both supervising the elections and training the National Guard in 1928, his requests were quickly granted. As one newspaper at the time reported, McCoy had "been made the Mussolini of Nicaragua." The State Department's priorities were clearly set out by Robert Olds, who instructed McCoy that the creation of the National Guard to replace American forces was the "most vital feature of the entire [American] program." The Guard would be the "cornerstone of stability for the whole country long after the election" was over.[38] The most important institutions of modern Nicaragua, the Guardia Nacional and the National Bank of Nicaragua, Limited, whose Board of Directors was dominated by U.S. citizens and met in New York, were being installed along with the election rules.[39] The result would be the creation of a new type of military leader whom the United States would support.

Secretary of State Stimson concluded in 1929 that the National Guard could handle Sandino and provide stability, which would allow for the gradual withdrawal of American troops.[40] In 1931, over the protests of American businessmen in Nicaragua, Stimson announced that the rest of the marines would be withdrawn by 1933 despite Sandino's continued attacks. In addition to his desire to end the intervention in response to criticisms at home and abroad, larger international problems were forcing the secretary's hand. As he wrote in his diary, a continuation of the marines' presence or other American interventions "would put me in the absolute wrong in China, where Japan has done all this monstrous work under the guise of protecting her nationals with a landing force."[41] The stability in Nicaragua was still, however, militarily imposed.

In Nicaragua, the Americans working with the government found it difficult to get along with President Moncada. His violent temper, drinking, and desire to use the Guardia Nacional against his political opponents forced them to seek out other contacts in the government. The man they turned to was Anastasio Somoza. The selection of Somoza as head of the National Guard placed him in charge of the most important institution in the country. The marine leadership in Nicaragua worried that the Guard lacked any senior officers who had not been involved in previous civil wars. The graduates of the officer academy were too young and lacked any experience as leaders to take over from the Americans. The chief director and other senior positions would have to be selected by the winner of the 1932 presidential election from a list of men who had previous military experience. The system adopted was the one suggested by the American legation, which meant that the person selected would gain the position of director because of his political position and ties to the winning party.[42]

American officials backed Somoza for this position. Hanna wrote the department that he was the "best man in the country for the position," a judgment confirmed by General Matthews and others.[43] The leading student of the formation and history of the Guardia Nacional, Richard Millett, has concluded, "The United States had given Nicaragua the best trained and equipped army it had even known, but it had also given that nation an instrument potentially capable of crushing political opposition with greater efficiency than ever before in the nation. . . . In addition, the danger of a break between the new *Jefe Director* and the Nicaraguan President existed before either of them had even taken office. This represented the real heritage left by the United States when the Marines turned over command of the Guardia."[44]

Only one obstacle remained in Somoza's way to complete power: Sandino. With the withdrawal of American forces, Sandino agreed, as promised, to enter into negotiations with the government. His main request was that the National Guard be disbanded and that power rest with the elected officials. In 1934, Somoza issued orders for Sandino to be killed. Somoza's men trapped him on the road after a meeting with Sacasa, took him and two of his generals to a field, and shot them. Somoza claimed the order received the approval of Arthur Bliss Lane, the U.S. minister in Nicaragua. Lane denied the charge and produced evidence that he had learned of the plan and warned Somoza not to attack Sandino.[45] Nonetheless, after the assassination of Sandino, Somoza remained the man the United States supported in Nicaragua, even if it did not endorse this specific act.

When in 1936 Somoza decided to take the presidency, even though he was prohibited as the leader of the Guard, Washington did not protest. Secretary of State Cordell Hull rejected pleas from Nicaraguan civilian leaders that the United States protect them from the military. He wrote that the "special relationship" between the United States and Nicaragua had ended with the final removal of the marines. To act now would be interfering in Nicaragua's internal affairs.[46] Indeed, the withdrawal of American forces had made it easier for Somoza to solidify his control over Nicaragua. Fighting broke out in May 1936, and Somoza quickly seized political power. The Roosevelt administration recognized the new government and extended it economic assistance. The United States wanted stability in the region and a government that would protect American economic and strategic interests. It was the job of the National Guard, and not the elected government, to do that once the marines were withdrawn.

In a volatile and ideological world, the need for order was seen as greater than ever. Hoover and Stimson, particularly after the onset of the Great Depression, had tired of the costs and the role of intervention. In addition, the promotion of elections apparently just furthered unrest. Turning to the local military force solved the dilemma of how to maintain order, protect American interests, and defeat Mexican-sponsored Bolshevism without having to send in the marines. American officials resolved the contradiction between nonintervention and allowing self-determination and the desire for stability by supporting Somoza. The decision created a new type of leader in Latin America that the United States would rely on in times of upheaval. There never were free elections in Nicaragua without the United States Marines, and Somoza and his two sons would rule Nicaragua with American support until 1979. The United States had developed an analysis of events to the south that transformed a complex nationalistic revolt into an upheaval by irresponsible groups influenced by communist agitators. Within that prism, the appropriate and necessary course of action seemed clear.

Limits of the Good Neighbor Policy

While the political situation in Nicaragua was being stabilized under the direction of the Guardia Nacional, the Hoover administration faced a new crisis in El Salvador. Events there would challenge the Republican policy of nonrecognition of governments that come to power by revolution and in 1932 would bring about a reversal of that policy. Responding to what the State Department viewed as a communist revolt in January 1932, the United States would informally recognize the government of General Maximiliano Hernández Martínez because he was seen as necessary to stability and anticommunism in the region. The Roosevelt administration, acting in the name of the Good Neighbor Policy, would accept the policies of the Republicans in Central America and extend formal recognition in January 1934.

The Hoover administration's recognition of the dictatorship of General Martínez marked the culmination of a decade-long development of

U.S. policy toward right-wing dictatorships in response to the changed international climate and revolutionary challenges that emerged from World War I. Martínez took power after the overthrow of El Salvador's first democratically elected president, Arturo Araujo, in December 1931. In keeping with the 1923 Washington Treaty, the State Department initially refused to recognize Martínez. After the peasant revolt in January 1932, this policy came into conflict with the overriding desire for stability. The department's interpretation, however, of the domestic unrest in El Salvador as being Bolshevist-incited and an assessment of the people of El Salvador as inferior and in need of a firm hand led the Hoover administration to ignore Martínez's responsibility for the *matanza* (massacre) that killed thirty thousand El Salvadoreans and to accept the murderous Martínez as the ruler of El Salvador. Driven by a desire for order and fear of Bolshevism, the policy toward El Salvador led to a cementing of the Republican-developed logic and rationale for supporting right-wing dictatorships.

El Salvador, dominated by the so-called forty families (the oligarchy), had been one of the most politically stable nations in Central America. Coffee, which had been introduced in El Salvador in the mid-nineteenth century, was the dominant crop of the nation, accounting for over 90 percent of all exports by the 1920s. The oligarchy's power rested in its control of the haciendas, which it had solidified in the 1880s, when in defending the principle of private property the government abolished all town communal landholdings. By the end of the 1880s, the state in El Salvador was organized for the "encouragement of coffee production, construction of railroads to the ports, elimination of communal lands, laws against vagrancy that permitted the state to force peasants to work for *hacendados* at low wages, and repression of rural unrest."[47]

The costs of these actions to the peasants were high. Tens of thousands were displaced from the lands they farmed, and the production of staple crops such as maize and beans was cut dramatically. During the 1920s, the amount of land devoted to coffee production increased 34 percent, and El Salvador became dependent on food imports from the United States.[48] While most peasants had survived on seasonal work and subsistence wages, the price of maize increased 100 percent and beans 225 percent during the 1920s. Sporadic peasant unrest was met forcefully by the National Guard. In addition to selling staple foods to El Salvador, United States banks loaned $21 million to the government and appointed a fiscal agent to supervise the collection of trade duties.[49]

Alberto Masferrer, editor of the daily newspaper *Patria*, summarized the impact of the expansion of the coffee lands in a January 1929 editorial. "It is extended like the conquistador," he wrote, "spreading hunger and misery, reducing the former proprietors to the worst conditions. . . . Is the income of the *campesino*, who has lost his land, adequate to provide maize, rice, beans, clothes, medicine, doctor, etc? So what good does it do to make money from the sale of coffee when it leaves so many people in misery?"[50] The coming of the Great Depression only made the situation worse. Coffee prices dropped from $15.75 per hundred kilograms in 1928 to $5.97 by 1932, devastating to a nation that drew over 80 percent of its national income from coffee. The income of plantation workers, which had barely provided a subsistence in 1928, was cut in half by 1932. Life for the campesinos was reaching a point of starvation and desperation.[51] These were the key reasons for the peasant revolt of 1932.

The domination of El Salvador by the oligarchy had provided political stability in contrast to the unrest in Nicaragua. The oligarchy had established the custom of having each president personally designate his heir, thereby preventing any internal factions from contesting for power. The presidents were "thorough-going dictators who ruled with an iron hand" in the interests of the oligarchy and the military.[52] In 1927, the candidate "elected" was Pío Romero Bosque. Romero Bosque, however, turned out to be a reformer who desired to open up the political process and hold free elections for the presidency. When the time came, he refused to name a successor.

This is not to say that Romero Bosque did not rule with absolute power. The pre-Depression years of his presidency featured a government-declared state of siege from December 1927 to February 1929. The American minister, Warren D. Robbins, reported that the state of siege was "in no way a hindrance to the general activities of the country and . . . merely facilitates the maintenance of order throughout the country."[53] Romero Bosque was viewed positively by the embassy, which reported that his "energetically friendly attitude to the United States" drew him criticism from the local intelligentsia.[54] As one report noted in March 1928, the president had a "clamp placed on agitators; attempted unfriendly demonstrations [were] suppressed; [and] objectionable articles [were] not permitted in the press" by anti-American propagandists.[55] In September, Bosque prevented a lecture on American policy in Nicaragua, deporting the speaker for his attempt.[56]

There were, however, problems in El Salvador, according to the American embassy. These problems were all linked to what was seen as Bosque's unwise attempt to open up the political process, a step embassy officials did not believe El Salvador was ready for. Given U.S. support of the oligarchy because of the stability it imposed on El Salvador, the economic advantages it provided Americans, and the paternalistic view State Department leaders held of Latin Americans that led them to believe they were incapable of democracy, the department saw no reason for change. Stimson believed that progress in the Central American republics was impaired by "difficulties of race and climate."[57] The department believed, therefore, that attempts at political change should be approached with caution or not at all.

In the fall of 1928, the chargé d'affaires, Samuel Dickson, reported that many "prominent Salvadoreans" believed that the government had become "entirely too lax with the censorship of the press; with the liberty permitted the students and labor organizations." Even under a declared state of siege, the "discontent being manifested against the present order is becoming rather alarming," and it appeared that the "nation is drifting into a state of chaos." Dickson concluded that he was "inclined to believe it is all too true. The President is drifting on a tide of political discontent."[58] In April 1929, Robbins, in his first report to Secretary of State Stimson, emphasized that President Bosque was "not a strong man . . . nor is he now very popular" with the landowners. Still, "Salvador, owing to several good years of coffee crop, is more prosperous than it ever has been and the rich landowners realize this." The view of the oligarchy was the only one presented in most reports. The minister was optimistic that as long as Bosque did not attempt many changes, he could produce "another quiet year."[59]

In June, Robbins worried about reports that Bosque was going to refuse to name a successor. He noted that the president "disapproved of the custom of succession and desires that a candidate should be chosen who demonstrates justly the choice of the people." This action caused a split in the oligarchy. Bosque was supported by a group of rich landowners, including Arturo Araujo, whom the minister characterized as having little political experience and, therefore, lacking an understanding of the danger such a move presented. As Robbins concluded, "This all sounds very well but what is really the wish of the people of El Salvador is [a] very difficult, if not impossible, question to find out."[60] Considering that the minister on at least one occasion discussed his worry of the danger with Romero Bosque and indicated his support for the tradition of succession, he clearly did not want to find out the answer to the question.[61]

The onset of the Great Depression and the fall in the price of coffee, coupled with the now open presidential race, brought about the rise of widespread vocal opposition to the oligarchy's rule and the status quo in El Salvador. Most of the opposition was unorganized peasants and the trade unions in San Salvador. In addition, the Partido Communista de El Salvador (PCS), headed by Augustín Farabondo Martí, was founded in 1929. His party never grew to include much beyond students and intellectuals in the capital. The crash of coffee prices, however, set off a series of protests in the nation. Eighty thousand people marched in San Salvador on May Day 1930, demanding a minimum wage for agricultural workers, an end to unemployment, and better working conditions. Smaller demonstrations followed in both the capital and small towns, particularly around Izalco in the Sonsonate province. The government moved quickly to put an end to these protests. President Bosque banned all demonstrations and the distribution of "leftist" literature. Mass arrests were made, and in the four-month period leading up to the election twelve hundred people were jailed.[62] The government's actions cut down the number of demonstrations but did not eliminate unrest in the nation.

In March 1930, the new American chargé, W. W. Schott, wrote to Stimson to report on the first upsurge of protest. There was some cause for concern, but he believed that prompt government action would quickly return calm to the nation. He wrote that he did not believe that "radicalism extends widely in the capital nor that the Government, by prompt and decisive measures, could not eradicate it entirely." Unfortunately, "it has not seen fit" to do so. Ignoring the conditions that prompted the protests or the demands being made, Schott laid the blame at the feet of "agitators" who were "spreading subversive doctrines." Even after reporting cases of violence on the large estates, the chargé stated that the ordinary Salvadorean "does not incline toward change." The danger was that because of their ignorance, they could be aroused by the PCS toward actions they did not understand. Still, the "situation could be controlled by no great energetic action."[63]

By August, after Bosque had banned all demonstrations, strikes, and distribution of subversive materials, what Schott labeled the "suppression of all Communist activities in the country," the chargé's reports indicated that El Salvador's problems had passed. The chief of police in San Salvador informed him that the president's action "affords him a strong weapon with which to deal with persons of Communistic tendencies, and that he anticipates eliminating the social evil in a very brief period."[64] Again tying the demonstrations and general unrest to the work of agitators and not real problems, Schott reported that the "people are not of the character to embrace Communism whole-heartedly." Amazingly, he then reported that the "problem of unemployment does not really exist, and the problem of life is not a serious one."[65] If there was no unemployment problem, as he claimed, then there was no basis for protests. The only conclusion to be drawn was the one Schott held to all along, that the basically happy Salvadoreans were being stirred up by a small group of agitators. Once they were eliminated, the difficulties would be gone.

This paternalistic and inaccurate view of the conditions in El Salvador was widely held by American officials. As late as 22 December 1931, exactly one month before the peasant revolt, Major A. R. Harris, the U.S. military attaché for Central America, reported to Washington his observations of El Salvador. His comments are much more revealing than he intended: "About the first thing one observes when he goes to San Salvador is the number of expensive automobiles on the streets. There seems to be nothing but Packards and Pierce Arrows . . . [and] nothing between these high-priced cars and the ox cart with its barefoot attendant. There is practically no middle class between the very rich and the very poor. . . . Thirty or forty families own nearly everything in the country. . . . The rest of the population has practically nothing. These poor people work for a few cents a day and exist as best they can." Harris did note that such a "situation is ripe for communism" but that the "authorities seem to realize that the situation is dangerous and are quite alert in their fight against communistic influences." Besides, according to Harris, the "people never go hungry. The poor can always get fruit and vegetables." In addition, "since they never had anything, they do not feel the want very acutely of things they have never had." Consequently, "they never become desperate."[66]

Given such reporting and the prevalent views of American officials, it is no wonder that the State Department could conclude in 1931 that El Salvador's political situation was the best and most stable in the region and would remain so as long as no one tried to institute too much change. The president needed only to maintain the support of the army and the oligarchy. The key to El Salvador's stability was that the Assembly was under the complete control of the president and approved whatever he wanted. This meant, the Division of Latin American Affairs concluded, that "in general the Governments of Salvador have been fairly good, not oppressive to the people and with very little danger of being overthrown by revolution." The secretary of state agreed. Stimson noted in his diary that El Salvador was the "second best" of the Central American republics because of its stability.[67] These views would soon be challenged by the peasants of El Salvador.

In this climate of unrest and mass arrests, the first genuinely free elections were held in El Salvador in January 1931. Six candidates entered the race, three from the now divided oligarchy, two generals, including General Martínez, and Arturo Araujo. While the other five represented the status quo and the interests of the oligarchy, Araujo campaigned as a liberal reformer. Even though he was a large landowner, he was known to pay his workers twice the normal wage. Araujo sought to model his political party after the British Labour Party and based much of his platform on Masferrer's ideas of *vitalismo*, "vital minimum," for all people to have a decent life. Labor and the peasants, lacking any political organizations of their own, supported Araujo. After a bitter campaign and a last-minute withdrawal by Martínez to become Araujo's vice president, Araujo led all the candidates with over one hundred thousand votes to sixty-two thousand for the second candidate and fifty-three thousand for the other three combined. Because there was no majority, the election went to the Assembly, where Araujo's election was ensured when the third-place candidate supported him.[68] Araujo's promises of land reform and legalized trade unions proved popular with the masses and indicated that many people in El Salvador desired change more than American officials believed.

Inaugurated on 1 March 1931, Araujo's government would last only nine months. The new government was ill-fated from the outset. On the one hand, the oligarchy went on "strike." Refusing to accept the results, El Savador's elite refused to allow its supporters to take any government jobs, thereby depriving Araujo of most of El Salvador's experienced professionals. On the other hand, having raised the expectations of the poor, Araujo found he could not satisfy his supporters. He was boxed in by the economic crisis of the Depression, which provided the government little capital with which to pursue reforms. Araujo attempted some limited land and tax reform, but the oligarchy succeeded in blocking his moves. As it became clear that Araujo was not going to be able to provide relief to the workers and peasants, protests mounted for immediate change. Peasant strikes and protests in the capital were repressed by the army under the command of Vice President Martínez, who was also minister of war. By July, martial law was declared. Araujo was relying on traditional methods to maintain his authority.

The beleaguered Araujo received little sympathy from the American embassy. His problems, embassy reports indicated, were of his own making because of his attempts at ill-considered reforms. Robbins wrote that the president "led many farmers and laborers to think that the millennium was likely" once he was elected.[69] By the late spring and summer, reports to Washington emphasized the folly of Araujo's attempt at democracy, the ineptitude of the president, the disaffection of the oligarchy, and the fear of rising unrest, which was tied to communism. The new American chargé, Harold D. Finley, reported in July that Araujo was a "very tired and harassed man."[70] Reporting the views of what he termed the "intelligent parts of the community," Finley declared that Araujo's government was unpopular and faced charges of corruption, inefficiency, and incapacity to rule. The imbalance of the economy and the intransigence of the oligarchy were not blamed for any of Araujo's difficulties.[71]

In the fall, Araujo lost the support of the army. The specific act that hurt him was his cutting of the military budget. On 2 December 1931, the army ousted Araujo and established General Martínez as the new president. Martínez was known as an eccentric who sold patent medicines and was a committed theosophist. He was called *el brujo* (warlock) by most people. Martínez's belief in reincarnation led him to respond to criticism of the *matanza* by stating that "it is a greater crime to kill an ant than a man, because the man is born again at death, while an ant dies forever."[72]

Martínez may have had little to do with organizing the coup, and he certainly was not involved in the specific plans of the junior officers who carried it out, but suspicion concerning his role remained and provided part of the reason for U.S. nonrecognition of his government. The junior officers were well aware that they would receive the support of the generals and the oligarchy because they all shared a distrust of Araujo and what they saw as his socialistic policies.[73] Because Martínez was vice president and minister of war in Araujo's government and was thought to have played a role in the planning, the State Department, in the midst of the Manchurian crisis, invoked the 1923 Washington Treaty and denied his government recognition. The other Central American leaders, believing the treaty protected them, joined with the United States.

From the outset of the army rebellion, Stimson was frustrated with the actions of the new American minister, Charles Curtis. Curtis had failed to inform the leaders of the revolt that the United States would uphold the "Hughes doctrine," as Stimson called it, of not recognizing any revolutionary government. "This was a lost chance," Stimson wrote in his diary, "because we have often been able to prevent a revolution by notifying the conspirators that even if they were successful, they wouldn't get any recognition."[74] Stimson wired Curtis that he needed to make this policy clear to the leaders of the revolt.[75]

Curtis replied with a lengthy dispatch the next day in which he argued that the revolution was in fact constitutional because the army had the right to protect the social order and had appointed the vice president and that Araujo's "great incompetence" made him "more unpopular than he deserved to be, and was easily overthrown." As for the 1923 treaty, Curtis admitted that "this matter was constantly on my mind" but that he regretted to "report that [he] did not bring it up to the attention of the revolutionary leaders until the success of the revolution was already certain." The minister defended himself by arguing that it was not clear who was in charge at the outset and that such notification would have had no impact. Curtis took the position that without any definite evidence, Martínez should be assumed innocent of complicity with the revolution. In addition, Martínez pledged to continue loan payments to American bankers and to hold new local elections.[76]

These reports infuriated Stimson. He thought the situation in El Salvador was "critical" and again expressed his belief that had Curtis acted "promptly when the revolution was brewing," he could have headed it off with the threat of nonrecognition by the United States. Moreover, Stimson expressed surprise at Curtis's "cables which indicated his sympathy with the revolution."[77] The secretary of state informed Curtis that new elections would not change the interpretation of the State Department that the 1923 treaty barred Martínez from being president. Stimson instructed Curtis to ascertain how General Martínez believed "a regime which can be recognized can be brought into office."[78]

Nonrecognition placed the United States in a difficult position. Martínez had the support of both the military and the oligarchy and thus the power to defy American wishes and remain in power. Without the threat of military intervention, clearly out of the question given Stimson and Hoover's position on the Far East and Nicaragua, how could the United States effectively influence events in El Salvador to uphold its policy while still ensuring stability? The problem could be solved only through a change in policy.

In his first effort to resolve this problem and arrange for a government in El Salvador that the United States would recognize, Stimson sent Jefferson Caffery to San Salvador on 19 December 1931 as a special representative of the Department of State. Caffery, who was currently the United States minister to Colombia, was a former minister to El Salvador and enjoyed the confidence of Stimson that Curtis lacked to carry out the secretary's policy.[79] Despite protests that the United States had no desire to interfere in the internal affairs of El Salvador, the Caffery mission was designed to obtain Martínez's removal and the creation of a new government headed by somebody, civilian or military, who could be recognized by the United States under the terms of the treaty.

Caffery immediately sought Martínez's resignation when he arrived. He told the general directly that "under no circumstances could [the United States] recognize him." His initial meetings, however, brought no movement by the president. Caffery informed Stimson that "unfortunately the better elements here are now supporting General Martínez because he offers for the moment a stable government." With Martínez refusing to step down, citing that as vice president he automatically became president when Araujo left the country, Caffery realized that any further efforts directed toward getting Martínez to resign would prove futile. The special representative turned his attention to the young officers who organized the 2 December revolt.[80] Caffery sought, in effect, another coup to remove Martínez and replace him with somebody who was not associated with Araujo's government and was, therefore, eligible for U.S. recognition. Caffery was able, so he believed, to convince the officers to "force Martínez out and replace him with someone" who was qualified under the treaty.[81] He informed the officers that the "Department of State would be glad to recognize anyone not debarred by the treaty." Responding to the "tactfully" expressed concern relating to the "well known charges regarding the United States forcing its will on the smaller Latin American countries," Caffery assured them that the United States "had not the slightest desire of doing anything of the kind; 'we are backing no candidates.'"[82] United States policy was in no way motivated by a concern to reestablish the democratic process, but rather by maintaining a treaty that was seen as a bulwark against revolutions and helped preserve U.S. dominance in the region.

Caffery returned to Washington, D.C., on 8 January 1932. Stimson termed his "rescue mission" a success because it had convinced the "people who are in control there . . . to abide by . . . our views of the situation."[83] Caffery, however, had been unable to obtain a commitment from the officers to a specific time or person to replace Martínez, and they made no move to oust the general. More than likely, they had told Caffery what he wanted to hear, not what they intended to do. Accustomed to the United States dominating events in the region, Stimson believed El Salvador would have to yield to U.S. desires.

The failure of Caffery's mission did not signal the end of American pressure. Stimson wrote the newest chargé, William McCafferty, on 13 January that "under no circumstances [could Martínez] be recognized" and that the department hoped that a government the United States could recognize "may be established in Salvador at the earliest possible moment."[84] Lacking a military threat or economic lever because of the Great Depression, Stimson could do little more. Yet a gradual shift in the American position was beginning to appear. Equating all unrest with communism, embassy reports regularly featured the danger of a communistic uprising. This fear led to a reevaluation of Martínez. Summarizing the concerns of the embassy staff, McCafferty reported on 20 January that for the "past three years and especially during the Araujo administration, communism has been permitted to spread throughout Salvador." The leaders, particularly the "notorious Augustin Marti," had "succeeded in inciting the farm laborers to take over control of several large coffee plantations," and only government force had kept control of the situation. Labeling the problem "serious," McCafferty was genuinely worried about a revolt.[85]

On 22 January 1932, thousands of Salvadorean peasants, armed mainly with machetes, attacked local government and army outposts in the western coffee regions of El Salvador. They were able briefly to hold a few towns, the largest being Sonsonate, a town of twenty thousand and a commercial center of the coffee area. While Martí and some other leaders of the insurrection were communists, the vast majority of the peasants were not. Unemployment, lack of land, starvation, and other long-standing political and economic grievances, not communist ideology, motivated the Indians and campesinos who revolted. The PCS tried to organize this discontent, but it did not create it, and its inability to control events became clear when the party's last-minute decision to call off the insurrection failed either to reach the peasants or to stop them.[86]

The rebellion was quickly crushed by the government. The insurrection had led to the killing of one hundred people.[87] The *matanza* that followed claimed up to thirty thousand lives. Wearing Indian dress, running from the security forces, or being suspected of left-wing beliefs made one a potential victim. Raymond Bonner describes a scene where the "roadways and drainage ditches were littered with bodies, gnawed at by buzzards and pigs. Hotels were raided; individuals with blond hair were dragged out and killed as suspected Russians. Men were tied thumb to thumb, then executed, tumbling into mass graves they had first been forced to dig."[88] Unions and all other political organizations were banned in the country. In the United States, a massacre of the same percentage of the population would have claimed 4.4 million lives.

The U.S. government, while trying to censor the full extent of the slaughter, argued that such severe repression was necessary because the peasants who revolted were communists.[89] American officials, having defined all unrest in El Salvador as communist-incited and having no relationship to the actual conditions of the country, and unwilling to side with or understand indigenous radicalism, accepted Martínez's explanation. The basis for a change in policy had been laid.

McCafferty set the tone with a report on 23 January which labeled the rebellion as communist. He ironically urged the State Department to help the government "in any way" because it "might prevent the threatened establishment of a communistic state here accompanied by much bloodshed." The chargé requested that American warships be sent to El Salvador and financial aid be extended to the government.[90] Two days later, he reported that the "large landowners against whom the venom of the Communists is naturally directed" remained scared.[91]

The chargé's reports created alarm in Washington. Responding to what Under Secretary of State William Castle termed the "serious situation in Salvador resulting from the Communistic outbreak," three American warships carrying marines were dispatched from the Special Service Squadron in Panama to El Salvador.[92] Stimson hoped that the marines would be unnecessary, "for it would make a bad impression in Latin America," but their dispatch was a precaution should the government lose control of the situation.[93] There was as well a search within the State Department for information on communism in El Salvador to support the reports being received from San Salvador. R. M. de Lambert of the Division of Latin American Affairs drew up a five-page memorandum, "The Growth of Communism in El Salvador," on 26 January 1932, for his superiors. Relying heavily on hearsay and fragmentary evidence, much of it supplied by Robert Kelley's Division of Eastern European Affairs, the memorandum linked all recent unrest to communists who had infiltrated El Salvador from Mexico. De Lambert dismissed any suggestion that local conditions had contributed to the unrest: "While practically all of the more valuable land of the country is held by a very small percentage of proprietors and wealth is concentrated in a few hands, and the very great majority of the people are extremely poor, nevertheless, even at this time, there appears to be very little unemployment in the country and, due to the nature of the climate and the fertility of the soil, there is practically no suffering from hunger or cold."[94]

The press was informed by the State Department that there had indeed been a genuine communist revolt, not a popular rebellion. Department officials laid the blame on leadership from Mexico. The situation had been serious, but the Martínez government was taking energetic action to suppress the rebellion.[95] In a review of accomplishments at the end of Hoover's presidency, the State Department continued to label the uprising as a "communist revolt" and argued that they "committed many atrocities." The *matanza* was ignored. Instead, the report noted only that the "Government . . . suppressed the uprising with utmost severity in a relatively short time and succeeded in restoring order. *This display of efficiency strengthened Martínez' position in the republic.*"[96]

Martínez's actions not only strengthened his position domestically—he was declared constitutional president by the Assembly on 5 February—but also brought about a reversal in American policy. Stimson's changing position was apparent immediately when he noted on 25 January that the "communistic revolution in Salvador . . . produces a rather nasty . . . problem, because the man who is president and who is the only pillar against the success of what seems to be a rather nasty proletarian revolution is Martínez, whom we were unable to recognize under the 1923 rule."[97] He wrote the U.S. minister in Guatemala that the question of recognition was now "a difficult one" because "Martínez appears to have strengthened his position . . . as a result of having put down the recent disorders and he apparently has a favorable majority in the recently elected Salvadorean Congress."[98] Of course, there was no opposition to challenge him.

By the beginning of February, McCafferty was reporting that the government was firmly in control and that order would be maintained as long as there were "sufficient funds to pay the armed forces."[99] He argued that the department should relax its legalistic opposition toward Martínez. The general was willing to give up the formal position of president while retaining actual control of the government. He would appoint the first designate as president, return to the vice presidency, and, therefore, be able to "resume the Presidency" should the first designate resign in "say 6 or 7 months." McCafferty informed Martínez that this plan would be seen as only an attempt to get around the treaty and that he doubted the administration would accept it. Yet he advised the department to agree. McCafferty, who never investigated the extent of the massacre, held to the position that communism still presented a problem in El Salvador and that Martínez was both popular and necessary for continued order. The situation was "extremely difficult" for the maintenance of U.S. nonrecognition, McCafferty concluded, because of the "fact that Martínez has been giving a very efficient and honest administration and the people of the country are generally [in] back of him."[100]

Stimson replied that the United States could not support Martínez's proposal. "It is clear that the plan contemplates an evasion of the terms of the Treaty" and would consist of U.S. recognition of Martínez's government. Yet Stimson wanted it made clear to Martínez that the department's actions were "not motivated by any unfriendliness against General Martínez for whom it has great regard." McCafferty informed Martínez that he believed the only thing he could do was resign outright.[101]

At this time, El Salvador announced that it was suspending payments on its 1922 loan from U.S. banks. A government decree on 27 February ordered that all customs duties that formerly were paid to the banks' American representative be paid to the treasury. American bankers insisted that the State Department act to ensure repayment on the defaulted loan. The State Department, however, declined to become involved. Although the stated reason was that it could not intervene with a government it did not recognize, the department may also have been acting out of its concern for the financial stability of Martínez's government, which it saw, whether recognized or not, as a bulwark against Bolshevism.[102]

Further actions by the department support this interpretation. In early March Stimson was willing to accept a different plan that allowed for recognition of a government in which Martínez maintained power. On 8 March, McCafferty telegraphed Stimson that "Martínez had decided to resign the Presidency outright." He would, instead, become the minister of war in the new government. With the situation in El Salvador, in McCafferty's estimation, "going from bad to worse without recognition," he wanted the department's opinion so that the process could proceed. He noted that it might take several weeks for the transfer to occur. The army and the oligarchy were, however, divided on who should assume the presidency, the first designate, Colonel Fidel Garay, or Colonel José Menéndez. Stimson responded that the State Department had no objection to that arrangement.[103]

When McCafferty met with Martínez on 2 April to discuss why the promised change had not occurred and when he could inform the State Department to expect the reorganization, Martínez replied that a change at that time would be a disaster. He argued that communism remained a serious problem, that the army wanted him to remain, and that he had the support of the public. In response to McCafferty's persistent queries as to whether he was going to step down, Martínez again said that he would after he worked matters out with the younger officers. The new target date was 1 June. On 8 June, Martínez announced that he was no longer going to try to find an arrangement to satisfy the 1923 treaty and that he would remain in office until the end of his term in 1935. Stability and the desire of the overwhelming majority of the people were his stated reasons for this move. McCafferty reported that nonrecognition was not seen as a problem by Martínez and his advisers.[104]

Stimson was faced with the decision of withdrawing the chargé and closing the legation or leaving McCafferty in San Salvador and thereby extending informal recognition to Martínez. Not removing McCafferty, supporters argued, would destroy the 1923 treaty and undermine U.S. ability to influence events in the region short of military intervention. It was, in effect, a choice between increasing American pressure and forcing Martínez out or accepting him in power. The secretary of state had, however, already reached the conclusion that Martínez was necessary for stability in El Salvador. Stimson had been trying since February to reach a solution that would technically satisfy the treaty without forcing Martínez to give up power.

It is not surprising, therefore, that a decision was reached almost immediately to keep the legation open. Edwin Wilson, chief of the Latin American Division of the State Department, acknowledged that closing the legation would "prove to be merely a futile gesture" that would easily be defied and would commit the United States to "a position which it might be awkward to recede from."[105] In addition, such a move could be seen as a signal of disapproval of Martínez and as the beginning of stronger measures to remove him. Both of these points ran counter to the views of the department that Martínez's continuation in power was necessary for the stability and development of El Salvador.

In November 1932, Costa Rica and El Salvador announced that as of 1 January 1934, they would no longer recognize the 1923 Washington Treaty. The State Department noted that if the treaty was abrogated, it "would resume its freedom of action and . . . judge each case upon its merits."[106] On 8 January 1934, Sumner Welles forwarded a State Department plan to President Roosevelt that would allow the United States to recognize Martínez formally. Nicaragua would recommend to Guatemala and Honduras that they continue to recognize the treaty among themselves "but not in force with respect to relations" with El Salvador and Costa Rica. Noting that reports from El Salvador "indicate that General Martínez has given his country a relatively efficient government and is strongly supported by public opinion," Welles argued that normalized relations "would constitute another and important step in the establishment of normal, friendly relations among all the nations of America." Roosevelt approved of the plan. On 24 January, following the initiative of Nicaragua, the three Central American states recognized Martínez's government, and the United States did the same on 26 January.[107]

Instead of hurting his standing with the United States, the *matanza* bolstered Martínez's position. It did not bring forth condemnation and statements that it was proof that the United States was correct in not backing such a government but rather a growing approval of the general and proposals for skirting around the legal problem of recognition. Finding no such method, the State Department simply quit in its efforts to "retire" Martínez, and in June 1932 informally recognized his regime. Without any debate, the Roosevelt administration recognized Martínez as soon as it was able to avoid the treaty restrictions. In the meantime, lack of formal recognition had not prevented the United States from demonstrating its support of Martínez. The dictator was now seen as essential for social peace and the development of El Salvador. His brutal regime, which began a fifty-year rule by the military in El Salvador, marks the beginning of modern history in El Salvador. In eliminating his opposition, Martínez began the polarization of El Salvadorean society that erupted in civil war in the 1970s and 1980s. The perceived benefits of stability, trade, and anti-Bolshevism overrode the problems of constitutionality and the desire to help limit arbitrary power in Central America.

The Roosevelt administration again accepted the Republican answer to the difficult problem of providing stability without direct American military intervention. Moreover, it was clear that while the United States nominally supported democracy and hoped to promote and protect it internationally, Washington was more concerned with instability and the danger of freedom in what it perceived to be politically immature nations. The key to development anywhere was order, which would minimize distress during difficult periods of transition to modern economic and, eventually, political states. Until then, evidence indicated that strong rule was necessary in many nations to ensure that they did not attempt self-rule until they were free of the dangers from the left. The United States would support authoritarian rulers as long as order was preserved, they did not form alliances with any power that threatened the United States, and investments and trade were protected. The policy pendulum had swung fully to a position of support for right-wing dictators.

Good Neighbor Batista

During his inauguration speech on 4 March 1933, Roosevelt announced that U.S. relations with the other American republics would be based on the "policy of the good neighbor . . . who resolutely respects himself and, because he does so, respects the rights of others."[108] Sumner Welles, an old friend of Roosevelt's, who would oversee the establishment of this policy, had recommended to the newly elected president that his top priority should be "the creation and maintenance of the most cordial and intimate friendship between the United States and other republics of the American continent."[109] Seeking to improve relations with Latin America so as to increase international trade, aid economic recovery at home, and forestall unrest, the administration renounced the use of unilateral American intervention in the affairs of those nations. The announcement of the Good Neighbor Policy received a positive reception on both sides of the Rio Grande. The seemingly bold declaration was in reality a continuation of Stimson's policy of ending direct American intervention while still preserving influence and stability. Only the methods, not the desired objectives of influence and stability, had changed.

Roosevelt's desire to end military intervention was similar to Stimson's. As early as 1928, he had stated that "single-handed intervention by us in the internal affairs of other nations must end; with the cooperation of others we shall have more order in this Hemisphere and less dislike."[110] The others too often turned out to be dictators. Roosevelt made his concerns clear in December 1933. He announced that the "definite policy of the United States from now on is one opposed to armed intervention." The problem of order remained. Roosevelt backed away from Wilson and Hughes when he stated that the "maintenance of constitutional government in other nations is not a sacred obligation devolving upon the United States alone." He then slightly shifted the central concern when he noted that "the maintenance of law and the orderly processes of government in this hemisphere is the concern of each individual nation."[111] This view left plenty of room for military rule and those who obtained power outside of constitutional means, such as Somoza and Martínez, as long as they followed policies that did not threaten American interests.

Roosevelt's own thinking about the region reveals the most important continuities. The president shared his generation's basic views and prejudices concerning the world. Roosevelt traveled to Europe eight times as a child and continued to travel to Europe, and once to Latin America, as an adult until stricken with polio. Like many, he confused this cosmopolitan behavior with knowledge about the world and its people. His view was in fact a rather limited one that saw the world through a Eurocentric lens. Similar to others who made American policy, Roosevelt assumed that because he and his advisers were reasonable men, all reasonable people in other nations would concur with their understandings of events and issues. When they did not, it was clear that the problem stemmed from either character flaws or racial inferiority. As one biographer has noted, Roosevelt "believed in the universality of American values and that peoples the world over would embrace those values if only they had an opportunity to do so."[112]

During the Wilson administration, Roosevelt, as assistant secretary of the navy, advocated military intervention in Mexico during the upheavals of its revolution, noting that "sooner or later the United States must go down there and clean up the Mexican political mess." He based these comments on his conviction that U.S. intervention was beneficial for civilizing "backward" people. For example, he remarked that Haitians were "little more than primitive savages" before the arrival of American occupation forces.[113] Given his positive view toward intervention, it was no wonder that he claimed during his 1920 vice presidential campaign that "I wrote Haiti's constitution myself, and if I do say it, I think it was a pretty good constitution."[114]

Once in office, Roosevelt's and other American officials' attitudes remained unchanged. Indeed, the adoption of the Good Neighbor Policy in many ways served to reinforce the ideas of Latin Americans' inferiority and the need for a strong hand to guide them now that the United States would no longer intervene to solve their problems. In discussions with Henry Stimson, Roosevelt asked whether Haiti was now stable and the job of American troops was finished. Stimson replied that he did not believe the stability was permanent and asked Roosevelt if "he knew any self-governing negro community which had stayed put." Roosevelt answered that he did not. Later he informed Stimson that while he agreed with the policy of removing American marines from Nicaragua, Haiti, and the Dominican Republic—so as to remove any legitimate grounds for criticizing United States policy—he believed that "Latin Americans would always be jealous of us" and therefore critical.[115] In developing his policy, Roosevelt relied on Welles. Welles had experience in the State Department working in Latin America and was active during the 1920s writing about United States policy and developing the good neighbor idea. In a 1924 debate with Samuel Inman in the *Atlantic Monthly*, Welles rejected the charge that U.S. policy toward Latin America could be characterized as imperialism. That, he believed, was true only for the period 1898–1901 when the United States acquired additional territory and colonies. Since then, American policy had been designed to aid the nations where American forces intervened.[116] Unfortunately, these interventions were met with hostility and, therefore, often failed to create the desired stability and financial order. For Welles, some other form of order was necessary to address problems before revolts broke out and eliminate the factors that created revolutions. Stability would allow for economic growth and rising educational levels that would benefit both those nations and the United States itself. The core of the Good Neighbor Policy rested on treating the nations of Latin America as sovereign, independent states and preventing the rise of conditions that produced revolutions.

Implementation of the new policy would be severely tested in Cuba. Roosevelt and Welles embarked on the Good Neighbor Policy at the same time that unrest was growing in Havana. Since 1903, the United States had claimed the right of intervention in Cuba through the Platt Amendment, and American troops had been dispatched there four times. Events in Havana in 1933 appeared to invite a fifth military mission. Between August 1933, when the Gerardo Machado regime collapsed, and January 1934, when Fulgencio Batista installed a government the United States supported, Cuba saw five different presidents in as many months, including one administration that lasted only two days. Having announced the Good Neighbor Policy, however, the Roosevelt administration could not afford to do an about-face and intervene directly to restore order, although the option was discussed. Yet the administration feared that the unrest would produce a radical government set on the course of social reform that would threaten established American interests. American investments in Cuba had increased from $50 million at the time of the Spanish-American War to $1.5 billion in 1929. Ultimately, the administration followed the course of its Republican predecessors and came to support a repressive military leader as the best solution for establishing order, protecting American investments, preventing communism, and governing a nation that did not appear to Washington able to manage democracy.

The Cuban dictator Gerardo Machado had ruled the island since 1924. In 1928, he subverted the constitution and guaranteed his continued rule, which was both corrupt and brutal. Reports of violence and torture of political enemies were common. The downturn in world prices for sugar caused by the Great Depression created extreme hardship throughout Cuba, leading to the island's economic collapse. Machado continued to rule only through the use of force. By 1933, the combination of brutal repression, economic crisis, and corruption brought forth intense opposition to Machado. In an act that exemplified how Machado ruled his country, the beleaguered dictator at one point had his agents put out a false announcement of his resignation. When four to five thousand people were celebrating in the streets of Havana, Machado's personal army, the Porra, began "firing into the crowd, killing twenty and wounding eighty."[117]

Despite his unconstitutional means of keeping power and his violence, the United States continued to support Machado. When Stimson met with Roosevelt in January 1933 to discuss world affairs and American foreign policy, the departing secretary of state informed the president-elect that "Machado had had unusual success in controlling his position" and that he "had not been obliged to give Cuba as much anxious thought as I had most other South American countries." The reason was the loyalty of the army, "which had been trained by American officers and had imbibed the American Army officers' doctrine of keeping out of politics and being loyal to their civil chiefs."[118] The period of his rule had been a profitable one for U.S. businesses in Cuba, and the desire for stability and the protection of American businesses had served as a shield against American opposition.

When Welles arrived in Cuba as ambassador in May, he set out to solve the building crisis by negotiating a new commercial agreement between the United States and Cuba. The State Department believed that the basic problem in Cuba was economic and that it could be solved through increased and regular trade. Economic recovery would bring political stability and quell the unrest. Continued upheaval might threaten U.S. interests and force the Roosevelt administration to do the one thing it had pledged the United States would no longer do, intervene directly. Hubert Herring aptly described Welles's dilemma at the time: "Mr. Welles had the task of intervening without intervention, of mediating without coercion, of playing the friend to Cuba without wielding a club."[119] Underestimating the opposition to Machado and the depths of the problem, Welles set out to establish a new treaty.[120]

After a week of negotiations, Welles wrote Secretary of State Cordell Hull of his optimism that an early economic agreement could be reached that would "not only revivify Cuba, but will give us practical control of the market we have been steadily losing for the past ten years."[121] Machado's continuation in power appeared necessary for this to happen. Welles wrote that "if the acute bitterness of feeling against the President . . . persists or becomes intensified during the coming year it would in all probability be highly desirable that the present chief executive be replaced . . . by some impartial citizen in whom all factions have confidence." Welles opposed a change at that time. He argued that "President Machado is able to preserve order joined with unquestioned loyalty and discipline of the Cuban Army. If some individual replaced him the loyalty of the Army would be questionable." With the opposition unable to agree on anything other than opposition to Machado, Welles feared "general chaos might well result" and the malcontents would try to force an American intervention "through the destruction of American property."[122]

Yet to obtain what he wanted, Welles had to pressure Machado to carry out reforms, placing himself on the side of the opposition and undercutting the dictator's rule. After months of negotiations and efforts to include opposition parties in his plans for reform, Welles found it impossible to stem the tide demanding Machado's removal. To be sure, there were moments when Welles's optimism that he could retain Machado in power returned, particularly when the Cuban president allowed political exiles to return and eased the censorship of the press. In July, Welles wrote Roosevelt that political unrest was near an end and that the "situation is distinctly encouraging, far more so than I had hoped six weeks ago." Yet two days later he acknowledged in a letter to Hull that Machado was not carrying out the promised reforms and that he was finding it difficult to alleviate the unrest without aiding Machado's opponents.[123] To preserve his power, Machado began attacking Welles, accusing him of meddling in Cuban affairs and lacking the support of the United States government. The truth was that Welles was fully in control of Cuban policy and had Roosevelt's complete backing.[124] Thus, when Welles decided to abandon Machado in August, Washington followed his lead.

On 4 August a general strike spread across Cuba, effectively ending Machado's ability to rule. Welles informed Machado that he was aware of the "obligation of the United States under the [Platt Amendment], but told him that the whole purpose of my mission . . . was to avoid the United States having to consider carrying out such obligations" to maintain order. He told Machado that to salvage the situation short of a revolution, he would have to resign. New elections, Welles now believed, would ease the crisis and alleviate the need for American intervention. He wrote Hull that the United States should withdraw its recognition of Machado's regime so as to force these elections.[125] The Cuban army solved part of Welles's problem when it revolted on 11 August, sending Machado into exile and allowing Carlos Manuel de Cespedes—whom Welles called a "most sincere friend of the United States"—to assume the presidency.[126]

Cespedes's government was doomed to be short-lived even with United States support. Welles hoped it could control the crisis and preserve order, but Cespedes's government lacked any significant support outside the United States embassy. Welles quickly sought to aid the new president by requesting a loan for the Cuban government and an increase in sugar purchases. These actions brought no relief to the unrest. As Welles noted just nine days after Machado's flight from the island, the situation was fraught with danger: "Government employees are in the greatest distress since salaries have not been paid over a period of many months. . . . All industry is practically at a standstill," and "poverty and destitution exist throughout the Republic." He concluded that "under such conditions no Government can stand, and particularly not a Government which has come into power under existing conditions." On 24 August he reported that he was "rapidly coming to the conclusion that my original hope that the present Government . . . could govern as a constitutional government for the remainder of the term for which General Machado had himself elected must be abandoned."[127] Welles had lost control over events in Cuba. After less than a month in power, Cespedes was overthrown on 4 September 1933 by the "Sergeants' Revolution." Led by Batista, the army installed Professor Ramón Grau San Martín as president. Grau promised reform and to "liquidate the colonial structure that has survived in Cuba since independence."[128] This program included a unilateral abrogation of the Platt Amendment, the suspension of payments on loans, and the seizing of some sugar mills owned by U.S. companies. Under the banner of "Cuba for Cubans," Grau refused to be intimidated by Washington.

Welles's response to the new government was overwhelmingly negative. He claimed that Cuba had fallen under the power of irresponsible elements, "extreme radical" students, and people who held "frankly communistic" ideas.[129] Welles described Grau as an "impractical and visionary leader" who led a government that was "incompetent in every branch." His support amounted to "only the students, a few radical agitators, and a small number of insignificant radical groups."[130] Welles be-

lieved that the "social revolution" in Cuba was producing "confiscatory measures designed to harm American interests." Grau, Welles emphasized, intended on "minimizing any form of American influence in
Cuba."[131] Reports of communist activity became a daily feature in embassy reporting and Welles's phone conversations with the State Department. Hull was so concerned that he had Assistant Secretary of State
Jefferson Caffery, who would replace Welles in December as ambassador
to Cuba, investigate the extent of communist activity and Soviet efforts
on the island.[132] Having raised the specter of communism, an exasper-
ated Welles advised Washington not to recognize the Grau government
and asked that American troops be sent to restore Cespedes to power
and to protect American interests. Welles strained to support his position by arguing that this landing, because it would restore the legitimate
government, would be consistent with the Good Neighbor Policy. Support of the new regime, on the other hand, would represent intervention by the United States to maintain a government that came to power
by a coup d'état.[133] Roosevelt and Hull agreed to nonrecognition but
stopped short of sending troops. Twelve ships were dispatched to the
Cuban coast to assure Americans there, and economic pressure was applied to hurt Grau's standing. Without recognition, the United States
would not negotiate a new sugar purchase agreement needed to alleviate the economic problems of the island.

Unable to unseat Grau quickly through nonrecognition and denied
the option of a military intervention, Welles shifted tactics and turned
to Batista for a solution to the problem. Batista, who had promoted himself to colonel and taken the post of army chief of staff after placing Grau
in power, was the most powerful person in Cuba. Instead of seeing him
as responsible for Grau's presidency, the ambassador saw Batista as the
best alternative to the current regime. Welles told him in October that
he was the "only individual in Cuba who represented authority." Grau's
supporters should be "studying in the university instead of playing politics." The ambassador emphasized that the United States would never
recognize such a government and that Batista should save himself and his
country by withdrawing his support for the government. He informed
Washington that Batista was popular with the respectable "commercial
and financial interests in Cuba" and, therefore, represented the best hope
for a return to stability. When the State Department indicated that it was
willing to reconsider the question of recognition, Welles protested that
it needed to give nonrecognition more time to work. He argued that as
"Batista becomes more influential the power of the students and Grau

San Martin diminishes." Welles's confidence that the policy of nonrecognition would oust Grau was increased when Batista informed him that he saw the government as "a complete failure" and that he planned to open up talks with opposition political leaders.[134]

Welles discounted the lack of protest and violence under Grau as the "quiet of panic" and continued to emphasize the disorder in Cuba and the danger of communism. Recognition of the Grau government would mean "economic ruin" for Cuba. It was the obligation of the United States not to saddle the Cubans "for an indefinite period [with] a government which every responsible element in the country violently opposed."[135] In December, Welles wrote Hull that Grau remained a figurehead for those "who are seeking to create a frankly communistic government in Cuba and those who are solely in the government for the profits."[136] When Caffery replaced Welles, his reporting was similar to his predecessor's. He too saw Grau's government as supported mainly by the "ignorant masses who have been misled by utopian promises" and unpopular with the "better classes in the country."[137]

The economic weapon eventually had the impact Welles sought. Nonrecognition eliminated any economic aid from the United States and hope for relief from the crisis of the Depression. Moreover, it harmed Grau because American opposition encouraged his opponents to hold out and avoid any compromise. They believed the United States would eventually bring about Grau's downfall. The one person who benefited from the fracturing of the political order was Batista, who held the power of the military. When Batista asked Caffery on 13 January what the United States desired in return for recognition of a government in Havana, the ambassador told him a new government.[138] Realizing that recognition would never come with Grau in power, Batista moved against the government. On 15 January 1934, he deposed Grau and placed Carlos Hevia in the presidency. His government lasted less than two days, when Batista pushed him out for the conservative opposition leader Carlos Mendieta. The State Department quickly recognized the new government, even though it had no more constitutional legitimacy than Grau's. Batista was now the real power in Cuba, and he assured the protection of American interests on the island.

As the unrest that marked the past five months persisted well into 1934, it became a truism in American discussions of Cuba that Batista had saved the country from disorder and anarchy. Reviewing the recent history of Cuba in February, the embassy reported that "communism appears to be concentrating its efforts on Cuba at the present time." The fault for this rested, of course, with the Grau administration, which made "little effort . . . to control communist agitation and none to suppress it." The report did note that Batista was undertaking "more energetic measures" to counter the communists, but the problem remained.[139] Thus Batista was seen as invaluable for Cuba. Caffery reported in April that although the danger of unrest and a communist revolt remained, Batista appeared to have the situation under control. He "continues in his calm, even way to direct the affairs of the Army," and "it remains a fact that no Government, this or any other, could last a day, if opposed by Batista."[140] The State Department concluded that Batista had saved Cuba from anarchy.[141] The Roosevelt administration supported that position by proposing a new commercial treaty and modification of the Platt Amendment designed to aid the new government. By May, the United States agreed to abandon the Platt Amendment and signed a new treaty with Cuba that increased its sugar quota and extended loans to increase exports.

According to Caffery, the communists sought to undermine the government before the positive aspects of these agreements could take hold. "The communistic organization," Caffery told Hull, "is energetically engaged . . . in promoting . . . disturbances, calculated to weaken the Mendieta Government." Their goal was to divide the American-owned estates among Cuban tenants, and "they believe that their activities will culminate in the overthrow of Mendieta and Batista." Caffery concluded that "the only real force . . . standing between a reasonable respect for property rights and chaos is Batista, and for that reason the elements of disorder are attempting to do everything possible to discredit him." Batista, Caffery approvingly noted, was standing by the government and continuing to maintain order. "He realizes that if the Mendieta Government is forced out of power by the Grau adherents . . . that the communistic elements would use Grau only for their own purposes and would continue their efforts at creating chaos in the Island."[142]

Batista was able to maintain control and in the process continued to gain support from the most powerful groups in Cuba. For example, Caffery informed Welles in September that former opponents realized that "if anything happens to Batista chaos will ensue, and that [they] well know that Batista is exceedingly able man with a great deal of sense, balance, and understanding."[143] Reports of communist activities continued in the fall, but American attention turned more to how Batista could preserve and improve his rule, rather than threats to it. As the Division of Latin American Affairs noted at the end of 1935, "It is difficult to believe that Col. Batista can keep himself absolutely free of any political entanglements in the coming elections. It is certainly unlike the Latin nature to pursue such an attitude." Events might force him to take direct control, but the Department was pleased that he was "trying to be as neutral as he safely can. . . . There is no doubt of his ability to enforce order during the holding of the elections."[144]

From the American viewpoint, Cuba had returned to stability and progress: Grau and his radical reforms were defeated, American interests preserved, and a dependable leader found. The official view was echoed in the press. The *Literary Digest* noted that while turbulence continued in Cuba, "the consensus . . . points to the man behind Mendieta as the sole visible hope in the situation. He is Fulgencio Batista . . . the dictator without portfolio." Batista retained Mendieta as president because he did not want the job and there was no one better available to put in his place. Expressing the prevailing paternalistic racism of the time, it approvingly concluded that in Cuba, "elections are impossible." Fortunately, the author found, "The army controls Cuba, and will for a long time to come—and Batista controls the Army. He will name the next President."[145] Herring reported in *Current History* that "Cuba has turned respectable. After pursuing strange gods for four months, she now comes back to the fold of the faithful, talks of stability, the payment of debts, the security of foreign capital." The man responsible was Batista, "the simple sergeant [who] proved himself to be something of a politician after all."[146]

The most glowing account of Batista's rule appeared in *Review of Reviews*. The story began: "In the sense that Emerson said 'an institution is usually the lengthened shadow of a single man,' the history of Cuba since September 4, 1933 may be told in the story of Colonel Fulgencio Batista." In tones that suggested a comparison to Mussolini, the author described Batista as having "a muscular obesity, for he weighs 180 and is but five feet five inches tall, which belies his intellectual grasp and dynamic character," and possessing the "prescience of genius." The article portrayed Batista as decisive in standing up to the communists on the island and maintaining order by a willingness to use force. In an analysis that could easily have been drawn up in Washington during the days of Theodore Roosevelt, Batista's politics were labeled clearly "pro–United States. He says the island is geographically a political accident, dependent on the United States economically, and must do all possible to cultivate its friendship. Batista's only other basic political creed is his anti-communism." Even though promised elections were continually postponed, the article reported that most Cubans were satisfied with Batista's control of the country. The support of the United States brought a new economic pact that "has saved Cuba from the almost hopeless dregs of the depression. It revived island trade like unexpected rain in a protracted drought." It concluded, "With these substantial benefits, Cubans, as well as tourists, are inclined to regard the political situation, even with its terrorism, quite tolerantly. Besides—there is Batista. Why worry?"[147]

Batista owed his power essentially to American support. Until the collapse of the Machado regime, the government controlled the military. The military coup that ousted Machado began the politicalization of the Cuban military. In succession, the military drove Cespedes, Grau, and Hevia from power when Batista decided they no longer served his interests. He settled on Mendieta because he was a popular counter to Grau. Mendieta, however, clearly understood that Batista held the real power. The fall of Machado and the rise of Batista also established the idea in Washington that Cuba needed strongman rule or it would be beset by disorder and vulnerable to radical ideas.

Benevolent Dictators

As long as rulers such as Batista and Somoza supported the United States and its foreign policy, World War II did not upset the fundamental support these dictators received. In 1938, for example, the embassy in Havana continued to report favorably on Batista's control over Cuban affairs. Summarizing the past five years, Ambassador J. Butler Wright wrote that "out of a widespread popular revolt of the masses has come military dominance—more or less benevolent at the time, but nevertheless fairly complete and in a position to be arbitrary."[148] Not surprisingly, as Batista moved to take formal power through elections in 1940, he had American support. Unfortunately, the election was a contested one, with Grau presenting the main challenge to Batista. The new ambassador, George Messersmith, fearing Grau might win, wrote Hull that "I am on the whole getting more of the opinion that we must take a stronger and firmer stand here, and that if we fail to do so we will be prejudicing seriously the interests of Cuba and ourselves."[149] The State Department was greatly relieved when Batista won, and he readily cooperated with the United States economically and militarily during World War II.

In 1942, Roosevelt hosted Batista at a state dinner in Washington. The president recalled for the audience the unrest in Cuba in 1933 and that his refusal to intervene, even though the United States was "compelled by . . . treaty, which was better know as the Platt Amendment," to do so, was the beginning of the Good Neighbor Policy. Engaging in some historical revisionism, he reported that he had told the representatives of all the Latin American republics that "I am not going to land a single American soldier or sailor on the soil of Cuba. I think this is an internal matter, which Cuba is fully competent to settle." Turning to Batista, Roosevelt stated that as "an army officer . . . he took part in that revolution of 1933 in a very modest way. Today the Cuban people are very happy that he is holding the office of Chief Magistrate of the Republic of Cuba." The use of force and extralegal means to gain power simply were not part of this review.[150] From the beginning of a rule that lasted with little interruption until 1959, Batista was seen as indispensable for Cuba.

Similarly, Somoza retained his favored status in Washington throughout the 1930s. Somoza was invited to the United States in 1939, a trip that included meetings with Roosevelt and an address to a joint session of Congress. The State Department report on Somoza prepared for Roosevelt was effusive in its praise of the dictator's rule. It skipped over Somoza's subversion of the electoral process on his way to power, merely noting that he became president in 1936 "for a term of four years. His term was extended early this year," and he "was reinaugurated on March 30 to hold office until May 1, 1947." Somoza's "rise to power in Nicaragua may be attributed principally to his political acumen and his pleasing personality rather than any profound abilities." Most important, "President Somoza is believed to have a sincere affection for the United States. He has consistently displayed a desire to cooperate fully with this Government and to cultivate our friendship." With World War II on the horizon, there was no good reason to question his method of ruling.[151] Dictatorships and military rule served American interests well by preserving order, controlling radical reform movements, and protecting American investments while obviating the need for U.S. intervention. Indeed, strong authoritarian regimes appeared necessary for the Good Neighbor Policy to succeed.

3 FROM ACCOMMODATION TO APPEASEMENT TO WAR
The Roosevelt Administration and Fascism in Europe

ranklin D. Roosevelt took his oath of office during the depths of the Great Depression. The winter of 1932–33 saw unemployment reach 25 percent, continued bank failures, and business closings, while breadlines and Hoovervilles dotted the landscape. By necessity, most of Roosevelt's efforts would be devoted to domestic policies and issues. His New Deal program for economic recovery was controversial from the outset, forcing Roosevelt to defend his legislation from attacks by conservatives and the Supreme Court. In 1935, in response to these pressures, he launched the so-called Second New Deal of reforms and then campaigned for reelection in 1936. Even though Roosevelt had an abiding interest in international events and had served under Wilson as assistant secretary of the navy during World War I, his attention and energy were focused on the home front. Still, international questions and developments were of great importance to the president, and he sought to make American influence felt when he could. Roosevelt was involved with the issues of international trade and economic recovery, the emerging territorial disputes in Europe, the problem of China and Japan in the Far East, and the establishment of the Good Neighbor Policy toward Latin America. Connecting many of these events was a quest for stability to allow for economic recovery and the peaceful resolution of issues. This concern was heightened by the growing appeal and power of the left in many nations and the questioning of capitalism that the Great Depression engendered.

While experimentation and change were called for at home, it was not a time for new initiatives abroad. Policies were pursued to enhance the status quo, not to challenge it. Moreover, globally the economic crisis created a movement away from parliamentary or democratic government in many nations to more authoritarian rule. There were no assurances that this upheaval was over or that the momentum might not swing to left-wing or radical nationalist movements. Given these circumstances and concerns, Roosevelt accepted and extended the policies and ideas of his Republican predecessors in most areas of the world. The tension between the U.S. desire for democratic governments and its quest for stability and nonradical political change was drawn even tighter during the 1930s. This would mean no fundamental changes in the ideology and policies toward right-wing dictatorships.

In Europe, Roosevelt continued the friendly relations with Mussolini's Italy, initially sought an accommodation with Nazi Germany, adopted a policy of neutrality toward Spain which aided Franco's fascist rebels, and supported the emergence of a protofascist government in Greece. Only during the latter part of Roosevelt's second term, when the pressure of German expansion snapped the tension and laid bare the central contradiction of United States policy, did the administration begin to reverse its position and come to oppose Germany directly. With the outbreak of World War II, support for right-wing dictators became anathema to most policymakers. Washington either distanced itself from such governments or openly opposed them. The policymaking pendulum swung from support to opposition of authoritarian governments as the first phase of United States relations toward right-wing dictators in this century came to an end.

The Fascist Challenge in Europe

Franklin D. Roosevelt and Adolf Hitler came to power within two months of each other. Though no one could have predicted it at the time, their fates, and that of their nations, became inexorably intertwined. Leaning on attitudes and ideas first developed during the 1920s, the Roosevelt administration developed its policies toward Germany and European fascism based on the favorable analysis and understanding gained from relations with fascist Italy. American policymakers and leaders had easily accommodated themselves to Mussolini's fascist regime. That experience provided the initial basis for policy toward the rise of similar regimes in Germany, Spain, and Greece. Employing the paradigm of moderate and extreme fascists, American leaders did not exhibit great concern about the dangers of these new dictatorships and found much to favor in these governments.

The advent of the Great Depression magnified earlier concerns for stability and fear of the left and Bolshevism. Strong right-wing dictatorships were seen both as necessary antidotes to unrest and essential bulwarks against communism. However much liberal democracies were preferred in theory, they were seen in many countries as too weak to withstand the global economic crisis. In the cases of Spain and Greece, American officials believed that attempts at self-government failed because the people were not prepared for the demands such governance created.

Yet the Nazis went beyond restoring stability. Germany's march to World War II severely tested the benign views and the ideological justifications for supporting right-wing dictatorships. In attempting to construct a policy during the upheavals of the 1930s, American statesmen faced a situation in which three different and powerful ideological visions vied for the support of the people of Europe: liberalism, fascism, and communism. As the decade unfolded, the question confronting American statesmen became how could they modify or contain the German challenge without relying on the Soviet Union and augmenting the influence of the European left. It was in this context that the Roosevelt administration moved from accommodation to appeasement. American policymakers already believed they understood the danger of communism and saw it as the foremost threat to Europe. Understanding fascism proved much more difficult and problematic.

A fixation on communism and fear that only Russia could benefit from a division among the Western states placed severe limits on American policymakers' ability to understand Hitler's policies or the nature of European fascism. As was true of many aspects of Roosevelt's presidency, his relations with European fascism and Nazi Germany did not always follow a clear and discernible path. There were twists and turns and finally a complete reversal of direction. The Roosevelt administration at first attempted to redress what it perceived as the legitimate grievances of Germany. When accommodation failed to provide a solution, Roosevelt adopted economic appeasement as a means to incorporate Germany into a Western-led liberal international order. After Munich, Roosevelt abandoned appeasement, and the United States moved to confrontation and eventually to war with Germany. In the process, the ideological premises for supporting right-wing dictatorships were questioned for the first time, and new ideas on the issue challenged the previously held positive assumptions concerning authoritarian regimes.

The decision to adopt a policy of appeasement was based in part on the American understanding of fascism gained from relations with Italy since 1922 and the Roosevelt administration's fear that another world war would lead to a protracted postwar era of social unrest and revolution. The United States had long held that Germany was the key to European prosperity and peace. This view, combined with the belief that the Treaty of Versailles and the postwar settlements were too harsh on Germany, led American leaders to agree that Germany had legitimate complaints concerning borders, reparations, and trade and to support revisions of the Versailles system. Hence the United States opposed the French occupation of the Ruhr in 1923, promoted German reconstruction, and provided financial support to Berlin through the Dawes Plan in 1924 and the Young Plan in 1929. Roosevelt agreed that European peace and prosperity depended on Germany and believed that revisions to the Versailles Treaty were necessary to return "that German sanity of the old type" that he remembered from his many visits to Germany in his youth.[1]

In addition, by the 1930s most of the members of the State Department in charge of European diplomacy were career Foreign Service officers whose shared outlook on the world centered around the dangers of communism. All studies of the U.S. Foreign Service at this time draw a similar composite portrait of these men. White, Protestant, and middle-class or wealthy men primarily educated in elite schools, they held a patrician's disdain for labor, minorities, and immigrants and a deep-seated fear of radical change. Most came to the Foreign Service around the time of World War I and adopted the prevalent hostility toward the Soviet Union and belief that any political upheavals were communist-inspired.[2] To the founding fathers of the U.S. Foreign Service, "communism was anathema. As Christian gentlemen, the diplomats were horrified at the assault upon family, religion, and simple decorum that gained popularity with the Bolshevist revolution in 1917."[3] This, along with their Eurocentric cultural bias, allowed them to accept antidemocratic, authoritarian regimes while at the same time condemning the Soviet Union as a dictatorship.[4]

Robert Kelley's Division of Eastern European Affairs worked hard to keep the communist menace at the forefront of the department's concerns. By the 1930s, the "containment of bolshevism was a constant in American diplomacy," shaped by a conservative set of "professionals in the State Department who found it hard to accept the implications of opposing rather than appeasing Hitler and Mussolini."[5] Many, including J. Pierrepont Moffat, head of the Division of Western European Affairs, William Phillips, under secretary of state and later ambassador to Italy, and Breckinridge Long, ambassador to Italy and under secretary of state during World War II, held strong anti-Semitic beliefs.[6] Moreover, the State Department was consistently suspicious of any diplomatic and peace initiatives that came from Moscow and believed that no matter what its course of action, the Soviet Union could not be trusted. The rising challenge of Nazi Germany was, for most of the decade, seen by these men as a secondary threat to that of communism. The conviction that "American and Russian national interests could never be compatible remained unshaken" down to the outbreak of war.[7]

To help understand the new German government, American officials turned to Italy. Roosevelt inherited excellent relations with Mussolini from the Republicans. Former secretary of state Stimson recalled that "the Italians in 1931 and 1932 were of all the great continental powers the least difficult" and that Mussolini was "a sound and useful leader."[8] Mussolini and his followers were viewed as nationalists who would provide for the maintenance of social order, a bulwark against Bolshevism, and an antidote for the illness of weak government in Italy. The State Department analyzed the Fascist Party as being divided into two groups, moderates and extremists. The extremists were blamed for the more unsavory aspects of Italian fascism. The moderates, led by Mussolini, could be counted on to keep Italy's policies on a "safe" course which featured domestic stability, anti-Bolshevism, and cooperation with the United States.

This analysis allowed American officials to ignore Mussolini's brutal repression of all opposition groups, destruction of Italy's constitutional government, and rule by violence. In developing American policy, officials in Washington were mainly influenced by Mussolini's establishment of a stable, noncommunist government that welcomed American trade and investments. In addition, the State Department believed that Mussolini's chest-beating speeches on foreign policy were made only for Italian domestic consumption and to appease the more extreme elements of the party. The Roosevelt administration added to this view the belief that Mussolini would provide a moderating influence on Hitler.[9]

In June 1933, in a letter to the American ambassador to Italy, Breckinridge Long, Roosevelt outlined his opinion of Mussolini. The president saw the Italian dictator as a moderate nationalist whose rule was having a positive effect on Italy. Roosevelt also saw Mussolini as a leader who would strive to maintain peace in Europe. The president wrote that he was "deeply impressed by what [Mussolini] has accomplished and by his evidenced honest purpose of restoring Italy and seeking to prevent general European trouble."[10] In July, Roosevelt wrote a friend who had sent a letter in praise of Mussolini that "I don't mind telling you in confidence that I am keeping in fairly close touch with that admirable Italian gentleman."[11] In the fall, Roosevelt wrote Long that with regard to disarmament and an overall European peace, "I feel that [Mussolini] can accomplish more than anyone else."[12]

While the administration maintained its positive evaluations of Mussolini, it was more cautious in its evaluation of Hitler and his program in Germany. The major concern was an aggressive Nazi foreign policy and Germany's greater military potential. From the very beginning, moreover, Hitler's anti-Jewish policies drew considerable attention to the repressive nature of his regime. Although never praising Hitler in the same manner as it did Mussolini, the State Department did find reasons to be optimistic about Hitler and the American ability to influence Berlin. The same criteria for judging fascist Italy would be used with Nazi Germany. The key factors would be Nazi economic and foreign policies, not the nature of Hitler's regime.

It was broadly accepted in the United States that Hitler's rise to power was the result of the harsh treatment of Germany under the Treaty of Versailles. This, combined with the unrest and instability caused by the Great Depression, led American leaders to worry about a threat from the left and to see Nazism as an understandable response by many to the multiple problems that beset Germany. As the American ambassador in Berlin, Frederic Sackett, stated on Hitler's coming to power, "From the standpoint of stable political conditions, it is perhaps well that Hitler is now in a position to wield unprecedented power." His Nazi Party promised a strong anticommunist force in Central Europe, stability, and order.[13] Sackett also feared, as did other Americans who studied the question of Germany, that if the Nazis failed, their collapse would open the door to communism in Germany.[14]

The State Department quickly drew favorable comparisons between Italian fascism and German Nazism. The most important aspect of this analysis held that, like the fascists, Nazis were split between moderates and extremists. This division was central to the course of action Germany would follow and could be exploited by the United States to obtain favorable policies from Berlin. As Norman Davis reported from Germany in April 1933, everything "depends upon Hitler's ability to withstand the radical leaders of his own party."[15] George Gordon, the American chargé d'affaires in Berlin, wrote the State Department that "there is no doubt that a very definite struggle is going on between the violent radical wing of the Nazi Party . . . and what may be termed the more moderate section of the party, headed by Hitler himself . . . which appeal[s] to all civilized and reasonable people." He concluded, "At the present moment in my judgment the more reasonable element has the upper hand."[16]

Besides Hitler, the other leading moderates were believed to be Hjalmar Horace Greeley Schacht, former president of the Reichsbank, who was appointed to run the German economy, and Hermann Goering. The Berlin embassy reported that Schacht promised that "in the field of economics and finance the Nazis will make no attempt" at economic adventure and that "American business in Germany had nothing to fear."[17] On the foreign policy front, assurances were sent to Washington that Hitler's "inflammatory statements regarding foreign policy and Germany's mission to expand in the East" were mainly propaganda. "The Nazi war talk . . . and posing is simply designed to impress their followers and should be discounted."[18] Early steps by the Third Reich to free itself of Versailles, such as leaving the League of Nations, were met with sympathy by the administration, and later efforts at rearmament and the occupation of the Rhineland were accepted without protest.

A 1937 State Department analysis summarized all of these points. The department believed that as a system, fascism was compatible with free trade and liberal governments. Germany could, therefore, be co-opted to reject self-sufficiency and territorial expansion and accept economic development in a liberal international order that emphasized economic cooperation among the leading industrial states. The central dilemma remained what forces to support when the democratic center was weak. The European Division's report explained the problems faced by policymakers in Europe: "When there is suffering, the dissatisfied masses, with the example of the Russian revolution before them, swing to the Left. The rich and middle classes, in self-defense turn to Fascism." Defining fascism as a natural movement by the respectable classes to defend the existing order and private property from Bolshevism, the department believed that where fascism was in power, "it must succeed or the masses, this time reinforced by the disillusioned middle classes, will again turn to the Left." The one problem was the issue of foreign expansion. As the report noted, "If Fascism cannot succeed by persuasion, it must succeed by force." The goal of the United States was, therefore, to ensure that Germany could recover economically. As the report concluded, "The problem of European peace . . . may be clearly defined: Can a compromise be found, or a price paid, which will satisfy the economic necessities of the German people, without war . . . ? If so, there will be no war; if no, war is possible, if not probable."[19]

Most of the discussion in the administration focused on economic cures and Eastern Europe. Roosevelt noted that Germany had needed raw materials, and he told Joseph Davies that he would explore the question of whether providing Germany "living room" would prevent war.[20] Long stated that the problem was that France and its allies "have put a military ring around Germany" and that German needs had to be addressed or "war is the only cure for the malady with which Europe is affected." Thus it was better to support Germany than to push toward war. The choice was aiding Berlin or Moscow: "There are only two Governments in Europe capable of being a real victor. One is Germany, and the other is Russia. . . . I shudder to think of a Russian domination of Europe. While a German domination would be hard and cruel—at least in the beginning—it would be an intensification of a culture which is more akin to ours than would that of Russia. Further than that, if Germany should be dominant throughout the greater part of Europe, she would act as a bulwark against the westward progress of Russia."[21] It was believed, therefore, that Hitler would, if given the chance by a proper redressing of Germany's grievances, follow the example of Mussolini and carry out policies that promoted stability and economic recovery while cooperating with the Western powers. Thus policy had to be designed to strengthen the position of the so-called moderates in Germany to reap the benefits of their control and avoid the danger of Germany adopting an adventurous foreign policy. A Germany cooperating with the West would bring about stability and prosperity while serving as a bulwark against Bolshevism.

In the first two years of the Roosevelt administration, Mussolini's stock continued to rise, and the belief was that Il Duce had a moderating influence on Hitler. Italy's mobilization of its army on the Brenner Pass frontier with Austria in July 1934 cemented the view of Mussolini as a peacemaker who had a constructive influence over Hitler. Mussolini's action was seen as the decisive step that caused Hitler to abort his attempt to absorb Austria into the German Reich. Under Secretary of State William Phillips stated the prevailing opinion of policymakers that it was Mussolini's action "which made Hitler realize that he could not fool with the Austrian State."[22] The Versailles Treaty needed to be revised by peaceful means. A February 1935 State Department report summarized the prevailing views concerning fascism in Italy. It noted that Mussolini's rule was necessary because of the danger of Bolshevism, the need for stability, and parliamentary government "was unsuited to Italian political life since it was imposed from above on a patchwork of peoples who were for the greater part illiterate." Moreover, Italy now held the "key position in the European concert" because of its relations with Germany and the problems of Central Europe. "Italy not infrequently holds and aims to keep the balance of power in Europe."[23] Thus Italy and Germany were linked in American policy to Europe and in the development of American appeasement.

The approach of the Italo-Ethiopian War forced President Roosevelt to give more attention to the building international crisis in Europe and Italy's position. In March 1935, he wrote Breckinridge Long: "These are without doubt the most hair trigger times the world has gone through in your life time or mine. I do not even exclude June and July, 1914, because at that time there was economic and social stability, with only the loom of war by Governments in accordance with preconceived ideas and prognostications. Today there is not one element alone but three or more."[24] Long replied that he agreed and that he too was worried that with "social unrest as widespread as it is, and with the certain exaggeration of it as the sequel to another war," he could "only shudder to think of our social situation a year after another conflict."[25]

Roosevelt did not fully elaborate on the three or more elements in his letter to Long. An examination of his writings on the question in 1935 and 1936, however, yields a general picture of the president worried that with the lack of economic and social stability in Europe resulting from the Great Depression, the aftermath of another world war would prove to be even more revolutionary than that following World War I. On 2 October 1935, Roosevelt spoke in San Diego about the danger of a "fierce foreign war" that was a "present danger at this moment to the future of civilization." Reflecting his concern about the building crisis in Ethiopia, Roosevelt referred to the Great War as "the folly of twenty years ago" and argued that the current danger in Europe was even greater than the outbreak and disruption of that war. A repeat would

On brink of WWII

"drag civilization to a level from which world wide recovery may be all but impossible."[26]

The outbreak of fighting in Africa prompted the president to make a major foreign policy speech on Armistice Day 1935. Roosevelt emphasized that people must come to understand "that the elation and prosperity which may come from a new war must lead—for those who survive it—to economic and social collapse more sweeping than anywhere experienced in the past."[27] The following February Roosevelt wrote Jesse Straus, ambassador to France, concerning his fears for Europe: "One cannot help feeling that the whole European panorama is fundamentally blacker than any time in your life time or mine." He compared the current crisis with the revolutions of 1848 and the Great War: "In 1848 revolutions in a dozen countries synchronized because of a general European demand for constitutional representative government; but at that time economics, budgets, foreign exchange and industrialism were not in the picture and the problem was ten times more simple than it is today. In 1914 the situation was eighty percent military, and again vastly simpler than today." His conclusion was that these "may be the last days of the period of peace before a long chaos."[28] Roosevelt feared another war because it would totally disrupt Europe. Thus began a search for a peace policy.

Cordell Hull shared the president's pessimism, and a similar view shaped the State Department's reaction to the approaching Italo-Ethiopian War. Hull recalled in his memoirs that his greatest worry during 1935, while the crisis on the horn of Africa mounted, was that it might somehow expand into a conflict between Italy and Great Britain. As Hull explained the American attitude to the French ambassador in July 1935, "A war between Italy and Ethiopia would be bad enough, but it is entirely within the range of possibility that it would in due time spread back into more than one part of Europe with its unimaginable, devastating effects."[29] It was not the Italian domination of Ethiopia that primarily concerned Hull but the danger of the military conflict spreading.

Mussolini's plans for the conquest of Ethiopia were well known to American officials by the time of the December 1934 border clash at Wal-Wal between Italian and Ethiopian forces which marked the beginning of the crisis. Thus President Roosevelt and the State Department had ample time to decide on a policy toward Italy's aggression on the horn of Africa. The major concern and the center of all discussions was how Mussolini's actions would influence events in Europe. Ethiopia itself was of little concern to American officials.

Ambassador Long kept both President Roosevelt and Secretary of State Hull fully informed of Italian plans and the reactions of various European nations. Long's correspondence concentrated on why the United States should not oppose Italy's colonial expansion. Italy's taking of African colonies was no different than British or French actions at an earlier time. Moreover, the important concerns of the United States were in Europe and the problem of Germany. Mussolini's actions in Africa should be tolerated because he held influence over Hitler and should not be alienated over a matter of no immediate interest to the United States. Too harsh a policy would push Mussolini toward Hitler and an alliance of the dictators.[30]

Long consistently focused the discussion onto Germany, the key to the building European crisis. Germany would have to be appeased, and Italy's role would be critical. It was unwise, therefore, to oppose Mussolini and push him into a position through sanctions that might lead his policy to fail, which could force him to lash out in frustration against Britain and bring about a larger war. Besides, Long noted, it was clear that the French had given Mussolini a free hand in Ethiopia.[31] The State Department agreed with the ambassador's analysis and adopted a very conciliatory position toward Italy in the time leading up to the war. Before the actual fighting began, officials downplayed the importance of the coming war and sought to avoid any identification of the United States with Ethiopia. The leaders of the department's Western European Division, J. Pierrepont Moffat and James Clement Dunn, opposed any actions against Italy out of both sympathy for Italy's economic needs and fear of the fighting spreading to Europe.[32]

Moffat also believed that though an Italian victory in Ethiopia would be bad for peace because it might encourage aggression, an Italian defeat might be worse. Defeat "would undoubtedly bring in its train not only revolution to Italy, but it would also bring nearer the inevitable day of German aggression." In addition, as Moffat wrote William Castle, an Italian defeat would be a disaster for European peace because "a strong Italy would seem to be essential in the eventual solution of the far more serious German problem."[33] Under Secretary of State Phillips summed up the State Department's view of the Italo-Ethiopian War when he noted that the department saw "Mussolini's 'enterprise' as a detail and felt that Germany remained the key to the whole European situation."[34] Italy's influence could not be squandered over Ethiopia.

On 3 October 1935, Italy invaded Ethiopia. The president reacted angrily to the news of the attack when it reached him while he was vacationing on board the USS *Houston*. He immediately instructed Hull to invoke the recently passed Neutrality Act so as to deny Italy access to American arms.[35] He did not wait for an official declaration of war, telling Harry Hopkins that "they are dropping bombs on Ethiopia—and that is war. Why wait for Mussolini to say so."[36] In addition, Roosevelt warned American citizens against traveling on belligerent ships and told American traders that they conducted business with the belligerents at their own risk. Because Ethiopia had no passenger shipping or access to American trade, both measures were directed against Italy. In October and November, Secretary Hull called for a "moral embargo" on the shipment of war-related items, including oil, copper, and scrap steel.

The administration would not, however, take any further steps, including an oil embargo that would cripple Italy's war machine. Actions were limited so as to not antagonize Mussolini to the point that he would precipitate a war with Britain or break relations. As Ambassador Long noted, an oil embargo would force Italy "to an early action and bring on a European war." Thus, in November, when Britain asked the United States if it would join in an oil sanction, Hull informed the Foreign Office that the United States would not participate in or support any such action by League members. Though cooperating independently on other matters, the United States was not willing to take this crucial step.[37] Hull's rebuke was followed by the disastrous Hoare-Laval peace plan, a secret plan devised by the British and French for partitioning Ethiopia and granting Italy economic dominance there. Only a strong negative reaction by the British public when word leaked out prevented the deal from being completed.[38]

Mussolini's methods, not his objective, led to Roosevelt's anger and the decision to try to isolate Italy. Washington was more concerned with European affairs. Along with their worry that Italy's actions might lead to a larger war, State Department officials feared that active opposition to Mussolini might lead to domestic unrest in Italy that could only benefit the left. American leaders saw the whole adventure as a colonial war and a misguided policy. Hull's meeting on 22 November 1935 with the Italian ambassador provided a clear demonstration of the administration's anger, understanding of the war, and unwillingness to revise its view on Mussolini and fascism.

Hull was astonished that the Italian ambassador had come to the State Department to protest that the application of the Neutrality Act discriminated against Italy. The secretary noted that both he and Roosevelt had "pleaded" with Mussolini to avoid war and obtain Italy's objectives through other means but had been ignored. Now Mussolini "expects us to furnish him with war supplies." Hull recalled his peace efforts, stating: "During the last three years I had almost worn myself out physically in an effort to aid in world economic rehabilitation so that Italy and other countries would have an adequate amount of international trade to afford contentment to their respective populations, and that the Ambassador could not begin to imagine the deep disappointment I feel at the effort to renew the practice which all nations have recently undertaken to abandon, relating to that of military aggression by any and all countries at any and all times." Hull then noted that he could not understand why Italy did not use economic means to accomplish its objectives of domination in Ethiopia, "why [the Italian] Government had not taken $100,000,000 to Ethiopia and brought back a key to the entire Empire instead of expending several hundred million dollars in its military conquest with all the worry and threat of danger to the balance of the world."[39]

Roosevelt and Hull would eventually swallow their anger, believing that Mussolini's Ethiopian adventure was a misguided policy rather than naked aggression that exposed the fundamental nature of his regime. No reevaluation of the favorable analysis of Mussolini as a moderate fascist, sincere in his desire for peace, took place. Instead, the administration began in 1936 to pay much greater attention to developments in Europe and to search for a means to satisfy German demands and avert another disastrous war on the Continent. The result was an American appeasement effort based on economic reforms designed to support the moderate elements in Germany. While U.S. policymakers refined their policies toward Germany and Italy, political crises were developing on both ends of the Mediterranean Sea that manifested further American endeavors to accommodate right-wing dictators.

Fascism on the European Periphery

In July 1936, civil war broke out in Spain, when General Francisco Franco's fascist rebels attacked the republican Popular Front government in Madrid. The United States joined with Great Britain and France in declaring their neutrality in the contest. Meanwhile, Germany and Italy aided Franco's forces and the Soviet Union provided materials to the Loyalists. Many commentators have argued that American nonintervention stemmed from a fear of the war in Spain spilling over the Pyrenees into a wider European conflagration. In addition, Washington sought to cooperate with London, and to a lesser extent Paris, to maintain unity in approaching the problems of Europe. Yet American policy toward Spain also fit with its overall approach to European events.

From its founding in 1931, American officials were skeptical of the Spanish Republic and predicted from the outset that there would be "a Bolshevistic turn" in Spain.[40] No one mourned the passing of King Alfonso XIII's rule, but there was great worry about what would replace the failed monarchy. From the outset, embassy officials feared that the new government was merely "a Kerensky interlude" preceding a Bolshevik takeover. The new government was seen as weak and its confiscatory policy toward foreign investments a clear indication that it was moving toward communism. Spain's economic policies and Popular Front governments had caused the relationship between the United States and Spain to break down almost completely before the civil war, and an anti-republican position dominated the State Department's thinking on Spain and led the United States to adopt a policy of nonintervention in the Spanish civil war.[41]

American officials had long held that the Spanish people were incapable of democratic government. Spain was seen as a backward nation, still governed by medieval institutions of the monarchy and the church, which prevented the political and economic developments that had advanced in the rest of Western Europe and accounted for the decline of Spain's empire, its easy defeat in the Spanish-American War, and the current poverty. Views of Spain were dominated by the "Black Legend," which portrayed the Spanish as a "treacherous, bigoted, and decadent people, thwarted in their progress." Spain's conquest of the Americas was characterized by an "insatiable greed and brutal destruction of the indigenous peoples," especially in comparison with the British. Americans saw Spain as an "anti-progressive nation because of its absolutism and influence of the Roman Catholic Church on Spanish government and society. In addition, they portrayed Spaniards as 'romantic, haughty, sometimes chivalrous, often cruel, [and] fanatical.'"[42]

Ambassador Irwin Laughlin described the Spanish in 1931 as "17th century minded . . . people," who, "captivated by Communistic falsities, suddenly see a promised land that does not exist."[43] Most Spaniards, he contended, were a "great inert mass of uneducated and mentally lethargic people" because they were controlled by the Catholic Church. The defeat of the proposal for a constitutional monarchy in favor of a republic was caused by the "characteristic . . . mentality of all Mediterranean peoples. They regard the ballot-box from the point of view of the Greeks who invented it; not as a means of choosing their governors, but of getting rid of them."[44] The main hope against Bolshevism, Laughlin wrote Stimson the month after the establishment of the republic, was that the "Spaniards are one of the Mediterranean races and they all react in pretty much the same way." In Greece in 1924, the Soviets had little luck convincing the peasants to support communism. Although there was every reason to fear "a Bolshevistic turn . . . I am hoping that this [a peasant rejection] will be the case here."[45]

Embassy reports remained filled, however, with accounts of communist activities, "anarcho-syndicalist revolt," and strikes of "a revolutionary and communistic nature," and the persistent fear of a communist takeover continued.[46] The appointment of Claude Bowers by Roosevelt as ambassador to Spain placed a sympathetic voice toward the republic in Madrid, but little changed in the State Department's understanding of events. From 1932 to 1935 it feared that the republic's instability, immature political institutions, and economic troubles could still lead to its succumbing to communism. These fears became more urgent in early 1936, when the Popular Front government in Madrid was formed. Modeled on the Soviet Union's call for a "united front" of progressive forces against fascism, this action seemed to be the final step toward a Bolshevik takeover.

American officials were suspect of the notion of a Popular Front from the outset. Under Secretary of State Phillips represented the department when he noted that Popular Front ideas were a cover-up for Soviet aggression and a different means of "encouraging communistic efforts in other countries."[47] Ambassador to the Soviet Union William Bullitt saw the united front as the "tactics of the Trojan horse."[48] Spain's action, therefore, was cause for alarm in Washington and the final step in the rupture of relations with the republic. Bowers reported in February 1936 that the "tremendous swing to the Left registered in the present elections is undoubtedly an expression of resentment by the masses against the ineffectual efforts" of the former center government to address the economic problems of the nation. The next month he described the leader of the socialists, Largo Caballero, as "the evil genius of the Spanish political situation" who is "largely responsible for the recent disorders in Spain." An avowed Marxist "and a communist at heart," Caballero had stated that it was time for the "Socialist party to come out squarely and declare that its goal is a proletarian dictatorship."[49] While Bowers still argued that the current government could prevent revolution, his reporting was encouraging the department to believe that the Kerensky period had arrived.

Bowers believed that Prime Minister Manuel Azana had to take "strong measures" soon or the situation would get out of control. While he tried to downplay the communist danger as much as possible, Bowers did note in his diary in March that "there are communistic elements in Spain that are working toward another French Revolution with its terror."[50] If Azana "fails to maintain the upper hand," Bowers informed Hull, the "danger exists that civil war or communism will ensue."[51] Meanwhile, reports began to arrive from Moscow and other capitals of Soviet support for the government. For example, William Bullitt reported from the Soviet Union that the Soviets were prepared "to take advantage of any opportunity which appears" and noted that "twenty young Spaniards trained in Moscow in the technique of the Bolshevik revolution" had recently departed for Spain.[52]

A later State Department white paper on American policy toward Spain reflected the attitudes of 1936. "Three eventualities seemed possible." The current government "might at last successfully consolidate its position by taking effective measures to control" the extremists; more "radical leaders of the left [might] assume power"; or the right "might attempt by a military coup d'etat to forestall the assumption of power by the radical Left." With these choices and the mounting evidence that the current government, "in an atmosphere of general unrest and lack of respect for authority, was earnestly striving to maintain public order but meeting with only limited success," it was almost with relief that the State Department received the news of Franco's revolt.[53] James Dunn of the Western European Division, Hull's closest adviser in the department, wrote just before the outbreak of the civil war that with the "Caballero Socialists . . . disposed to support the Communists," the situation of "the masses [was] getting out of hand."[54] He later told a reporter that the department saw the Loyalists as "a lot of hoodlums."[55] William Phillips was concerned about the "great enthusiasm in Moscow" for the Loyalists. He reminded Secretary of State Hull that the Popular Front was supported by "Socialists, Communists, and even Radicalists."[56]

Hull held several long meetings with his chief advisers on 4 August to determine American policy toward the Spanish civil war. Phillips laid out the problem facing the United States. If the Loyalists could not buy weapons in Europe, "they will undoubtedly turn to us and we shall be in an embarrassing situation since we have no legislation authorizing us to refuse the export of such materials even though they are destined for what amounts to a communistic government." Phillips continued, "If the [Spanish] government wins, as now seems likely, communism throughout Europe will be immensely stimulated."[57] Now that the issue was clearly defined as a revolt against a communist government, the solution was to deny the Loyalists arms. Hull and Phillips decided to impose a "moral embargo" on all weapons sales to the Spanish Republic. They won over a reluctant Roosevelt, and American neutrality became policy.

Although nonintervention came under heavy attack from many in the United States, American policy would not shift until it was too late to help the Loyalist cause. Moreover, to many, a rebel victory was seen as an attractive prospect that would bring order to Spain while preventing Bolshevism. Franco and his followers were seen as mainly nationalists rather than fascists. Assistant Chief of Western European Affairs Harold Tittman noted that "from the outset of hostilities . . . high echelon officials were strongly pro-Franco."[58] The embassy in Madrid reported that Franco's "primary object" was to stop the "soviet revolutionary movement" from making Spain "a socialist or communist state," while Bowers wrote Hull that Franco, "while clearly hostile to democracy," was "not a Fascist."[59]

Even German and Italian aid to Franco was interpreted in the best light possible. Phillips reported from his new post in Rome that "Italy has been forced to concern herself with the Spanish situation because of the original actions of Soviet Russia in seeking to communize Spain with the consequent menace to established systems in neighboring countries." Ambassador William Dodd in Berlin, who was known for his anti-Nazi position, wrote that while Germany was indeed aiding Franco, "regard should be paid to the . . . antipathy of Hitler and Mussolini toward the establishment of a 'Red' Government in Spain which unquestionably is a motivating factor in their Spanish policy."[60] Moffat and Dunn agreed that Italy and Germany "considered that Russia had intervened in Spain and that they were merely acting defensively."[61]

Roosevelt would later regret that he allowed his Spanish policy to be set by the State Department's appeasers, but at the time he concurred with them. No change was enacted until 1939, when it was too late to reverse the outcome of the war. By then, the president had abandoned appeasement in all of Europe. Spain would serve, however, as one of the rallying points for opposition to the policy of supporting right-wing dictators during World War II and after. In particular, the U.S. decision to recognize the Franco regime would be challenged and used as an example of the shortsightedness of such a policy. The first push to the policy pendulum was delivered, as discussed in the next chapter, during the debates that began over Spain in the late 1930s.

The Fourth of August Regime

The U.S. policy toward General John Metaxas's establishment of a dictatorship in Greece on 4 August 1936 has been largely overlooked by American historians, yet it provides an excellent example of American policy toward right-wing dictatorships and is particularly illuminating given the other events in Europe at that time. U.S. policy toward Greece demonstrated how universal and persistent the well-developed rationales and ideological justifications for supporting right-wing dictatorships had become in the State Department. In the midst of increasing German aggression, the Roosevelt administration welcomed the overthrow of the Greek republic by an avowed admirer of fascism as beneficial to Western interests in the region. Metaxas defended the suspension of the constitution, dissolution of parliament, and declaration of martial law—with King George II's approval—as necessary to save Greece from a communist revolt. Although Greece was clearly within Great Britain's sphere of influence, and American direct interests and influence there were small, State Department officials nonetheless invoked the fear of Bolshevism, instability, and the inability of the Greeks to govern themselves democratically as justifications for American support of Metaxas's government. American officials believed that the dictatorship was warranted to prevent communism in the region and to bring stability and necessary modernizing reforms to Greece. Moreover, it would serve the interests of the United States by preventing "another Spain" while providing Britain with a stable ally.[62]

The Greek republic, established in 1924, had never been accepted by a minority of ardent royalists and other conservatives, particularly in the military. For the next decade, politics centered around the rivalry between the followers of the Liberal Party leader Eleftherios Venizelos and the Populist Party, led by Panayiotis Tsaldaris, which during the 1920s and 1930s was generally associated with the monarchy. The onset of the Great Depression served to add further strain and heighten the tension of the "National Schism," as the division was known, and increased the activity of the rival factions for power. The Depression cut Greek exports, mainly in agricultural goods such as tobacco, olive oil, and currants, in half by 1934 and, along with a drop in immigrant remittances and shipping, increased the Greek debt to a point that two-thirds of the state's expenditures were servicing the debt.[63]

Regularly scheduled elections in September 1932 failed to bring an overall majority for the ruling Liberal Party. Venizelos allowed Tsaldaris to form a minority government, which quickly collapsed and forced new elections in March 1933. This time, the Populists defeated the Liberals and along with other anti-Venizelists and royalist forces put together a majority coalition in parliament. Republican officers in the army, surprised by the election results and the formation of an anti-Venizelist government, attempted a coup under the direction of General Nicholas Plastiras. This was done, he claimed, to protect the republic from its enemies. The coup failed, but it did open "up . . . all the old wounds caused by the National Schism" and "was to have a disastrous effect on the stability of the Greek political system."[64] Once again talk arose of a restoration of the monarchy.

The lingering suspicions by the Venizelists of the Populists and fear of the influence of Metaxas and the royalist forces on the government led to another coup attempt in 1935, the so-called March Revolt, by republican officers. The revolt, successfully put down by a Liberal general, George Kondylis, served to strengthen the power of the royalists as the Tsaldaris government responded with massive purges of Liberals and committed republicans from both military and public office. Leading officers implicated in the revolt were shot by firing squad. Yet Metaxas, who was made a member of Tsaldaris's cabinet after the revolt as a concession to the right, quickly resigned because he felt the government refused to carry out a necessary "bloody reprisal."[65] The March Revolt helped to pave the way for the Metaxas dictatorship by seriously weakening republican forces and unifying the reactionary right.[66] This was the political climate that awaited Lincoln MacVeagh when he arrived in Athens on 4 September 1933 as the new American ambassador.

MacVeagh's initial reports on the political situation emphasized the control Prime Minister Tsaldaris had over political matters and the ambassador's dislike of Venizelos. Weekly reports followed the continual struggle between the government and the Venizelists, with occasional references to the ambitions of the military, particularly Generals Kondylis and Metaxas.[67] The ambassador's overall assessment of Greek politics before the March Revolt was optimistic. Tsaldaris, he believed, had consolidated his control at the expense of both the Liberals, whose power he saw eroding, and the royalists. MacVeagh claimed that Tsaldaris was keeping a close watch on the royalists. In addition, the prime minister was improving the economy and pursuing policies that might well "confer a lasting benefit to the country at large."[68] The prime minister deftly blocked Venizelos's chances for the presidency in the fall of 1934. The defeat led Venizelos to withdraw from Athens to his native Crete, where he continued to attack the policies of the government. To MacVeagh, these were all desperate measures stemming from the breakup of Venizelos's political power and did not represent a real danger of the destruction of the republic. In the face of "improved economic and fiscal conditions on which the Government is consolidating its strength," the ambassador saw little reason for concern.[69] As for the military and the royalists, MacVeagh acknowledged that Tsaldaris needed General Kondylis, but the general needed the premier as well because he was not "strong enough to face the country alone." In any event, MacVeagh reported that the "Premier is watching his Minister of War very carefully."[70]

Given this analysis of Greek politics in early 1935, the ambassador and the State Department were taken off guard by the March Revolt and shocked by subsequent events. Initially, MacVeagh was optimistic in the wake of the March Revolt, which he interpreted as an indication of the waning influence of Venizelos and not a matter of constitutional violations. In a lengthy dispatch on 13 March 1935, MacVeagh noted that the failure of the republican officers was a shattering blow to the Liberal Party's prestige and power. He believed that "a difficult period in the country's history" had passed "with credit to those in charge." The main result was that "there is not likely to be any more trouble with the Opposition [Liberals] for some time. The Venizelists are stunned, and the Government will have its way." What MacVeagh failed to see was that the immediate impact was not the decline of the Liberals but the rise of the reactionary right.[71]

MacVeagh was quickly forced to take notice of the new threat from the right. On 17 March, the ambassador wired the State Department that talk of bringing the king back was everywhere and that the government was forced to bring Metaxas into the cabinet as a concession to the extremists. He reminded the department that Metaxas was "one of the most bitter and violent of the opponents of Venizelos."[72] In early April, MacVeagh noted that if Metaxas were to gain power, it "would justify the recent revolt in the eyes of many Greeks [and] the country might easily fall a victim to a real civil war."[73] In a clear contrast to Metaxas, MacVeagh characterized Tsaldaris and his party as the group who "stand for wisdom and moderation" and credited him with keeping the reprisals to the shooting of only two generals.[74] While the "execution of these two officers is a disquieting indication of the strength of the extreme reactionary faction in the Royalist ranks," the ambassador noted that Metaxas had quickly resigned because the cabinet was unwilling to carry out more extensive killings and that "it is generally conceded . . . that this victory of moderation and sanity" owed much to the responsiveness of the government to British, French, and American pressure.[75]

Elections in June delivered an overwhelming victory for Tsaldaris over Metaxas of 287 to 7 seats in the 300-seat parliament but still failed to resolve matters. First, the Liberals had boycotted the election, leaving Tsaldaris and Kondylis as the sole defenders of the republic. Second, the prime minister had already promised a plebiscite for the fall as a means for resolving the question of restoring the monarchy, now the central issue in Greek politics.[76] The Populist victory, therefore, did little to satisfy the defenders of the republic or the proponents of restoration.

On 3 July, General Kondylis, in a surprise move, publicly declared his support for the monarchy. He claimed that he did not believe the republic could any longer preserve order in Greece and that "if the monarchy is able to assure this, it will save Greece." This move forced Tsaldaris to set a definite date, 10 November, for the plebiscite. But the royalists, seizing their opportunity, were not willing to wait and take their chances on a popular vote. The military stopped Tsaldaris's car on 10 October and demanded an immediate restoration of the monarchy. When the prime minister refused and reiterated his position to hold a fair plebiscite, the military took over with Kondylis as prime minister.[77]

These developments caused Ambassador MacVeagh to reverse his position, and in his analysis of events he sided with the royalists. Numerous conversations with the British minister, Sir Sydney Waterlow, and consideration of Great Britain's position influenced the ambassador.[78] MacVeagh described Kondylis's July announcement as the shock "that broke the hard core legal sentiment of the majority of the country which would have defended the regime on principle."[79] The ambassador began searching for new explanations for what had changed or gone wrong and was now concerned for the stability of Greece. This led him to emphasize the lack of political sophistication of the Greeks, reevaluate the "maturity" of their political institutions, and discover a communist threat to Greece that mandated strong action. These worries formed a new analytical base and provided the rationale for supporting first the restoration of the monarchy and second the Metaxas dictatorship.

Two new features gained prominence in his analysis: a new supposed communist threat to the country and the inability of the Greek people to govern themselves. In September, MacVeagh drew in the specter of Bolshevism for the first time. He wrote to Hull that "serious observers are not unaware that large portions of the Opposition [Liberal Party] are moving distinctly to the Left in the face of governmental uncertainty and private squabbling. Communism is spreading, and with it alarm for the survival of ordered government itself." [80] Following the royalist coup in October, MacVeagh began his first full report by stating that "one thing which undoubtedly aided General Kondylis and his henchmen in maintaining order was the apathy and disgust of the majority of the onlookers at this new proof of the ineptitude of self-government in Greece." [81]

MacVeagh's analysis also now built on views of Greece widely held in the United States. Writing in the establishment journal *Foreign Affairs* in 1926, Charles P. Howland, in his article "Greece and the Greeks," presented the conventional wisdom. He found that the Greeks "in their present stage of evolution are not especially suited to an era whose dominating principle is industrial and political organization." They possessed a "very sensitive nervous organization, a constitutional restlessness and habit of disputation" and "are volatile in their political allegiances." Their "effervescent temperament and tendency to oscillate between intense activity and repose make the political future a problematic one. It is an open question whether the Greeks can subordinate their nerves and emotions to the excellent understandings in the fashion required for the successful working of democracy." [82] Writing ten years later in the same journal, William Miller found that the Greek problem, "which lies at the root of the national character," was getting the people to submit to authority and work together. [83] Another writer at the time noted that the Greeks suffered from a "disinclination to obey a leader and the concomitant tendency to split up into cliques and groups." These characteristics were "hindering the social evolution of Modern Greece." [84]

The coup had been carried out so that the return of the king would be a certainty. At the end of October, MacVeagh wired the State Department to inform it that there would still be a plebiscite in early November "only to legalize decisions already taken." [85] As expected, the monarchists won an overwhelming victory, gaining 97 percent of the vote, with a total of over four hundred thousand more votes than had ever been cast previously in a Greek election. [86] Though clearly fraudulent, the vote provided a legal blessing to the king's return later in the month. MacVeagh accurately reported the British support for the restoration of the king of the Hellenes and said that the British minister was to advise the king personally on instructions from London. [87]

Writing President Roosevelt on Thanksgiving Day 1935, MacVeagh summarized recent events by explaining that in Greece politics "is a game"; it "is subject to peculiar rules which everybody recognizes." Barely hiding his amusement and displeasure, MacVeagh noted that while "Governments rise or fall by the ballot . . . whenever the minority feels hopelessly up against it, it is considered all right for it to turn the majority out by a *coup d'état*, if it can manage to do so." The army, MacVeagh explained, was the "chief piece on the board." Having simplified Greek politics to a game akin to the way Americans "follow the races, baseball, or the stock market," and thereby removing any legitimacy from the battles over the future of the republic, MacVeagh virtually ignored the issue of the destruction of Greek democracy that was under way. Returning to recent events, the ambassador explained that the king owed his throne to a minority interest and the British. The minority could have its way because it had the support of the army, and the Liberal Party press was "muzzled and the Opposition leaders arrested." Yet the "people accordingly accepted the revolution as a *fait accompli*," strengthening MacVeagh's belief that the Greeks were inept at self-government.[88]

Elections sponsored by the king were held on 26 January 1936 to elect a new assembly under the restored monarchy. The results were indecisive, with the Liberal Party and its allies gaining 141 seats, the Populist Party and its allies, including Metaxas, 143 seats, and the communist-led Popular Front 15 seats. While the Liberals and Populists discussed forming a coalition government, each side was also engaged in secret talks with the communists to see if they could form a government without the other powerful bloc. The Communist Party, fearing a fascist takeover, was seeking protection by participating in the government.

MacVeagh updated Roosevelt on the political developments in Greece in a lengthy letter on 29 February. His discussion centered around his agreement with the king's statement to him that Greece needed "more Anglo-Saxon ideas in this country." MacVeagh praised George II and expressed sympathy for his difficulties in trying to reform Greek politics. "He has shown himself," MacVeagh wrote, "to be a serious-minded and genuine person determined to do his best as Monarch of the entire country and not simply one party." The ambassador's overall portrait was that of a nation that lacked "true" political behavior and was in need of firm leadership. While MacVeagh believed the king was willing to provide that leadership, he badly misread his partisan intentions and in particular his reliance on General Metaxas.[89]

In April, the king resolved the political impasse by naming Metaxas premier. The Populists provided the context and the rationale for this move by accusing the Liberals of plotting with the Communist Party to undermine the state. In the midst of charges and countercharges, the assembly voted to adjourn for five months, until 30 September, and leave power to the new prime minister. The king and Metaxas argued that such drastic, but "temporary," measures were necessary to save Greece from the danger of Bolshevism. Ambassador MacVeagh quickly took up the government's arguments that an unstable Greece, with a politically immature population, was threatened by communism and in need of strong measures. He worried only whether the necessary steps would be taken soon enough and with enough strength. MacVeagh's reports from April until the official establishment of the Metaxas dictatorship in August concentrated on the danger of Bolshevism and comparisons of Greece with Spain. Given that example, the State Department welcomed a firm right-wing dictatorship in Greece.

With the "adjournment" of the assembly, the embassy reported that the "Government has been run as a virtual, if temporary, dictatorship of the King." This was not, however, to be a cause for concern. As MacVeagh argued, given the king's popularity and the "weariness of the electorate after a troubled year, it might be qualified as a dictatorship with the consent of the dictates." Demonstrating his approval, the ambassador wrote that in gaining a free hand from the "professional politicians," a term he always now used in a pejorative manner, the king had "gained a great victory. But to do so he had to use the steamroller." MacVeagh concluded that it would soon be known "what progress, if any, the King can make in giving this country 'more Anglo-Saxon ideas.'" [90] It is not clear whether MacVeagh intended the irony of this last statement, given the king's reliance on Metaxas and the general's well-known hatred of parliamentary government "and his admiration of fascism." Metaxas, however, believed he had a "personal mission, as the nation's savior from the vicissitudes of representative government, and from the vulgarity of partisan politics." [91]

Unrest increased in early May. Hit hard by the drop in markets for Greek exports, tobacco workers in Salonica led a series of protests. In his full report to the State Department on 29 May, MacVeagh laid the blame for events on the communists. He described a situation of escalating unrest prompted by the "presence of communist agitators in the crowd." The police, who had responded to the strikes with violence and would be replaced by the army to prevent more bloodshed, were defended as being "deliberately goaded into shedding blood." "Cries of 'Long Live Spain'" were frequent, the ambassador added, along with the known communist ploy of using the corpses of "'martyrs' in exciting further riot." Having established the source of the problem, MacVeagh lamented that the authorities did not fully recognize the scope of the trouble or move with enough speed to suppress it. Arguing that the "troubles in the north constitute the most serious labor disturbance in Greece's history," MacVeagh noted that they "afford a couple of lessons which the Greek Government would do well to heed." The primary lesson was the "extent to which organization has supplemented mere agitation in Northern Greece." The strike could "only be the product of a centralized directing force," which MacVeagh linked to Moscow. Referring to the "old adage that 'Satan finds work for idle hands to do,'" MacVeagh wanted the government to recognize the fertility of the fields the communists were tilling in Greece.[92]

MacVeagh was particularly worried that communist influence was spreading quickly in the nation. Workers elsewhere were watching, and it was almost "inevitable . . . that communistic influence should extend to the miserably low-paid workers of the textile and other industries of Salonica." The government, therefore, needed to suppress the communists and at the same time improve conditions, or MacVeagh feared that Salonica might be "destined to become another Barcelona and spread the infection of economic revolt." MacVeagh noted that he was doing his best to bring Metaxas and others around to this understanding. "The Government can still turn the flank on this country's incipient communism," MacVeagh emphasized, "by assuring to the poor a modicum of . . . contentment." If the government failed, both with political repression and economic reform, MacVeagh feared that the "country may well be the next victim of the social revolution. This, I fear, is the real significance of the recent strike."[93] A turning point had been reached.

The Department of State was alarmed by MacVeagh's report and shared the ambassador's concerns and analysis of the events. Wallace Murray summarized the department's opinion when he wrote MacVeagh that "you have convinced us that the Greek Government is storing up serious trouble for itself in not taking in hand the labor situation in Macedonia and Western Thrace." At a time when events in Spain were about to erupt into civil war, the department feared a similar occurrence on the other side of the Mediterranean. And again, any government in alliance with the left was unacceptable, while a right-wing dictatorship was not only tolerable but now seemingly necessary.[94] This was Metaxas's position as well, and he was finding important support for it in London and in Washington.

British minister Waterlow welcomed Metaxas's coming to power because he was willing to be the "strong man" Greece needed. The end of normal parliamentary rule did not bother Waterlow. He believed it would provide a "breathing space" for the king and Metaxas to bring order to Greece and deal with the danger of communism. The Foreign Office agreed that Metaxas should have a stabilizing effect on Greece.[95]

MacVeagh's esteem for Metaxas grew throughout the summer. The ambassador now described him as "charming and sympathetic" and noted approvingly that Metaxas shared the king's dislike of politicians because "he has a desire to get things done." MacVeagh believed that the general needed to act with more vigor and introduce a program "capable of turning the flank of the Communists." The military metaphor represented the approach MacVeagh hoped to see used. But MacVeagh feared that the government, "honest as it may be in its efforts to make Greece orderly and efficient in spite of [it]self," might not be able to do the job. The ambassador even went so far as to characterize trouble and ineptitude as "normalcy in Greece."[96] Unless the government remained on its guard, "the King's good intention of bringing 'more Anglo-Saxon ideas' to this country may easily be wrecked on the shoals of the Greek temperament."[97]

MacVeagh was en route to the United States to campaign for Roosevelt's reelection when Metaxas officially dissolved the constitution, instituted martial law, began the suppression of the opposition press and labor unions, and established his dictatorship on 4 August 1936. Harold Shantz, the chargé d'affaires, who had recently come to Athens from Moscow, reported to Washington without question the official explanation for Metaxas's action. It was necessary to "forestall general strike called [for 5 August] . . . to protest recently decreed compulsory labor laws; background causes ascribed to rapid spread of communism among laborers and farmers." In addition to the danger of Bolshevism, Shantz also believed that the "endless political quarrels leading to inability of the present chamber to form a responsible government" was the other primary reason why Metaxas's move was necessary.[98]

In a lengthier dispatch prepared four days after the establishment of the Fourth of August Regime, Shantz emphasized that the establishment of the dictatorship was an antidote to political instability in Greece caused by the Greeks' inability to rule themselves and the growth of Bolshevism. This instability had provided an opening for communism in

Greece that had to be blocked. In addition to the recognition of the communist danger and placing an end to the instability on which it bred, Shantz found that there was great potential for the Metaxas regime to carry out positive political and economic reforms and allow for a political maturation in Greece. The chargé welcomed the coming of the dictatorship by quoting as fact a government report that demonstrated the spread of communism and how, by "profiting by the 'political anarchy which the incurable quarrels of the political parties created,' it reached the moment for overthrowing the social regime; and how the twenty-four hour strike was to be prolonged until it assumed the character of a civil war." Shantz added that "with this in mind, and with the tragic accounts of Spain filling the local press, it is not surprising that the Metaxas Government, with the King's support, took the steps it did." The lack of popular support for Metaxas or the dictatorship did not bother the embassy. The Greeks, after all, had demonstrated their inability to govern themselves and make wise decisions. Shantz, however, neatly turned this problem into a show of support: "The apathy with which the dictatorship was greeted seems to indicate that the people in general were heartily sick of squabbling politicians." Shantz concluded that the "Metaxas Government has a great opportunity to effect much needed reforms."[99] Metaxas moved quickly to consolidate his power, and by 22 August, Shantz was able to report that Greece was "as quiet as a lamb" now that Metaxas had suppressed the "communist menace." Regarding the needed reforms, he found that "much has been done already," and he optimistically predicted that the regime would "last for a long time."[100]

The State Department adopted the embassy's analysis of events in Greece, and in light of British policy and the civil war in Spain, it supported the coming of the dictatorship. Outlining the State Department's interpretation, Murray wrote to Under Secretary of State Phillips on 5 August that the establishment of the dictatorship was necessary because of the political chaos in Greece, which had led to "no workable basis for the formation of a cabinet," and had created the danger of Bolshevism in the nation. The "establishment of an authoritarian regime" was needed because of the "widespread labor troubles in Greece and the growth of the Communist party." Metaxas was the "most gifted soldier of modern Greece" and a "strong, capable leader, with an active mind and physically young for his sixty-five years."[101]

Ambassador MacVeagh, upon his return in September 1936, endorsed the analysis of the embassy sent to Washington during his absence. "Mr. Metaxas," he wrote, "has now turned the eyes of the indigent to himself rather than to Moscow, and in that sense, and to the degree in which he puts adequate welfare measures into force, may be considered *as a savior of the country*."[102] MacVeagh's own report, however, contained enough information to undercut his and the State Department's analysis and to support an argument that there was no parliamentary paralysis or danger of a Bolshevik revolution. The Liberals had been ready to form a government back in April and again in the fall, when the assembly's five-month "recess" was over. But this would have meant Metaxas and the king accepting a coalition government that included the Communist Party in April or a triumph of a republican coalition that fall. These conditions were equally unacceptable to Metaxas and to American representatives in Greece.

MacVeagh's reports provide little evidence that he saw the political parties as representing competing interests in Greece. Instead, they became, with the rise of the strikes in 1936, intolerable excesses that had to be eliminated. There was, however, no political impasse in April. The Liberals would have formed a government headed by Themistocles Sophoulis. Only when negotiations with the Communist Party became public did the agreement collapse out of "fear that this 'scandal' would become the excuse for a coup d'état." Moreover, in August there was no communist threat.[103] Yet the communist danger came to dominate embassy reporting. Only the invocation of the specter of Bolshevism could square American policy with the fact that the Greek people consistently voted for parties that supported the republic.

Nonetheless, MacVeagh held to the position that, though the communists may not have been planning a revolt in August, Metaxas was correct when he claimed that communism "would have created such an overturn in the great bourgeois centers, spreading their influence gradually to the smallest centers, that we should have entered . . . a revolutionary atmosphere from which we surely could not have emerged without bloodshed."[104] The specter of Spain haunted the ambassador. MacVeagh concluded that though the new government was not ideal, it did provide stability and it had rescued Greece from communism.[105] The king's continued support was safe, MacVeagh reported, because he believed a dictatorship was necessary "for the turbulent Greeks. This, together with his natural fear of renewed parliamentary bickering, sufficiently explains . . . his support of Mr. Metaxas."[106] The king had told the British minister that ideally "there is only one real solution, and that is that Greece should be taken over by your civil service and run as a British colony. If only it were possible." Waterlow believed that after twelve years of "civilized life" in London, the king faced the task "in the spirit of one carrying the white man's burden among the tribes of the jungle."[107]

Much, however, remained to be done. As MacVeagh reported the next month, Metaxas still had not succeeded "in changing [the Greeks'] undisciplined habits. . . . Greece is still Greece, slowly modernizing out of its backward depths . . . and inveterately disobedient and individualistic whenever immediate and constant pressure is not applied." Apparently the dictatorship would be needed for a long time to come. Combined with the growing international crisis and German-Italian pressure in Eastern Europe, MacVeagh, in the words of John Iatrides, while "fully aware of [Metaxas'] unpopularity and sinister side . . . had little difficulty in accepting the dictatorship as a necessary evil."[108] Neither did the State Department. Foy Kohler summarized the view in 1939 when he wrote that Metaxas should be appreciated "for a sincere and reasonably successful attempt to bring the country through a difficult period . . . when endless and excessive political strife of republican Greece might have proved disastrous."[109] As MacVeagh wrote Roosevelt in 1938, "Mr. Metaxas is quite the ablest man in Greek political life today." He warned that if "Mr. Metaxas should die, the position would . . . be difficult in the extreme."[110] The view that Metaxas had foiled a potential communist uprising, brought stability to a Greece that could not digest "more Anglo-Saxon ideas," and promised needed reforms before Greeks could take on the task of self-government had become a truism for American leaders. With stability being secured at each end of the Mediterranean, the Roosevelt administration could concentrate its efforts on the development of its German policy.

Economic Appeasement

In 1937, Roosevelt seriously began to explore the means to achieving a general European peace. At the core would have to be a settlement of the German question. The policy the Roosevelt administration settled on was one of economic appeasement. In essence, the United States would attempt to meet Germany's economic demands while opposing territorial expansion. By appeasement, American policymakers meant an accommodation with Hitler that would maintain peace in Europe while providing Germany redress from the burdens of the Versailles system. Economic arrangements were believed to be the best method to secure greater international trade, settle the demands of Germany, achieve peace, and prevent the two feared alternatives that threatened Europe should these efforts fail: a world of closed economic systems or wars of aggression that would lead to instability and revolution. The key officials in developing this policy were the new under secretary of state, Sumner Welles; William Phillips, now stationed in Rome; Norman Davis, who served as an ambassador-at-large for the president; and Assistant Secretary of State Adolf A. Berle. All of these men were personal friends of the president and advocates of appeasement and the continued isolation of the Soviet Union from European affairs.[111]

The American pursuit of appeasement was a well-developed policy that appeared to preserve U.S. interests while offering the prospect of a genuine peace. It was neither a shortsighted policy in the sense that officials did not realize that by the late 1930s Germany presented a grave threat nor an attempt to drive Germany to the east to fight the Soviet Union. The United States did not want to see any wars in Europe, including one between Germany and the Soviet Union, because it feared that fighting would inevitably spread to the whole Continent, further destabilize existing institutions, and provide a spark for revolutions. Economic appeasement is best understood as an attempt at an overall economic and political settlement to bring about stability, trade, and the restoration of Europe's economy while insulating the United States from direct political commitments in Europe.

A crucial component to the thinking of Roosevelt and his leading advisers was their disillusionment over World War I. By 1936, American leaders were unsure whether any benefits had resulted from that war, and they were fearful that another conflict in Europe would have disastrous effects. The most tangible results of the war seemed to be communism in Russia, the Great Depression, and Hitler's rise to power in Germany. Roosevelt and the State Department were convinced, therefore, that another war in Europe would necessitate American involvement, bring about another period of postwar disorder, and foster revolutions. Appeasement, a term that had yet to gain its postwar opprobrium, appeared to be worth the effort, particularly given the belief that fascist regimes were not in and of themselves necessarily incompatible with Western liberalism and trade. This view was based on the State Department's belief that the current tensions in Europe were rooted in Germany's economic problems. Germany threatened aggression because it needed markets and raw materials, not from the dictates of fascism as an ideology.

"Germany," the department's Western European Division concluded in a lengthy February 1937 analysis, is "at the center of the problem of peace and war. If there is to be war, it will probably take the form of a drive by Germany for sources of raw materials." The report continued by stating that "it is widely appreciated among far-seeing statesmen that Germany should . . . have access to raw materials." Berlin's demands, therefore, were not "wholly unreasonable," and a means to help underwrite German recovery had to be found. The German adoption of economic autarky was viewed as a misguided policy by the Nazis that they could be persuaded, in their own interests, to abandon. A program designed to ease the crisis appeared capable of persuading the German moderates to redirect Germany away from economic self-sufficiency to international cooperation. "The immediate objective, then, of an intervention on the part of the United States . . . would be to precipitate the movement for a general political and economic settlement which would obviate the necessity for Germany to strike out to obtain the resources of raw materials in markets deemed by the German leaders necessary to maintain the standard of living of the German people."[112]

This strategy fit well with the administration's global efforts to increase trade through the Reciprocal Trade Agreement program. Secretary of State Cordell Hull firmly believed that economic rivalry was the cause of war and that greater international trade and interdependence among nations would serve to avoid conflicts.[113] It would also mean a more stable world order. To ensure stability and economic recovery while seeking to prevent war and concomitant revolutions, economic appeasement was adopted as a comprehensive policy for solving the growing problems of Europe. The administration was confident that its plan could work. Roosevelt wrote Hull in February 1936: "I get it from a number of sources in England and Europe that your policy and mine, working toward the long view program of general increased trade, is beginning to get under their skins and that they are getting heartily sick of mere bilateral agreements."[114] As one State Department memorandum summarized the strategy in 1938, "the development of our trade program will automatically put economic pressure on Germany" as more nations engaged in freer international exchange. "And in this we have a ready forged weapon in hand to induce Germany to meet world trade and political sentiment."[115] Once its trade began to improve, Germany would see that its interests were better served through cooperation with the Western democracies than in combating them. This in turn would end Germany's need to expand and would prevent a disastrous war in Europe. From 1936 to 1938, therefore, Roosevelt pursued appeasement in an effort to induce Germany to turn away from aggression toward economic cooperation as the best means to achieve its goals. The State Department had concluded that "economic appeasement should prove to be the surest route to world peace." [116]

Good relations with Italy and Mussolini's influence on Hitler were considered to be important components of this overall plan. Phillips's appointment as ambassador was a signal to Rome that although the United States opposed Italy's aggression in Africa and would not recognize Italian control, European affairs were of much greater importance and that Washington sought to restore its former close relations with Italy. Phillips wrote a series of favorable reports and letters to Roosevelt and the State Department concerning Mussolini and fascism. These communications demonstrated that Mussolini's image as a peacemaker and a moderate fascist remained intact. In January 1937, Phillips wrote Roosevelt that though fascism as a "form of government is anything but desirable from our point of view, I am greatly impressed by the efforts of Mussolini to improve the conditions of the masses." Phillips concluded that "the fascists honestly believe that they represent a true democracy in as much as the welfare of the people is their principal objective. Certainly they have much evidence in their favor." [117]

Turning to foreign policy, Phillips wrote in April that while Mussolini continued to use strident language when making public speeches, his "bellicose language and the rattling of the sword . . . is in [Mussolini's] opinion necessary to keep alive [the] new spirit of the Italian people," which had emerged under fascism. [118] Ambassador Phillips was reviving the old pre-Ethiopia argument that Mussolini's words were merely for domestic consumption and that they had little correlation to how he would act. That is, though Mussolini might engage in small colonial wars to rally the Italian people to the fascist state, Phillips believed that he did not intend to bring Italy into a war with any European nation.

The ambassador had little but praise for Mussolini and his programs. He believed that fascism had brought the Italian people out of a "slough of despond" and had created a new, proud spirit in Italy. "Through his dynamic personality and great human qualities," Phillips wrote Roosevelt, Mussolini "has created a new and vigorous race throughout Italy. He is essentially interested in bettering conditions of the masses and his accomplishments in this direction are astounding and are a source of constant amazement to me." Phillips concluded that Mussolini had no further aggressive intentions. Fascist aid to Franco's rebellion in Spain was not to be understood as part of a policy of aggression. Mussolini's only intention in Spain, the ambassador argued, was to prevent the establishment of a communist state in the Mediterranean. Phillips concluded that Mussolini, desiring to concentrate on domestic matters, was already tired of the war in Spain.[119]

The State Department concurred with the new ambassador's analysis. Hugh R. Wilson openly admired Italy's "achievements" in Ethiopia, writing that "the Italian effort was magnificent, the road construction was superlative, the health of the Army something that had never been seen when Westerners were fighting in tropic conditions."[120] James Dunn noted that Mussolini's intention to remove his forces from Spain indicated that he was "sincerely on the side of peace."[121] In a June 1937 report, the State Department reiterated the analysis of fascism which had guided its policy since 1922. Fascism "has brought order out of chaos, discipline out of license, and solvency out of bankruptcy." Italy's importance in influencing Germany and in maintaining the peace of Europe should not, therefore, be undercut by an unfriendly policy.[122]

Now that relations with Rome were back on track, the administration turned its attention to Germany. In a July 1937 speech at the University of Virginia, Welles made it clear that the United States would welcome a general settlement to Europe's problems through a revision of the Versailles Treaty. The treaty, he declared, had left Germany with intolerable "moral and material burdens."[123] In a national radio speech that same month, Welles stated that "the causes of the ills from which the world suffers today revolve primarily about the fundamental fact that the injustices and maladjustments resulting from the Great War have never yet been rectified."[124] In short, German revisionist demands had some legitimacy and a way had to be found to satisfy them.

Roosevelt outlined his own thinking at the same time in a letter he sent to Mussolini. The keys to peace were international trade and disarmament: "The two things must go hand in hand. It seems clear to me that if the nations can agree on armament reduction, even if it be in the form of a progressive reduction over a period of years, they can far more effectively discuss practical instruments for reduction of trade barriers, thus building up employment in industry to take the place of employment in armament." The president even hinted at concessions for Italy when he added, "I recognize that as a part of the discussion of increasing trade, every consideration should be given to a more ready access to raw materials' markets for those nations which in themselves do not produce the raw materials necessary to industry."[125] The barrier of the Italo-Ethiopian War was removed, and the main components of Roosevelt and Welles's appeasement policy of late 1937 and 1938 had been formed.

In October, after much searching and questioning, Roosevelt adopted Welles's idea for peace. Roosevelt knew that there was no easy answer and that whatever direction he turned had its difficulties and shortcomings. He set out his dilemma in a pair of letters to Phillips. Roosevelt began to doubt one piece of the appeasers' position: that communism, not Nazi Germany, was the greatest danger to Europe. "Every week changes the picture," the president mused, "and the basis for it all lies, *I think*, not in communism or the fear of communism but in Germany and the fear of what the present German leaders are meeting for or being drawn toward." [126] In May, Roosevelt stated that the "more I study the situation, the more I am convinced that an economic approach to peace is a pretty weak reed for Europe to lean on. It may postpone war but how can it avert war in the long run if the armament process continues at its present pace—or even for that matter at a slower pace?" Yet he wondered what else was available. Collective security meant some agreement with the Soviet Union, and disarmament was tied to economic recovery. "How do we make progress if England and France say we cannot help Germany and Italy to achieve economic security if they continue to arm and threaten, while simultaneously Germany and Italy say we must continue to arm and threaten because they will not give us economic security?" The president's thinking kept returning to economic solutions and an appeasement of Germany as the only way out of the problem. [127] Unable to advocate or accept collective security, which would have to include the Soviet Union and might lead to war, Roosevelt saw no other way to approach the German problem. The prevailing interpretation of fascism gave him hope that a solution was possible.

The plan Welles developed consisted of the United States calling a world conference along the lines Roosevelt had described to Mussolini in July. In a lengthy memorandum for the president, Welles outlined his objectives and reasons for the conference. Nations must reach an agreement on how they "may obtain the right to have access upon equal and effective terms to raw materials and other elements necessary for their economic life." Achieving this goal would necessitate a revision of the Versailles Treaty. As Welles pointed out, "Before the foundations of a lasting peace can be secured, international adjustments of various kinds may be found in order to remove those inequities which exist by reason of the nature of certain settlements reached at the termination of the Great War." [128]

The under secretary received support from many in the State Department. Moffat joined Welles because he feared that a war against the fascist nations would augment the influence of communism in Europe.[129] The ambassador to Poland, John Cudahy, echoed these ideas when he wrote Roosevelt, "It was wrong that the proud, capable, ambitious, and warlike" Germans were prevented by the post–World War I arrangements from obtaining prosperity while the "crude and uncouth" Russians, who were three centuries behind civilization, had an empire.[130] Norman Davis hoped to see Welles's plan adopted because he feared too much emphasis was being placed on a moral condemnation of "the dictators" that would only serve to drive them into "a closer alliance." A formula needed to be found "which would enable . . . them to come back to a cooperative" movement. Adolf Berle supported Davis, noting that "the State Department is divided. About half of it is following a Wilsonian moral line which in my judgment would lead eventually to our entry into a war on the British side. The other half, headed by Sumner and myself, is still endeavoring to steer matters into an ultimate conference."[131]

As Welles later recalled, the general aim was an "understanding between this country and the leading powers of Europe to achieve economic co-operation." The conference would help create "an ultimate international economy based upon reduced armaments, a greater common use of world resources, and the improvement and simplification of economic relations" among nations.[132] The first attempt to implement Welles's plan was blocked by Secretary Hull, who did not want Roosevelt taking the initiative in European affairs.[133] But Welles revived the idea in January and secured the secretary of state's agreement so long as Roosevelt first advised the British of Welles's plan. Again, central to the idea was an economic reordering of world trade. "It is my belief," Welles wrote Roosevelt, "that the proposal in itself will lend support and impetus to the effort of Great Britain, supported by France, to reach the basis for a practical understanding with Germany both on colonies and upon security, as well as upon European adjustments." On 11 January, Welles advised the British ambassador, Sir Ronald Lindsay, of his plan. Despite the endorsement of the British Foreign Office, Prime Minister Neville Chamberlain rejected the proposal because, he argued, it would interfere with his own appeasement efforts currently being negotiated with Italy and Germany.[134]

Roosevelt and Welles were upset by Chamberlain's rejection and his apparent decision to exclude the United States from participating in a settlement. American leaders believed that a general settlement of Europe's problems had to be reached, while Chamberlain pursued a bilateral and piecemeal approach of political and territorial adjustments with

Germany and Italy. As the prime minister informed Roosevelt when he turned down the president's offer to call for a world conference, it would "delay consideration of specific points which must be settled if appeasement is to be achieved."[135]

In particular, American officials worried about negotiations Britain was conducting with Italy. Roosevelt and Welles feared that the British would give away the lever of recognition of Ethiopia without settling other problems. As Roosevelt noted in his reply to Chamberlain, one concern was over the "harmful effect" de jure recognition of Italy's empire would have on "the course of Japan" in China. Moreover, Roosevelt believed that although U.S. recognition of Italy's conquest was inevitable, recognition should be granted only as part of securing Mussolini's assistance in reaching a general European settlement. "The recognition of the conquest of Ethiopia," Roosevelt wrote, "which at some appropriate time may have to be regarded as an accomplished fact, would seem to me to be a matter which affects all nations which are committed to the principles of non-recognition and which should be dealt with as an integral part of measures for world appeasement."[136]

Welles informed Ambassador Lindsay that the recognition of Italy's empire was "an unpleasant pill which we should both swallow" to obtain Mussolini's aid in a settlement, but that Roosevelt wished that "we should both swallow it together."[137] Chamberlain, finally persuaded by Foreign Minister Anthony Eden, decided to delay his talks with Italy and reopen discussions with the United States. Rapidly changing events on the Continent, however, culminating in Hitler's annexation of Austria on 12 March 1938, brought an end to any discussions of peace based on Welles's plan.

In the wake of the *Anschluss*, Chamberlain reopened negotiations with Mussolini. By the end of March, Britain had reached an agreement with Italy which traded de jure recognition of Italy's control of Ethiopia for the removal of Italian forces from Spain. The prime minister believed this was a major achievement in weakening the relationship between Rome and Berlin. The British Foreign Office pressed the United States for approval of its actions. Welles, supported by Phillips, urged Roosevelt to issue a public statement in support of the British in order to aid in their effort at keeping Mussolini out of Hitler's orbit. Phillips believed that because the *Anschluss* was so unpopular in Italy and Germany so distrusted by the Italians, it was possible to divide Mussolini permanently from Hitler.[138] Welles, his faith in Mussolini and the use of Italy as the road to peace unbroken, saw any move that would weaken the Axis as one that the United States had to support. On 19 April, the president released a statement that the United States had "urged the promotion of peace through the finding of means for economic appeasement" and that it viewed the Anglo-Italian agreement with "sympathetic interest because it is proof of the value of peaceful negotiations."[139]

By September 1938, while the Czechoslovakian crisis grew daily, Roosevelt was more pessimistic than ever. Writing to Phillips, the president indicated that he now saw war as inevitable: "Chamberlain's visit to Hitler today may bring things to a head or may result in a temporary postponement of what looks to me like an inevitable conflict within the next few years." Voicing his depression over events in Europe and sense of powerlessness to stop the oncoming crash, Roosevelt continued: "Perhaps when it comes the United States will be in a position to pick up the pieces of European civilization and help them save what remains of the wreck—not a cheerful prospect."[140] The president's mood, however, swung to optimism the next week.

Czechoslovakia, yielding to British and French pressure, announced it would surrender the Sudetenland to Germany. Roosevelt and other officials began to believe, for the last time, that war might still be averted and a means to appeasement obtained. Roosevelt contacted the British, French, Germans, and Czechs, urging them to continue negotiations. At this juncture, the president again turned to Mussolini. On 27 September 1938, Roosevelt wrote the Italian dictator that "I feel sure that you will agree with me as to the destructive and tragic effects of a war in Europe." Roosevelt asked Mussolini to "extend [his] help in the continuation of the efforts to arrive at an agreement of the questions at issue by negotiation."[141] Berle noted that the "reconstruction of the Austrian Empire unit under Germany" was "probably necessary and . . . not alarming."[142] He advised Roosevelt that with Germany about to absorb "some, if not all" of Czechoslovakia, the United States should not let "emotion" obscure its judgment. If it were anyone but Hitler, the action would be viewed as "undoing the unsound work of Versailles." Despite growing hostility toward Nazism, "a successful great Germany" will not "forever be the hideous picture it is today."[143]

When Hitler agreed to a meeting in Munich, American officials believed, as Ambassador Phillips stated, that "there was no doubt that the Duce played a strong hand at this critical moment" in bringing about the conference and avoiding war.[144] Chamberlain's announcement that he would meet Hitler and Mussolini in Munich prompted Roosevelt to express his opinion in a two-word cable: "Good Man." [145] The State Department's leading advocates of appeasement believed that the Munich meeting could lead to an overall settlement of the problems of Europe. Moffat stated that the department agreed that the "work for peace should not be reduced but redoubled." The "opportunity for real appeasement resting on sound economic foundations was at hand." [146] Sumner Welles declared in a radio speech on 3 October that because of Munich, "today . . . more than at any time during the past two decades, there is presented the opportunity for the establishment by the nations of the world of a new world order based upon justice and upon law." [147]

The optimism over Munich quickly vanished, however, in the face of Germany's intransigence on negotiations and the renewed repression of German Jews. It was now irrevocably clear to Roosevelt that appeasement had failed. Time was running out, as Roosevelt told Secretary of the Treasury Henry Morgenthau: "These trade treaties are just too goddamned slow, the world is marching too fast. They're just too slow." [148] On 15 November, Roosevelt called the American ambassador to Berlin, Hugh Wilson, home for consultation. He never returned. The State Department began what Berle called its "death watch" on Europe. Roosevelt concluded that Hitler was a fanatic, "a pure unadulterated devil," who would have to be stopped by force.

The Pendulum Moves

American views on right-wing dictators had been thrown into flux. Germany's aggression provided room for questioning the whole basis for previous ideas and whether American interests were actually served by supporting such regimes. Roosevelt's thoughts on Mussolini in 1939 demonstrate the difficulties, contradictions, and continuity of old ideas concerning dictators. In January 1939, Roosevelt wrote his secretary Stephen Early a candid memorandum outlining his understanding of Mussolini and dictatorships. His main thesis was that Hitler had changed the central aspects of fascism and was the cause of all the present difficulties. In effect, Hitler had corrupted a viable system. Previously, Roosevelt recalled, "there were many, including myself, who hoped that having restored order and morale in Italy, [Mussolini] would, of his own accord, work toward a restoration of democratic processes." Therefore, the question needed to be asked "as to whether, if Hitler and Nazi-ism had not risen in 1933 and gone to such extreme lengths, Mussolini could have survived alone, could have put through a greater absolutism, or whether he would have been compelled to reestablish some form of popular representation." Remarkably, Roosevelt concluded that the "development of Fascism in Italy was of great importance to the world, but it was still in the experimental stage" before Hitler.[149] Phillips concurred with the president. The ambassador to Italy recalled that Mussolini had done great things for Italy, but his "craving for greatness" and the influence of Germany "had led him astray."[150]

Roosevelt and Welles's meeting with the new Italian ambassador to the United States, Prince Ascanio Colonna, on 22 March 1939, reflected these views and demonstrated both the persistence of the favorable analysis of Mussolini's dictatorship and the view that Mussolini held, in Roosevelt's words, the "key to peace."[151] The president began his meeting with the Italian ambassador by impressing upon him, first, that American resources and materials would be available to those who opposed Germany, and, second, that American opposition to Germany did not stem from an ideological opposition to fascism or dictatorship per se but to aggression. "It was not," Roosevelt said, "a question of an insistence by the people on the form of government which European peoples should have, but on the contrary a deep-rooted opposition to the carrying out on the part of any nation a policy of military domination" that threatened world peace and the interests of peaceful nations. It is difficult to imagine an American president or policymaker expressing similar views about a communist government.[152] These statements suggest that at this late date, Roosevelt and others still believed that authoritarian governments were necessary transition stages for some nations and that there was no fundamental conflict between support for them and American interests. The main problem had been an alliance with a powerful nation that was now an enemy of the United States, not the nature of the regimes in and of themselves.

The policy pendulum, however, had begun to move. The fascist threat in Europe loosened its moorings, and four long years of fighting would open up the debate on relations with right-wing dictators to a broad range of opinion. Because of the demands for wartime supplies, the Roosevelt administration did not want to upset the flow of goods by challenging any government that sided with the Allied cause. This necessitarian approach led as well to military arrangements with Admiral Jean Darlan and the Vichy France forces in North Africa and to the recognition of the Badoglio government in Italy. It is also true that the original views developed during the 1920s were never fully discarded during the war and that the origins of American involvement in World War II lay in German aggression, and not the type of ideological opposition that would motivate so much of American postwar policy and hostility toward the Soviet Union and communism during the Cold War. One could still argue that in many other nations the need for authoritarian rule to provide stability, combat Bolshevism, and protect economic opportunities remained as long as those states did not align with Germany.

Nonetheless, the push that proclamations such as the Atlantic Charter and the Four Freedoms gave to the pendulum set in motion a change of American policy. The members of the State Department who held to what Berle termed "a Wilsonian moral line" gained ascendancy. In the process, they attacked Argentina throughout the war for its refusal to break relations with Germany and prepared to use the power and influence of the United States to force dictators to adopt constitutional methods or give up power once the war was over. In 1946, the Truman administration would adopt an official policy of opposition to all right-wing dictatorships. This change would prove, however, to be short-lived. With the emergence of the Cold War, the administration would reverse course and return, albeit with some important modifications, to the policy of the interwar years.

4 DISREPUTABLE GOVERNMENTS OR ALLIES? The Truman Administration and Right-Wing Dictatorships

The Allied victory in World War II appeared to mark more than the defeat of Germany, Italy, and Japan. It was to be, for many, the beginning of a new epoch. Central to that vision was the defeat of fascism and the triumph of democratic ideals and values over dictatorship and authoritarian rule. The world's nations had not only joined together in an antifascist coalition on the battlefield. They also produced documents such as the Atlantic Charter and the Charter of the United Nations that extolled human rights, self-determination, and freedom. At home, Roosevelt spoke the lofty language of the Four Freedoms, criticized tyranny and colonialism, and talked of the expansion of American institutions to other parts of the world. For Americans, the postwar period promised a vindication of their nation's values and institutions, which they were sure others would want to emulate and adopt. It was an article of faith that the world's peoples desired the things that the United States represented and that the values of America were universal. To make sure that these words and doctrines were not merely empty phrases and symbolic gestures, Americans believed that this time they had to take command of the world and accept the obligations of world leadership that they had rejected in 1919. From this realization emerged the remarkable achievements in postwar West Germany, Italy, and Japan of establishing democratic governments and the rebuilding of Western Europe's and Japan's economies.

In other areas of the world, events looked equally promising. In Africa and Asia, independence movements were on the march that would end the discredited vestiges of European imperialism. Dictatorships appeared to be on the wane and destined to become a thing of the past, particularly in Latin America, where U.S. influence was the greatest. Two long-term dictators, Martínez in El Salvador and Jorge Ubico in Guatemala, fell in 1944, and in 1945 Argentina, under intense pressure from the United States, became the last nation to break relations with Germany and join the Allied coalition. Other dictators, such as Somoza in Nicaragua and Rafael Trujillo in the Dominican Republic, had been forced to express support for basic freedoms, even if they were still no more than platitudes on their part. The fledgling United Nations refused to admit Spain, and most nations agreed with its request that they withdraw their ambassadors from Madrid in protest over Franco's rule. Outside of the Soviet Union and the areas the Red Army controlled, it seemed that democracy was the force of the future and that the spread of democratic ideals, governments, and institutions was one and the same with the interests of the United States. The spread of democracy would lessen, if not completely eliminate, the threat of another war and foster an international environment of free trade and cooperation led by the United States. In 1946, opposition to dictators was adopted as official policy by the State Department.

Even the postwar disputes with Moscow and the emerging Cold War with the Soviet Union, at first, seemed to demand, in the name of Allied unity and consistency with American criticisms of the governments being established in Eastern Europe, that Washington oppose dictatorships and support the establishment of free governments. Yet as the Cold War deepened, older attitudes toward dictatorships reemerged. Committed globally to opposing communism, the Truman administration sought stability and cooperation with U.S. foreign policy from the nations of the newly named Third World. While it would be best to allow free institutions and governments to struggle and take hold, there did not appear to be time. Communist forces would take advantage of unstable conditions and people who lacked a history of self-rule. Moreover, administration officials doubted the capacity of the newly emerging nations and those in Latin America to establish free governments and stable societies. To overcome the apparent contradiction between their condemnation of Soviet-supported governments and the dictators the United States supported as members of the "free world," officials began to make a clear distinction between what were termed traditional authoritarian dictatorships and communist or fascist regimes. By 1950, the outlook on right-wing dictators and relations with them was reversed from the opposition and intolerance at the end of World War II to at first a grudging acceptance and then an open embrace.

The Truman administration witnessed the most extensive discussion to date of the issue of how the United States should respond to right-wing dictators. The debates concentrated mostly on Latin America, but the ideas were broadly applicable. By the time of the Korean War, the administration had added a new component to the already existing arguments about stability, anticommunism, and the inability of certain peoples to govern themselves. Support of right-wing dictatorships was not only a recognition of existing realities, a necessity for order, and a protection of U.S. economic interests; it was now viewed as vital to the defense of the free world and the development of liberal institutions. Right-wing dictatorships could bring order and control and provide direction for a nation to establish democracy. Authoritarian rulers were, therefore, often a necessary stage for the emergence of democracy, while a communist government was seen to preclude freedom forever. Outside of Latin America, this same view led, most notably in Southeast Asia, to cooperation with the reestablishment of colonial rule to block communism until the people were "ready" for independence. Thus the United States found itself in the position of supporting some of the world's most brutal regimes in the name of promoting freedom.

Democracy and Dictatorship in Latin America

Then ambassador to Cuba Spruille Braden sparked the initial discussions in the Truman administration concerning right-wing dictators when he submitted a statement titled "Policy re Dictatorships and Disreputable Governments" in January 1945. At the request of Assistant Secretary of State Nelson Rockefeller, Braden expanded his thoughts into a longer memorandum on the topic in April. The State Department subsequently sent his document out to each embassy in Latin America for comments. From October to January 1946, the Division of American Republics prepared summaries and policy statements based on Braden's proposal, the responses, and internal discussions. This discussion set out the full parameters of American policymakers' thoughts and concerns surrounding the question of American policy toward dictator-ships in the Western Hemisphere, the promotion of democracy, and what best served the interests of the United States. With the new presi-dent's and his chief advisers' attention focused on the end of the war, postwar settlements in Europe, the occupation of Japan, and the recon-version of the economy to peacetime conditions, the State Department officials in charge of Latin America had great leeway in the discussion and development of policy.

Braden's opening of the discussion represented the confidence of those who wished to see the United States take a more active position against dictatorships. The war demonstrated to them the correctness of the liberal position in the State Department that supporting dictators worked against the best interests of the United States. The fundamental premise of Braden's argument was that the "interests of the United States require like-minded, friendly, sympathetic neighbors . . . and since de-mocracy must prevail in the Latin-American countries before such con-ditions can be assured, it should be the policy of the United States Gov-ernment to encourage democracy by demonstrating a warm friendship for the democratic and reputable governments and to discourage dicta-torships and disreputable governments by treating them as something less than friends and equals, i.e., by maintaining with them a relation-ship courteous and proper, but at the same time aloof and formal."[1]

This position, he and those who supported him believed, was the logical extension of the Good Neighbor Policy and wartime diplomacy. Braden argued that if being a "Good Neighbor" meant, in Roosevelt's words, one "who resolutely respects himself, and because he does so, re-spects the rights of others," this stance could not be attained if the United States maintained friendly and cooperative relations with dicta-torships. In support of his argument, Braden cited the "Department's Se-cret Instruction no. 4616 of November 1, 1944" informing American representatives that military dictatorships and unconstitutional govern-ments "are to be deplored. . . . While the Department will continue to maintain cordial relations with all established and recognized govern-ments, it is not incompatible with those policies to state unequivocally the self-evident truth that the Government of the United States can-not help but feel a greater affinity and a warmer friendship for those governments which rest upon the . . . freely expressed consent of the governed."

Braden, therefore, proposed that the United States should recognize all governments that held power, but it should "treat these petty tyrants with aloof formality, respecting the sovereignty of their nation but avoiding any identification with them. We should refuse to be inveigled into collaborations, which disregard the discrepancy between the despots' announced international objectives and their internal abuses." He offered several means for implementing his ideas. Most important, the United States should refrain from extending to dictators any loans, economic assistance, invitations to Washington, or honors. Public statements of praise, even if to note a constructive endeavor, should be prohibited because they could be misunderstood. Silence was the best course of action. In particular, military cooperation had to be avoided. The time had passed when assistance to any dictators was necessary to the defense of the hemisphere, meaning that the "military equipment supplied to a dictator may too frequently be utilized to maintain himself in power or to forge new chains wherewith to shackle his fellow citizens."

To help foster democracy, American representatives in nations ruled by dictators needed to develop a wide base of contacts with all classes of people and encourage honesty in government operations because it "will prevent many of the excesses and may even, given the underlying urge for democracy which pervades this hemisphere, develop in the direction of human liberties whereas dishonest administrations will inevitably move in the opposite direction." In conclusion, Braden thought that "with democratic and constitutionally elected regimes we can and should be tolerant, patient, and generous, but with the dictators we should be exacting and demand the scrupulous fulfillment of their agreements with and commitments to our government." "A careless tolerance of evil institutions" may "endanger our future self-preservation by leaving receptive media open for infection and employments by the Nazis, who are now going underground, and by others opposed to democracy."

Ambassador Braden recognized some problems and possible limitations with this policy, notably the question of nonintervention in the internal affairs of other nations. While that should be respected, the United States was not obligated to accept all nations "as equals and friends." Furthermore, it was dangerous for the United States not to take up an active position against dictators. "If . . . we fail to sustain and augment the enthusiasm for the practice of democratic ideals" that World War II had brought forth, "the void will be filled by pernicious 'isms' imperiling our way of life." On the other hand, "even implicitly to evidence an apparent approval of the dictators may not only intrench them, but may serve to spread the system elsewhere."

All the ambassadors who responded to the department's request for comments agreed in principle with Braden's aims, and the majority thought that his ideas should be implemented as policy. The most enthusiastic endorsement, not surprisingly given his tenure in Spain during the late 1930s, came from Claude Bowers in Chile. Bowers believed that the continuation of dictatorships in Latin America was being challenged by democratic forces awakened by the war. The United States should fully aid these groups. It was, he wrote, "utterly untenable an attempt to discriminate between a government avowedly fascist or nazi and a dictatorship resting on force, since under a military dictatorship the liberty of speech, the freedom of the press, the right to assemble to petition for the redress of grievances are no more tolerated . . . than under the systems of Hitler, Mussolini and Franco." Some of the supporters argued for greater flexibility than Braden's points allowed for and worried about how to define a dictatorship, but overall the department found little in the responses to "strengthen the case presented by Ambassador Braden."

The department did find, however, that the "arguments arrayed against the proposed policy are formidable." The opposing views can be grouped into two categories: general opposition to the policy and reasons to oppose it because of conditions in Latin America. The most important points in the first group were that the adoption of Braden's proposal as policy would violate American pledges of nonintervention, provide for noncooperation from the dictators on matters important to the United States which might lead them to decide to align with other nations, and, therefore, prove unworkable in practice. The arguments that were specific to Latin America recycled familiar claims from the prewar era. Those opposed emphasized that the adoption of such a policy would be unfair to such backward nations and would potentially open the door to communism in the region. The department summarized these ideas by using Haiti and Honduras as examples. The application of this policy in those nations, with their "low standard of living, little education, and almost no political knowledge and understanding, might result in the penalizing not only of a very good friend of the United States but also of the most progressive government which the country has any prospect of having." The choice at this time was not necessarily between "dictatorship and democracy but between dictatorship and chaos." Moreover, denying cooperation and assistance to nations ruled by dictators in areas such as "public health, education, agriculture, exchanges of students, and visits of professional men, including military men, technical assistance in government, the work of the Office of Inter-American Affairs and of the Export-Import Bank, etc.," would deny these nations access to activities that raise the standard of living and "create the conditions favorable to democracy." Yet providing such assistance to nations was vital in combating the potential threat of communism in the region.

The Division of American Republics report sided with the opposition on most points. It too endorsed the general principles laid out by Braden but found that the proposal's "force is diminished by the fact that it does not contain any recognition of the differences existing among the various countries." The emerging view within the department was that as a policy, Braden's ideas were in some aspects impractical and failed to consider fully the local conditions in Latin America that made implementation of the policy in the manner outlined by the ambassador problematic. Central to these concerns was the lack of consideration of the sensitivity of Latin Americans to "anything approaching intervention" and a failure to provide "due consideration to the low standard of living and political immaturity existing in some of these countries." The promotion of democracy required "a sound foundation in the socio-economic condition of the people," a quality the division found sorely lacking in most nations to the south. The report concluded that "in spite of the desirable objective of the proposed policy and the admitted need for a new policy, the arguments presented so far have not demonstrated an urgency great enough to warrant the adoption of the proposal in its present form." If adopted, it needed to be modified with "due consideration for the low standard of living, the lack of education, and the political immaturity prevailing in a number of the other American republics."

As the discussion moved up higher in the State Department, more qualifications were added. The department set out to establish a policy that held to the general principle of supporting democracy and opposing dictators, but it modified the specifics to take into account the objections already raised. Central to these concerns were the impracticality and "unfairness of applying the policy to a 'backward country.'" Moreover, it reemphasized that in these nations the "choice might not be between dictatorship and democracy, but between dictatorship and chaos, and that a dictator may offer the most nearly progressive government that a country has the prospect of enjoying." In support of this argument, the Division of American Republics claimed it was "historic fact . . . that many dictators have wittingly or unwittingly prepared the way for more nearly democratic or popular self-government." No examples, however, were provided. In the end, a "slower but more hopeful approach to the problem" was advocated. In its final form, the "Recommended

Policies toward Dictatorships and Disreputable Governments," adopted in February 1946, endorsed, albeit in modified form, Braden's proposal as official policy. The United States should "maintain proper and courteous (but not cordial) relations with dictatorships." U.S. diplomats should avoid "all acts which might be interpreted as indicating approval of the nature of their governments . . . whenever it is possible to do so without giving serious offense to the people upon whom this government depends for the eventual establishment of democracy in those countries." On the most important aspects of relations, it specified that the "United States should avoid the granting of favors to dictators." "Economic assistance should be given only where it is clear that it will benefit the people of a country generally and will help in the development of democracy and honest government," and "no military equipment or assistance should be given except where such a policy is agreed upon by international action, or where it is clearly necessary for reasons of security to the United States." [2]

The new policy would first be implemented against Argentina. At the beginning of 1945, relations with Argentina had been strained for four years because it failed to break relations with Germany and join the Allied wartime coalition, conflicts over the two nations' differing visions of hemispheric unity, and a clash between the antifascist position of the United States and the makeup of the Argentine government. Relations reached their nadir in late 1944. In response to Edelmiro Farrell and Juan Perón's taking power in early 1944, the Roosevelt administration withheld recognition of the government, and in June it recalled Ambassador Norman Armour. [3] The basis for this position was summarized by Assistant Secretary of State Edward Stettinius in a memorandum for Roosevelt. The difficulty with the regime in Buenos Aires was that it was controlled by a "military-Fascist combine. This group is pro-Nazi, anti–United Nations and is determined to stimulate the formation of the same type of government in other South American republics." As long as Farrell and Perón remained in power, the United States would continue to oppose the government. "Unless there is a real turnover in Buenos Aires," Stettinius wrote, "the Department will do everything possible to maintain the 'quarantine' to the full extent in political relations, and to the maximum extent consistent with the war effort in economic relations." [4]

The impasse was finally broken on 27 March 1945, when Argentina declared war on the Axis. This action brought a brief period of improved relations. Led by those who placed primary emphasis on economic concerns, hemispheric solidarity, and the establishment of an inter-American collective security arrangement, the State Department quickly moved to restore relations. Rockefeller announced that the United States would extend recognition on 9 April. The Farrell-Perón government had joined the rest of the hemisphere in its defense, leaving no reason to continue to isolate the government in Buenos Aires. Further, Argentina agreed to the provisions of the Treaty of Chapultepec, based on the premise that peace in the Americas was indivisible, that an attack on any nation was an attack on all, and once the war was over the American nations would meet to establish a formal defense agreement. In turn, the United States sponsored Argentina's membership in the United Nations (UN), over Soviet objections, to maintain regional solidarity. In defense of his actions, Rockefeller noted that the totalitarian nature of the Argentine government was not a matter of concern to Washington, and U.S. policy was to avoid intervention in the internal affairs of Latin American nations. "A policy of intervention may be necessary in war-torn Europe," Rockefeller declared, but in the "Western Hemisphere we have developed other methods of encouraging democracy . . . you can't superimpose democracy from the outside." Roosevelt approved the action and appointed Braden as the new ambassador.[5]

Relations were no sooner seemingly repaired and Argentina successfully included as an original member of the United Nations when new problems arose. The declaration of war and inclusion in the UN did not change anything for opponents of cooperation with dictatorships. Argentina's leaders had collaborated with Nazi Germany, held profascist sympathies, and maintained a government that was undemocratic. Braden's appointment as ambassador in April 1945 ensured that the wartime opposition to the Farrell-Perón government and the conflict with Argentina would continue. Braden, who was once described by Dean Acheson as the only bull who carried with him his own china shop, immediately began to attack the Argentine government, and Juan Perón in particular, upon his arrival in Buenos Aires.[6] He saw this as an opportunity to place into action and demonstrate the value of the policy against dictators while the department was still considering it. Braden refused to forget Argentina's long neutrality during the war and was determined to force Farrell and Perón out of power through American opposition and to foster democratic rule in Argentina. In particular, the ambassador attacked the continued crackdown by Perón on his political opposition and demanded a return to constitutional government. Good relations with Argentina, he insisted, depended on U.S. ability to "win the respect, confidence and friendship of the Argentine people" and not the government. The department, he wrote at the end of May, must "recognize that a leopard does not change its spots and that Peron and associates are fundamentally unfriendly to us, totally unreliable, self-seeking . . . and would double-cross us instantly if they deemed it advantageous to do so." In support of his approach, Braden claimed that the present government "has no (repeat no) popular support." The United States "must (repeat must) stand on principle" and refuse any cooperation with the government.[7] With the war in Europe over, there was no need to accommodate the rulers of Argentina.

At first glance, Braden's efforts appeared to yield the desired results when Farrell announced that elections would be held in early 1946. Yet the ambassador kept up the attack and his criticisms of the government, its ties to the Axis, commitment to fascism, and danger to the hemisphere, and he sought to rally public opinion in the United States. The Roosevelt administration's endorsement of Argentina for membership in the UN was unpopular at home. Liberals in particular condemned cooperation with a government that continued to protect Nazis, while some conservatives worried about Argentina's restrictive trade policies. *Time* magazine published a cover story on Braden and Argentina in November 1945 that endorsed the ambassador's actions. Swastika symbols were used to denote Argentina's position on the accompanying map of Latin America. Braden's attacks on Argentina, documentation of the imprisonment of political enemies of the government, and the blocking of free speech and press were well received by a public that had spent four years fighting to eradicate fascism.[8] In an apparent endorsement of his actions, the newly appointed secretary of state, James Byrnes, brought Braden back to Washington in the fall to replace Rockefeller as assistant secretary of state for inter-American affairs.

Critics of Braden's approach placed a higher value on hemispheric cooperation. The opposition of conservative senators, particularly Arthur Vandenberg and Tom Connally, was most significant. They had agreed to accept Argentina's membership in the United Nations to foster hemispheric unity and secure a regional collective security organization. Their focus was already more on the Soviet threat to the Americas than on the lack of democracy in Argentina. But because Byrnes and Truman were focusing attention on Europe and Asia, Braden was able to dominate the making of Latin American policy and continue his battle against fascism in Argentina. Braden's reports from Argentina were replete with attacks on Perón and warnings against any cooperation with the regime in Buenos Aires. In what must be one of the earliest uses of the Munich analogy, Braden wrote on 4 September 1945 that if the United States were to "appease now and allow the situation to drift, we will either be faced for a long time to come with a Fascist anti-U.S.A. Govt. under German tutelage and or eventually revolution in Argentina in which case supply of foodstuffs from this country might cease." Referring to 1938 directly, Braden continued, "If we could not then turn our back on a European threat to our security still less can we do so now [that] we have won the war for democracy in respect to a danger from within the American Hemisphere." Opposing Perón and nipping his "maneuver for pseudo elections in the bud we probably will not only defeat it but likewise would avail ourselves of our best chance to destroy the Nazi-dictatorial-militaristic system in this country and the danger of its spread elsewhere in the hemisphere." Three days later, Braden wrote Byrnes that the "fundamental point to remember is that Peron (with his clique) is Fascist-minded dictator who will not change his spots even though he may shift tactics."[9]

That fall, now working as assistant secretary, Braden announced that because of the totalitarian nature of the Argentine government, the United States could not enter into any military assistance agreement that included that nation. The United States, therefore, canceled the foreign ministers meeting set for October to finalize the collective security arrangements called for at Chapultepec. At the same time, he launched a department study, the so-called Blue Book, to document the fascist nature of the Argentine government and to discredit Perón, who was the leading candidate for president in the upcoming election, and secured Secretary Byrnes's endorsement of the Larreta doctrine. Uruguayan foreign minister Eduardo Rodríguez Larreta had proposed that American nations take multilateral action against any country that violated human rights. Braden contended that no violation of nonintervention pledges would occur because the action was not designed to "injure the government affected, but rather it must be recognized as being taken for the benefit of all, including the country which has been suffering under such a harsh regime."[10] To Braden, this was exactly what was necessary to combat fascism in Argentina.

The Blue Book, which consisted of almost 150 pages of documents and analysis, proved that Argentina's government had collaborated with Germany during the war, received direct support from Nazi Germany, supported fascist efforts at recruitment in other Latin American nations, and protected German economic interests in Argentina. Further, the report concluded that Argentina continued to seek to undermine the inter-American system and is "vested in a partnership of Nazi 'stay behind' leaders and capital with a coalition of Argentine totalitarian elements, both military and civilian." Actions such as the declaration of war after the failure of Germany's last offensive and professions of a desire to cooperate were a "defensive strategy of camouflage." All other conciliatory actions and "repeated avowals of pro-democratic intentions proceeded from this strategy of deception." Why these promises remain unfulfilled was clear to the department: "Behind the record of broken promises and repeated pledges of cooperation we have proof positive of complicity with the enemy." The only corrective was a new government.[11]

Immediately after the State Department adopted Braden's policy as expressed in "Dictatorships and Disreputable Government," it sent the Blue Book to the respective ambassadors of Latin American nations in Washington and publicly released it on 11 February 1946. In response, Perón launched a sustained attack against Braden and American imperialism. The ambassador's criticisms represented, he claimed, a direct and unprovoked intervention in Argentina's domestic affairs designed to weaken the nation and open it for the exploitation of American business. Adopting the slogan "Braden or Perón," Colonel Perón swept to a landslide victory on 24 February. The State Department's action undoubtedly exploded in its face and contributed to the size of Perón's victory.

Braden's failure to oust Perón provided an opening for those who advocated a different approach. Argentineans were not alone in Latin America in seeing the Blue Book as a case of North American intervention. It was, along with the Larreta doctrine, widely criticized throughout the hemisphere. After all, many other repressive governments in the region had reason to fear such criticisms and possible intervention against their rule.[12] Critics in the United States who wished to have the Rio de Janeiro conference on military assistance meet, and who believed that the primary objective of United States policy had to be meeting the Soviet challenge, began to mount a campaign to change policy. Their most important act was obtaining the appointment of George Messersmith as the new ambassador to Argentina in April 1946.

Messersmith immediately set out to repair relations. Although it is an overstatement to claim, as one historian has, that "Messersmith fell under Peron's spell almost as soon as he had landed in Buenos Aires," the ambassador did take a much more sympathetic stance on Argentina's actions and slow compliance with its international agreements.[13] In the first of numerous lengthy reports back to the department, Messersmith noted on 15 June that he was optimistic that the problems between the two nations could be worked out and "encouraged by the developments in the situation so far." He characterized past policies as "errors that have been made in good faith," but mistakes nonetheless. His objective, as he understood it, was the "consolidation of the closest collaboration in the political, economic, social, and defense field among all of the American republics." Such cooperation was impossible without the "wholehearted collaboration of the Argentine." Perón would be in power for at least six years so the United States had to "deal presently with a government which is largely controlled by the will of a single individual."[14]

Argentina, the ambassador believed, was willing and eager to cooperate with the United States. Perón had made it clear to him that "he desires to arrive at a new and proper situation" and that he planned to "safeguard the rights of property of foreign interests." Perón even concurred that Argentina had been historically too focused on Europe and that it "must look to the Americas" more in the future. The problem, therefore, was that "some of the agencies of our government are still proceeding in actual practice as though the war were still on and are endeavoring to apply war-time considerations and measures." This not only prolonged the problem, it misplaced the focus of policy. The "collaboration among the American States," Messersmith wrote, "is essential to our peace and security in this hemisphere . . . it is the first line of defense for us and . . . can be one of the bulwarks in the world structure for security and peace." Messersmith noted that he was aware, even if most people were not, that the situation in Europe was "an armed truce." Thus the United States had to have security in the Western Hemisphere to meet this challenge. Continued attacks against Perón were, from this perspective, not only ineffective but self-defeating. Perón was president, and it was "useless and more than useless to discuss the methods by which he was elected. There is no doubt that he had the complete support of the military and also labor." In complete contrast to Braden's views and current department policy, Messersmith argued that "we have to forget the past as much as we can and take him at his word and his expressions of good faith and desire for our friendship and collaboration at their face value, for if we do not we will lose the one opportunity we have." The Argentine military desired to sign the defense pact, and the government was ready to meet the requirements of the proposed treaty.[15] The basis for a change in policy had been outlined.

The policy of opposition to dictators, however, still held sway for most of 1946. In July, Braden completed a review of American-Argentine relations and sent it to President Harry Truman, who affirmed the continuation of the policy that there must be "deeds and not merely promises" before the United States would enter into a military arrangement with Argentina.[16] Therefore, the proposed Rio conference would continue to be delayed. This decision led to a barrage of letters and communications from Messersmith, often deliberately going around Braden and leaking information to the press, in an effort to change the policy and discredit the assistant secretary. In one representative fifteen-page letter on 15 August, Messersmith provided Byrnes with a detailed critique of Braden's views and analysis. He stated that from his meetings with the secretary and the president it was his "understanding of these conversations that it was our desire, in view of the world situation . . . and in view of developments in the Argentine situation, to endeavor to bring about a normalization of our relations with the Argentine." Messersmith believed evidence existed that Argentina had made concessions and was well on its way to the "compliance necessary for the normalization of relations." In a detailed examination of the July document, he charged that Braden did not wish to recognize these realities and sought to continue his personal war against Perón. The United States, Messersmith concluded, had to "give faith and confidence" to the acts of the present government. Policy should shift from the "present condemnation and opposition and antagonism" to "one of understanding what is happening in the country." Continuation of current efforts would destroy the "basis of the whole American system and . . . the confidence in us of every one of the other American republics."[17]

Relations between Braden and Messersmith were strained as each vied to determine the direction of American policy. The next day, Messersmith wrote Truman, Acheson, and Byrnes again, directly criticizing Braden. He charged that Braden's position was hampering the work of the department and that he was interested only in protecting his personal policy. Both Acheson and Truman responded that they did not find the situation as bad as Messersmith described it and that the differences were over approaches and not policy.[18] Failing to gain satisfaction from the administration, Messersmith took his anti-Braden campaign to the press, writing Arthur Sulzberger of the *New York Times* a detailed letter of his complaints and view that relations with Argentina had to be improved. He stressed that Perón was not a dictator, that Argentina had made significant progress toward compliance with the terms of the Chapultepec agreements, and that Argentina was a strong bulwark against communism. *Time* magazine picked up the story and this time placed

Messersmith on the cover and outlined the divisions within the department over policy.[19]

Although the State Department ordered Messersmith to stop writing to the press, policy was beginning to swing to his position. In 1946 the department took an increasingly hard line toward the Soviet Union that submerged regional issues to the broader mandates of the emerging Cold War. From Washington, events in Europe since the end of the war began to take on an ominous cast. Soviet actions in Eastern Europe and the Middle East came to be seen as aggressive measures that threatened American interests and plans for postwar peace and prosperity. American officials were determined that the United States would seize its "second chance" to shape the postwar world. It was an article of faith to American internationalists that the United States should accept responsibility for postwar leadership and see to it that the world adopted American ideals of self-determination, free trade, arms limitation, and collective security. These aims were not only good for the United States but beneficial to all nations. To ensure that the American understanding of self-determination and the open door were able to flourish, it was necessary to combat closed spheres of influence. No one nation or group of powers could be allowed to establish a system that competed with the American one.

It was also axiomatic to Truman and his advisers that political and economic freedoms were interrelated and that American prosperity was dependent on world economic recovery along liberal economic lines. Any restrictions of trade would lead, it was feared, to a repeat of the 1930s. Truman clearly outlined these views in early 1947. He declared in a speech at Baylor University that "peace, freedom, and world trade" are inseparable. "The grave lessons of the past have proved it." There was, Truman believed, "one thing that Americans value even more than peace. It is freedom. Freedom of worship—freedom of speech—freedom of enterprise." They, too, could not be separated. Americans' devotion to freedom of enterprise was contingent on the other two freedoms. It "has deeper roots than a desire to protect the profits of ownership. It is part and parcel of what we call American." A free trade system, rather than a state trading system, was essential. If trends continued, however, the government would "shortly find itself in the business of allocating foreign goods among importers and foreign markets among exporters and telling every trader what he could buy or sell, and how much, and when, and where. This is precisely what we have been trying to get away from as rapidly as possible, ever since the war. It is not the American way.

It is not the way to peace."[20] Limiting a Soviet sphere was, therefore, mandatory.

Truman was convinced by the end of 1945 that it was time to "stop babying the Soviets." "Unless Russia is faced with an iron fist and strong language, another war is in the making."[21] The arrival of George Kennan's long telegram from Moscow in February 1946 served to provide coherence to the developing hard line against the Soviets. Kennan argued that the Soviet Union was motivated by a combination of traditional Russian desires to expand and by Marxist ideology that taught there could be no cooperation with capitalist states. There was, therefore, no room for compromise or negotiation. The Soviets would take advantage of all sincere efforts at peace and honor agreements only when doing so was expedient to their goals. The obvious conclusion for Kennan, and the one drawn by the Truman administration, was that the Soviets had no legitimate grievances. A policy of opposition and the containment of Soviet power was the only wise course to follow.[22] The next month, former British prime minister Winston Churchill delivered his Iron Curtain speech, sounding the call for an Anglo-American alliance against the Soviet Union.

Problems seemed to be multiplying around the world, and from the White House it appeared that more often than not the source of the difficulties was Moscow. In Asia, revolutionary nationalist movements, often headed by communists, were fighting against the restoration of Europe's colonial empires, while civil war between the American-supported Guomindang and the communists resumed in China. In Europe, economic recovery from the war was slow, food and other essential goods in short supply, and communist parties, particularly in France and Italy, gaining ground. Soviet-installed governments in Eastern Europe were seemingly becoming entrenched, and a civil war raged in Greece between the British-backed royalist forces and the communist-led rebels. To many officials, it appeared that Western Europe could collapse and communism sweep the region. Time for action was apparently running short.[23]

The emerging hard-line position was supported by the development of the idea of "Red Fascism." A popular analogy that merged Nazi Germany and Soviet Russia together as totalitarian states, Red Fascism served to support the demonization of the Soviet Union and provided a historical lesson—no more Munichs—to apply to current problems. There could be no appeasement of the Soviet Union as there had been of Nazi Germany.[24] The notion that dangers to the United States were to be found only in communist states that were now the definition of totalitarian regimes was also revived. No matter what the crimes of other nations, as long as they were anticommunist they would never fall under this rubric and demand the same opposition.

On 15 August 1946, Truman endorsed a policy memorandum drawn up by his senior advisers stating that the "time has come when we must decide that we shall resist with all means at our disposal any Soviet aggression." In particular, Turkey and the Turkish straits were identified as vital to American interests, and military action might be necessary to keep them out of Russia's control.[25] Truman also asked Clark Clifford to prepare a summary of all the agreements the Soviets had violated. The final report, prepared by George Elsey, went beyond the initial request and presented the president with an outline designed to provide a coherent outlook on relations with the Soviet Union. Drawing heavily on Kennan, Elsey's document set out the problem of relations with Russia as an ideological challenge that had to be met. Soviet foreign policy was expansive, and the United States had to be prepared to meet it with military force.[26]

The British announcement in February 1947 that they were pulling out of Greece spurred the Truman administration into action. London could no longer afford the war, and it asked the United States to take it over. Rather than viewing the conflict as a long-standing division in Greek society over the nature of its government and institutions, American policymakers now interpreted it as part of a Soviet effort to expand. Dean Acheson told congressional leaders that the "Soviet Union was playing one of the greatest gambles in history at minimal cost." In an early version of the domino theory, he compared the situation in Greece to a barrel of apples infected by one rotten one: "The corruption of Greece would infect Iran and all to the east. It would also carry infection to Africa through Asia Minor and Egypt, and to Europe through Italy and France." The United States alone was "in a position to break up the play."[27]

In March, the president announced the Truman Doctrine. The central theme of his speech was that there was a global contest between two competing and incompatible ways of life: democracy and totalitarian communism. Democracy represented government "based upon the will of the majority" expressed through "free institutions, representative government, free elections, guarantees of individual liberty, freedom of speech and religion, and freedom from political oppression." Communism meant the "will of a minority forcibly imposed upon the majority.

It relies on terror and oppression, a controlled press and radio, fixed elections, and the suppression of personal freedoms." The course of action was clear. "I believe," Truman declared, "that it must be the policy of the United States to support free peoples who are resisting attempted subjugation by armed minorities or by outside pressures." American foreign policy was now based on a bipolar worldview of inherent conflict between the United States and the USSR and the containment of communism.[28]

The adoption of containment as the global policy of the United States had a dramatic effect on the conflicts in the State Department over policy toward noncommunist dictatorships. It did not matter that the Greek government, controlled by the discredited forces of the oligarchy that supported the prewar fascist government, more nearly resembled Truman's description of communism than democracy. Other factors became more important than the particular composition of a government and whether or not it was democratic. World War II was no longer the dominant paradigm for forming policy toward right-wing dictators. If it was a contest between only two ways of life, governments had to fit into one side of the divide or the other. There was no room for any other distinctions. Right-wing regimes were part of the free world no matter what the composition of their governments. It would be ideal if they were democratic, but they must be anticommunist. Communism was the danger and the Cold War the new paradigm that ushered back in the positive evaluations of authoritarian governments in the worldwide struggle with the Soviet Union. The wartime view of fascism as the enemy had yielded to the danger of Soviet expansion. In this new understanding of the world, there was little room for moral arguments against right-wing dictators. They would be wedged into the free world, no matter what their record of abuses, as nations capable of being set on the course to democracy. No such hope existed for communist nations.

The Truman administration's ideological division of the world led to the ascendancy within the government of those who believed unity in the noncommunist world was the single most important policy objective. Relations with Latin America, Asia, and Africa and the question of relations with right-wing dictatorships were now subsumed to the policy of containment. The most important consideration was where a nation stood in relation to the Cold War and how readily it supported American policies and actions. This policy guaranteed a lack of attention, knowledge, and concern about local conditions and that the nations on the periphery of the Cold War would receive high-level attention only in times of crisis. Older ideas reemerged to provide justifications for moving away from the policy of opposing dictatorships to embracing them as part of the free world. With the appointment of General George Marshall as secretary of state at the outset of 1947, policy toward Latin America and its dictators began to gain the same clarity as policy toward the Soviet Union. Continued acrimony over Argentina and the rift between Braden and Messersmith could no longer be tolerated. Relations needed to reflect the politics of the Cold War. In this context, the original arguments against Braden's policy were revived and used to reverse course.

Marshall favored normalizing relations with Buenos Aires and the conclusion of a mutual defense pact within the Americas. Braden's policy had failed to oust Perón from power, was blocking efforts at implementing the mutual assistance pact called for by the Treaty of Chapultepec, and was, therefore, hampering the U.S. ability to resist Soviet expansion. It had to be abandoned. In April 1947 a joint committee of the State, War, and Navy Departments recommended that the United States make American weapons available to Latin American nations to prevent those countries from turning to the Soviet Union and providing Moscow with "political leverage potentially dangerous to U.S. security interests."[29] Argentina was the most likely first candidate to break ranks. As Messersmith wrote Marshall, continued hostility toward Argentina was "serving the interests of only one country, and that is the Soviet Union."[30]

The final change in policy occurred when Truman invited Argentina's ambassador, Oscar Ivanissevich, to meet with him on 31 March. With Acheson and Senators Vandenberg and Connally in attendance, Truman informed Ivanissevich that the only obstacle remaining to good relations was that some twenty to thirty Nazi agents were still in Argentina.[31] On 3 June, Truman announced, after meeting again with the Argentine ambassador, that because Argentina had taken steps to fulfill its obligations to inter-American unity, "no obstacles remained" to the normalization of relations and the completion of the mutual assistance treaty.[32] That same month, both Braden and Messersmith were asked to resign. In the fall, the Rio Pact was completed and closer cooperation with the various military forces in Latin America begun. Secretary of War Robert Paterson believed that the United States would reap great benefits from "permanent U.S. military missions and the continued flow of Latin American officers through our service schools. Thus will our ideals and way of life be nurtured in Latin America to the eventual exclusion of totalitarianism and other foreign ideologies."[33] As the new ambassador, James Bruce, reported to Truman in November, relations with Perón "could not be better," and the United States could "count definitely on the Argentines as friends and allies."[34] In October 1953, Truman recalled Braden as "that crazy guy" who "got mixed up in the elections of Argentina" and was responsible for Perón's getting elected. Messersmith "did a very good job of healing things up," although some ill feeling caused by Braden's actions continued. In an indication of the low priority placed by his administration on Latin American affairs, the former president did not "know how the situation is developing now."[35]

In February 1950, Assistant Secretary of State for Inter-American Affairs Edward Miller traveled to Buenos Aires to meet with Perón. Relations had again become difficult, although it now had nothing to do with the nature of Argentina's government. The disagreements stemmed from Perón's continued independence within the American system and desire to play a leading role in South America. The embassy reported to Acheson that the "value of Mr. Miller's visit was very great" in improving relations. Miller's presence and discussions with Perón provided the dictator with "a suitable medium" for toning down his anti–United States rhetoric and moving toward greater cooperation.[36] Commenting on his visit, Miller noted that some would prefer that the United States refuse to conduct relations with Argentina "in light of the Perón regime's disregard of civil liberties. But no Western Hemisphere country (except Uruguay) observes civil liberties in the same way as the U.S. Such a standard would be impractical and would play into the hands of the Russians." The United States had vital interests in Latin America and placed a high priority on hemispheric unity. It could not "gear its actions to the repeated governmental shifts in particular countries" without negating the whole "purpose of the Inter-American system."[37]

Messers X and Y

Nonintervention was to mean again that the United States would cooperate with any right-wing dictatorship in Latin American (and elsewhere) as long as it was anticommunist and aligned with the United States. When the promotion of democracy and efforts to contain communism came into conflict, containment won out under the banner of allowing self-determination. The change of views was dramatically outlined in a comprehensive area policy statement by Louis Halle for the Division of American Republics in 1948. The United States, he noted, has "confronted a dilemma that arises, in part, out of its own moral scruples and high expectations" in Latin America. The problem stemmed from dictatorships that denied their citizens "the freedoms that all the American republics have pledged themselves to respect. While we are firmly pledged not to intervene unilaterally for the purpose of reforming or replacing such governments, the degree to which we may cooperate with them is a matter on which we have considerable freedom of decision." Those who advocated a continuation of the 1946 policy to refrain from cordial relations with dictatorships based their position on three points. Cooperation "impedes the progress toward liberal democracy," compromises "our moral position in Latin America and the world as the chief advocate of liberal democracy," and prevents true unity within the hemisphere "since inter-American solidarity is based on a common devotion to freedom." Opponents in the State Department argued that this position should be rejected because the "prime need is to assure for ourselves the cooperation of all the other American republics, whatever the nature of their particular governments," in the defense of the hemisphere. Moreover, "dictatorial government is, where typical, a consequence of social conditions rather than of the motives and machinations of men." It was, in other words, endemic to the area because of the "poverty and ignorance of the masses rather than . . . the wickedness of individual dictators who profit thereby." Finally, the United States should not act as a judge "since we would not tolerate such judgments by others upon ourselves." Halle agreed and was glad to note that the critics' views now constituted American policy. During the war, the United States maintained cordial relations with all governments as long as they supported the war effort. It was only after the war that "we embarked upon a new policy of non-cordiality with dictatorial governments in Latin America." This position proved unwise, and with "our growing awareness of Soviet Russia's aggressive policy . . . we have now swung back toward a policy of general cooperation that gives only secondary importance to the degree of democracy manifested by the respective governments" to the south.[38]

The change in policy had an immediate effect on relations with other nations. In 1948, the military forces in Peru and Venezuela overthrew democratically elected governments and established dictatorships. Several meetings and discussions were held to consider what the United States response should be. The State Department issued a statement that reiterated American commitments to "encourage democratic and constitutional procedures," expressed its "growing concern with respect to the overthrow of popularly elected governments by military forces," and noted that the "use of force as an instrument of political change is not only deplorable, but is usually inconsistent with the acknowledged ideals of the American republics."[39] These words were, however, mere platitudes. The United States quickly recognized the new dictatorships and concluded that it would be "unproductive and possibly damaging to inter-American relations" to call a meeting of foreign ministers to discuss this issue.[40] The Policy Planning Staff believed that no "useful purpose would be served by a protracted withholding of recognition" and that there appeared in Venezuela "to be greater likelihood of an orderly political procedure, eventually involving popular elections and peaceful regularization of government, if the new regime is encouraged to carry out its present promises." The army was greatly concerned that the supply of oil from Venezuela remain uninterrupted and thought that the new government of Marcos Pérez Jiménez "may be expected to provide more adequate security measures for the oil production area than a reinstated Gallegos Government which would depend for a part of its support on unions sympathetic to Communistic aims." Further, the military government would permit the "continuance of the U.S. Army Mission in Venezuela, and the subsequent influencing of a generally pro–United States element."[41]

The Central Intelligence Agency (CIA) found that both coups stemmed from the fear within the officer corps of declining influence of the military in "liberal or left-wing governments." These changes would have no adverse effect on U.S. interests. Similar actions in other nations could be expected because "in the absence of a broad, stable basis for civilian political power—a condition which depends upon the long-term solution of social and economic problems—the armed forces of most Latin American states will constitute the social group most eager and most able to exercise authority." Supporting these governments was merely "a frank acknowledgment that present difficulties can be most easily controlled by semi-military methods."[42] A Council on Foreign Relations Study Group that included Assistant Secretary of State for Inter-American Affairs Edward Miller reached the same conclusion. Its report stated that "it should be recognized that the attainment of a stable constitutional democracy in each member nation . . . cannot be achieved overnight." It required "a long period of education and political development, particularly in the case of those nations that are less advanced." Consequently, it should be expected that progress toward democratic government would be interrupted "in the form of revolutions, coups d'etat and local dictatorships." The best course of action for the United States was to "exercise patience and tolerance toward these regrettable but inevitable manifestations as long as they do not involve Western Hemisphere security . . . or totalitarian infiltration."[43] By totalitarian, the group meant communist. A new distinction was beginning to appear in official conversations and reports.

The two military takeovers did not, the State Department concluded, pose any threat to United States interests in the region or indicate a trend toward fascism in Latin America, as many in the press were claiming. In fact, the department argued that the takeovers were positive indicators for a democratic future: "Rather than constituting a trend towards fascism in this Hemisphere, it is our belief that all of this is the result of the impact of a new social consciousness on a society which until recently had been comparatively static for centuries." The key influence was the United States and its values, which created "an excessively rapid trend towards the adjustment of social rights which could not but result in a greater degree of political instability." In nations such as Venezuela, this instability meant, before the coup, the danger of left-wing parties coming to power. The military moves were necessary to provide order during this time and to ensure that the left did not take advantage of the period of flux. The department concluded in 1950 that "no clearer proof" of the correctness of its decision to recognize the Jiménez regime "can be adduced than the recent step towards return to constitutional government in Venezuela."[44] Dictatorship, apparently, was the best route to democracy.

The department continued to focus on the question of relations with Latin American dictatorships over the next two years. A 1949 State Department problem paper designed to enumerate the "principles which should govern the formulation of U.S. policies concerned with inter-American relations" spelled out in greater detail the reasons behind the reversal of policy. The report began with a background review of Latin American history that was to provide the necessary context for understanding and supporting current dictators. The United States had to realize that its colonial experience of "representative partial self-government" inherited from Great Britain was in "sharp contrast with the background of revolution and the founding of new institutions in Latin America." Spain and Portugal had no democratic institutions. "Democratic self-government was not only alien to the mother countries, but incipient tendencies toward it in the colonies were deliberately suppressed." The church and crown dominated all aspects of society. The new Latin American nations were forced to "assume a 'developed stage without first having had the preliminaries.'" Progress had been made, but it was "extremely slow," and with each new crisis the "basic instabilities reassert themselves in political upheavals throughout the area." The result was that "most Latin American countries have not been able to establish stable and democratic political systems." Independence did not bring about a "clean break with the authoritarian political tradition of the colonial regime. The church, the landed gentry, and the military successfully defended their economic and political prerogatives." These problems were further "complicated in some instances by the efforts to assimilate millions of Indians who are heirs to a different type of civilization." In an analysis that became central to justifications for supporting right-wing dictators throughout the Cold War, the report emphasized that in determining policy toward these nations "it is important to determine if a dictatorial regime is of the traditional Latin American military or authoritarian type, or if it is of Communist, Nazist, or other police state type." This distinction was crucial. The former was acceptable, but the latter was grounds for "legitimate concern." Further, it was necessary to distinguish "between dictatorial governments whose influence is effective beyond their own borders and those whose actions are far less likely to be a threat to international peace and security." Communist states fell into the first category but authoritarian regimes did not. The conclusion was clear. Right-wing dictatorships were historically part of Latin America and its heritage and, for the foreseeable future, unavoidable in the region.[45] Nor were they by definition negative. An Army Intelligence Report made the same point more bluntly: "Where dictatorships have been abolished, the resulting governments have been weak and unstable."[46] Dictatorships would be supported in the name of nonintervention and anticommunism. "Public statements of our support of democratic institutions and practices are desirable," the report noted, but "there should be no effort to impose our own particular form of government and institutions upon other peoples."[47]

The change in policy was undergirded by the persistence of the paternalistic racism and lack of knowledge about Latin America that had always characterized American policy. President Truman, as his most recent biographer, Alonzo Hamby, has shown, might have "remained a racist only in the narrowest sense of the word and was considerably less so than the vast majority of white Americans in the years after World War II." Still, he used words such as "nigger" in private to describe blacks and held to the racial categories and stereotypes of his youth.[48] He found Latin Americans to be, "like Jews and the Irish, 'very emotional' and difficult to handle."[49] Dean Acheson admitted upon becoming secretary of state in 1949 that "he wanted to know more about the situation in South America" because he was "rather vague on this particular point." Was it "richer or poorer, going Communist, Fascist or what?"[50] He believed that the problems in Latin America stemmed from the "Hispano-Indian culture—or lack of it." The combination of "an explosive population, stagnant economy, archaic society, primitive politics, massive ignorance, illiteracy, and poverty—all had contributed generously to the creation of many local crises tending to merge into a continental one."[51] State Department records are riddled with comments such as how Guatemalan leaders were known for their "mental deviousness and difficulty thinking in a straight line," or that trying to reason with Latin Americans was "rather like consulting with babies as to whether or not we should take candy away from them." Descriptions of Latin Americans as children were common. Spruille Braden opined that "our Latino friends were playing at economics, just as a child will pretend in his games to be something he isn't and has no immediate possibility of becoming."[52]

The full development of the favorable policy toward right-wing dictators was completed in 1950. At the meeting of the United States chiefs of mission in Rio de Janeiro in March 1950 the question of American relations with dictators was again raised. The chief participants were George Kennan, in his only trip to Latin America, and Louis Halle. Kennan focused his attention on the communist threat to the region. In particular, he worried that while the United States worked with "local governments, business interests, and advanced circles, the Communists are influencing schools and labor groups. What they are doing," he warned the assembled ambassadors and diplomatic staff, "is more important and deeper than are our efforts." He also expressed concern that the problem with American policy was that too often it seemed "too wishy-washy, thereby giving the impression of weakness." Foreign governments had to be "impressed by our importance and our ability to be tough if necessary." The communists would exploit any signs that we were not willing to stand up to them and support governments that were anticommunist. The final answer "might be an unpleasant one," but the United States "should not hesitate before police repression by the local government. This is not shameful since the Communists are essentially traitors." One could not "ignore the effectiveness of police action, and the cases of Turkey and Portugal are examples of nations which . . . have been successful in repressing" communism. "It is better to have a strong regime in power than a liberal government if it is indulgent and relaxed and penetrated by Communists."[53]

On the direct question of the form of government in Latin America, Kennan noted that "while we have our own system in which we believe," it is still "experimental." When considering other countries with different histories and political conditions, "we may like one government and dislike another, but our likes and dislikes should have nothing to do with our relations." Those feelings needed to be "put aside" and a criterion established based on "whether or not the governments are maintaining satisfactory relations with us." Too rigid a policy left open the question of what to do "about a benevolent authoritarian rule." Certainly the "best assurance against Communism was a working democratic system but . . . this cannot always exist." In that case, authoritarian rule was necessary and even desirable. In general, Halle concurred with Kennan. The starting point for American policy in Latin America was the solidarity of all the nations "as the foundation of our security." He agreed that though it was not in the best interest of the United States to "indulge in denunciation of other governments, or pass judgment on domestic affairs," it was necessary to keep alive and speak of certain ideals. All nations in Latin America shared these broad ideals and, with the possible exception of Argentina, "were moving in the direction of democracy, even where they had undemocratic government." Dictators, he argued, fostered democracy, as in the case of Guatemala, where he claimed that "Ubico . . . was a dictator . . . who kept alive the ideal of democracy and actually steered the country in that direction." In an effort to discern the difference between noncommunist and communist dictatorships, Halle remarked that "a clear-cut distinction might be made between the concept that the state exists to serve the individual and the concept that the individual exists to serve the state."[54]

Both Kennan and Halle further developed their ideas that year in two documents, one hidden away in the records of the State Department, the other submitted for publication, which demonstrated the policies and attitudes that guided American policy. Their reports were produced at the same time as NSC-68, with its dire portrait of the world situation in the wake of the communist victory in China and the Soviet detonation of an atomic weapon the previous fall.[55] Following his return from Latin America, Kennan composed a memorandum for Secretary of State Acheson outlining his views on Latin America as a problem for United States foreign policy.[56] The overarching theme was how best to integrate Latin America into a noncommunist international system and check communist influence in the region. "The military significance to us of the Latin American countries," Kennan wrote, "lies today . . . in the extent to which we may be dependent upon them for materials essential to the prosecution of a war, and more importantly in the extent to which the attitudes of the Latin American peoples may influence the general political trend in the international community." The aim of the Soviet Union in the region was the "destruction of American influence . . . and the conversion of the Latin American peoples into a hotbed of hostility and trouble for the United States."[57]

Latin America, according to Kennan, provided fertile soil for communist efforts because of its poverty and "formidable body of anti-American feeling already present." In addition, Kennan held the peoples to the south in very low esteem. "It seems to me," he told Acheson, "unlikely that there could be any other region of the earth in which nature and human behavior could have combined to produce a more unhappy and hopeless background for the conduct of human life than in Latin America." Poor climate combined with Spanish colonial rule "superimposed a series of events unfortunate and tragic almost beyond anything ever known in human history." The Spanish brought little but "religious fanaticism, a burning, frustrated energy, and an addiction to the most merciless cruelty." Intermarriage with Native Americans and blacks originally brought over as slaves "produced other unfortunate results which seemed to have weighed scarcely less heavily on the chances of human progress." Given the conditions "in these confused and unhappy societies," the necessity of the region to American defense, and the danger posed by communism, Kennan believed the United States had to create "incentives which will impel governments and societies of the Latin American countries to resist communist pressures, and to assist them and spur them on in their efforts, where the incentives are already present." Echoing his statements earlier in the month in Rio, Kennan declared that in achieving its goals the United States could not "be too dogmatic about the methods by which local communists can be dealt with." The best solution was undoubtedly a strong democratic state. "But where they do not exist, and where the concepts and traditions of popular government are too weak to absorb successfully the intensity of the communist attack, then we must concede that harsh governmental measures of repression may be the only answer; that these measures may have to proceed from regimes whose origins and methods would not stand the test of American concepts of democratic procedure; and that such regimes and such methods may be preferable alternatives, and indeed the only alternatives, to further communist successes."[58]

To justify his claims, Kennan invoked the history of American nonintervention and exceptionalism. Those who historically opposed intervention have "allowed for the possibility that our own political institutions might be the product of a peculiar national experience, irrelevant to the development of other peoples." Quoting John Quincy Adams, Kennan argued that in Latin America "arbitrary power, military and ecclesiastical, is stamped upon their education, upon their habits, and upon all their institutions." He said that he took "particular occasion" during his stay in Latin America to investigate this question. Experience, therefore, demonstrated that "democratic institutions . . . are not universally native to Latin America" and should not be anticipated in the near future. Nothing the United States could do "in the way of direct interference" could alter that situation. Moreover, it should be recognized that the "difference between democratic and authoritarian forms of government is everywhere a relative, rather than an absolute, one and that the distinctions between the two concepts are peculiarly vague and illusive against the background of Latin American psychology and tradition." To base policy on "moral discrimination addressed to the internal-political personality of Latin American regimes" would mean taking responsibility for their domestic affairs. Kennan stressed that the only basis for deciding policy was a nation's "conduct in their relations with us and as members of the international community."[59]

The second document, Louis Halle's article "On a Certain Impatience with Latin America," was published anonymously as "Y" in the journal *Foreign Affairs* in July. The parallels to Kennan's 1947 "X" article, "Sources of Soviet Conduct," published in the same forum three years earlier, are obvious. Both pieces were intended as public statements of policy and designed to influence popular attitudes. Acheson had asked for the preparation of an article on American policy "similar to the 'X' article." A public rationale for the change in policy from the end-of-the-war opposition to right-wing dictators to support was necessary. When he sent the finished paper to Acheson, Assistant Secretary of State Miller termed it an "excellent restatement of our Latin American policy."[60] Unlike Kennan's report, Halle's statement of the issues was considered a more acceptable public explanation of the harsh realities.

Halle's title indicated his appeal to the prevailing paternalistic perceptions held about Latin America to explain American policy, while his epigraph by Edith Hamilton on fifth-century Athens, that "democracy even under a tyranny continued to advance," placed the support of dictators in the context of advancing liberalism. "Public opinion," Halle began, "has shown a sporadic impatience at the failure of many Latin American republics to achieve a greater degree of political democracy." The continuation of "dictatorships in our midst throughout a war fought for democracy was a moral embarrassment. The establishment of new dictatorships after victory seemed to some like a rejection of what we fought to achieve." The public would have to realize that Latin Americans were basically like children and "less mature" than citizens of the United States. Thus a policy of "*noblesse oblige*" was called for on behalf of Washington to guide these nations forward in the same manner a stern father would his own children. In an interesting historical analysis, Halle set out the argument that the United States had gained its independence "because we had come of age and were ready for it. The other Americans gained theirs because the mother country was struck down." The nations to the south "were quite unready to assume the responsibility of self-government. The result was a sordid chaos out of which Latin America has still not finally emerged." Democracy had to be achieved by "evolution rather than revolution. Those whose animus is against dictatorships have propagated a common delusion that democracy is the absence of dictators." This idea was naive, Halle thought, because many other worse conditions, such as anarchy or communism, existed. Democracy, rather, was "political maturity." Without that, the "overthrow of dictators, as we have so often seen, may result only in the chaos that leads to renewed dictatorship." "Maturity," however, "is not guaranteed by lapse of time." It is denied to many nations by "poverty and the sordid necessities of their circumstances": lack of education, leadership, and tradition. The tradition in Latin America, Halle found, was one of "political behavior marked by intemperance, intransigence, flamboyance, and the worship of strong men." Latin American politics resembled the "conduct of schoolboy gangs" rather than that of "mature men and women." "Worship of the 'man on horseback' . . . is another manifestation of immaturity. It is characteristic of adolescence."[61]

Halle proceeded to follow the line of argument used in April by Assistant Secretary of State Miller. Miller favorably reviewed American interventions in Latin America under Presidents Theodore Roosevelt, Wilson, and Coolidge. He termed these actions "necessary evils" and opined that "if the circumstances that led to protective interventions by the United States should arise again today, the organized community of American states would be faced with the responsibility that the United States had once to assume alone." Specifically, the nonintervention clause of the Organization of American States (OAS) Charter was not an absolute. If communism threatened any state in the region, the group would have to act in the interests of all members.[62] As Halle framed the issue, the question of "whether the backward countries of Latin America were to be regarded as responsible adults or as irresponsible children was first answered by us in the early years of the twentieth century. With the construction of the Panama Canal we felt that we could no longer tolerate disorder and the lack of responsible government." Through the Roosevelt Corollary, the United States would "in effect . . . be responsible for keeping order among the children in our own yard." "Consequently, when chaos threatened our interests and those of other mature nations, we did not scruple to land armed forces and establish military governments of our own in the Dominican Republic, Haiti, and Nicaragua." The situation, unfortunately, remained much the same. In conclusion, Halle requested continued patience from his readers. "The other American republics are younger and less mature than the United States. Their historic drive is in the direction of the orderly practice of political democracy. They have made progress since the days when Bolívar . . . said that America was ungovernable." The United States had to expect growing pains and continued problems. While "they govern themselves today more or less badly, more or less well," they were, most important, still "free of iron curtains." The United States had to make sure that situation continued. Tolerance of dictators and the necessary role they had to play in preventing communism was called for. Latin America, similar to Athens, could advance toward democracy while under tyranny.[63]

The full extent of the reversal of policy and its meaning can be seen through an examination of policy toward two of the longest-standing dictators in Latin America, Somoza in Nicaragua and Trujillo in the Dominican Republic. Both Somoza and Trujillo were under pressure at the end of World War II to implement reforms. The American adoption of the policy of opposition toward dictatorships had given rise to domestic opposition, a loosening of control, and a fear by both dictators of the loss of United States support. Somoza and Trujillo each moved to lessen criticism by granting more freedom and going so far as to call for presidential elections in 1947. American policy, it appeared, was having a positive effect. A State Department summary prepared for Secretary of State Marshall in January 1947 expressed the negative view of dictators that was then official policy. Somoza held power through "repression and trickery. He has constantly tried to convince the Nicaraguan people that we support his regime and, in doing so, he has tended to turn many of the better element against us." The report further noted that the dictator "runs the country for his own financial benefit" and was attempting to rig the upcoming vote in favor of his hand-chosen candidate, Leonardo Argüello. Because the opposition's complaint that the election would not be fair was accurate and Argüello would be Somoza's puppet, the United States should "avoid any step which could be misinterpreted as approval for continuation of the dictatorship."[64] This statement repeated points from a March 1946 memorandum drawn up in response to Somoza's efforts to visit Washington as he had done in 1939. The department saw this as a bid to convince the Nicaraguan people that the United States supported his continuation in office. His suppression of "freedom of speech, press and assembly" and "evasion of constitutional provisions against re-election" made it important "to our relations with the entire hemisphere that we not give even the appearance of lending our support" to him.[65] The department went so far as to withdraw recognition of the government from June 1947 to May 1948 after Somoza overthrew his own presidential candidate because he proved too independent.

Similar views were expressed with regard to Trujillo's continued control of the Dominican Republic and the elections he planned for May 1947. He was portrayed in the report as "a ruthless and unprincipled dictator." The State Department was taking every precaution "in conformity with its attitude toward dictatorships and disreputable governments and its stated policy of warmer friendship for and a greater desire to cooperate with those regimes which rest on the periodically and freely expressed consent of the governed" to avoid any acts that could be construed as supporting Trujillo or the continuation of his rule.[66] Again, this represented policy that was adopted at the end of World War II. Byrnes wrote Truman in late 1945 that "because of the generally disreputable nature of the present Dominican regime," a "minimum of cordiality" should be shown to its ambassador when he visited the president. In March 1946, Byrnes described Trujillo as "the most ruthless, unprincipled, and efficient dictator in this hemisphere. He holds the country in an iron grasp, [and] rules by fear." He is well "aware of this Government's disapproval of his methods and practices in imposing his tyranny on the Dominican people," yet he claims he enjoys United States support. "His regime is completely unsavory and we should scrupulously avoid even the appearance of lending him any support."[67]

Yet by 1952, both dictators had returned to a favored position in Washington, and each visited President Truman. Both came for the same reason. Somoza and Trujillo stressed their anticommunist credentials at a time when Cold War fears were peaking and their ability to maintain order in regions where upheaval seemed to be the norm.[68] With concern about the course of reforms in Guatemala growing, Somoza promised support against what American diplomats saw as a communist outpost in the Americas. By 1949, the State Department feared that should Somoza fall, it "would expect years of political turmoil bringing with it the usual economic chaos." Such an eventuality would return Nicaragua to the 1920s and the end of José Santos Zelaya's dictatorship. "When Zelaya fell, political and financial chaos ensued until Somoza took over as dictator."[69] Ambassador Capus Waynick observed in 1950 that Somoza had "his foot firmly on the spark of communism here." The dictator's main attributes were that "he does preserve order," that he was "insistently 'Americanista,'" and that the United States can get from him as President or strong man of the country any wanted cooperation or concession."[70] Assistant Secretary Miller found in 1951 that the Nicaraguan people were strongly pro-American and that Somoza was "a most convivial and delightful character."[71]

A Council on Foreign Relations Study Group on Inter-American Affairs examined the question of communism in Latin America and stated that the State Department needed to prevent the "establishment of totalitarian regimes in this Hemisphere." One question went to the heart of the matter. Would this mean opposition to Nicaragua and Somoza? Francis Adams Truslow, a New York lawyer and chairman of the group, responded that the policy did not apply to Nicaragua because Somoza's dictatorship only "involves autocratic rule." Totalitarianism was "autocratic rule, plus total, absolute control of economic life, as for example, communism." Truslow continued, "totalitarianism we refuse to cooperate with," but with "dictatorships we will."[72] This analysis helped push the pendulum back to support of right-wing dictators.

The complete reversal of attitudes toward Somoza since the end of the war was most evident in the memorandum Acheson sent President Truman in preparation for his meeting with the Nicaraguan dictator. Prepared by the Latin American Division, it emphasized that "Somoza is an able man with an engaging personality. He is informal, genial, energetic, persuasive and politically astute." The memorandum also noted that he was "impulsive, vain and egocentric." Nonetheless, though his methods had often been criticized, he had "restored order to Nicaragua and in recent years has been less repressive." The key to the return of this favorable view was that "Nicaragua has consistently supported United States foreign policy. The government and the people give every evidence of friendship to the United States and our prior occupation of Nicaragua has left no residue of ill-feeling. Somoza, himself, is a great admirer of this country and he considers his official visit in 1939 as guest of President Roosevelt a highlight of his career." Somoza was currently interested in economic development, particularly road construction, and his administration "has greatly improved Nicaragua's financial and economic position."[73]

The views of the members of another Council on Foreign Relations Study Group on political unrest in Latin America summarized the attitude that now prevailed in the United States. They found that Somoza's continued rule was beneficial for Nicaragua. The discussion emphasized that he had "maintained stability," and none other than Spruille Braden observed that "it was to Somoza's credit that he had been consistently anti-communist through the years." The group concurred with one member's conclusion that "if every Latin American country had a Somoza, there would be no need for a discussion of political unrest in these countries. It must be remembered that few Latin American countries are ready for democracy."[74]

A Friendly, Stable, and Independent Spain

The reversal of American policy toward Spain was even more dramatic than that toward the dictators of Latin America. Franco had been helped into power by Nazi Germany and fascist Italy, and his Falange Party was modeled after the other fascist movements of Europe. In the closing months of the Spanish civil war the United States had come to oppose Franco, and the widespread opposition to him in the United States from the civil war years continued into World War II. As a signatory of the Anti-Comintern Pact of 1939 with Germany, Italy, and imperial Japan, Spain was seen as a part of the Axis. Wartime efforts to keep Spain neutral and the limited cooperation with Franco's regime up to 1945 did not change the fundamental American position that his government was one of the three fascist regimes that had brought war to Europe. At the end of the fighting in May, the only difference between Franco's regime and those of Hitler and Mussolini was that his fascist dictatorship had yet to be destroyed. Yet by the 1950s the United States had established good relations with Franco and entered into a military alliance with Madrid. In a span of less than seven years, Franco and Spain had moved from fascist dictator and pariah nation to trusted friend and ally. Other enemy states had, of course, become friends, but in Germany, Italy, and Japan, the old regimes were destroyed and new political systems installed. In Spain, there were no fundamental changes; they all came from the American side and were the result of the Cold War.

There was no doubt in the United States that at the outset of World War II Spain actively supported Germany. Spain provided a variety of aids to the Axis cause, from propaganda to war materials, and came close to entering the war in 1940. Spain was kept out of the war only by Germany's refusal to satisfy Franco's imperial ambition for territory in North Africa. Still, Franco was sure of a German victory and wanted to maintain his close ties with Hitler. As an indication of Spain's commitment, Franco dispatched his Blue Legion of fourteen thousand soldiers to join the Germans on the Russian front in September 1941 and changed Spain's official status from neutral to "nonbelligerency" to indicate a more active support of the Axis. When Germany's fortunes began to fade in the cold of the Russian winter and it became clear that Great Britain and the United States would continue to control the western Mediterranean, Franco moved back to neutrality and began a limited cooperation with the Western Allies.

Franco's shift was welcomed by Roosevelt for pragmatic reasons. In a move similar to the Darlan deal and the support of the Badaglio government in Italy, Roosevelt was willing to cooperate with avowed fascist forces and withstand the criticism that came with these decisions, as long as that effort aided the war against Germany. Military decisions were a higher priority than political considerations. Seeking to keep Spain from striking at Gibraltar and using its large army in Morocco against the Allied forces planning to land in North Africa, Roosevelt, at the suggestion of Ambassador Carlton Hayes, wrote directly to Franco to express American friendship and provide him assurances against attack. On 2 November, one week before the Allied landings in North Africa, Roosevelt pledged that the United States would "take no action of any sort which would in any way violate Spanish territory." Roosevelt reiterated these points in a second letter on 8 November, the day military action began in French North Africa. He expressed a hope for continued Spanish-American friendship and provided Franco his "full assurance that these moves are in no shape, manner, or form directed against the Government or people of Spain or Spanish Morocco or Spanish territories—metropolitan or overseas. . . . Spain has nothing to fear from the United Nations."[75]

Hayes worked over the next two years with great success to maintain Spanish neutrality. By 1944, he was reporting that Spain was actually working to enhance the interests of the Allies, and the fact that "we do not like its ideology should not stand in the way of our realistically obtaining advantages from it in the war against Germany." That fall, when he submitted his resignation, Hayes wrote Roosevelt that the "mission . . . has now been discharged. Spain not only did not enter the war on the side of the Axis or jeopardize Allied military operations in North Africa in 1942, in Italy in 1943, or in France in 1944, but has actually accorded us, during the past two years and a half, an increasing number of facilities helpful to our war-effort."[76]

Although Franco certainly preserved his regime by staying out of the war, he also hoped that his wartime actions would gain him recognition and aid from the victorious Allies. In the United States, Ambassador Hayes made just such an argument on behalf of friendly postwar relations with Spain. Upon his return home in February 1945, Hayes prepared a seventeen-page report for the president and the State Department on past and future relations with Spain. "General Franco," Hayes argued, "should not be underestimated. He is a cautious and clever politician" who would remain in power for the foreseeable future. Hayes recounted the actions Franco had taken to support the Allies, a policy he termed "benevolent neutrality," and believed that they formed the basis for a lasting relationship. Turning to the central problem, Hayes wrote that he fully recognized the "obstacles at present in the way of the adoption by the United States Government of that especially friendly attitude toward Spain which the Spanish Government and the Spanish people desire." He noted that public opinion was "predominantly hostile to the existing régime in Spain, expectant of its speedy collapse, and opposed to any measure or indication of a collaboration with it which might conceivably serve to strengthen or prolong it." He hoped the U.S. government would counter this view with a more realistic appraisal and pursue a friendly policy.[77]

"We may not like the existing régime in Spain," Hayes argued, "but we are seriously misinformed and unrealistic when we assume that its collapse is imminent—unless, of course, we are ready to employ Allied armed forces to collapse it." The United States had to stop allowing the losing side in the civil war to determine its policy. "After all . . . General Franco represents that part of the Spanish nation which finally won a three years' civil war; and it would indeed be quite a novelty in human history if the victors in such a war should say to the vanquished only five or six year afterwards: 'We are sorry; we shouldn't have won . . . we will restore you to power.'" Using the American Civil War as a comparison,

Hayes asked the reader to "imagine General Grant saying anything like that to the leaders of the Southern Confederacy in the midst of our own post–Civil-War Reconstruction!" Hayes contended that though all nations would like to have every other nation adopt their institutions and values, the United States should be under no illusions "about the present ability of the mass of Spaniards to create and maintain a democratic republic." Unless the United States intended to "occupy and police the country and . . . ensure free and honest elections over a long period of time, we shall discover sooner or later to our grief that a restored republic in Spain will be the harbinger of a new cycle of disorder, chaos, civil war, and great popular suffering and distress." Spain should be left alone to handle its internal affairs. Franco would oversee a slow "liberalizing [of] the institutions, laws, and practices of the country," which outside opposition would only impede. Meanwhile, good relations with Madrid would be "very serviceable to American interests at the present and in the future."[78]

Roosevelt appreciated Hayes's "solid diplomatic achievements won largely by your own efforts" during the war in Spain and noted in his 14 March reply that his recommendations would receive "the closest attention and respect." He wrote, however, that "whatever this policy may eventually become, I believe you will agree that at the present time it must inevitably take account of the fact that the present regime in Spain is one which is repugnant to American ideas of democracy and good government." Cooperation with Franco had been a matter of wartime expediency. With the war coming to a close in Europe, no need existed to continue to act in a friendly manner toward Spain. It was to be treated as an enemy state. Roosevelt was even more direct four days earlier when he wrote to the new ambassador to Spain, Norman Armour. He was writing, the president told Armour, because he wanted him "to have a frank statement of my views" regarding Franco and Spain. "Having been helped to power by Fascist Italy and Nazi Germany," Roosevelt stated, "and having patterned itself along totalitarian lines the present regime in Spain is naturally the subject of distrust by a great many American citizens who find it difficult to see the justification for this country to continue to maintain relations with such a regime." Its past support of the Axis and the actions and utterances of the Falange "cannot be wiped out by actions more favorable to us now that we are about to achieve our goal of complete victory over those enemies of ours with whom the present Spanish regime identified itself in the past spiritually and by its public expressions and acts."[79]

Formal diplomatic relations and wartime actions "should not be inter-preted by anyone to imply approval of that regime and its sole party, the Falange, which has been openly hostile to the United States." In an indi-cation that the removal of Franco from power would be one of his post-war objectives, Roosevelt declared that "our victory over Germany will carry with it the extermination of Nazi and similar ideologies." Although it was not the policy of the United States to interfere in the internal af-fairs of other nations, Roosevelt stated that he would be "lacking in can-dor . . . if I did not tell you that I can see no place in the community of nations for governments founded on fascist principles."[80] Roosevelt had clearly expressed the liberal position toward Spain, which saw Franco, from the days of the civil war, as a pawn of Hitler. His actions during the war did nothing to change that view, and victory would relieve the United States of the need for any tolerance and free it to move against the government.

Consistent with U.S. opposition to dictatorships immediately after the war, this view was quickly implemented into policy. In June 1945, at the general conference in San Francisco that adopted the United Na-tions Charter, the United States supported the exclusion of Spain from membership. At Potsdam in July, Truman responded positively to Jo-seph Stalin's desire to overthrow Franco. In a line similar to Roosevelt's, Stalin made it clear that it was "not to the fact that the Franco regime was a dictatorship to which he objected but the fact that it owed its ori-gin to Fascist intervention."[81] The Potsdam Declaration stated that the Big Three "feel bound . . . to make it clear that they for their part would not favor any application for membership [in the UN] put forward by the present Spanish Government, which, having been founded with sup-port of the Axis powers, does not, in view of its origins, its nature, its rec-ord, and its close association with the aggressor States, possess the quali-fications necessary to justify such membership."[82]

In September, the State Department, with President Truman's ap-proval, published a copy of Roosevelt's March letter to Armour in the *New York Times* to demonstrate the consistency of American policy at San Francisco and Potsdam with the former president's views. Moreover, as Acheson noted, it "would operate as a further indication to the present Government of Spain, and especially to the people of Spain, of our po-sition and to this extent may help on the evolution which we hope will take place there."[83] The letter's publication served to counter critics who believed that the policy was influenced mainly by Great Britain's Labour government and undercut the Spanish position that the current policy was not in keeping with Roosevelt's views. Franco's appeals for support were rebuffed mainly because of his association with Hitler and Mussolini, not simply because he was a dictator.

The ostracism of Spain continued until 1947. On 4 March 1946, the United States issued a joint statement with the United Kingdom and France that restated the position that "so long as General Franco continues in control of Spain, the Spanish people cannot anticipate full and cordial association with those nations of the world which have, by common effort, brought defeat to German Nazism and Italian Fascism, which aided the present Spanish regime in its rise to power and after which the regime was patterned." The nations disavowed any intention of interfering in Spain's internal affairs, noting that the "Spanish people themselves must in the long run work out their own destiny" and that there was no desire to see the "Spanish people . . . again be subjected to the horrors of civil war and bitterness of civil strife." The statement then contradicted its nonintervention stance when it declared, "On the contrary, it is hoped that leading patriotic and liberal-minded Spaniards may soon find means to bring about a peaceful withdrawal of Franco, the abolition of the Falange, and the establishment of an interim . . . government under which the Spanish people may have an opportunity freely to determine the type of government they wish to have and to choose their leaders." The new government would have to welcome back all political refugees and extend political amnesty to all members of the opposition. The incentive was that the Allies would grant "full diplomatic relations and the taking of such practical measures to assist in the solution of Spain's economic problems" to such a government.[84]

In a striking parallel to its policy toward Argentina and the publishing of the Blue Book in February 1946, the State Department issued, in conjunction with its joint declaration, a white paper on Spain. Composed of captured German documents, it demonstrated the extent of Franco's support of the Axis and collaboration with Hitler during World War II.[85] In December 1946, the United States supported a UN resolution that continued to exclude Spain from the organization and recommended that it be "debarred from membership in international agencies established by or brought into relationship with the United Nations." Claiming that the Franco government did not truly represent the people of Spain because it "was imposed by force upon the Spanish people with the aid of the Axis Powers," the General Assembly called on all member nations to "immediately recall from Madrid their ambassadors and ministers."[86] The United States complied by not filling the then empty ambassadorship.

Franco responded to the Western pressure with a series of moves designed to make him appear less dictatorial. In July 1945, a new constitution was proclaimed that contained a Bill of Rights for the Spanish people. At the same time, Franco replaced several of his ministers who were members of the Falange Party with people associated with other parties. The next year he hinted that the monarchy might be restored and finally announced in March 1947 that Spain was again a monarchical nation, albeit without a king or queen. All the while, Franco made numerous overtures to the United States and Great Britain declaring his anticommunist position and seeking support for his country. Even if most of the changes were cosmetic, Western pressure was producing some relaxation of Franco's rule.[87] None of these moves, however, produced any responses from the United States.

The treatment accorded to the other dictator on the Iberian Peninsula, Antonio Oliveira Salazar in Portugal, was in marked contrast. Because Portugal possessed the Azores, it had been considered a strategically important nation since the outbreak of World War II. If an enemy gained control of the islands, the National Security Council explained, it "would hold a position directly astride our lines of communication to our most probable war area."[88] Salazar came to power in 1928 after a long period of instability which saw sixteen revolutions between 1910 and 1926. The United States believed that his coming to power through the army "was welcomed by the public, in the expectation that the military dictatorship would end the governmental chaos." His rule was described by the CIA in 1949 as a "comparatively benevolent dictatorship." During the war, Portugal was neutral, but its actions generally benefited the West. It had never joined in any agreements with Germany or Italy, and it allowed American military access to the Azores both during and after the war. Salazar's support for Franco was understandable because "his policies have allayed Portuguese fears of Communist penetration of the Iberian peninsula, as well as because of the moral strength Salazar derives from the existence of a similar authoritarian government in the adjoining country." Another reason for supporting Salazar was that his government was seen as an authoritarian, not totalitarian, regime, as Franco's was at the time. "In its origins," the CIA reported to the National Security Council, "unlike the dictatorship of Generalissimo Franco in Spain, which was imposed through the assistance of foreign powers and the active intervention of their military forces, Salazar's dictatorship developed as a completely native movement, backed by the Portuguese Army. It has had, therefore, much wider popular support and has evoked less international antagonism than the present Spanish regime." Indeed, there was no opposition to Portugal's entry into the United Nations or as an original member of the North Atlantic Treaty Organization (NATO).[89]

Dean Acheson, in particular, was impressed by Salazar. He found that the dictator was popular and that "there was a remarkable lack of tension in Portugal. It did not have any of the indicia—the emotional indicia of a dictatorship." Rather, he believed the people were content. The government differed "very much from the regimes of personal power which we were used to in Italy and Germany and Russia." Although Salazar's views were "certainly not democratic or libertarian in any way," his actions were not "coercive in the sense of exercising violence on people."[90] In his memoirs, Acheson described Salazar as one of the few people he was immediately drawn to upon first meeting. He had come to power "to run a country that for twenty years had been sinking into economic chaos and political anarchy." Acheson recalled that he saw Salazar not as "a dictator in his own right as Stalin was, but a dictator-manager employed and maintained by the power of the Army . . . to run the country in the interest of the middle class." Democracy and political liberty did not exist, but they "would probably be incompatible with the economic stability and growth" that Salazar had created. "A convinced libertarian—particularly a foreign one—could understandably disapprove of Salazar. But," Acheson wrote, "I doubt that Plato would have done so."[91] Acheson was concerned about the question of succession and who would rule after Salazar. If a suitable replacement was not found, "Portugal will go back into the confusion out of which he brought it."[92] That, however, was a problem better faced at a later time. For now, the benefits of Salazar's rule were, from the State Department's view, all too obvious.

In 1947, which saw shifts in policy toward the rest of Europe through the Truman Doctrine and the Marshall Plan, a reversal of course in Japan, and the abandonment of opposition toward dictators in Latin America, policy toward Spain also changed. As Hayes's 1945 memorandum indicates, the currents were always present, but the hardening of the Cold War was the catalyst for the United States, in the words of Under Secretary of State Robert Lovett, to "quit kidding ourselves as to our interest in Spain and to reorient our policy in relation thereto." In December 1947, in "Report on U.S. Policy toward Spain," the National Security Council (NSC) set out the case for change. It noted that the current policy was "unsatisfactory not only from the political point of view," because it had failed to oust Franco from power, "but from the viewpoint of our military planners." The reality was that "General Franco remains firmly in power and that his regime has actually been strengthened by demonstrations of international hostility." All agreed it would be "highly desirable to bring about the replacement of Franco by a regime fully representative of the Spanish people, if it were possible to do so without violent internal or external repercussions." That was not the case. There was "no evidence of effective opposition to Franco . . . which could bring an orderly change in government." Any effort was open to "serious doubt as to the results to be expected from such a course." Any weakening of the regime would bring "an ensuing political struggle leading only to internal chaos and resultant advantage to the Communists with all its ominous implications." Therefore, "it is believed that, in the national interest, the time had come for a modification of our policy toward Spain" to normalize relations. No public announcement of this change should be made, but relations needed to be restored "to a normal basis, irrespective of wartime ideological considerations or the character of the regime in power." Restrictive economic policies should be "quietly dropped, so that normal trade may be resumed between the two countries." This would be followed by private trade and the possibility of economic assistance for Spain. The United States would provide Spain with the "opportunity . . . to develop its resources and play a normal part in the revival of world commerce and industry." The final outcome was to be a friendly relationship with Spain "in the event of international conflict." The proposals were approved by Marshall and Truman in January 1948.[93] The CIA recommended a similar course of action because Spain would provide an excellent site for air and naval bases for controlling the western Mediterranean. Improved relations were necessary because the United States "requires a friendly, stable, and independent [i.e., noncommunist] Spain." Franco provided all of this.[94]

The public was finally made aware of the new policy in January 1950. Secretary of State Dean Acheson sent a statement to Senator Connally that characterized the past policy as a failure and a mistake. He blamed "organized propaganda and pressures" for keeping the old "controversy alive here and abroad." It had "served to stimulate more emotional feeling than rational thinking." The principal problem had been how to force change without intervention. Franco gave no indication that he was willing to step down, and it was hard to imagine the Spanish opposition being able to lead a revolt under his police state rule. Continued pressure would only unite Spain against democratic ideas or renew the civil war. Acheson noted that since 1947 the United States had opposed the actions of the United Nations with regard to Spain because the Franco regime posed no danger to world peace, and he called for a repeal of the ban on sending ambassadors. More to the point, the regime was stable and willing to cooperate. Given the heightened fears of the time, this was more than enough justification for seeking an alliance with Franco. The only consequence of past actions was to isolate Spain from normal relations with Western Europe, which hindered both economic recovery and the defense of the West. The United States would rectify this situation through normalized relations, trade, and negotiations.[95]

Although President Truman was never fully comfortable about dealing with Franco and the British and the French strongly objected, the State Department and the military, particularly Generals Marshall and Omar Bradley, were adamant about obtaining air and naval bases in Spain. High-level negotiations on economic assistance to Spain were conducted throughout 1950 to prepare the way for the military agreements, two leading American banks extended loans to Franco's government while Standard Oil invested in Spanish refineries, and Truman's friend Stanton Griffis was named as the new ambassador to Madrid in December. Truman approved making available credits from the Export-Import Bank of up to $25 million for Spain.[96] The adoption of NSC-68, which defined the Soviet challenge as global, and the outbreak of the Korean War in June 1950 provided the final impetus toward a military agreement. In February 1951, Truman endorsed National Security Council report 72/4, "United States Policy toward Spain." The immediate objectives were to develop the "military potentialities of Spain's strategic geographic position" for the common defense of the West, not just Spain alone; acquire "such facilities as bases for long-range bomber and fighter operations and behind-the-lines staging areas" along with naval bases; provide military assistance for Spain's forces; and improve Spain's relations with the other members of NATO in order ultimately to "obtain early Spanish participation" and membership in the alliance.[97]

The "changing conditions resulting from Soviet-inspired aggression and the consequent increasing danger of global war" made these steps imperative. Spain's value grew "steadily in direct proportion to the deterioration of the international situation." Spain, having been "spurned for several years" by the West, could opt for neutrality in the event of a Soviet attack on Western Europe. The National Security Council feared that "the longer we delay before seeking Spanish cooperation, the more we encourage this neutrality sentiment."[98] Cooperation with Franco was necessary, accompanied, as the planners knew, by support for his dictatorship. Once the bases were established, Franco's ability to maintain stability and order would become part of the defense of the free world.

Negotiations progressed rapidly. After consultations with the British and French governments, Griffis was instructed on 7 March to open direct talks with Franco. The generalissimo readily agreed to the establishment of U.S. bases as long as the United States furnished adequate military assistance. He acknowledged that at this time Spain's admission into NATO was impossible but assured Griffis that Spain would comply with all the commitments of the North Atlantic Treaty and the common defense of Western Europe in case of a Soviet attack. Griffis reported that "any location in Spain or its possessions was at the immediate disposal of the United States for air, military or naval bases." In a June progress review of NSC 72/4, the National Security Council recommended more economic assistance for Spain to facilitate the negotiations. In July, Admiral Forrest Sherman, chief of naval operations, went to Spain to begin discussions on which airfields and ports were to be modernized and how to improve Spain's transportation system to enhance military movements. The next month a military survey team arrived to examine the sites, and an economic mission came to evaluate the costs and Spain's financial needs.[99]

The next year, Lincoln MacVeagh was brought to Spain to conduct the final negotiations. MacVeagh's long experience included a second term as ambassador to Greece, negotiation of the base arrangement with Iceland, and most recently Portugal's entry into NATO and the securing of the base in the Azores. Negotiations slowed down because of the continued objections of the British and French, the Korean negotiations, the 1952 presidential campaign, and Truman's frustration over Franco's delays in carrying out promises to allow greater religious freedom in Spain. It took the State Department four months to construct a suitable reply to Franco's 17 March letter to Truman. Franco indicated that Truman was unjustifiably concerned about a lack of religious freedom in Spain and implied that it was probably the work of people who sought to block good relations between the two countries.[100] Truman, however, took this issue very seriously. He worried about reports of persecutions of Protestants and Masons and had told Acheson in August 1951 that he had "never been happy about sending an Ambassador to Spain, and unless Franco changes his treatment of citizens who do not agree with him religiously I'll be sorely tempted to break off all communication with him in spite of the defense of Europe."[101]

Such outbursts were common for Truman, but his threat was empty. The logic of strategy and the Cold War had long since overwhelmed this question of principle. In the end, Truman's reply noted "fundamental differences between the views you have expressed and the attitude of the United States on this subject" but concluded that he shared Franco's hopes that the current negotiations would have a successful outcome and lead to closer friendship and understanding between the two nations. It was to the "mutual benefit of both countries to develop these ties and to find means for working together to help strengthen the defense of the Western nations against the danger that confronts us all."[102]

The final agreement was reached in September 1953 with the signing of the Pact of Madrid. This treaty created a formal alliance between the United States and Spain and, through the United States, linked Spain to the defense of Western Europe. The United States would build three air force facilities, a large naval base that could serve as a submarine repair center, storage facilities, radar installations, and other smaller supply stations throughout Spain in the next decade at a cost of $226 million. The agreement also called for extensive American financial assistance to Madrid. Over the next ten years the United States provided $400 million in military appropriations to Spain and almost $1 billion in nonmilitary aid in an effort to ensure stability and Franco's rule.[103] Truman fully realized that Franco was a son of a bitch, but he was firmly on the side of the United States.

Anticolonialism to Anticommunism in Vietnam

The same convergence of events and ideas that led to the return to the policy of supporting right-wing dictators after 1947 resulted in the United States supporting France's efforts to reclaim its colonies in Southeast Asia. Roosevelt had originally intended to place the region under a UN trusteeship after the war. This, he believed, was necessary to allow for a proper transition and time to prepare the people for independence. A combination of European pressure, the unfavorable course of events in China and elsewhere in East Asia, and the onset of the Cold War brought about an abandonment of this effort. Instead, the Truman administration provided support for France and by 1950 recognized the French puppet regime of Bao Dai and began paying most of the cost of the

French war. Containment, anticommunism, and the desire for stability had placed the United States in direct opposition to Ho Chi Minh's revolutionary nationalist movement, the Vietminh, and placed the United States in the position of supporting the first of a series of unpopular and nondemocratic governments in Vietnam.

As Roosevelt explained his policy to Hull in 1944, "It was perfectly true that I had, for over a year, expressed the opinion that Indo-China should not go back to France but that it should be administered by an international trusteeship. France has had the country—thirty million inhabitants—for nearly one hundred years, and the people are worse off than they were at the beginning." Thus the case for taking the region away from France was "perfectly clear. . . . The people of Indo-China are entitled to something better than that."[104] This position was consistent with Roosevelt's other wartime pronouncements, his view that the war in the Pacific was in large part the result of European imperialism, and belief that colonialism in Asia was a dying system.[105] It also fit with his view that the Vietnamese, along with many other Asians, were not yet prepared for self-government. "With the Indo-Chinese," Roosevelt noted, "there is a feeling they ought to be independent but are not ready for it." They needed to be educated in the same manner that the Filipinos were. In that case, "it took fifty years for us to do it." He agreed with Queen Wilhelmina of Holland that because of Dutch rule the "Javanese are not quite ready for self-government, but very nearly," and would soon gain independence. In contrast was the case of New Guinea, where the people were described as the "lowest form of human life in the world, their skulls have least developed." They were "probably two hundred years behind the rest of the world."[106]

Such paternalistic views ensured that Roosevelt and his immediate successors would rule out independence for Vietnam and helps explain why the president began to back away from his position that France had to be kept out of Indochina in 1945. The larger aim remained the same; the American "goal must be to help [colonial people] achieve independence." But when asked in March if he had "changed his ideas on French Indo-China," Roosevelt first answered no, then hesitated and added, "If we can get the proper pledge from France to assume for herself the obligations of a trustee, then I would agree to France retaining these colonies with the proviso that independence was the ultimate goal."[107]

When Roosevelt died in April 1945, Truman inherited a policy in a state of flux. In the rush of events surrounding the end of the war in Europe, relations with the Soviet Union, the Potsdam Conference, the decision to drop the atomic bombs, and the end of the war in Japan, French colonial policy and Vietnam did not command much of Truman's attention and energy during his first months in office. It was not surprising, therefore, that he took a cautious, and what must have appeared to him safe, course in deciding his policy. In May, after a review of policy by both the European and Far Eastern Divisions of the State Department, Truman approved the decision that the United States would allow a French return to Indochina and instructed the State Department to inform France that the United States did not question its sovereignty there.[108] France was expected to ensure that the region would be open to all for trade and to work toward the establishment of a "democratic national or federal government to be run for and increasingly by the Indochinese themselves . . . so that within the foreseeable future Indochina may be fully self-governing and autonomous."[109] These were details to be worked out in the future. The immediate concern was stability. The door was opened for a French return with American support.

Before the French could secure their position, Ho Chi Minh declared Vietnam's independence on 2 September 1945. Sporadic fighting between the Vietminh and the returning French soon broke out, and after failed efforts at negotiations, the conflict escalated into full-scale war in late 1946. The American response was mixed. On the one hand, the United States sought to aid its French ally and secure access to Indochina's raw materials and markets for France's economic recovery. Unity in Europe was a high priority, and there were few advocates of support for Ho. As Acheson tersely noted in December 1946, officials had to "keep in mind Ho's clear record as agent international communism." Indeed, as Archimedes Patti observed, now "all official references to Ho were prefixed 'communist.'"[110] On the other hand, the Truman administration did not want to tie the U.S. reputation directly to European imperialism and refused to grant France the direct aid it requested. Washington still hoped that France would grant more autonomy to the Vietnamese to undercut the nationalist appeal of the Vietminh. But neither would it condemn France's actions or prevent it from diverting aid sent to Paris to the war effort in Southeast Asia.

In 1947, after the announcement of the Truman Doctrine, American policy became clearer. Secretary Marshall informed American diplomats in France and Vietnam that the "key [to] our position is our awareness that in respect [to] developments affecting position [of] Western democratic powers in southern Asia, we [are] essentially in same boat as France." As the region moved toward independence, a "relaxation of

European controls . . . could plunge new nations into violent discord . . . [and] anti-Western Pan-Asiatic tendencies could become dominant force, or Communists could capture control. We consider as best safeguard against these eventualities a continued close association between newly-autonomous peoples and powers which have long been responsible for their welfare." Regarding the fighting in Vietnam, the United States believed that the Vietnamese "will for indefinite period require French material and technical assistance and enlightened political guidance which can only be provided by nation steeped like France in democratic tradition and confirmed in respect for human liberties and worth of the individual."[111] Marshall wanted to be sure that "we do not lose sight [of the] fact that Ho Chi Minh has direct Communist connections and it should be obvious that we are not interested in seeing colonial administrations supplanted by philosophy and political organization emanating from and controlled by the Kremlin."[112]

The question was raised as to whether the United States should support Ho rather than sticking with the French. Those who advocated abandoning the French and supporting the Vietminh argued that "United States . . . support [of] France . . . will cost us our standing and prestige in all of Southeast Asia." Moreover, "whether the French like it or not, independence is coming to Indochina. Why, therefore, do we tie ourselves to the tail of their battered kite?" Several answers were provided. There was no reason to think that the French effort was fundamentally doomed, and just because the odds were against them was no reason not to back their effort given the alternative. The United States should not place itself in the position of eliminating the opportunity for a noncommunist Vietnam. The last point was, of course, at the center of the issue. With France's agreement in 1949 to establish three associated states in Indochina within the French Union, placing Bao Dai at the head of the state of Vietnam, it was acknowledged that Bao Dai's chances were "not brilliant," but the United States had to help provide him a chance to succeed.[113]

The United States, therefore, welcomed this move by the French and changed its policy to open support. Acheson bluntly eliminated any alternative position in May 1949. The "question [of] whether Ho as much nationalist as Commie is irrelevant. All Stalinists in colonial areas are nationalists. With achievement [of] natl aims (i.e. independence) their objective necessarily becomes subordination [of] state to Commie purposes and ruthless extermination not only [of] opposition groups but all elements suspected even slightest deviation."[114] In 1950, the State Department outlined the options. They were to support either "Bao Dai (or a similar anti-communist successor) or Ho Chi Minh (or a similar communist successor); there is no other alternative." That meant supporting the French or "face the extension of Communism over the remainder of the continental area of Southeast Asia and, possibly, farther westward." It would be a "case of 'Penny wise, Pound foolish' to deny support to the French in Indochina."[115]

On 8 May 1950, the United States formally recognized the government of Bao Dai as an independent state within the French Union and announced that it would send aid to his government, thereby joining the war in Vietnam. Acheson argued that this move was necessary because it would provide "encouragement to national aspirations under non-Communist leadership for peoples of colonial areas in Southeast Asia, the establishment of stable non-Communist governments in areas adjacent to Communist China," and support to an important European ally.[116] American prestige and interests were now best served by a direct association with the French in Vietnam. As far as the State Department could predict, "French forces appear to be the sole effective guarantee that communist forces will be resisted."[117] The first order of business was to defeat communism. All other questions concerning full independence and the type of government in Vietnam would have to wait until the Vietminh were defeated and Vietnam was stable.

In Defense of the Free World

The problem that confronted the Truman administration in Vietnam over supporting the French was fundamentally the same as that concerning policy toward right-wing dictators. The United States would have preferred in Vietnam a stable, independent, pro-Western government, just as it wished to see stable democracies established in Latin America. But leaving these matters in local hands was fraught with danger. In the case of Vietnam, it was clear that the transition to independence, if decided only by the Vietnamese, would allow Ho Chi Minh to come to power and establish a communist government. In Latin America, the problem was that truly democratic governments would likely be unstable for a period of time or pursue dramatic economic reforms, providing opportunities for communist forces to exploit. In both cases, order and stability needed to be established and strong governments in place to prevent negative outcomes. This meant supporting the French in Vietnam and dictators in Latin America. A 1952 State Department summary of policy toward Vietnam illustrated that the United States had to accept nondemocratic solutions to prevent communist gains. "We believe that, as a practical matter, US objectives in Indochina can be achieved only through the French." Given the inability "of the native governments to assure the territorial integrity of the area for the foreseeable future without outside help and the unlikelihood that other friendly nations than France are able or willing to participate in the defense of the area, individually or collectively, we are obliged to support the only practicable means available to us, which in this case is the French."[118]

The same logic guided the State Department's final regional appraisal of policy toward Latin America, which was forwarded to President Truman on 11 December 1952. It provides a useful summary of American policy toward right-wing dictators on the eve of the transition to the Eisenhower-Dulles years. The importance of Latin America to the United States for security and economic reasons was to provide American access to vital raw materials in case of war. Fully 35 percent of all U.S. imports now came from South America, at a value of $2.9 billion. Almost half of these goods "consisted of strategic materials" such as quartz crystals, oil, copper, and tin. "Furthermore, Venezuela, Brazil and Chile are becoming increasingly important suppliers of two of the basic ingredients of our steel industry, namely iron ore and manganese. Any disruption in the import of the more than a billion dollars' worth of materials, not listed as strategic, such as coffee, sugar and bananas, would have extremely serious consequences throughout the United States." Likewise, Latin America was a major purchaser of American goods, of which about $2.7 billion were exported there in 1950 and over $6 billion in direct private U.S. investments. Thus, "notwithstanding the imperfections which mar the actual practice of democracy, the area is to be regarded as an effective part of the Free World."[119]

The stability of the area was threatened by three interrelated problems: "a popular demand for immediate reform which produces instability"; the "great disparity of wealth and power between the United States and Latin America" which generates nationalism and anti-American sentiments; "and communism, which exploits both of these conditions." The question was, Did the lack of democratic governments exacerbate the problems or provide a solution? The lack of a middle class was identified as the key feature missing in the development of Latin America, which meant that "political developments have not kept pace with the times. Venality on the part of public officials is common. . . . Suffrage is ineffectual and, where it exists, the people are often unprepared to assume full responsibilities of citizenship." Thus power was left in the hands of an alliance between the military and property owners "with forms of government varying from pure military dictatorship, illustrated by the Trujillo regime in the Dominican Republic, to governments, such as the one in Chile, which do not have the strength and discipline essential to an effective administration of the affairs of state."[120]

This appraisal came as no surprise to the department, given that these societies derived their independence from Spain and Portugal, leaving the "political, social and economic patterns . . . largely frozen in the same status in which they had developed in Spain and Portugal during medieval times." The result was unrest throughout the area, "a weakening of respect for property rights," and revolutionary nationalist movements that were often "controlled by immature and impractical idealists . . . who are not only unprepared to conduct government business efficiently but lack the disposition to combat extremists within their ranks, including communists." Latin America was in flux, and the area was "passing through a period of inevitable and very far reaching adjustments as between classes." Leaders from a variety of nations had gained power by promising change. "One of the consequences of these internal adjustments is political instability which is itself enfeebling." It was exactly these situations which communists sought to turn to their advantage. Communism was "a force which exploits and makes articulate nationalistic aspirations and which supplies organizational and directive guidance to all anti-American elements." All of this made supporting reform in the area a dangerous business and demanded a rethinking of some positions.[121]

The report recognized that while dictatorships can sometimes "set in motion violent forces and invite instability, in the present state of world affairs revolutionary governments" were much more dangerous. Revolutionary nationalists "observe the form" of democracy "in order to destroy the substance of democratic processes." Further, they open themselves up to communist influences, "which not only makes it difficult for us to obtain the cooperation we need but precipitates economic crises which in turn produce more unrest and instability." Only the enemies of the United States could benefit from such a situation.[122]

Right-wing dictators, to be sure, often created resentment and opposition, but until the danger of communism was removed, stability had to be assured. Dictators provided a necessary and useful protection. Most notably, the doctrine of nonintervention had to be clarified. It did not "mean that the United States must sit by with crossed hands if a clearly communist regime should establish itself in the hemisphere. Our agreements on this subject are with sovereign American states and their protection would not extend to the satellite of a foreign imperialistic power."[123]

The implications of these points were far-reaching. The logic set out was based on the premise that communists could not be nationalists. They exploited nationalist movements and legitimate grievances only for their own aims, which were directed by Moscow in the service of the Soviet Union. The United States should, of course, use its "influence to promote an orderly evolution towards democracy" and American principles "through the example which we set." This was not, however, always possible given the historic instability of certain areas and the danger of communist infiltration. The only road available, therefore, was the "economic development of the Latin American countries" so as to produce the missing middle class on which stability seemed to depend. That meant, of course, that it was essential to "protect the legitimate rights of United States investments in the area, defending them against abuses and discrimination which are the product of extreme nationalism."[124] Again, dictators were necessary to provide the stability for what would later be termed economic takeoff.

The problem for the Truman administration in producing the desired middle class was that there were not enough funds to extend to Latin America. Europe and Asia were the places where the Cold War was the hottest, and they received the lion's share of American foreign aid. Truman's Point Four program provided only limited funds, and Latin America ranked last of all regions of the globe, receiving only 2.4 percent of foreign aid.[125] As Acheson and others continually emphasized, the money for development had to come from private sources.[126] Investors, however, were hesitant to send capital to nations that appeared unstable. One solution was American military spending. In this area, certain nations in Latin America were seen as a priority. U.S. security, the State Department reported, was "synonymous with hemisphere security." Because of the "prevalence of economic instability in Latin America," the United States needed to extend greater military support for its southern neighbors to "meet the added responsibilities that have emerged since the Korean crisis."[127] In response, Congress passed a military assistance program of over $38 million for Latin America that the administration had long sought. It was designed to strengthen local armies under U.S. supervision. Latin American forces were not to be used outside the region, and the money was intended mainly to provide for internal security. With thirteen military dictatorships in the twenty Latin American republics, the United States was now directly arming the dictators.[128]

The Truman administration's decision to extend military aid to Latin America was seen as necessary for the nations of the hemisphere to maintain internal order. Acheson described the danger of unrest to the south as "a very acute one." He explained to the Senate Foreign Relations Committee (SFRC) that Soviet agents were actively fomenting trouble and presented "a very considerable sabotage menace to the oil fields, shipping facilities, trade routes, air fields and all that sort of thing." Acheson did acknowledge there was a danger. "How do you tell in Guatemala or Nicaragua or some other place what is a Communist-front organization and what is not?" He was concerned that Latin Americans did not have "as much experience with that sort of thing as some of us." They could miss the real communists or use the resources to "put their political opponents in jail."[129]

Senator Theodore Green of Rhode Island struck at the heart of this issue when he asked if the U.S. program was not actually encouraging the establishment of dictatorships. Acheson agreed it was a possibility. As he began to elaborate, Green cut in and wondered if this "was a dangerous question to bring up." Again, Acheson agreed that the program created potential for dictatorships, but to refuse to aid Latin American militaries was an even greater risk. To leave the threat of communist subversion unchecked was the "gravest danger." The proper way to view the issue, Acheson argued, was to realize the United States was combating the "danger to the internal security of a country growing out of the international subversive movement." Green was satisfied with this distinction, and the rest of the discussion centered on how best to describe the program's objectives.[130]

The United States had, in effect, intervened to support dictators not just in the name of stability but to protect freedom. With peace indivisible, these actions were justified in the national defense. Support for right-wing dictators was seen as a legitimate activity in holding together the free world. Autocratic rulers provided stability and order, welcomed and protected investments, and were bulwarks against communism. Moreover, they were now seen, along with the military, as able to provide the conditions that would lead to an evolution toward democracy. From this perspective, they were forces of modernization that would protect the nations during the most difficult transitions to modern institutions and ideas. Until that time arrived, the United States had to support right-wing dictators lest revolutionary forces take over, bringing communists to power and closing the door to any possible movement toward liberalism and freedom. The groundwork was set for American interventions of the 1950s and 1960s in Iran, Guatemala, the Dominican Republic, and Vietnam.

5 THANK GOD THEY'RE ON OUR SIDE
Eisenhower, Dulles, and Dictators

When Eisenhower became president, he found little to be optimistic about concerning international affairs and American foreign policy. With the exception of Truman's successes in Europe with containment, the Marshall Plan, and the creation of NATO, all of which Eisenhower supported, the new president found reason to criticize all other areas of his predecessor's foreign policy. The most obvious problem was the stalemate in Korea. Not wanting to damage the war effort or the ongoing negotiations, Eisenhower kept his comments during the 1952 presidential campaign to a minimum and promised only that he would go to Korea. That pledge was enough, however, to indicate his displeasure with the Democrats' handling of the war and policy in Asia. Eisenhower saw the outbreak of the Korean War and its continuation as a consequence of Truman's broader failures to confront the Soviet challenge outside of Europe. Eisenhower never went as far as the McCarthyite wing of his party, which accused the administration of allowing communists to conduct its Asian policy, or his vice president, Richard Nixon, who recklessly spoke of Dean Acheson's "cowardly College of Communist Containment," but he did believe that Truman mishandled the civil war in China and failed fully to appreciate the communist challenge throughout Asia. With domestic anti-communism at its peak, the Republicans battered the Democrats with the charge that they had "lost" China for the free world and feared that Southeast Asia would be next.

Similarly, Eisenhower and his secretary of state, John Foster Dulles, were greatly concerned with the problems they found in the Middle East and Latin America and the progress of communism they saw in both regions. The decline of British and French control in the Middle East and Western support for the state of Israel opened the way for radical nationalists from Iran to Algeria to attack Western influence and imperialism. The United States sought to distance itself from aspects of European policy and searched for an effective counterforce to the angry nationalists who threatened to exclude all Western, including American, companies from the oil-rich region. The most pressing danger was in Iran, where Prime Minister Muhammad Mossadegh's move to nationalize Iranian oil had driven the British from their predominant position and appeared to open the door to communist penetration throughout the region. Eisenhower believed that the Truman administration had alienated most of the Latin American nations through a policy of neglect. Here, too, the rise of nationalism presented the first stage of the problem that could be exploited by communists to create confusion, hostility toward the United States, and eventually communist rule. This was the administration's understanding of events in Guatemala, where the reform government of Jacobo Arbenz was seen by 1954 as on the brink of becoming a communist state that would serve as a base for the spread of Soviet influence throughout the region.

In his memoirs, Eisenhower recalled that the "problems challenging the new administration were complex and urgent. Two wars, with the United States deeply engaged in one, and vitally concerned in the other, were raging in Eastern Asia; Iran seemed to be almost ready to fall into Communist hands . . . [and] Red China seemed increasingly bent on using force to advance its boundaries." Moreover, "European economies were not yet recovered from the effects of World War II," eroding their control over their colonies, and "Communism was striving to establish its first beachhead in the Americas by gaining control of Guatemala."[1]

Eisenhower, however, had no bold new proposals, such as a Marshall Plan for Latin America, to combat these problems. Instead, he sought to stabilize the direct conflict with the Soviet Union in Europe to allow the administration to concentrate on the nationalist and communist challenge in the Third World. Here, the Eisenhower administration did initiate a new approach: covert action through the Central Intelligence Agency. The Cold War would be waged on two separate levels. The United States would recognize the existing Soviet sphere of influence in Eastern Europe and pursue improved bilateral relations with Moscow but seek to prevent any further extension of communism in Asia, Africa, and Latin America. In this context, right-wing dictators came to play an expanded role in American efforts to combat communism and create stability.

Whatever criticisms the Republicans had concerning Truman's foreign policy, they readily accepted the necessity of supporting authoritarian regimes. This continuity in policy was not, as some charged at the time, caused by simple neglect of the Third World, a lack of concern for democracy, or ignorance of the consequences of aiding such regimes. Rather, it stemmed from Eisenhower's clear sense that the Soviet challenge, or what the administration and commentators generally called "International Communism," had shifted from Europe to the Third World, and it was part of his administration's efforts to ensure stability and implement containment across the Great Crescent from the Middle East to Japan and in Latin America. In doing so, Eisenhower and Dulles accepted the reasoning of administrations from Harding to Truman that, at least in the short run, supporting right-wing dictators provided the necessary stability and anticommunist bulwarks in nations too weak or politically immature to have viable democratic governments. This does not mean that the Eisenhower administration gave no thought to the issue. On the contrary, it periodically discussed the problem and dilemmas inherent in this approach, but each time it reached the same conclusion that American interests would be served by continuing to aid right-wing dictators. Some officials acknowledged that supporting dictators could lead to a backlash of opposition, anti-American sentiment, and damage to American prestige in the ideological battles with the Soviet Union for support of other nations. Eisenhower's advisers, however, saw these as necessary risks because the alternatives always appeared to be worse. In its efforts to moderate the risks, the administration turned to private development and nation building, most notably in Vietnam, to help create modern institutions and stability that could withstand the difficult transition to democracy.

Nation-building

During Eisenhower's second term in office, his administration would confront the shortcomings and consequences of American support for repressive right-wing dictators. The attacks on Vice President Nixon during his 1958 tour of Latin America, a series of military takeovers in

Asia and Africa in 1958 and 1959, and the Cuban revolution shocked the administration and served to reopen the debate on policy toward authoritarian regimes. The overthrow of Batista's dictatorship by Fidel Castro's 26th of July Movement brought about the exact scenario critics had predicted would result from supporting authoritarian governments: an anti-American sentiment that fostered a revolutionary, and ultimately communist, movement that looked to the Soviet Union for support. Right-wing dictators eliminated the center of politics and any other alternative route to change. In response, the administration adopted a two-track policy. It spoke more forcefully about the need for democracy and publicly distanced itself from certain dictators. Yet the administration sought reforms that came from above rather than through the sharing of power with opposition groups or revolution from below. Moreover, Eisenhower continued the military aid and other programs that maintained authoritarian rulers around the world. The struggle to fashion a new policy toward the Dominican Republic in 1960 demonstrated the limits to the Eisenhower administration's ability to reject the existing policy and respond to right-wing dictators in a different manner. The administration's commitment to containment and stability still demanded support for authoritarian rulers and enforced order rather than taking chances on what were seen as weak and unstable democratic movements that could open the door to communism.

Lesser of Two Evils

Consistent with all administrations since Wilson's, Eisenhower's agreed that U.S. interests were best served by the existence of other stable democratic and capitalist nations and spoke publicly about promoting democracy and freedom abroad. The problem, as Eisenhower and Dulles understood it, was in areas lacking a history of free government. New democratic governments tended to be weak and faced a myriad of challenges in their efforts to establish order and create prosperity. It was, therefore, considered a gamble to support such governments when the Soviet Union appeared to be active in all areas and communists were apparently poised to take advantage of instability or nationalist reform movements. Dictators who protected Western interests, provided stability, and suppressed communism were a much better bet in such a context and had to be supported until their nations matured politically or, given the logic of the domino theory, whole areas would fall to communist forces. With their Manichean view of the Cold War, neither Eisenhower nor Dulles could tolerate revolutionary nationalism and other challenges to the status quo in the Third World.

The fundamental premise for this policy remained the idea that too many of the world's people were not yet trained or were unable to govern themselves democratically. With enough time and tutelage they could possibly develop democratic systems, but communist forces were waiting to take advantage of any signs of instability and the weaknesses of new democratic governments. The time necessary for the transition from colonial status or authoritarian government to democracy was a luxury the United States did not appear to have. In addition, an agent theory of communist activity and revolution saw all disturbances and radical movements as emanating from the Kremlin. Communist forces were seen as having a discipline and zealousness that democratic groups had difficulty matching.

Distrust of the abilities of other people came instinctively to the senior members of the Eisenhower administration, stemming from their general attitudes toward people in the nonwhite world. Eisenhower and his advisers invariably talked about the nations and peoples of Asia, Africa, and Latin America as "backward" and in need of direction and Western supervision before they were ready for full independence.[2] The president described Mexicans as "rascals at heart. You can't trust them," and he endorsed William Knox's view that the government in Argentina was still in its "adolescence" striving for maturity.[3] He saw Indians as "funny people," was convinced that Arabs "simply cannot understand our ideas of freedom or human dignity," and contrasted all nonwhites to the English-speaking world with its duty to act as "a model for the necessary cooperation among free people."[4]

Dulles and others held similarly paternalistic views. When Eisenhower proposed in February 1953 that one possible solution to the deterioration of relations with Latin America would be to send notable Americans and university professors on tours of various countries to demonstrate that the United States was not ignoring its neighbors, Secretary of State Dulles found this idea to be "a very good way of doing things" because "you have to pat them on the head and make them think that you are fond of them."[5] Thomas Mann, a Latin American expert in the State Department, put the negative view of Latin Americans more forcefully when he stated, "I know my Latinos. They understand only two things—a buck in the pocket and a kick in the ass."[6]

Eisenhower thus remained attached to the simplistic notion that visits by prominent Americans would create goodwill and cement positive relations with Third World nations. In August 1953, he returned to this idea. He wrote Under Secretary of State Walter Bedell Smith that he was concerned that the State Department was "not properly organized to give to the sensitive South Americans the feeling that they are really important in our scheme of things." As a possible solution, he proposed the creation of an ambassador at large just for Latin America.[7] The department rejected this idea, preferring instead to send special missions such as the one recently completed by the president's brother Milton Eisenhower to investigate conditions and report on possible future actions.

In 1956, the president responded positively to Ambassador Henry Cabot Lodge's suggestion that the State Department sponsor trips by high-ranking American officials, accompanied by their wives, that were mainly social exchanges. According to Lodge, such junkets would undercut the perception "that we are forever lecturing, telling people what to do and generally assuming an attitude of insufferable superiority." A suspicion existed that "Americans, like European colonial powers, are willing to work with the 'natives,' but are not willing to play with them and treat them as social equals." Lodge emphasized that while the travelers could pick up some useful information or correct misunderstandings along the way, "the main point would be simply to be agreeable and to make them feel that *we* think *they* are attractive." The ambassador first saw the value in his idea, he informed Eisenhower, when he and his wife visited Khartoum in the Sudan. Lodge wrote that the "Foreign Minister (who was coal black) danced with my wife and I heard later from our U.S. representative that the word went out all over town that the Americans were not stuffy." Eisenhower found that Lodge's points "make good sense" and again passed the idea along to the State Department.[8]

The president mused in June 1953 that the "tricky problem that is posed these days is this: if firm opposition to the spread of Communism requires fighting, as in Korea and Indo-China, how can the free world turn its attention to the solution of these great humanitarian problems which must be tackled in order to eliminate the conditions that promote Communism?"[9] As Eisenhower's comments indicate, the administration understood the need for social change in the world and recognized that the United States had to adjust its approach to relations within the hemisphere and elsewhere in the Third World. Dulles told the Senate Foreign Relations Committee in April 1953 that he realized social problems and instability would be present in the world without the Soviet Union, "but what makes it a very dangerous problem for us is the fact that wherever those things exist, whether it is in Indo-China or Siam or

Morocco or Egypt or Arabia or Iran . . . even in South America, the forces of unrest are captured by the Soviet Communists." In a peaceful world without the threat of the Soviet Union, the United States "could do very much more in the way of promoting . . . reforms and advancing self-government than we can do under present conditions." The secretary of state believed that it was necessary "to take a realistic view of the situation and recognize that at this time, to support a somewhat backward situation, it is the lesser of two evils, because the possibility of a peaceful change is very much diminished by the fact that you have constantly with you, for instance, the tactics of the Soviet Communist forces which take advantage of every opportunity to capture and lead the so-called reform and revolutionary movement." The United States was forced to back dictators. "Syngman Rhee, Chiang Kai-shek, and so forth . . . are not the people, under normal circumstances, that we would want to support." Others would be preferable, "but in times like these, in the unrest of the world today, and the divided spirit, we know we cannot make a transition without losing control of the whole situation."[10]

The solution to the dilemma of how to bring about social change and an evolution toward democracy without setting off revolutions and aiding the spread of communism was to be found in supporting strong leaders who would heed American advice. The rule of various dictators, therefore, was viewed positively by the new administration. For example, Vice President Nixon, discussing South Korea, exclaimed in 1953 that "they are hard to work with, but thank God they're on our side. With all the things that are wrong with [South Korean President Syngman] Rhee, the Communists are a lot worse."[11] Eisenhower commented in June that, given the recurring crises in Paris, "he himself was beginning to feel that only a strong man could save France."[12] Favors and honors were extended to shore up the rule of certain dictators, such as Marcos Pérez Jiménez of Venezuela. The State Department found Venezuela to be an "outstanding example to the rest of the world of cooperation between foreign investors and the government" for the benefit of both sides.[13] For his efforts, Jiménez was invited by Eisenhower for a state visit in Washington in 1956 where he was presented the Legion of Merit medal, the highest award the nation can bestow on a noncitizen. Advocates of greater military aid for Somoza argued that Latin American military leaders, such as the Nicaraguan dictator, worked more closely with the United States than any other groups, and those who "come to this country and see what we have and what we can do are frequently our most useful friends in those countries."[14]

To enhance this relationship, NSC 5432/1, adopted in September 1954, called for closer relations with military officers, recognizing that they "play an influential role in government."[15] A National Intelligence Estimate noted that the United States faced a dilemma in the "conflict between 'democracy' and 'dictatorship' in the Caribbean." The dictators "present themselves as guarantors of stability and order and of cooperation with the United States. The reformists, by definition, are an unsettling influence, but they contend that the United States, as a progressive democracy dominant in the area, has a moral obligation to foster social and political development." Conversely, the region's dictators "resent any indication of US support for reformist regimes as a betrayal of the 'true friends' of the United States."[16] Early the next year, Secretary of State Dulles made it clear where the administration stood on this question when he instructed State Department officials to "do nothing to offend the dictators; they are the only people we can depend on."[17]

In a February 1955 discussion on the progress of the implementation of NSC 5432/1, the National Security Council considered the question of communism and dictatorships in Latin America. Secretary of the Treasury George Humphrey told the council that it must realize "that a strong base for Communism exists in Latin America." Moreover, "wherever a dictator was replaced, Communists gained." The United States had to "back strong men in Latin American governments." Nelson Rockefeller responded that the "dictators in these countries are a mixed blessing. It is true, in the short run, that dictators handle Communists effectively. But in the long run, the U.S. must encourage the growth of democracy in Latin America" if it wished to defeat communism in the region. The discussion of relations with dictators reminded the president of a comment made by Portugal's Antonio Salazar, which he did not dispute: "Free government cannot work among Latins." Eisenhower noted his general agreement with Rockefeller "that in the long run the United States must back democracies" without providing any indication of when and how that would come about. It was, however, the short-run challenge of communism that had to be attended to.[18]

In both the crises in Iran and Guatemala, Eisenhower and Dulles believed that the situation had moved from a theoretical problem to an actual danger of communist rule. Both governments exhibited all of the problems policymakers associated with weak and ineffective democratic governments. They were creating a climate of confusion that would either pave the way for a communist takeover or had already permitted communists to penetrate their governments. The evidence for this view was found in Iran's efforts to nationalize the oil industry and Guatemala's pursuit of land reform. These policies, the administration noted, were exactly the same ones that communist nations adopted. Even if the people in power were not communists, they were doing the work of the Kremlin. In these cases, the administration found it necessary to help remove the dangerous government and support leaders who would maintain order, suppress communism, and align the countries with American foreign policy. The Truman administration had allowed the situation in these nations to reach the crisis stage. Establishing and supporting right-wing dictators, covertly and through announced policy, appeared to be the only option outside of direct military intervention to prevent the creation of full-blown communist states.

The administration formally set out its policy on covert action in March 1954, when it adopted NSC 5412. Greater suspicion of nationalist movements required new measures to combat these forces and shore up traditional forms of authority. Based clearly on the bipolar worldview and concern that the Soviet Union had redirected its efforts from Europe to the Third World, the National Security Council believed that "in the interest of world peace and U.S. national security, the overt foreign activities of the U.S. Government should be supplemented by covert operation." The CIA's activities could expand beyond espionage and counterespionage actions to include discrediting and reducing the strength of international communism and its parties; countering "any threat of a party or individuals directly or indirectly responsive to Communist control to achieve dominant power in a free world country"; orienting peoples and nations toward the free world and the United States by increasing the "capacity and will of such peoples and nations to resist International Communism"; and developing resistance movements and covert operations in areas "dominated or threatened by International Communism." These actions were to be coordinated with the State and Defense Departments to ensure that "covert operations are planned and conducted in a manner consistent with United States foreign and military policies" and carried out in such a manner that "any U.S. Government responsibility for them is not evident . . . and that if uncovered the U.S. Government can plausibly disclaim any responsibility for them." The operations would include "propaganda; political action; economic warfare; preventive direct action, including sabotage, anti-sabotage, demolition; . . . subversion against hostile states or groups including assistance to underground resistance groups, guerrillas and refugee liberation groups; [and] support of indigenous and anti-communist elements in threatened countries of the free world." [19]

At the same time, Eisenhower appointed a committee headed by General James Doolittle to conduct a study of the CIA and the need for covert activity. The committee's conclusion, which Eisenhower received in October 1954, set the issues out in stark and dangerous terms: [20]

> It is now clear that we are facing an implacable enemy whose avowed objective is world domination by whatever means and at whatever cost. There are no rules in such a game. Hitherto acceptable norms do not apply. If the United States is to survive, long-standing American concepts of "fair play" must be reconsidered. We must develop effective espionage and counterespionage services and must learn to subvert, sabotage and destroy our enemies by more clever, more sophisticated, and more effective methods than those used against us. It may become necessary that the American people be made acquainted with, understand and support this fundamentally repugnant philosophy. [21]

Covert activities were to fill the gap between the need to maintain order and prevent the spread of communism and the desire to avoid direct intervention. The United States was entering a new phase of the Cold War and relations with right-wing dictators.

In a 1956 interview, Secretary of State Dulles captured the intentions and problems confronting the administration. The secretary explained that American policy was designed to ensure freedom from communism for all the nations of the world. What nations did "with their freedom after they get it is a second problem. We naturally would like them to have the same kind of freedom and exercise it the way we do, with our same democratic processes." This was not, he realized, the case. Nor was it a major concern of the United States. Democracy was the best system, but it "is a system which can only be spread throughout the world gradually, and as I say, today there are not many parts of the world where that particular system prevails." [22] To insist on it, then, would damage American interests and create openings for the Soviet Union to exploit. Better to stay with loyal friends than experiment with change and new people in a dangerous world.

Second Chance in Iran

The first place the administration implemented its more active approach to establishing and supporting strong pro-Western leaders was in

Iran. On 28 April 1951, riding a wave of virulent anti-British nationalism, Muhammad Mossadegh became prime minister of Iran. His sole agenda was the nationalization of the Anglo-Iranian Oil Company. The Truman administration found itself in a bind. Iran had long been part of the British sphere of influence, and Washington worried about the impact of England's decline on regional stability, and in particular on the flow of vital oil supplies. Still, American diplomats generally agreed that the British had unfairly exploited Iran, thus producing hostility and legitimate grievances. The administration spent the next two years trying to find some middle road between the removal of the British from Iran and London's desires to return complete control over Iranian oil to Anglo-Iranian, a company in which the British government held the majority interest.[23]

With the British leading a boycott, no oil was coming out of Iran and world reserves during the Korean War were becoming dangerously low. In an effort to mediate the dispute, Acheson convinced Averell Harriman to head an American delegation to Tehran to negotiate with the Iranians and British during the summer of 1951. Both sides resisted Harriman's attempts to forge a workable compromise that would provide Iran with more revenues and control over its oil while preserving the company's ownership of its assets and decision making. Acheson saw Mossadegh as a "demagogue of considerable shrewdness and ability," aided by the "usual and persistent stupidity of the company and the British Government in their management of affairs." Truman informed London that the United States sought stability in Iran and would extend developmental aid to Tehran. At this juncture, the administration feared that if Mossadegh fell, the communists would come to power. Some accommodation had to be reached, but the president made it clear to both sides that he had no intention of joining an anti-British coalition or attacking America's closest ally.[24]

By the end of 1952, the administration had given up on any hope of striking a deal with Iran as long as Mossadegh remained in power. Acheson's attention, as well as that of the British, turned to restoring the young Shah to power. The idea of supporting a coup against Mossadegh was first discussed in a meeting with British foreign minister Anthony Eden. Eden stated that "at some stage it might be necessary . . . to impress on the Shah the need" to remove the Iranian prime minister from power.[25] Acheson believed that it was an "illusion that some other moderate leadership existed between the Tudeh Party Communists and the feudal reactionaries and mullahs." The establishment of an authoritarian government under the Shah was the only hope he saw for preventing a descent into communism or chaos.[26]

The Eisenhower administration shared Acheson's concern. It did not oppose Mossadegh and reform in Iran per se or the prime minister's efforts to gain a greater share in the operations of the Anglo-Iranian Oil Company for his country. The problem was that Mossadegh, by continuing to pull the tail of the British lion instead of agreeing to a settlement, was continuing to foster political unrest in the country and appeared to be losing control of the situation. Only the well-organized Tudeh Party could benefit from the persistence of this confusion. In his first full report on Iran to the National Security Council, Allen Dulles, the new head of the CIA, noted that Mossadegh had painted himself into a corner and could not afford to reach an agreement with the British. To do so would undercut his political support. The next week, Dulles informed the NSC that a dangerous political vacuum was being created in Tehran, where, if "the Shah's power was completely gone, it would be extremely difficult to find any constitutional alternative to Mossadegh if he were driven from power. The possibilities that the Communists would fill this power vacuum had been heightened." It came down to either the Shah regaining power or the continuation of Mossadegh's rule, which would mean a communist takeover.[27]

In early March, Secretary of Defense Charles Wilson summarized the problem faced by the administration. The United States needed an answer to the problem of how, with the obvious collapse of colonialism, to counter the "Communists' new tactics in exploiting nationalism and colonialism for its own purposes." Where could it find a stabilizing authority? "In the old days, when dictatorships changed it was usually a matter of one faction of the right against another, and we had only to wait until the situation subsided." Now, as in the case of Iran, "when a dictatorship of the right was replaced by a dictatorship of the left, a state would presently slide into Communism and was irrevocably lost to us." As long as the prime minister hung on, Dulles believed, the situation was salvageable, "but if he were to be assassinated or otherwise disappear . . . the Communists might easily take over." The consequences of such an eventuality would be enormous. The free world's loss of Iranian oil production and reserves to the Russians would be the least of the problems. "Worse still . . . if Iran succumbed to the Communists there was little doubt that in short order the other areas of the Middle East, with some 60% of the world's oil reserves, would fall into Communist control."[28]

Covert Action In Iran

Having decided Iran would fall to communism, soon be followed by the whole Middle East, and given the limited options available, it is not surprising that the administration turned to covert action to oust Mossadegh and reestablish the authority of the Shah. In fact, discussions with London for a covert operation to oust Mossadegh had already begun. Foreign Minister Anthony Eden sent a delegation to Washington in early February to begin planning. Ambassador Loy Henderson's analysis supported the CIA's interpretation and called for American action. The State Department found his points to be an "accurate expression of the situation and national state of mind in Iran, so accurate in fact" that it sent Eisenhower lengthy excerpts to read. Henderson argued that covert action was necessary to prevent Iran from falling to communism. It was difficult, the ambassador acknowledged, for most Americans to "understand the lack of appreciation of the Iranian public of [the] disinterested efforts made by individual American nationals in Iran for the benefit of Iran." Yet no amount of goodwill or public relations efforts would change this situation as long as the current rulers were in control. "Only those sympathetic to the Soviet Union and to international communism have reason to be pleased at what is taking place in Iran." Thus the overthrow of the existing government was the only way to save the situation. This was possible, Henderson contended, because "most Iranian politicians friendly to the West would welcome secret American intervention which might assist them in attaining their individual or group ambitions."[29] In other words, prominent elements of the military and royal family were willing to cooperate in a coup.

The successful coup was greeted with enthusiasm in Washington, and the administration acted quickly to help consolidate the Shah's rule.[30] Henderson praised the Shah for his "vigor, decisiveness, and certain amount clear thinking which I had not found in him before." The Shah requested immediate American aid, arguing that this "was Iran's last chance to survive as an independent country." Henderson agreed that "if the present government should fail, Communism seemed to be the only alternative."[31] The National Security Council found "real hope for . . . stability and for [an] improvement in Iran's economic and financial situation." It predicted that "the Tudeh Party would be ruthlessly curbed" and forced underground. The most urgent issue was extending financial aid to Tehran promptly so that "Iran will again assume its place in the pro-Western grouping of nations." Secretary Dulles stated that the United States now had a "second chance" after "all hope of avoiding a Communist Iran appeared to have vanished." Funds would have to be sent immediately to assist the new regime and work begun on reaching a permanent oil settlement.[32] On 3 September, $23.4 million in Point Four technical assistance was granted, followed two days later by the announcement of an economic assistance loan of $45 million. In his announcement of the aid, Eisenhower expressed his hope that "with our assistance, there will be an increase in the internal stability of Iran which will allow the development of a healthy economy to which an early effective use of Iran's rich resources will contribute."[33]

Maintaining the Shah's rule and stabilizing his regime became a central preoccupation of the Eisenhower administration. NSC 5402 noted that owing to Iran's "key strategic position, oil resources, vulnerability to intervention or armed attack by the USSR, and . . . to political subversion, Iran must be considered as a continuing objective of Soviet expansion." The loss of Iran would be "a major threat to the security of the entire Middle East, as well as Pakistan and India," enhance Soviet military capabilities while damaging U.S. prestige with neighboring nations, and cause a "serious psychological impact elsewhere in the free world." The installation of the Shah in August provided a "better opportunity to achieve U.S. objectives with respect to Iran. The Shah's position is stronger and he and his new Prime Minister look to the United States for counsel and aid." An oil agreement was a must because external aid could not "create real stability, permit development or avoid future emergencies." This is a problem that "any non-Communist . . . government would encounter." If the oil industry were placed "on a sound basis, Iran should be in a position to establish a self-supporting, stable government, and carry out much needed economic and social welfare programs."[34]

Vice President Nixon's visit in December 1953 confirmed the positive evaluation of the Shah and the need for an agreement with Iran concerning its oil. He praised the Shah's decisive rule and saw a promising future for relations with Iran. "Now that Mossadegh is out of the way things should be a lot better. What he did to that country is enough to hang him."[35] An end-of-the-year evaluation of conditions in Iran found that while the Shah had placed "a good many of the leaders of the Tudeh Party into jail," there was little or no progress in the crucial area of social and economic reform. The key was an oil agreement with the British. Its delay was blamed on London. Until a deal could be reached, the United States would provide up to $5 million monthly in emergency aid.[36]

The alliance with Iran and the Shah was sealed in 1954. The final agreement established a consortium between Iran and British, Dutch, and American oil companies. Iran was granted ownership of the oil assets within its borders, and the Anglo-Iranian Oil Company received compensation for its lost assets. The real power and operation of the National Iranian Oil Company was in the hands of the oil companies that made up the consortium. Profits would be split fifty-fifty, similar to other arrangements in the Middle East.[37] Iran was immediately rewarded with a new aid package of $127 million. Between 1953 and 1960, over $1 billion in economic and military aid was sent to Iran by the United States to shore up the Shah's rule.[38]

The Eisenhower administration saw the Shah's rule as a long-term necessity for a strategically important Iran and quickly came to depend on him to provide stability in the region. His greatest asset was his reliance on the United States for advice and protection. In 1954, Henderson expressed the widely held view that "so long as international communism is determined take over Iran, so long as Iran leaders and people are what they are, so long as Iran is in such a dreary economic and social state, and so long as Iran has no defense against Soviet Union . . . danger of Iran being lost to free world will continue . . . [and] Iran will continue [to] need our guidance and for some years our aid."[39] The Shah was hosted three different times by Eisenhower, and in 1959 the Shah returned the favor when Eisenhower visited Iran as part of an eleven-nation trip. That same year Iran and the United States entered into a bilateral defense pact. The State Department's background material for the Shah's 1958 visit described him as "a loyal friend of the United States and . . . a firm supporter of the Free World." He is "very intelligent and sincere" and "has greatly matured in recent years and is deeply mindful of the important role that he plays in Iran, where virtually all authority is concentrated in his hands." In many ways he was seen as a model ruler for such a nation, pursuing reforms and modernization from above. The Shah was "pushing ahead with a vast economic development program and other reforms designed to bring lasting political stability and social progress to his country."[40]

Iran represented the type of "constructive nationalism" that Eisenhower thought the United States should support.[41] Here was a strong dictator in a nation not ready for democracy who protected the interests of the West, aligned himself with the United States, and sought to institute needed reforms in his nation. Given the president's view that people in the Middle East "simply cannot understand our ideas of freedom and human dignity," a ruler such as the Shah was the best he could hope for in the region.[42] In the short term, U.S. interests were served. Critics, however, charged that the United States was supporting a "conditional" nationalism in the Third World, which in the long term bred anti-American feelings that would eventually erupt. As long as these nations aligned with the West and did not threaten private business, the United States would support them against European colonialism. But when efforts at reform challenged private property or threatened too much independence in international relations, such governments had to be opposed. Guatemala provided a perfect case in point.

Reversing Guatemala's 1944 Revolution

The Eisenhower administration's successful overthrow of the Guatemalan government in 1954, along with the Bay of Pigs operation, is the most well known and studied example of CIA covert activity. It is unnecessary to recount here all of the planning and the operation itself.[43] What is relevant to this discussion is how Guatemala represented to the administration the dangers of weak democratic states and why Eisenhower and his advisers believed that at certain times it was better to support a dictator than a freely elected government. As Thomas Mann later stated, the government in Guatemala demonstrated that the United States should not necessarily "support . . . all constitutional governments under all circumstances."[44]

The overthrow of Ubico's dictatorship in 1944 by the middle class and students ushered in the first truly democratic government in Guatemala's history. In the presidential election held that year, Juan José Arévalo defeated General Federico Ponce. Arévalo initiated a series of reforms to institutionalize democratic structures and distribute power more broadly. In 1951, Jacobo Arbenz Guzman, the winner of the 1950 presidential election, took office and began to extend the reform movement begun under Arévalo to include social welfare programs and land reform. Arbenz believed that agrarian reform was essential if Guatemala were to progress economically and become a stable democratic society. Arbenz's program called for the expropriation with compensation of all idle lands greater than 223 acres. Between 1952 and 1954 the government distributed over 1.5 million acres of land to one hundred thousand families. The United Fruit Company lost four hundred thousand acres, for which the government offered $1.2 million. The company rejected this settlement and demanded $75 an acre, for a total of $30 million. The ambitious attempt to create small landowners out of the mainly peasant population brought the Arbenz government into conflict with the

United States and the United Fruit Company, the largest landowner in the nation.[45]

The Truman administration worried about the direction events were taking in Guatemala and the influence of communism in that nation but took no direct action against the government. From the outset, the Eisenhower administration demonstrated far greater concern about the events in Guatemala. Eisenhower saw Arbenz as a communist "dupe" who would soon lose control of his nation.[46] In February 1953, Allen Dulles described the overall relations of the United States with Latin America as deteriorating and noted that his agency saw signs that the "Kremlin was exploiting this deterioration." The United States "was confronting in Latin America a basically revolutionary movement not altogether unlike what existed in the Middle East." The trends toward "economic nationalism, regionalism, neutralism, and increasing Communist influence . . . posed a direct danger to United States sources of supply for such strategic materials as copper, petroleum and tin." The "most serious immediate situation was in Guatemala, where the development of pro-Communist influence was such as to mark an approaching crisis."[47]

In March 1953, Eisenhower approved NSC 144/1 as the basis for policy toward Latin America. It called for the United States to mobilize the hemisphere to combat Soviet communism, "eliminate the menace of internal Communism," and support "orderly political and economic development." Quoting directly from the State Department's December 1952 final report on Latin America for the Truman administration, it expressed concern that too many of the leaders in South America were "immature and impractical idealists" who lacked both the necessary training for government leadership and "the disposition to combat extremists within their ranks, including communists." In light of this problem, and given the "overriding security interests" of the United States, unilateral intervention might be necessary if a "clearly identifiable communist regime should establish itself in the hemisphere."[48] The National Security Council acknowledged that U.S. intervention "would be a violation of our treaty commitments . . . and would probably intensify anti-U.S. attitudes in many Latin American countries." A better option, therefore, was strong local control.[49]

The State Department's analysis of the situation in Guatemala supported these views. Under Secretary of State Smith wrote the president that although Arbenz contended that Guatemalan communists followed "Guatemalan not Soviet interests, and visit Moscow to study Marxism, not to get instructions," they were "in fact disciplined agents of international communism, preaching authentic Soviet-dictated doctrine and openly affiliated with numerous international Communist labor and front groups." The United States had repeatedly expressed its concern to the Guatemalan government "because of the merciless hounding of American companies" by taxes, strikes, and the inadequate compensation for seizures of land under "a Communist-administered Agrarian Reform Law."[50] A National Intelligence Estimate concluded that communists were represented in all areas of the government and that "their influence will probably continue to grow as long as President Arbenz remains in power."[51]

The impending fall of Guatemala to communism was confirmed for the administration by the first reports it received in December 1953 from John Peurifoy, its new ambassador to Guatemala. Peurifoy's first meeting with Arbenz on 16 December consisted of a six-hour discussion in which Arbenz "showed depth of his feeling against United Fruit Company and his admiration for Guatemala's Communist leaders, leaving no doubt he intended to continue to collaborate with them." At one point, Peurifoy reported, the president went so far as to say that "if there were a choice, it would be for Guatemala to live under Communist domination than live for fifty years with Fruit Company." The ambassador could only conclude that "if President is not a Communist he will certainly do until one comes along, and that normal approaches will not work in Guatemala." Six days later, Peurifoy wired the department that he was "convinced Communists will continue to gain strength here as long as [Arbenz] remains in office." Given the lack of results through diplomatic channels to that date and the rejection of all American efforts to persuade the president to separate himself from the communists, Peurifoy found "no alternative to our taking steps which would tend to make more difficult continuation of his regime in Guatemala."[52] From the administration's perspective, Arbenz was doing the dirty work for the Kremlin, and only the establishment of a strong ruler, that is, a dictator, could prevent the nation from falling to communism.

Immature peoples and their impractical leaders in Latin America could not be allowed to pursue policies that Washington deemed dangerous no matter how representative the government might be. In January 1954, Dulles told the Senate Foreign Relations Committee that "in the old days we used to be able to let South America go through the wringer of bad times, and then when times would get better it was right there where it was; but the trouble is that now, when you put it through the wringer, it comes out red." The situation in Guatemala was difficult because it was clear to the United States that communist agents were at work, yet the nations of Latin America, owing to the "sensitiveness of the Latin American people against what they call interference with their internal affairs by this country," were wary of the steps necessary to counteract the Kremlin's actions. Dulles, however, planned to turn the tables on this issue at the upcoming Caracas Conference of the Inter-American Council. The United States was seeking to have the nations adopt "an expression of opinion that Communism is, itself, an interference with the internal affairs of these countries, that [it] is a foreign conspiracy and therefore to eradicate these Communist groups is not an interference, but an elimination of the interference." If that effort was successful, the administration could invoke the Monroe Doctrine and justify actions against Guatemala on the basis of defending the hemisphere.[53] Dulles's ideas went back to NSC 144/1. Unilateral covert action was the only available option.

The administration denied playing any role in the overthrow of Arbenz and stretched the limits of credulity in its praise for the independent actions of Guatemalans to preserve their freedom. Dulles informed a national radio and television audience that the events in Guatemala represented a victory over the "evil purpose of the Kremlin to destroy an inter-American system." He lectured that "for years international communism has been probing here and there for nesting places in the Americas. It finally chose Guatemala as a spot which it could turn into an official base from which to breed subversion which would extend to other American Republics." It was not the Arbenz government per se "that concerned us but the power behind it." With Arbenz's overthrow, Dulles claimed that the "people of Guatemala have now been heard from. . . . Led by Colonel Castillo Armas, patriots arose in Guatemala to challenge the Communist leadership—and to change it." The future, he declared, now "lies at the disposal of the Guatemalan people themselves."[54] Eisenhower echoed his secretary of state when he stated in a series of speeches that summer that the "people of that region rose up and rejected the Communist doctrine."[55]

The overthrow of a democratic regime for the establishment of a military dictatorship was applauded as a victory for freedom. John Foster Dulles called it the "biggest success in the last five years against communism."[56] The United States quickly recognized the Armas government and began to extend extensive economic aid to his regime, totaling over $46 million in three years. A more compliant figure than Armas would have been difficult to find. He returned all of the United Fruit Company's land, reversed the various other reforms undertaken by Arévalo and Arbenz, and imprisoned his political opponents.[57] In his tour of Central America in early 1955, Vice President Nixon found much about Armas's rule to applaud. He impressed Nixon "as a good man with good intentions" and informed Nixon that he wanted the United States to "tell me what you want me to do and I will do it." Nixon believed that "for this if for no other reason we must not allow the new government in Guatemala to fail," and he recommended holding it up to the world as a picture of success. Noting that the "first concern of the United States with the Central American republics related to the maintenance of their political stability," the vice president found reason to be optimistic, and he compared Armas favorably to the other American client in the region, Somoza, who also "really desires to do what the United States wants him to do."[58]

That the new government was a repressive military dictatorship did not bother the administration or cast a shadow on the supposed success of American policy. Rather, the administration saw Armas and the military as all that prevented "greater instability, a return of open communism, and a return of a more severe nationalistic, anti-American government."[59] In November 1955, Armas was treated to a hero's welcome when he visited the United States, including a ticker-tape parade in New York City. The purpose of his visit was "to show our friendly support of his government." Nixon, substituting for an ailing president, declared at the state dinner for Armas that the United States "watched the people of Guatemala record an episode in their history deeply significant to all peoples. . . . Led by the courageous soldier who is our guest this evening, the Guatemalan people revolted against Communist rule, which in collapsing, bore graphic witness to its inherent shallowness, falsity and corruption."[60] No mention of elections or a return to the constitution of 1944 marred the event.

When Armas was assassinated in 1957 by his former bodyguard, the United States continued to support the military rulers of the nation. His successor, General Miguel Ydígoras Fuentes, had been rejected by the CIA in 1953 for leadership because of his close ties to the Ubico dictatorship. While it was acknowledged that he favored "a dictatorial form of government, and . . . is certainly politically on the right," he was welcomed as a staunch anticommunist and friend of the United States. He was believed to be popular "because of his personal prestige and because he represents the strong government which so many Guatemalans seem to want."[61] When Ydígoras wrote Eisenhower in 1960 raising the specter of a new communist threat to Guatemala, this time from Cuba, the United States quickly extended emergency economic aid to his government. Eisenhower replied that the situation confirmed his conviction that the "countries in this Hemisphere face . . . a very definite threat to our democratic way of life and to our American system that requires our constant vigilance and resolute action." He believed "it would indeed be a tragedy for us all and a great triumph for Communism if your country having once freed itself of the Communist yoke should again find that yoke reimposed." The president approved $9.6 million in loans and credits and indicated that further requests would be considered.[62] In countries where Washington deemed dictators necessary to protect the people from themselves, an anticommunist stance was all a strongman needed to be deemed a protector of the democratic way of life.

A Synthetic Strongman

As Dulles trumpeted the 1954 coup in Guatemala as the greatest success in American foreign policy in five years, simultaneous events in Vietnam were causing grave concern about the advances of international communism. The French military effort to hold onto its colony was defeated at Dienbienphu, and the Geneva Conference on Southeast Asia provided for communist control of Vietnam north of the seventeenth parallel and elections within two years to unify the nation. The efforts of Eisenhower and Dulles to prevent a complete defeat and salvage some of Southeast Asia centered on the establishment of Ngo Dinh Diem as the president of the newly declared nation of South Vietnam and would again lead to U.S. support for a dictator in the name of establishing order, promoting freedom, and blocking communist expansion. Drawing on precedents in Greece, the Philippines, Iran, Korea, and Guatemala, the administration saw the establishment of a dictator supported by the military as the best solution to protect the free world and prevent the further spread of communism.

At the outset, the Eisenhower administration saw the situation in Vietnam, according to Dulles, to be "even more dangerous in its global aspects than is the fighting in Korea, for a collapse in Indo-China would have immediate grave reactions in other areas of Asia."[63] When Eisenhower stated in his inaugural address on 20 January 1953 that "freedom is pitted against slavery; lightness against the dark," Vietnam was one of the places he had in mind. The struggle conferred "a common dignity upon the French soldier who dies in Indo-China . . . [and] the American life given in Korea."[64] Eisenhower called on the nation to do more in the Far East and proposed that Congress "make substantial additional resources available to assist the French and the Associated States in their military efforts to defeat Communist Viet Minh aggression."[65] The administration increased the amount of aid the United States provided the French from $10 million to $400 million while pressuring Paris to grant more independence to Vietnam, Cambodia, and Laos as a means of better prosecuting the war.

Eisenhower summarized the importance he placed on Indochina to the free world at his famous press conference on 7 April 1954, when he outlined the "domino theory": "First of all, you have the specific value of a locality in its production of materials that the world needs. Then you have the possibility that many human beings pass under a dictatorship that is inimical to the free world. Finally, you have broader considerations that might follow what you would call the 'falling domino' principle. You have a row of dominoes set up, you knock over the first one, and what will happen to the last one is the certainty that it will go over very quickly. So you could have the beginning of a disintegration that would have the most profound influences." Eisenhower noted that for the first point, tin, tungsten, rubber, and other items would be lost. More important, the free world could not afford greater losses in Asia, where "already some 450 million of its people" had fallen "to the Communist dictatorship." Finally, the loss of Indochina to communism would lead to the loss "of Burma, of Thailand, of the Peninsula, and Indonesia" and threats against Japan, Taiwan, the Philippines, and eventually Australia and New Zealand. In addition, it would deny Japan that region where it must trade or "Japan, in turn, will have only one place in the world to go—that is, toward the Communist areas in order to live. So, the possible consequences of the loss are just incalculable to the free world."[66]

There were limits, however, to how much pressure toward independence the United States could exert on the French. If pushed too hard, France might pull out, leaving no force to oppose Ho Chi Minh. The greater trouble was how to carry out the shift to self-government. It was not difficult in the legal sense, as a juridical matter. "The trouble comes," as Dulles explained to the SFRC in 1953, "when you come practically to translating that change of attitude into the life of the community. What you have got there is a bunch of people who have been colonialists all their lives, and it is in the actual working relations, who has what house, do you bring them into your clubs, and do you allow them to be trained in units larger than a battalion . . . are what really makes the difference." Change would not come easily because of the lack of abilities among the Vietnamese and because "we all know how difficult it is to change social relations which have grown up over a long period of years, which reflect the white man's sense of superiority, the ruler's sense of superiority over the natives."[67]

Dulles lamented in January 1954 that French promises of granting independence in Vietnam were fine, but the "principal difficulty in the way now of achieving independence there is the lack of political maturity on the part of the people themselves, and their inability to make up their own minds as to what it is they want." The secretary of state continued by stating that he was "a great believer in the general idea of giving independence to people who want it, but I think that—I don't know really whether some of these people are qualified, well qualified yet for independence. I am not sure that these people are qualified to be fully independent." The communists tested the Filipinos' capacity for independence, but they had years of American tutelage and "quite a lot of experience and training and development." In other areas, such as Indonesia, "it has yet to be proven whether independence . . . is the proper thing." Granting "independence to a lot of these people in a world where the Communists are prowling around to grab you, it is not a thing which is easily accomplished." The great question to be overcome remained who one would work with and "whether there is a political maturity among the people to organize their own institutions, establish a strong government needed to meet the disturbing conditions that prevail there."[68]

The Senate Foreign Relations Committee returned to this same point the next month during a meeting with Under Secretary of State Walter Bedell Smith. The French, Smith argued, were making a great sacrifice and should receive more understanding and sympathy for their problems. If they could "get a little more leadership from Bao Dai" to shore up the Vietnamese forces fighting in the war, success was possible. When questioned by Senator J. William Fulbright whether he thought Bao Dai could ever be a real leader, Smith replied in the affirmative: "The man is brave; he is a courageous man. . . . Why it is that he is a little reluctant to assume leadership I do not know, and it may be that he is not yet convinced himself that the French really mean what they say when they promise sovereignty." Still, Bao Dai himself was not the complete issue here. As Smith noted, "If you handle it properly you can make a synthetic strong man out of almost anyone who is not a coward, if he is will-ing to go out." [69]

Fulbright responded that this was the key to a solution to the problem in Vietnam. A strong native leader was needed who would take charge. The United States, he argued, has too "often gone overboard in talking about democracy in countries such as this; what you need here is a man comparable, we will say, to Ataturk in Turkey; that you cannot expect this country to respond to democratic ideas, that you have got to have a tran-sitional period here with a real strong leader, and a native leader." Such leadership would undermine the communists' advantage in guerrilla warfare. "The only way to stop it is a strong native leader who really can rally the people, and it cannot be done by B-26s or any other kind of thing that we can put in." Smith agreed that this was the critical ques-tion. Fulbright continued by stating that the necessary sort of native leader could not be created synthetically. It would have to be "one who is a leader after the fashion of Kemal Ataturk, who made Turkey over. It is the best example of what should be done in an undeveloped country that I can think of in the last 30 years." [70]

Smith indicated that the State Department was working on this very idea and that "we have speculated in almost every direction . . . and con-sidered . . . providing certain religious leadership or religious cause for background for something to fight for in addition to the country." He did not want to provide any more details, but he informed Fulbright that he had "stated the case very patly there." The exchange returned to Bao Dai and whether he could be the one to turn the situation around or if the United States "ought to get another one." Fulbright was "very strongly in favor" of the State Department "taking a strong lead in trying to de-velop a really effective man" and providing the nation with incentives to fight. The French had no more desire to stay on, so what was there to fight for by "a people who do not understand democracy?" All that was left, Fulbright concluded, was the desire to rule in their own manner. That message was working for the communists. "We have got to have a leader who can inspire those natives" if the noncommunist forces were to overcome the Vietminh and keep Vietnam from "falling into the hands of the Communists." [71]

In response, Smith recalled his days as a young officer in the Philip-pines when he was told that they were going to get their independence: "I just did not believe it, and I was being the same minor satrap that we all were, and that is what a lot of the French colonial officials have been doing up until recently." He now realized he was wrong and that the chances of success in Vietnam would greatly improve when the local leaders realized they would have independence. Senator Hubert Humphrey added that Korea was a similar positive example of how a strong leader could provide the basis for the native population to defend itself from communism.[72] A road away from the French and toward success had seemingly been found. A strong dictator was what Vietnam needed until its people gained the maturity to rule themselves democratically and still resist communism. At some point, the United States would have to break free of France and go it alone.

Vice President Nixon's report on his tour of Asia in late 1953 brought further support for these views. His general conclusion was that in nations that had strong leaders, such as South Korea, Taiwan, and the Philippines, the communist danger was under control and relations with the United States positive. Elsewhere, notably in Indonesia, Burma, and Thailand, the lack of strong leaders made these countries vulnerable to communist subversion. In the case of Indonesia, while Nixon found Sukarno to be the "greatest and most powerful leader there," he was "naive about Communism," his country needed more strong men in the government, and was, along with Burma, in a race "as to which is the weakest and most liable to go Communist." In the whole region, American policy "has to be one of babying . . . because they are young governments, terribly sensitive, lacking power and stability." When he asked an American officer what was necessary for success in Vietnam, he replied: "I hate to admit this, because he's a real S.O.B., but what they need there is a Rhee." Nixon endorsed this view. Any negotiation that led to a French withdrawal would result in communist domination. The "only capable leadership at the present time in Vietnam is Communist leadership. The anti-Communist Vietnamese leadership is not built up to this point." A leader such as Rhee or Ramon Magsaysay of the Philippines had to be found.[73]

The momentum was building toward unilateral action on the part of the United States to save the situation. The day before Eisenhower's "domino theory" news conference, the president and secretary of state made it clear to the NSC that the time for action was quickly approaching. Dulles again argued that the French would have to "internationalize" the war and grant true independence to the nations of Indochina if the situation were to be saved. When Secretary of the Treasury George Humphrey asked if this attitude was not leading the nation to a stance of "policing all the governments of the world," Dulles responded, not at

Eisenhower, Dulles, and Dictators

all. The issue was communist aggression, whether it was internal sub-version or external attack. "We can no longer accept further Commu-nist take-overs," he said, and "no longer afford to put too fine a point on the methods." As evidence, Dulles noted that the Franco government in Spain was not one that we particularly liked, but no effort was being made to destroy it. Eisenhower agreed, telling Humphrey that "you ex-aggerate the case. Nevertheless in certain areas at least we cannot afford to let Moscow gain another bit of territory."[74]

The French defeat at Dienbienphu in May 1954 had to be turned into an opportunity. The problem, therefore, had to be redefined. Their de-feat meant that it was best to remove the French altogether and start anew with an American-selected leader and American advisers. Dulles em-phasized that the fundamental question was independence; this was "a war for independence, not a war for colonialism." From that perspec-tive, the United States could now intervene directly. There should be, he told the Congress, "a more effective participation by the United States in the training of native forces," building on past successes in Greece, the Philippines, and Korea, where the "United States has done an excel-lent job of training other people." The United States could clearly suc-ceed where France had failed. "I think we have shown a certain aptitude," Dulles declared, "and developed a type of officer who can do that sort of thing." There was plenty of local manpower; it just needed the proper direction and training, which the United States could provide.[75] Dulles was ready to embark on the task of building a new nation to block com-munist control of all of Southeast Asia and to provide a showcase for American-supported independence which would be a middle ground or third way between colonialism and communism.

The Geneva Accords provided for an armistice and a temporary mili-tary partition of Vietnam at the seventeenth parallel with the Vietminh pulling its forces to the north and the French to the south. These were to be administrative units designed to separate the two armies. Neither side was to allow foreign military bases or enter into military alliances. The political question was to be resolved by elections, supervised by an international commission, to be held within two years to establish a uni-fied Vietnam.

Dulles immediately made it clear that the United States was not bound by the settlements reached at Geneva. He indicated to the Senate Foreign Relations Committee the administration's intentions to work against the complete enactment of the provisions: "You have to realize that in fact the military regrouping will be apt to gradually become a live de facto political division." Dulles certainly did all he could to make sure this was the case. In particular, he noted that in Vietnam, unlike Germany or Korea, the United States "was not anxious to see an early election" held "because as things stand today, it is probable that Ho Chi Minh would get a very large vote."[76] Eisenhower wrote in his memoirs that "I have never talked or corresponded with a person knowledgeable in Indochinese affairs who did not agree that had elections been held as of the time of the fighting, possibly 80 per cent of the population would have voted for the Communist Ho Chi Minh as their leader rather than Chief of State Bao Dai." He continued by noting that the lack of leadership demonstrated by Bao Dai had led the Vietnamese to believe they had nothing to fight for. "What Vietnam needs," as one Frenchman told the president, "is another Syngman Rhee regardless of all the difficulties the presence of such a personality would entail."[77]

Ideally, Dulles would favor "genuinely free elections" in Vietnam, but currently it was not possible. "At the present time in a country which is politically immature, which has been the scene of civil war and disruption, we would doubt whether the immediate conditions would be conducive to a result which would really reflect the will of the people." The situation was similar to other areas, such as East Germany, where "the people were so terrorized, so misinformed, that quick elections held there under existing conditions could not be expected accurately to reflect the real views of the people and their intelligent judgment." Further, the United States would not "stand passively by and see the extension of communism by any means into Southeast Asia."[78] Dulles did not believe that the people of Southeast Asia could govern themselves. Without continued guidance from the West, these nations would fall to communism. Until they gained the political maturity that American guidance had provided the Filipinos, the Vietnamese would need support and the United States was obligated, in the face of France's failure, to provide it. What was needed was a strong anticommunist leader who could combat Ho's forces and develop South Vietnam with the backing of the United States. That would allow time for the people to learn the benefits of a U.S.-supported government as opposed to the current conditions. At that point, they would be better informed to cast ballots.

Success in South Vietnam would take two years, Dulles believed, "and would require in large part taking over the training responsibility by the US."[79] Still, it could be done. Dulles did not wish to be bound by an unreasonable and unbending commitment to the principle of territorial integrity. One of the reasons for the failure in China was that "the territorial integrity of China became a shibboleth. We finally got a territorially integrated China—for whose benefit? The Communists."[80] This judgment combined with the ever-increasing confidence of the administration in its ability to create a viable new nation in South Vietnam. Over and over, administration officials pointed to the examples of Greece, Iran, Guatemala, and most notably the Philippines as proof that it could be done. As Dulles told a friend, with the French defeat "we have a clean base there now without a taint of colonialism. Dienbienphu was a blessing in disguise."[81]

American policymakers saw the progress of the Philippines from chaos to order and the defeat of communism as a remarkable success story they could take full credit for, a shining example of American leadership and nation building. The United States had backed Ramon Magsaysay first for the position of secretary of defense and in 1953 for president at a time when the communist-led Huk rebellion threatened to overthrow the government in Manila. He was credited with suppressing the Huk uprising and averting economic collapse in the archipelago, mainly because, officials believed, he was willing to listen to and follow American advice. Magsaysay had secured a strategic outpost of the United States, established order, and turned the newly independent former colony firmly toward the West.[82] If the United States could successfully create a stable, independent, pro-U.S. Philippines, it could do the same in South Vietnam.

The man the United States entrusted to effect its political will in Vietnam was Ngo Dinh Diem, who was appointed as premier of South Vietnam by Bao Dai on 17 June 1954. Diem was far from an ideal candidate. He was a Catholic in a predominantly Buddhist nation and had spent the entire war for independence in Europe and the United States. His nationalist credentials consisted of quitting his position in Bao Dai's government in the 1930s because of French restrictions. Diem overcame these shortcomings by gaining important political support in the United States, particularly from leading Catholic politicians such as Senators Mike Mansfield and John Kennedy. After meeting with Diem, Ambassador to France Douglas Dillon wrote Dulles that "on balance we are favorably impressed but only in the realization that we are prepared to accept the seemingly ridiculous prospect that this Yogi-like mystic could assume the charge" of leading the government "because the standard set by his predecessors is so low."[83] Having supported similar undemocratic figures in various countries for years, the United States assumed that any character, as long as he was backed by Washington, would succeed.

In August, the United States informed France that it intended to deal directly with the new state of South Vietnam and that it would no longer funnel aid through Paris or have its military advisers work with French officers. This would ensure that the states of Indochina were "completely independent, that they establish strong and stable governments and that, to assure the latter end, the United States will henceforth channel the bulk of its aid, both economic and military," directly to the new governments. Dulles informed the American ambassadors in London, Paris, and Saigon that "we do not wish to make it appear that Ngo Dinh Diem is our protege or that we are irrevocably committed to him. On the other hand, we do believe the kind of thing he stands for is a necessary ingredient of success and we do not now see it elsewhere." The secretary of state's message to the French government started by noting that the American decision was motivated by the desire it shared with Paris that "in South Vietnam a strong Nationalist Government must be developed and supported if the world is not to witness an early Communist take-over in Indochina and a still greater menace to South and Southeast Asia with repercussions in Africa." In a direct slap at Bao Dai, Dulles noted that the Americans believed that Diem "has a better chance of rallying and holding nationalist sentiment than most of the Vietnamese who seem now to be on the scene, or in the wings." To help ensure its success and "preserve freedom in Vietnam," the United States would now treat Diem's government as an independent state, and American assistance would be sent directly to it "rather than through the French government."[84]

Everything seemed to rest on Diem's ability, with the assistance of Colonel Edward Geary Lansdale, to rule with a strong hand. Lansdale was selected to assist Diem because he was seen as an expert in nation building. He had been the closest American adviser to Magsaysay in the Philippines and was brought to Saigon to repeat that performance. The key question was whether Diem could become a strong leader, or as Walter Bedell Smith again phrased it in September 1954, "Can we make a synthetic strong man of him, and can we associate with him competent people who may compensate for his deficiencies in administrative ability and governing capacity?" Was it possible to build around Diem "a government which with our . . . support will be relatively enduring and may eventually attract the allegiance of the three sects and the Army?"[85] With Lansdale on the scene, the administration believed the answer to all these questions was yes.

That Lansdale had few raw materials with which to make Diem into a synthetic leader hardly deterred the administration. Dulles, in response to questions concerning the lack of a stable foundation for Diem's government, responded that "this is, of course, the familiar hen-and-egg argument as to which comes first but I would respectfully submit that the U.S. could profitably undertake two courses of action in Free Viet Nam: one to strengthen the government by means of a political and economic nature and the other, to bolster that government by strengthening the army which supports it."[86] When the Pentagon complained that it was difficult to "do a satisfactory job of building up and training the Vietnamese native forces in the absence of a stable government in South Vietnam," Eisenhower replied that "in the lands of the blind, one-eyed men are kings." He wanted a force that would support Diem and was sure this could be accomplished. "The obvious thing to do was simply to authorize General O'Daniel to use up to X million of dollars . . . to produce the maximum number of Vietnamese military units on which Prime Minister Diem could depend to sustain himself in power." As Dulles had stated earlier, the United States "could no longer afford to put too fine a point on the methods."[87]

Still, American officials in Vietnam doubted Diem's ability to consolidate his power. General Lawton Collins, Eisenhower's special representative in Saigon, saw Diem as incompetent and uncooperative and believed he had to be removed if a U.S.-backed government were to succeed. Diem's stock, however, rose immensely in the spring of 1955, when his army was able to defeat the powerful sects with their private armies and establish his government as the only noncommunist force in the nation. Collins's efforts to have Diem removed were cut short. The administration was now fully committed to Diem and was determined not to fail. Dulles informed the French a year after the fall of Dienbienphu that the United States believed "that Diem has the best chance of anyone of staying on top of the revolution and keeping it within 'tolerable' limits. Diem is the only means US sees to save South Vietnam and counteract revolution. US sees no one else who can." Furthermore, whatever questions there had been in the past, "today US must support Diem wholeheartedly. US must not permit Diem to become another Kerensky."[88]

With American support secure, Diem informed Ho's government in Hanoi that he would not participate in the elections stipulated by the Geneva Accords. The State Department encouraged Diem in this position. An intelligence analysis in 1955 found that "almost any type of election would . . . give the Communists a very significant if not a decisive advantage." Instead, Diem held a referendum to form a republic with himself as the president. The choice was his new government or the continuation of the monarchy under Bao Dai. In an election that would have made any communist government in Eastern Europe proud, Diem garnered over 98 percent of the vote.[89]

For his efforts, Diem received unvarnished praise in Washington. Apparently a Magsaysay, or at least a Rhee, had been found for Vietnam. Before Diem's defeat of the sects and blocking of elections, Dulles was still hedging his bets. In January 1955 he saw events on a "slight upgrade" but noted that "there were moments both in Iran and Guatemala when many people thought the situation was hopeless, but we kept a stout heart, kept our courage up, and then all of a sudden things began to go better, and that is a possibility in Vietnam."[90] The next year he reported to the Senate that this faith had been rewarded. The "situation has immensely improved. . . . We stuck with Diem at a time when many people, including some in our own Government, felt he should be abandoned." Diem, he continued, "has done a wonderful job, of course with our help, in cleaning up his sect armies," and "Diem's authority throughout the area is now generally accepted." Not all the problems were yet solved, but Diem had "brought central authority into the country to a degree which is really quite amazing." Furthermore, "Bao Dai has been eliminated, and there is a chance for really building a strong and effective anti-Communist regime in an area where for a time it looked as though it would be swept away as a result of the French defeat . . . and by the unfavorable armistice terms."[91]

Senator Kennedy praised Diem for making South Vietnam "the cornerstone of the Free World in Southeast Asia, the keystone in the arch, the finger in the dike," while Mike Mansfield argued that the fact "that a free Viet Nam exists at the present time . . . is the result of the efforts of Mr. Diem."[92] The *Saturday Evening Post* referred to Diem as the "mandarin in a sharkskin suit who's upsetting the Red timetable,"[93] and *Life* magazine, with no apparent sense of irony, justified Diem's refusal to hold the unification elections on the grounds that Ho would win. "Diem saved his people from this agonizing prospect simply by refusing to permit the plebiscite and thereby he avoided national suicide."[94] The *New York Times* titled its 1957 profile on Diem "An Asian Liberator." The paper of record applauded his work to "save his country from falling apart" and how he "tirelessly toured the countryside so that the people would get to know him and perhaps like him more than they did Ho Chi Minh." This effort was paying off as the "Vietnamese learn to respect their new Government and their new leader."[95]

American officials, having supported dictators for so long, believed that even a synthetic leader of their own creation could provide a stable anticommunist government that would serve as a model, or a third way, for other nations in Asia and Africa to follow as they gained independence. The temporary successes Diem enjoyed served to mask the fundamental flaws in American policy. Policymakers viewed and understood Vietnam primarily as a symbol of the Cold War, not as a real and distinct place with a history and people who were acting on their own local needs and desires. The agent theory of communist aggression allowed policymakers to ignore the ongoing revolution in Vietnam and talk instead of containment, nation building, and falling dominoes. The administration established an autocratic government that met all the existing conditions for American support and appeared to provide the bulwark against communist expansion in the region that it desired. The shortsightedness and the dangers of supporting right-wing dictators were, however, about to be vividly demonstrated in both South America and the Caribbean.

A Policy in Trouble: Nixon's Trip to Latin America

Signs of unrest in Latin America spurred the new assistant secretary of state for Latin American affairs, Roy R. Rubottom, to recommend to Dulles in late 1957 that he embark on a tour of South America early the next year. Rubottom warned the secretary of state that the "situation in Latin America has changed substantially in the past year." Economic conditions "in the whole area [have] deteriorated due to the catastrophic price drops in metals" and declines in the price of staples such as coffee. This downturn provided openings for the communists, who "are on the alert to whatever political opportunity appears." A trip by Dulles would be the "extra effort . . . required" to hold onto the "reservoir of friendship and good will in Latin America" he believed the United States currently enjoyed and would effectively counter the communists' propaganda that Washington did not care about its neighbors to the south. Dulles informed Eisenhower that he thought a trip an excellent idea but that he would be unable to travel until the summer. An alarmed president told Dulles that he "urgently believed something should be done" and recommended that Nixon go in place of the secretary of state. The trip was finally arranged for May; the vice president would attend the inauguration of Arturo Frondizi, the newly elected president of Argentina, and then visit other nations, particularly Peru and Venezuela, where dictators had recently been removed from power. A trip designed to "contribute greatly to the cementing of our good relations with Latin America" became, ironically, a symbol of the gulf that existed between United States perceptions of South America and the anger and discontent harbored by its residents against U.S. policies, in particular its support of repressive dictatorships.[96]

On every stage of the journey, Nixon was heckled and harassed by students and others who denounced U.S. policies in the hemisphere, blamed American imperialism for the problems in the region, and condemned Washington's support of dictators. In both Peru and Venezuela, Nixon was physically attacked. The most serious incident occurred in Caracas, where the vice president's car was nearly seized by an angry mob, which the embassy claimed was "undoubtedly . . . organized by the Communists." Enraged that the United States had allowed the recently deposed Jiménez and his chief of the secret police, Pedro Estrada, to enter the United States, the mob broke the windows of Nixon's car and roughed up the embassy's naval attaché. Only the arrival of troops with drawn bayonets cleared a path for the car to escape the crowd. Nixon's trip renewed the discussion within the administration over U.S. relations with right-wing dictators and the constant dilemma American policymakers faced concerning this question. The State Department's analysis stressed the communist responsibility for the hostile demonstrations. "The Communist bloc has intensified its efforts in the economic, political, and cultural fields in Latin America in the past few years . . . [and] the preponderance of U.S. influence in Latin America is being challenged." The problem was that the nations with the worst disturbances, Peru and Venezuela, were emerging from dictatorships and characterized by "political instability and weak governments." The communists were exploiting "numerous alleged or real grievances" against the United States, "particularly the issue of U.S. relations, both past and present, with dictatorships in the area."[97]

While the communists were blamed for most of the disturbances, it was granted that they had fertile soil to till. A broader explanation of the problems was needed. As Allen Dulles told his brother, "There would be trouble in Latin America if there were no Communists."[98] The CIA's analysis was that the demonstrations in Lima and Caracas, "although undoubtedly Communist instigated . . . did give expression to a popular sense of grievances against certain phases of US policy, and general feeling that with our preoccupation with Europe, Asia and Africa, South America has been relatively neglected." While moderate opinion deplored the actions of the mobs, the "general public reaction . . . has been that the shock brought South American problems to our attention as nothing else could have done and hence may have long range benefits for South American countries." For the communists, then, these demonstrations "were at least a temporary success."[99]

Nixon's reports to the cabinet and the National Security Council concerning his Latin American trip addressed the question of democracy and dictatorships. In speaking to the cabinet, Nixon emphasized the communist inspiration for the riots and dismissed particular aspects of American policy toward the individual nations. He did believe, however, "that the political complaint against the United States for harboring refugee dictators was more important than the various economic complaints." He stressed that Latin Americans "much prefer to be friends of the United States rather than Russia." The problem was how to cultivate this friendship given the emergence of "the lower classes into the political scene" and the long-standing ties of the United States to the traditional elite.[100] The vice president expanded on these points the following week in the discussion with the National Security Council. Again, he began by emphasizing "that the threat of Communism in Latin America was greater today than ever before."[101] The question was why? What were the conditions that made this so?

Paradoxically, for Nixon, part of the problem was because the nations of South America were "evolving toward a democratic form of government." Although this would normally be cause for celebration, it was a development fraught with danger and "may not always be in each country the best of all possible courses, particularly in those Latin American countries which are completely lacking in political maturity." Where dictators were being replaced, Nixon explained, the new leaders, such as Frondizi in Argentina, were advocates of reform and influenced by Marxist thinking. They were not drawn from the "old upper-class" but instead from the middle class and the intelligentsia. "Being the kind of men they are, they are very naive about the nature and threat of Communism, so much so that their attitude is frightening. They regard the Communists as nothing more than a duly-constituted political party." This attitude was in part understandable because the communists often aided the new rulers in overthrowing the dictators, but it still indicated to Nixon a serious problem with the maturity of these nations and caused concern about their future ability to see the problems of the region in the same terms as they were understood in Washington.[102]

Moreover, these new leaders were afraid to deal "harshly with the Communists" out of fear they would lose public support, mainly that of the middle class, university students, professors, and the labor movements. How did Nixon explain this failure? It "stemmed from the fact that the people of most of these countries were so weary of dictatorships that they felt that the danger of the old-fashioned dictatorship was much more to be feared than any danger from communism." Thus the paradox: "While we are witnessing the development of democracy in Latin America, we are at the same time witnessing the development of a serious communist threat." For example, Uruguay "was the most democratic country in the Western Hemisphere after the United States and Canada." Yet it "was in the greatest danger of a Communist take-over." It was impossible to get the Latin Americans to face the danger of communism. They could focus only on their economic problems.[103]

While Nixon argued that the United States had to promote better economic development projects, he did not find much to fault in current United States policy. "Our policies and actions were generally correct, but the problem was essentially more subtle and hence more difficult to solve. We must join the battle in Latin America on the field of propaganda. Otherwise the Communists would ultimately win out." He suggested, therefore, that the United States demonstrate a clear preference for Latin American democracies over dictatorships and establish a distance from the ruling right-wing dictators it currently aided. Nixon's position was based "on the understanding that dictatorship now constitutes the most emotional issue in Latin America." From this premise, the United States should attack "communism not as Marxist economic thought but as a dictatorship and, worse than that from the Latin American point of view, a foreign-controlled dictatorship." Hungary would serve as the perfect example.[104] The new approach, as Nixon phrased it one time, should be "a formal handshake for dictators; an *embraso* [embrace] for leaders in freedom."[105]

Such sentiments reminded John Foster Dulles of Bradenism. "The genius of the Eisenhower Administration was to get along with all countries" in Latin America.[106] "If we attempt to adjust our relations according to our appraisal of their government," Dulles claimed, "we would become involved in their internal affairs."[107] Dulles informed the cabinet that he agreed with the analysis of the problem but not with Nixon's solution. He argued that the difficulty in responding to it was "that since democracy as we know it will not be instituted by the lower classes," these new groups "will bring in a dictatorship of the masses."[108] The secretary of state was concerned about the "definite swing away from the old-fashioned ruler or king, in favor of the kind of dictatorship of the proletariat which was represented by a Nasser or a Sukarno, with their mass appeal." They were leading their nations toward communism. The old type of American-supported dictators were not a problem. The distinction for Dulles was critical and one that had to be kept in mind.[109]

Dulles told Nixon that he was worried about the impact criticizing traditional dictators would have on U.S. relations with South America and the nation's security. Nixon's trip had prompted renewed congressional criticism, headed by Senator Wayne Morse (D.-Oregon), of the administration's relations with the various dictators who ruled in Latin America, most notably Trujillo in the Dominican Republic. To counter the hostility emerging from the south and to prevent opportunities for communists, Morse and others were calling on the State Department to take action against such regimes. He told Nixon that he did not think "our Amb[assador]s should be operators running around nor that we should graduate our treatment according to whether [rulers] are dictators." Dulles emphasized that "there are a whole series of gradations of dictators."[110] In an effort to forestall any public comments from the president or changes in policy and actions against any of the right-wing regimes, Dulles spoke privately with Eisenhower and criticized Nixon's "attitude about dictatorships." He argued "that while there was merit in this point of view, it did not explain everything, and it was not possible in a brief trip to many countries to come back with a formula of solution."[111]

Eisenhower, however, wanted to address this problem actively, but with his administration split he moved cautiously and no clear new direction emerged. The president saw the problem as revolving around the "use of the term 'capitalism,' which means one thing to us, [but] clearly meant to much of the rest of the world something synonymous with imperialism." He suggested to the National Security Council that it "try to coin a new phrase to represent our modern brand of capitalism."[112] Following this idea, the administration changed its public posture to emphasize a concern for democracy and criticism of arbitrary rule. In August 1958, Eisenhower welcomed the new Venezuelan ambassador in a public ceremony and stated that "authoritarianism and autocracy of whatever form are incompatible with ideals of our great leaders of the past."[113] The president dispatched his brother Milton on another fact-finding mission that fall. His January 1959 report called for a greater effort by the United States to provide economic assistance to the nations of Latin America and to provide more encouragement to the trend in South America away from dictatorships and toward democracy. Eisenhower found that everywhere he went the "charge arose that while the

United States treasures freedom and democracy for itself, it is indifferent about these in Latin America—indeed, that we support dictators." This was, he insisted, a misunderstanding on their part, but he did acknowledge that the United States had made "some honest mistakes in our dealings with dictators," particularly by decorating many of them with medals. He recommended following Nixon's suggestion that Washington provide an embrace "for democratic leaders and a formal handshake for dictators." He stopped short of recommending any cessation of relations and specifically stated that all current programs be continued. All that should be done was "refrain[ing] from granting special recognition to a Latin American dictator."[114] There was, therefore, no immediate change in policy. The administration did not desire any more weak democracies that might cause the unrest and instability that it saw the communists exploiting.

Milton Eisenhower's other recommendation, that the United States provide greater economic assistance to Latin America, did prompt new programs by the administration. These expressions of support for political democracy were accompanied in 1959–60 by new economic initiatives that served as a precursor to Kennedy's Alliance for Progress. Eisenhower concluded that relying on private capital would not solve the economic problems of Latin America or prevent the spread of communism. The State Department believed that the "Latin American republics had got off to a rather late start in terms of their economic development. Like our own South, they had long been wedded to an agrarian economy." To break this cycle would require inducing "the Latin American republics themselves to follow consistent and sound economic policies" along with greater U.S. assistance. The availability of capital would serve as the incentive to greater economic responsibility.[115] In its last two years, the Eisenhower administration committed approximately $850 million in economic assistance.[116] The 1959 Cuban revolution served, however, as the immediate catalyst for making these monies available, and the fear of revolutionary nationalism and communism, and not a commitment to progress and change, served as the context for the Eisenhower administration's rethinking of its policy toward dictators in its last two years of power.

The Fall of Batista

Fidel Castro's overthrow of Fulgencio Batista's government in January 1959 and eventual establishment of a communist state in Cuba marked the greatest challenge to the U.S. policy of supporting authoritarian rulers since World War II. Moreover, events in Cuba provided compelling support to critics' arguments that Washington's close relations with dictators such as Batista blocked any effective means for the necessary progressive reforms in their nations, destroyed the political center, and created a backlash of anti-American sentiment that would open the door to radical nationalist and communist movements to take power as the people looked to revolutionary change as the only possible route to redress their problems. In conjunction with Nixon's Latin American trip and events elsewhere in the world, the success of Castro's 26th of July Movement in wresting control of Cuba from Batista forced a reexamination of American policy toward right-wing dictatorships.

Batista had enjoyed American support since 1934, when he worked closely with Sumner Welles and Jefferson Caffery to bring down Grau San Martín's nationalist government. Since then Batista dominated the political life of Cuba either directly as president or through his control of the army, and in 1952 he returned to power in a coup that ousted President Carlos Prío Socarrás. Batista's rule further enhanced U.S. economic domination of the island. By 1958, 80 percent of all Cuban trade was with the United States, direct American investments on the island increased from $686 million in 1952 to $1 billion, and Cuba remained dependent on the U.S. sugar quota to market its largest crop. Batista welcomed organized crime figures to run Havana's casinos and increased his ties to both U.S. business interests and government agencies to help maintain his dictatorship.[117] As Assistant Secretary of State Edward Miller noted after Batista's return, "From the cold-blooded standpoint of U.S. interests, we have nothing to worry about Batista who is a proven friend of ours and who might possibly be tougher on the commies than Prio was."[118] Although the State Department "naturally deplores the way in which the Batista coup was brought about," Acheson recommended to Truman that the United States quickly extend recognition to his illegal government. As the American ambassador to Cuba stated, "If this had to happen Batista was the best material for the job."[119]

This support was undergirded by the persistent view of Latin Americans as politically immature, excessively emotional, and childish and the Cubans as suffering from "excessive pride."[120] That the Cubans were unable to govern themselves democratically remained a given to policymakers. Support of the military and dictators such as Batista continued to be necessary to keep order and block communist advances. As Dulles noted in 1956, "a good many dictators that we have as friendly countries, we do not always like the way they conduct their internal affairs," but as long as they provide stability and "as long as their international policies do not threaten the United States," there is no basis for "interference in their internal affairs." When members of Congress questioned State Department officials concerning the continuation of military aid to Batista's Cuba, the response was that the areas with "military-type governments" are "of some value to us for maintaining order in those areas, so we do not have that problem on our backs." The United States "must help maintain law and order, presuming that the government in the country is a government that is anti-Communist."[121]

When Nixon traveled to Cuba in 1955, the State Department instructed him that the army, which was the "key to the situation," firmly backed Batista and described the dictator as a "master politician" who "is friendly to the U.S., admires the American way of life, and believes in private enterprise." What problems existed stemmed from the fact that Cubans suffered from "a sense of inferiority which promotes exaggerated nationalism." Upon his return, the vice president described Batista as a "remarkable" and "strong and vigorous" man. At the same time, the American ambassador reported that there was no mistaking that Cuba "has had a rebirth, and a genuine resurgence" because of Batista.[122]

By 1958, however, Batista was proving to be a political embarrassment to the Eisenhower administration. Castro's movement was gaining favorable attention in the United States and throughout Latin America, while Batista's harsh measures enacted in an attempt to suppress the rebellion were bringing unfavorable light to the practices of American clients. Senator Mansfield expressed the view of many critics when he asked Rubottom if he found supporting Batista to be "the kind of policy that is likely to help this country keep its reputation of devotion to freedom among the people of Latin America?"[123]

More and more the answer administration officials gave to such questions was a qualified no. The administration concluded that Batista would have to be replaced but was divided and unclear about how that should be done and who should replace him. As events unfolded, Batista proved that authoritarian rulers were rarely what policymakers thought they were. Washington had first overestimated his power, and then, when his government was in trouble, misread his willingness to act as the administration wanted and step aside. The only point of agreement over Cuban policy in the Eisenhower administration was that it should not support Castro. Ambassador Earl Smith rejected any accommodation with Castro and peppered the State Department with negative reports. Smith consistently argued that Castro was unpopular and that his 26th of July Movement lacked the ability to take power. Moreover, the ambassador could see no alternative to Batista or military rule. "If Batista were assassinated," Smith believed, "there is no responsible group able to take over the government. Vandalism, chaos and bloodshed would surely ensue."[124]

In an attempt to preserve the existing order in Cuba, the United States took steps to try to force Batista to moderate his actions. In March, the State Department imposed an arms embargo on Cuba to prod Batista into enacting reforms. It quickly became apparent that these efforts were too late. On 1 April the department conceded that "the chances for a peaceful solution to the Cuban political crisis appear to have vanished." Even the moderate opposition to Batista had concluded that he must go, "leaving no room for compromise." A "showdown involving violence and bloodshed appears inevitable." Batista had to be replaced, but the question was by whom? There was little about the 26th of July Movement and "its top leadership to inspire confidence that it would show the qualities of integrity, moderation, and responsibility which will be needed to restore order and tranquility to Cuba." Although there was no concrete evidence to support Batista's "charge that Castro is a communist, it does suggest that he is immature and irresponsible." Further, his chief lieutenant, "the Argentine Dr. Ernesto Guevara, makes no secret of his anti-American feelings and shows definite indications that he has been subject to Marxist influences." The department, therefore, sought "a possible third alternative to a continuation of Batista, or the installation of a revolutionary regime dominated by Castro," in the form of the "emergence of a military-civilian junta which would oust Batista but not permit Castro a dominant position."[125] The administration believed it had time to work out this problem. As Allen Dulles reported to the National Security Council in April, Castro's efforts to launch a general strike had failed and he would have to revert to guerrilla warfare. The government, because of the loyalty of the army, "has the situation in hand at the moment."[126] For the rest of the year the administration searched for a compromise that would remove Batista but keep Castro out of power.

The effort to find a third alternative to Batista and Castro failed. Policymakers discovered only after the fact that there was no longer a moderate, pro-U.S. group in Cuba to which it could turn. Moreover, Batista refused to surrender power just because the State Department requested it. The administration's last hope that a peaceful change could be orchestrated came from Batista's promise to hold free elections in November 1958. The elections, however, were rigged, and the State

Department dispatched William Pawley to Havana to convince Batista to yield power to a military junta. Again he refused. The United States would have to try to reach an accommodation with Castro.

Batista fled Cuba on 31 December, and Castro took power the next day. The Eisenhower administration's initial responses were mixed as it demonstrated a willingness to work with the new government. In January 1959, Allen Dulles contended that Castro had demonstrated "great courage" in his fight against Batista and that he was not a communist agent, although the situation would bear watching. As for the executions of Batista supporters, Dulles told the Senate Foreign Relations Committee in executive session that upheaval was to be expected and that Cuba would go through a "little French Revolution." "When you have a revolution, you kill your enemies." Dulles concluded that Castro "apparently has very wide popular backing throughout the island." Still, the CIA director informed the NSC that the new Cuban leaders "had to be treated more or less like children. They had to be led rather than rebuffed. If they were rebuffed, like children, they were capable of doing almost anything."[127] Two months later, Rubottom found "a potential for greatness in this revolution in Cuba, and everybody hopes that it will be able to achieve this potential" and provide Cuba with an "honesty and high level of competence" in its government. In the long run American business would profit from this revolution.[128]

After Castro's visit to the United States in April 1959, Christian Herter, who replaced an ailing Dulles as secretary of state, wrote Eisenhower that he believed Castro would remain in the Western camp, although "his position here must be regarded as uncertain." He worried that the land reform program Castro intended to enact "may adversely affect certain American-owned properties" and that it was clear that he did not "have the same idea of law and legality as we have in the United States." Herter concluded that "on balance, despite Castro's apparent simplicity, sincerity and eagerness to reassure the United States public, there is little probability that Castro has altered the essentially radical course of his revolution." The administration would make "a serious mistake to underestimate this man. With all his appearance of naiveté, unsophistication and ignorance on many matters, he is clearly a strong personality and a born leader of great personal courage and conviction." It would be best to wait and see what he did "before assuming a more optimistic view than heretofore about the possibility of developing a constructive relationship with him and his government."[129]

Good relations with Castro were, however, short-lived as he moved to implement his revolution and redress the inequalities in Cuban society. Genuine change in Cuba had to and did harm various American interests. Castro socialized the sugar industry, expropriated land, increased his denunciations of the United States, and announced that he would be neutral in the Cold War. By 1960, Castro had established trade relations with the Soviet Union. All this brought a predictably negative response from the Eisenhower administration. It understood the need for some reforms in Cuba, but not to the extent that Castro was going.

The new leadership in Cuba and the Eisenhower administration saw the historical relationship between their two nations in dramatically different terms. For Castro, social progress and prosperity could come to Cuba only when it gained independence of U.S. domination. So accustomed were American leaders to having Cuban affairs conducted to the benefit of the United States that they could not understand this position. In October 1959, Eisenhower told the press that he did not know why Cuba was hostile toward the United States: "Here is a country that you would believe, on the basis of our history, would be one of our real friends. The whole history—first of our intervention in 1898, our making and helping set up Cuban independence . . . and the very close relationships that have existed most of the time with them—would seem to make it a puzzling matter to figure out just exactly why the Cubans and the Cuban Government would be so unhappy when, after all, their principal market is right here, their best market. You would think they would want good relations."[130]

By this time, the administration had given up all hope of working with Castro. It saw his basic program as designed to foment "anti-American sentiment in Cuba and seeking to do so in other Latin American countries," as well as to provide support for other revolutionaries in the Caribbean. In response, the administration increased its criticisms of Castro, enacted an economic boycott to pressure him into abandoning his more radical reforms, and continued to seek "a coherent opposition consisting of elements desirous of achieving political and economic progress within a framework of good United States–Cuban relations" to check or replace Castro.[131] Castro was now seen as "a very conspiratorial individual who tries to create the impression that he and Cuba are beleaguered . . . an extreme Leftist." Without direct intervention, the "only solution would come through the development of a moderate and responsible force from within Cuba."[132] On 17 March, Eisenhower approved an American covert plan to support an invasion of Cuba by armed exiles. The purpose was to "bring about the replacement of the Castro regime with one more devoted to the true interests of the Cuban people and more acceptable to the U.S." without revealing American complicity in these events.[133]

All of this opened up the questions of how the United States found itself losing influence and power in a nation it had dominated since the turn of the century and what change, if any, the United States should adopt in its relations with Latin America. Moreover, should the United States change its policy toward right-wing dictators? Would abandoning rulers such as Batista aid in the finding and promoting of moderate democratic forces or would it just open the door for another Castro? John Foster Dulles held to the position that a change in policy was unnecessary and might create even greater problems. Such a step could unleash forces that would be difficult to control. The problem was better seen as how to manage change to preserve order. Invoking the standard paternalistic views that guided policy toward Latin America throughout the century, the secretary of state argued that the "most significant fact that we must recognize was the fact that throughout much of the world and certainly in Latin America there had been in recent years a tremendous surge in the direction of popular governments by peoples who have practically no capacity for self-government and indeed are like children in facing this problem." He reminded the National Security Council that "our Founding Fathers realized that it would take considerable time before the new United States could safely practice government by direct democracy." Hence the election of presidents through the electoral college and not direct suffrage. But "unlike ourselves, many of the Latin American states are leaping ahead to irresponsible self-government directly out of a semi-colonial status. This presents the Communists with an ideal situation to exploit." The question was how to "move in, take control over, or guide" these nations toward democracy. Dulles was convinced that even if all concrete problems between the United States and Latin America were solved, "the problem of irresponsible government would remain."[134]

Yet the pressure from Congress and Latin American nations in conjunction with fear of further revolutions seemed to demand some modification in American policy. The National Security Council took up the question of overall U.S. policy toward Latin America shortly after Castro took power. The council's Planning Board recommended that military assistance no longer be extended to dictators as part of a general effort to counter the impression that the United States favored dictatorships in the region. The full NSC rejected this idea. Under Secretary of State Dillon explained that the State Department rejected this idea because it believed "that in the matter of dealing with dictatorships, it was important for the U.S. to maintain an adequate degree of flexibility, inasmuch as many of the governments of many of the Latin American countries were subject to frequent change." He agreed with the president, who thought a cautionary word was sufficient. The director of the U.S. Information Agency, George Allen, added that one had to keep in mind "that it was often thought that there were both good and bad dictatorships in the world." It was agreed that the United States did not want to establish a policy of opposition to dictators per se and would continue to evaluate this question.[135]

The difficulties the administration confronted as it reexamined its policy of supporting dictatorships was compounded by Castro's efforts to support forces trying to oust Trujillo in the Dominican Republic and Somoza in Nicaragua. As Secretary Herter pointed out, "If the U.S. Government sided with the dictatorships, it would find itself in serious trouble with many other Latin American Republics. On the other hand, if we did not do something, the fire would spread very fast."[136] But could the United States reject supporting dictatorships unless it was sure it could find a moderate democratic replacement? Another Cuba was unacceptable. As Herter was posing this dilemma, events in Asia and Africa prompted the State Department to investigate this very problem.

Political Implications of Military Takeovers

Responding to the military takeovers of civilian governments in Burma, Iraq, Pakistan, Sudan, and Thailand in the past year, the State Department prepared a study in May 1959, "Political Implications of Afro-Asian Military Takeovers," that investigated the "short and long-range policy implications for the U.S. found in this trend . . . in parts of Asia and the Near East." The guiding premise of the document was that "political and economic authoritarianism prevails throughout the underdeveloped world in general and represents the predominant environment in which the U.S. must associate its interests with those of the emergent and developing societies." Of course, the United States would prefer "benevolent and experienced civilian politicians who have a broad popular base and are held to some form of accountability by a parliament or organized opposition." Unfortunately, that was not the case, and most of these nations lacked any history of stable civilian rule. The United States had to subordinate its ideals "to the practical and the possible for many years to come."[137]

The military takeovers did provide, the department found, "certain short-run advantages to the United States." Authoritarian governments were better able to withstand communist pressures and generally represented what the United States saw as the best segments of the societies. Most important, they were seen as conduits to modernization and necessary stages for a society to develop. Reflecting the influence and jargon of modernization theory, the report asserted that "our experience with the more highly developed Latin American States indicates that authoritarianism is required to lead backward societies through their socio-economic revolutions." Moreover, if the "break-through occurs under non-Communist authoritarianism, trends toward democratic values emerge with the development of a literate middle class." Right-wing dictators would "remain the norm . . . for a long period. The trend toward military authoritarianism will accelerate as developmental problems become more acute and the facades of democracy left by the colonial powers prove inadequate to immediate tasks." The question was what the United States could do to take advantage of this situation. The key was working with both the soldier and civilian to encourage "both to modernize their societies by some 'middle way' between private enterprise and Communism, thus preserving the residue of human rights and dignity essential to the growth of democratic values."[138]

The State Department found three additional reasons why the United States "must support military regimes at this stage of Free Asia's development." First, "a real security threat confronts Red China's free neighbors." In that context, the "officer groups are often the most disciplined, and educated institution-in-being on which backward societies can draw in time of crisis." Second, military intervention in government "will continue to be necessary to supplant ineptness, corruption or slippage toward Communism." Finally, military guidance was necessary because it would "take decades for Free Asia to develop those institutions which establish in more advanced countries civilian control of the military." In these circumstances, the "essential test . . . should be whether a particular military regime responsibly confronts the problems facing it—security and developmental progress—and, in doing so, successfully resists Communist techniques." Up to this point, Burma, Pakistan, and the Sudan in particular earned high marks.[139]

The report outlined the fundamental dilemma in this policy, the potential long-range threats, and the possibility that supporting right-wing dictators could damage American prestige.

> It is of course essential in the Cold War to seek to promote stability in the under-developed countries . . . where instability may invite Communism. A new, authoritarian regime, though less "democratic" than its predecessor, may possess much more stability and may well lay the ground for ultimate return to a more firmly based "democracy." These are compelling reasons for maintaining relations with regimes in power. On the other hand, to become identified with an authoritarian regime and its policies makes us a target for anti-regime propaganda . . . and creates the impression that we approve of authoritarianism and repression so long as our self-interest is thereby satisfied. This impression . . . discredits our sincere dedication to the principles of freedom, democracy, economic progress and development, and respect for human dignity.

In addition, there were no guarantees that authoritarian leaders would successfully lead their respective nations forward. No doubt influenced by the recent events in Cuba, the department warned that a failure to achieve "developmental revolutions . . . encourages a parallel trend toward 'second stage revolutions,' e.g. revolutions engendered by the dissatisfaction or stifling of opposition groups (labor, students, intelligentsia, dissident younger officers)." It was possible that the "incidence of political authoritarianism . . . weakens the fiber of democratic values and points the way toward an easier acceptance of economic controls which tend toward Communist controls." A developing society could "be lost to Communism short of military aggression and by failure to manage the developmental revolution."[140]

Yet these were risks well worth taking. "In the bipolar world of the Cold War, our refusal to deal with a military or authoritarian regime . . . could lead almost necessarily to the establishment of that regime's friendly relations with the Soviet Union." More optimistically, the State Department believed the right "happy medium from the standpoint of U.S. interests" could be reached that would consist of a "military regime 'civilianized' to the greatest extent possible and headed by a military leader who saw security and development in perspective and thereby evidenced political leadership of the type required in a developing society." It was the task of the United States to discover "techniques whereby Western values can be grafted on modernized indigenous developmental systems." All this could be done with no loss of prestige to the United States. "Our image will depend basically on the example of our own democracy at work, our unequivocal support for the independence and development of emergent nations, and our assisting the regime in power to satisfy popular aspirations." The best route was to offer assistance and attempt to influence the course of events rather than to leave those decisions solely in the hands of these nations.[141]

The report, presented to the National Security Council by Henry Ramsey of the State Department on 18 June, was followed by a lengthy discussion by its members. Secretary of Defense Neil McElroy expressed his agreement with the analysis presented: "Military leadership has basically represented a conservative element in the societies of newly developing countries," and "while in some instances, the military can be troublesome, it remained true that in these backward societies, it was desirable to encourage the military to stabilize a conservative system." As an example, he cited the positive military role in Indonesia. Citing its organization and clarity, President Eisenhower praised the report as the "finest" ever presented to the NSC. The study raised an even larger question: "Can our system of free government stand the strains which it must endure because of our tolerance of pressure groups and other kinds of uninformed thinking?" Another stress was the budget. The administration was "anxious to keep our economy strong and stable" while keeping a balanced budget, but it "seemed to be in need of doing more to assist such backward countries as Mr. Ramsey had been describing in his report."[142]

The focus of the discussion shifted to how best to influence foreign military leaders. Admiral Arleigh Burke, of the Joint Chiefs of Staff, responded to Eisenhower that the key was developing "responsibility by the members of governing groups." Accordingly, it was essential for the United States to train the "young people of these backward countries so that they could develop the requisite sense of responsibility." CIA director Allen Dulles concurred. He reminded Admiral Burke that in a letter to him the previous fall he had "stressed the need for our military attachés and for the personnel of our Military Assistance Advisory Groups (MAAGs) to be carefully selected so that they could develop useful and appropriate relationships with the rising military leaders and factions in the underdeveloped nations to which they were assigned." Eisenhower vigorously supported Dulles's view. He noted that the "young military leaders in these underdeveloped countries could probably be most effectively influenced by our MAAG personnel" and suggested that there be "more civilian instructors in our higher military schools in order to instruct our own military people on the importance of other than purely military considerations in their relationships with their opposite numbers" wherever they were assigned.

The president's special assistant for national security affairs, Gordon Gray, complained that in too many of the NSC policy papers on different nations "there appeared boiler-plate language with respect to objective calling for 'strong, stable, democratic governments with a pro-Western orientation.'" Yet, "as Mr. Ramsey's paper indicated, this was not always going to be possible and we must look into these objectives more carefully in the future." The president endorsed this point and stated "that it seemed to him likely that the trend toward military takeovers in the underdeveloped countries of Asia and Africa was almost certainly going to continue." Given that reality, "we must do our best to orient the potential military leaders of these countries in a pro-Western rather than pro-Communist direction." This process would take time and would not immediately result in democratic governments. He cited the Philippines as a perfect example: "If we had not trained the Filipinos in democracy for some forty years, the Philippines would now have become a military dictatorship."

There was some dissent. Eisenhower's special assistant for foreign economic policy, Clarence Randall, disagreed with the report's conclusions and the opinions expressed in the meeting. He noted that this was the "biggest issue which he had heard discussed in this body in a very long time." Acknowledging that he was "doubtless in a small minority," he still believed that "Ramsey's paper was much too complacent . . . too much readiness to give up pushing for the democratic ideal." He wished to see more emphasis on the education of civilians in "these backward countries." Randall believed that institutions such as the "American University in Beirut had accomplished wonders for democracy in the Near East . . . [and] profoundly advanced our American and Western ideals in the areas in which they were located."

Eisenhower stated that he found the American University to be "under considerable Communist influence" inasmuch as it had advised against a visit and speech by Secretary Dulles. Furthermore, he was wary of the prospects for the success of democracy in the region. "If you go and live with these Arabs," Eisenhower claimed, "you will find that they simply cannot understand our ideas of freedom or human dignity. They have lived so long under dictatorships of one form or another, how can we expect them to run successfully a free government?" In such circumstances, military dictators were better than communist ones. Under

Secretary of State Dillon, who earlier had noted that the report "reflected State Department views at the top levels," argued that it was incorrect to claim that the department was endorsing a continuation of military regimes forever in the Third World. Rather, it insisted that "in the short range, parliamentary democracy simply will not work in these countries as it works in the U.S." (No one mentioned that the United States does not have a parliamentary system either.) "Accordingly, our best bet was to try to civilianize these military regimes as far as possible in the interest of ultimate victory of democratic government."

Eisenhower supported Dillon by pointing out that it was absolutely necessary "that before these colonies did become free countries their citizens should be trained for freedom. It was indeed pretty difficult if such colonies became independent before they had trained any of their people in the art of government." The president alluded to what he termed the "paradoxical situation in Nicaragua. After years of a heavy-handed dictatorship" under Anastasio Somoza, his son "permitted and encouraged the development of a number of freedoms in Nicaragua such as freedom of speech, freedom of the press, and the like. For his pains Luis Somoza was now confronted by a revolution against his relatively mild authoritarian regime."

Council members raised two other potential risks: that the greater centralization of power increased both the danger of communist subversion and military aggression against neighboring states. Eisenhower quickly dismissed these points by stating that he was "quite sure that these risks had been calculated," a position Ramsey affirmed. It was decided that the State Department would continue to monitor these issues and that the conclusions of the report would be used in "preparing recommendations with regard to the Afro-Asian area." The administration was fully aware of the dangers of its policy of supporting right-wing dictators. The problem was that too often it could see no alternative beyond American intervention for maintaining stability and keeping these nations in the free world. In the short run, the benefits of continuing to support authoritarian rulers seemed clear, and it was difficult to look beyond the immediate crises. As George Allen concluded, the United States should be "a little more friendly to the democratic regimes" without abandoning the dictators. Or at least that was "the ideal to keep in mind as our ultimate goal." Just maybe with the right set of leadership, luck, and economic development, the dictators would allow for an evolution to democracy.

Policy for the last year and a half of Eisenhower's term was guided by these ideas. The United States publicly distanced itself from dictator-ships in Latin America and attempted to do more to promote peaceful change to democratic rule while quietly maintaining support for dicta-tors in nations it believed to be unprepared for democracy and where their role was viewed as necessary for providing stability and preventing communism. Completely severing ties with right-wing dictators was seen as unnecessary and even unwise until noncommunist alternatives were ready to take over. The administration's struggle to implement a new policy toward the Dominican Republic and replace the brutal dic-tator Rafael Trujillo demonstrates the limits to change the administra-tion was willing to accept. Its overall policy continued to place a priority on containment and stability through the support of right-wing dictators rather than taking chances on weak and unstable democratic govern-ments that might open the door to communism.

Pendulum Swing?: Preventing Another Cuba

The turmoil and unrest in Latin America became acute in the Do-minican Republic in 1960. The tottering of Generalissimo Trujillo's re-gime appeared to provide an ideal opportunity for the Eisenhower administration to counter the criticism that it was committed to main-taining the status quo and protecting the economic and political elites that had for so long dominated the area. As Eisenhower stated in 1960, it was necessary to show that the United States did not support a "feu-dal system [that was] grinding down the masses of people."[143] Opposi-tion to Trujillo and efforts to remove him from power, however, were conducted within rigid parameters. Washington sought to prevent Tru-jillo from becoming another Batista while continuing to uphold the pri-macy of order and anticommunism for Latin America.

In February 1959, the National Security Council reasserted the pre-vention of communism as the foremost U.S. priority in Latin America. NSC 5902/1 called for the United States to provide "special encourage-ment" to the establishment of representative government, focusing on security questions. The other nations in the hemisphere played a "key role in the security of the United States. . . . A defection by any significant number of Latin American countries to the ranks of neutral-ism, or the exercise of a controlling Communist influence over their governments, would seriously impair the ability of the United States to exercise effective leadership of the Free World."[144] In responding to the challenges posed by the Cuban revolution and promoting change in

Latin America, the priorities had to remain order and anticommunism. Dulles defended military aid to all nations in Latin America and worried that if one supported only democracies, "the practical result would be that many friendly governments would collapse and Communism would take over." As Herter declared: "A more urgent value—security and survival—must take precedence over an absolute commitment to the promotion of democracy."[145] While reform appeared to be the only alternative to revolution in the hemisphere and the administration sought to establish new initiatives in Latin America, it was still bound by its bipolar Cold War understanding of events.

For most of his thirty years as dictator of the Dominican Republic, Trujillo enjoyed unwavering American support. He provided the stability Washington desired after the removal of American troops in the 1920s. With the onset of the Cold War, Trujillo had been a loyal supporter of American policies, and the Pentagon had constructed a missile-tracking station in his country. Support for his repressive regime attracted congressional critics of military aid programs, most notably Senators Fulbright, Frank Church, and Morse, who sought to cut off funding to nondemocratic governments. Relations began to deteriorate in 1958, when the Dominican Congress, in response to these criticisms, voted to end all technical and military cooperation with the United States. The next year, fearing a fate similar to Batista's, Trujillo cracked down on his domestic opposition by arresting more than a thousand persons, including pro-American members of prominent Dominican families. Moreover, finding himself the focal point of the revolutionary and antidictator tide sweeping the Caribbean, Trujillo embarked on efforts to topple the governments in Cuba and Venezuela. In an effort to isolate Trujillo and force him from power, President Rómulo Betancourt of Venezuela brought charges to the Organization of American States that the Dominican leader was guilty of human rights violations. Reports were regularly reaching Washington that pro-Castro forces were preparing to overthrow Trujillo.[146]

By 1959, the State Department was increasingly concerned that Trujillo was about to fall from power and that it had another Batista on its hands, creating the conditions for a communist takeover. Trujillo had to be replaced. The question was, again, who would succeed him? The United States wished to remove Trujillo from power without allowing a pro-Castro group to take control. The solution was to turn to members of the professional and commercial class for moderate leaders to replace the aging dictator. Unfortunately, as the embassy in Santo Domingo reported in May, these were the people that "benefitted directly from the Trujillo regime." Castro's actions frightened them, and they were unwilling to demonstrate any opposition to the government out of fear that so doing would aid radical elements. The Cuban revolution increased their reliance on the military for order and protection, and they would only support a gradual "transition to a much more democratic regime through which their personal interests would continue to be protected." The "anticipation of violence" resulting from efforts to oust Trujillo "inclines most people to 'bear the ills they have rather than fly to others they know not of.'" The final factor, the embassy emphasized, that could not be overlooked in any analysis of the political future of the Dominican Republic "is the fact that the people are not now politically educated to accept democracy as it exists in the United States." Whoever emerges after Trujillo "must be a forceful leader," albeit not necessarily as extreme as the generalissimo.[147] In December, the embassy repeated its warnings that it would be difficult to find "an experienced leadership friendly to the United States to fill the vacuum in the Dominican Republic if and when the Trujillo regime goes." The government had "effectively liquidated and enfeebled virtually all potentially rival and democratic leadership." That left the only organized opposition aligned to those caught up in the "current 'anti-dictatorship' feelings of Latin America" and provided an "opening to the radical leadership supported by Castro and . . . infiltrated by pro-Communist elements."[148]

The National Security Council took up the question of replacing Trujillo in January 1960. Under Secretary of State for Political Affairs Livingston Merchant informed the council that U.S. policy was to ensure a successor government of moderate elements friendly toward the United States while blocking any pro-Castro groups from coming to power. This task was difficult because the "moderate elements who have opposed Trujillo are widely dispersed so that the only active anti-Trujillo groups in the area at the present time are either Communist or Communist-infiltrated." There were, however, "some elements of hope in the professional, business and academic groups. Our actions in the months ahead will be designed to coalesce these groups."[149]

By the next month, the need to take action appeared urgent. Herter warned Eisenhower that the situation was deteriorating rapidly and that the "Trujillo government is acting against the moderates and may soon create a situation like that in Cuba where the opposition is taken over by wild radicals."[150] Trujillo had conducted another round of political arrests against opponents whom he charged were conspiring to overthrow his regime. In March, in an effort to persuade Trujillo voluntarily to step down from power, Eisenhower agreed to retired general Edwin Clark's proposal that he secretly visit Cuidad Trujillo (Santo Domingo) to discuss this possibility with the generalissimo. A quick downfall of the Trujillo government with no plan for its replacement would create "bloody, chaotic conditions" and "might be a prelude to the establishment of another Communist regime." Clark believed that Trujillo wished to retire but that he could not see a way to do so without endangering his wealth. Clark's scheme was based on the establishment of a trust fund from the fortune Trujillo had accumulated over the years to be administered by former Latin American and U.S. presidents for the benefit of the Trujillo family and the nation. With this protection of the dictator's wealth, it was hoped he would not see it necessary to hang onto power. The United States would then oversee the establishment of a provisional government that could provide for elections in the future and forestall "a radical, anti–United States, pro-Castro government." Trujillo, however, rejected this and other efforts to have him abdicate his power.[151]

The overriding concern remained the prevention of a Castro-type government. In March 1960, the State Department analysis of the Dominican problem reaffirmed that the goal remained working with "all possible assets to assure that a successor government comes in which is friendly to us, stable, and as 'democratic' as Dominican realities will permit it to be." But "this ideal is not in harmony with the facts as they exist and there is, therefore, imposed on us the inescapable necessity over the next year of assigning priorities between our 'negative' objective of keeping Castro out and our 'positive' objective of working towards a more democratic regime." The United States needed to ride both of these horses simultaneously for as long as possible, but it had to recognize that "if they come to a parting of the ways when a real possibility of a Castro . . . takeover of the Dominican Republic exists, we must be prepared to jump solidly on the 'stop Castro' animal." The only choice might be "between the continuation of Trujillo and the assumption of power by a Castro-oriented government."[152] The Eisenhower administration was finding that supporting right-wing dictators created long-term problems. In typical fashion, Trujillo had worked diligently to prevent any organized opposition, not just communist, to his rule. There were, therefore, few alternative leaders outside of the military that the United States could turn to when the continuation of the regime began to be threatened and American interests no longer found it useful.

The National Security Council again took up the question of how best to prevent a pro-Castro takeover in the Dominican Republic on 14 April. Allen Dulles reported that a real danger existed that Trujillo could collapse and "if there is a gap between his departure and the establishment of the new regime, the radical pro-Castro elements might have an opportunity to seize power." The moderate groups were still disorganized, and many leaders were in exile. A military junta was probably necessary to replace the dictator, but the danger existed that efforts to create a peaceful transition of power to moderate elements would be a case of too little, too late. Nixon believed that "we could not let Castro ... take over the Dominican Republic even if we had to intervene in order to prevent such a takeover." The council concurred that the United States had to be prepared to take quick action. Dillon added that if Trujillo could be removed "while pro-Castro elements were prevented from seizing power in that country, our anti-Castro campaign throughout Latin America would receive a great boost."[153] Eisenhower approved a new initiative to "forestall a pro-Castro takeover by seeking actively to bring about the early overthrow of Trujillo provided that we can make prior arrangements with an appropriate civil military leader group in a position to and willing to take over the Dominican Government with the assurance of United States support."[154]

When its own efforts to remove Trujillo failed, the administration turned to the OAS. The forthcoming meeting in August appeared to provide an excellent opportunity to obtain sanctions against the Dominican Republic and increase the pressure on Trujillo to leave. The United States recommended that nations withdraw their recognition of the government and impose an arms embargo, measures that were adopted. Eisenhower, however, thought more had to be done. He believed that it was "necessary to settle the Trujillo situation because it appears impossible to shake the belief of Latin America that the Trujillo situation is more serious than the Castro situation. Until Trujillo is eliminated, we cannot get our Latin American friends to reach a proper level of indignation in dealing with Castro."[155]

Herter proposed to the president that the OAS should become an "anti-dictatorial alliance." As long as dictators such as Trujillo ruled, they would continue their "aggressive and interventionist policy." The OAS needed to take over the situation in the Dominican Republic, force Trujillo out, and supervise elections. He saw his plan as the best means to promote a peaceful transition of power, avoid a revolution, and serve as a precedent for possible later action against Cuba.[156] In August, the United States broke relations with the Dominican Republic while it continued the arms embargo it had begun in 1958 and increased its contacts with opposition groups. Again, these new measures failed to convince Trujillo to leave voluntarily or to bring forward a group the United States could support to replace him. The dictator continued to cling to his power in defiance of Washington's wishes.

Along with these failures came new notes of caution about forcing Trujillo out of power. In October, Dillon advised Eisenhower that the time was not right for the dictator's removal "since no successor is ready to take power, and the result might be to bring an individual of the Castro stripe into power there." [157] The next month the State Department's director of intelligence wrote Herter that since the August meeting of the OAS, U.S. prestige in Cuidad Trujillo "among the moderates has been declining steadily and these moderates have been losing influence to the pro-extremists." Locally the "tide is running against the US and the longer the current impasse continues, the more unfavorable to US interests the outcome is likely to be when the Dominican pressure-cooker finally explodes." [158] Eisenhower gave the go-ahead in his last days in office for limited covert action against Trujillo, but the situation remained unresolved when he left office.

Although nobody phrased it that way, these effort to remove Trujillo were strikingly similar to the policies advocated by Spruille Braden after World War II. Yet the policy pendulum did not swing to the position of opposing all dictators. Braden and his supporters were committed to the removal of dictators without worrying about the spread of communism. Eisenhower's and Herter's actions were primarily motivated by containing Castro and preserving order in the Dominican Republic. They opposed Trujillo because his continuation in power increased rather than decreased the chances of a successful revolutionary movement. The administration's opposition to Trujillo's oppressive regime was a singular case rather than an overall shift in policy. It attempted to move beyond a reliance on dictators for order and anticommunism and sought leaders who were willing to promote reform, "rising living standards and a more equitable distribution of national income within the general framework of a free enterprise system and through peaceful evolutionary means rather than violent." [159] Whether they could be found remained to be seen. And what if the process of change created an opening for more radical forces to come to the fore in a nation? Who would prevent further Cubas in Latin America and elsewhere?

Eisenhower's time in office ran out before he was compelled to find a complete answer to these issues, and the problems were left to John Kennedy and Lyndon Johnson to confront and attempt to solve. Two different lessons were drawn from the events in Cuba and elsewhere in Latin America over the past two years: pursue reform and distance the United States from autocratic and military regimes or support right-wing dictators no matter what to block further radical nationalist and communist gains. During the difficult days of the early 1960s, the Democrats would try both approaches. The next four years would witness intense efforts by the Kennedy and Johnson administrations to find a suitable stopping point for the policy pendulum.

6 NEW FRONTIERS?
Kennedy, Johnson, and the
Return to Intervention

ohn F. Kennedy's 1960 campaign for the presidency was based on
the premise that he and the Democratic Party could do a better job
than Nixon and the Republicans in combating communism and
winning the Cold War. Kennedy charged that the Eisenhower
administration allowed a missile gap to develop that placed the United
States dangerously behind the Soviet Union in weapons and space technology and that the United States was losing the struggle for the allegiance of the Third World. More Cubas could be expected unless action
was taken quickly. It would be difficult to overstate Kennedy's fixation
with Castro and his determination, at almost any cost, to prevent another
successful communist revolution in the Western Hemisphere. Kennedy
spoke so often during the campaign about Cuba and Castro that those
who did not follow politics could be forgiven if they came to think he was
running against Fidel Castro and not Richard Nixon. Some of this over-
heated rhetoric was political payback for the Republicans' charges during the 1952 campaign that the Democrats had lost China and were soft
on communism. Still, Kennedy was determined to catch up and surpass
the Soviets on missiles and in space, take the initiative once again in the

Cold War struggles in the Third World, and deal more effectively with Castro.

Kennedy devoted his entire inaugural address to foreign policy and made it clear that his would be an activist administration. Kennedy declared, "Let the word go forth from this time and place, to friend and foe alike, that the torch has been passed to a new generation of Americans— born in this century, tempered by war, disciplined by a hard and bitter peace, proud of our ancient heritage—and unwilling to witness or permit the slow undoing of those human rights to which this nation has always been committed." He continued, "Let every nation know, whether it wishes us well or ill, that we shall pay any price, bear any burden, meet any hardship, support any friend, oppose any foe to assure the survival of liberty." The president saw the moment as a pivotal one in history. "In the long history of the world, only a few generations have been granted the role of defending freedom in its maximum danger. I do not shrink from this responsibility—I welcome it."[1]

To do all of this, new approaches to the problems of the Third World and containing communism were necessary. In the wake of the disastrous failure at the Bay of Pigs to oust Castro, Kennedy initiated the Peace Corps and the Alliance for Progress to promote peaceful change in Latin America. These programs, which represented efforts at creating change from above rather than revolution from below, focused on agrarian reforms and improvements in housing, education, and health opportunities as the best means to combat communism. The bold new rhetoric and idealism of the Alliance for Progress was, however, always connected to the administration's primary focus on containing Castro. Reform had to be balanced with military assistance to ensure stability. The programs, therefore, had from the outset an internal contradiction that the administration would be unable to escape.

The situation in Vietnam was similar. Intensive fighting between Saigon and the National Liberation Front (NLF) turned the Cold War hot, and Kennedy increased the American commitment of advisers, aid, and programs while escalating the American military presence and emphasizing new counterinsurgency measures to defend South Vietnam. When Diem failed to produce military victories or the reforms urged upon him by American advisers, the Kennedy administration abandoned his government in favor of military rule.

Central to these new efforts to win the Cold War in the Third World would be a change of policy toward right-wing regimes. Kennedy and his advisers concluded that right-wing dictators had proven to be ineffective and even dangerous bulwarks against communism. They upset political stability as much as they protected it by frustrating desires for change and democracy, and they nurtured support for left-wing and communist opposition to their rule. The problem was how to break the dependence on right-wing dictators for order and to promote change without unleashing revolutionary movements and allowing the political forces on the left to take over. This was a dilemma the Kennedy and Johnson administrations never resolved. Riding the wave of ten new governments that replaced dictators in Latin America in the late 1950s, the Kennedy administration adopted a policy of opposition to all new military governments in the hemisphere and distanced itself from authoritarian regimes. This shift was not, however, primarily motivated by an ideological commitment to support constitutional governments at all times. Rather, it was seen as a better means to contain communism, and the administration's actions never matched the bold rhetoric of the policy. Confronting the problem of the·Dominican Republic, Kennedy noted that there were three possibilities, "in descending order of preference: a decent democratic regime, a continuation of the Trujillo regime or a Castro regime. We ought to aim at the first, but we really can't renounce the second until we are sure that we can avoid the third."[2]

When the movement toward democratic governments receded in the next two years and Kennedy's policies came into conflict with the difficult problems of poverty, underdevelopment, and deeply divided societies, the administration backed away from its policy of opposition to dictatorships and began to find reasons to provide aid to military governments. In the face of the continuing challenges of revolutionary nationalism and the choice between order and social change, the Kennedy and Johnson administrations opted by 1963 to support military dictators over democratic governments they feared were slipping toward communism. This swing of the pendulum back to supporting right-wing dictators took on the now-familiar ring of the need for stability in nations that were too politically immature to defend themselves against communism. The democratic rulers the dictators replaced were believed to be weak, ineffective, and dangerously naive about or unprepared to handle communist subversion.

The repositioning of the pendulum back on the right was completed in the first months of the Johnson administration. Following the assassination of Kennedy, Lyndon Johnson backed away from much of the idealistic rhetoric and policies of the Kennedy years, particularly the Alliance for Progress. Facing continual unrest in Latin America and a rapidly deteriorating military and political situation in Vietnam, Johnson sought to impose order. The Johnson administration again turned to right-wing dictators and military rule that appeared to have worked so well in the past. In 1964, the administration made the return to the old policy evident when it supported the Brazilian generals who overthrew the government of João Goulart. The announcement of the so-called Mann Doctrine, which trundled out all the familiar rationalizations for supporting despots, soon followed. Security and stability took precedence over promoting social change and democratic rule.

By 1965, Johnson feared that unless the United States exerted a greater effort, the communists would achieve victories in the Western Hemisphere and in Vietnam that would destroy his presidency and ability to carry out his Great Society reforms at home. In the Dominican Republic, the local strongmen supported by the United States failed to create stability and block communism. Johnson decided that the United States would have to impose order through military intervention until the immediate communist threat was crushed and local forces could again act as sentries on America's frontiers. In Vietnam, however, Johnson and his advisers sought in vain for a capable general to take control of the government in Saigon and effectively prosecute the war. The success of the marine landing in Santo Domingo added to the confidence of those who advised escalation in Vietnam. Misplaced confidence in right-wing dictators and the U.S. ability to find the right ruler led officials to believe that an American solution could be found to the problem of Vietnam. Johnson's actions carried American support of right-wing dictators to its logical and tragic conclusion.

Anticommunist Manifestos

Kennedy's Task Force on Latin America, chaired by Adolf Berle, delivered a clarion call for action by the administration. The proposals in the final report to the president were based on the assumption that "in Moscow and Peiping revolutionary seizure of parts of Latin America appears to have been agreed on as an early target in the 'Cold War' now active in the Caribbean littoral." All members of the task force agreed that "the greatest single task of American diplomacy in Latin America is to divorce the inevitable and necessary Latin American social transformation from connection with and prevent its capture by overseas Communist Power politics."[3]

To achieve this goal, American policy toward right-wing dictatorships had to change. Washington must emphasize human rights, recognize that "genuine freedom necessitates advancing social and economic well-being for everyone," and uphold the "principle that governments take their legitimacy from the free assent of their peoples and therefore can from time to time be changed without force. This carries with it the general conclusion that the only legitimate governments are freely elected governments." The report emphasized that the "present ferment in Latin America, which facilitates Communist penetration, is the outward sign of a tide of social and political change the United States cannot and should not check." With the whole continent undergoing a social revolution, "American policy should aim at coordinating and supporting the widespread democratic-progressive movements throughout the area which are pledged to representative government, social and economic reform (including agrarian reform) and resistance to entrance of undemocratic forces from outside the hemisphere. It cannot stabilize the dying reactionary situation." Continued support of the "few remaining dictatorships or regimes based on plutocracies or oligarchic landowners would mean supporting doomed reactionary groups whose downfall would leave the United States in an untenable popular position."[4]

Yet now that Latin America was an active theater of the Cold War, "sufficient order must be maintained and defended if social and economic plans are to be feasible." The United States "must, therefore, seek to bring about stability at a tolerable level of social organization without leaving the transformation to be organized by Communists." Support had to be provided for economic development and to the "political parties and movements already in existence in most of Latin America" that desire peaceful social transformation and cooperation with the United States. "The foundation of the 'Alliance for Progress' must be cooperative programs for economic and social development." For most countries in the hemisphere "it is a realistic objective to bring the area within a decade into economic step with the modern world." This would necessitate abandoning the Eisenhower administration's reliance on private investment, which "amounted to saying that whatever was good for General Motors would be good for the Latin American countries." The Republican approach failed to recognize the weak middle classes in most nations, the inequitable tax structures, poor distribution of wealth, and disincentives to investments and "lent plausibility to the Communist charge that America's only interest was to enlarge her investment opportunities and markets, and to the Marxian charge that American capitalism equated to imperialism."[5]

New resources had to be marshaled from both the public and private sectors to provide investments, loans, and technical assistance. Berle summarized the new approach when he wrote Kennedy:

The present struggle will not be won, and can be lost, by opportunist support of transitory power-holders or forces whose objectives are basically hostile to the peoples they dominate. Success of the American effort in Latin America requires that at all times its policy be based on clear, consistent, moral democratic principles. I do not see that any other policy can be accepted or indeed stands any real chance of ultimate success. The forces sweeping Latin America today demand progress, and a better life for the masses of their people, through evolution if possible, or through revolution if that price must be paid. A preponderance of these forces want the resulting forms to provide liberty, rejecting tyranny whether from the right or from the left.[6]

The intellectual underpinnings of these plans were the modernization theories developed by social scientists throughout the 1950s, and particularly the work of Walt Whitman Rostow, who moved from MIT to Kennedy's National Security Council staff. Modernization theory was based on the idea that economic development followed discernible paths in Western Europe and the United States, and it could be followed by other nations. Nations went through stages of growth along a continuum from traditional societies to industrialized ones. The key was the transferal of Western value systems and economic institutions. As one economist stated, "If economic development is to proceed, value systems, attitudes, and economic institutions, relations and organizations must correspond more closely to those of the West with their greater emphasis on material gain." The goal was to transform traditional agrarian societies dominated by landed oligarchies into complex, urban, secular, industrial states.[7]

Furthermore, officials believed development was an evolutionary process that stemmed most directly from underdeveloped nations having contact with more advanced states. The United States, therefore, should involve itself in all levels of a society to diffuse its values and institutions through foreign aid, education, military training, and technical assistance. Central to this theory was economic growth. Once economic development occurred, modern ideas and institutions would spread to the social and political realms. Rostow, exhibiting the hubris of his generation, asserted in his 1960 study, *The Stages of Economic Growth: A Non-Communist Manifesto*, that once one understood the impulses under which "traditional, agricultural societies begin the process of their modernization" and how regular growth became a built-in feature of a society, an effective means to eliminate poverty and combat the attractiveness of communist thought would be available. His work, as the subtitle indicates, was designed to "constitute an alternative to Karl Marx's theory of modern history." Rostow concluded his study by claiming that "the lesson of all this is that the tricks of growth were not all that difficult." He posited five stages of growth: traditional society, the precondition period, the takeoff stage, maturity, and the final period of a diffusion of wealth on the basis of durable consumer goods. The Alliance for Progress was designed to move Latin America from the stages of traditional societies or nations in the precondition period to and through the take-off stage and into maturity.[8]

Rostow believed that the Third World was experiencing a "truly revolutionary" period, and it was this "revolutionary change which the Communists are exploiting with great energy." They believed that the "weak transitional governments that one is likely to find during this modernization process are highly vulnerable to subversion." The communists were the "scavengers of the modernization process" who knew that once the "momentum takes hold in an underdeveloped area—and the fundamental social problems inherited from the traditional society are solved—their chances to seize power decline." Rostow declared that "Communism is best understood as a disease of the transition to modernization." These conditions necessitated strong rule in the Third World until the modernization process had developed enough to allow "these societies [to] choose their own version of what we would recognize as a democratic, open society."[9]

In preparation for the announcement of the Alliance for Progress, Rostow confidently informed Kennedy that "it is likely that a good many of the countries in the underdeveloped world will, during the 1960s, either complete the take-off process or be very far advanced in it." The 1960s represented to Rostow the time of "peak historical requirement for special external aid," and he predicted that in Latin America, Argentina, Brazil, Colombia, and Venezuela would attain the level of self-sustaining growth by 1970. Success in these areas would "keep them off our necks as we try to clean up the spots of bad trouble," most notably the Congo, Cuba, and Vietnam.[10]

At the same time, the historian and special assistant to the president Arthur Schlesinger Jr. advised Kennedy that the fundamental issue to be addressed in Latin America "is the problem of the *modernization* of Latin American society." Schlesinger had written in 1960 that the most urgent issue in the Third World was how to address those nations' desire to "compress centuries of social experience into a single generation and to advance from the ox-cart to the steel-mill in a single leap." The new nations needed to develop "social discipline which will see traditional societies through the ordeal and tumult of transition." Under such circumstances, it was not surprising that these nations turned to what Schlesinger termed "heroic leadership" as "the most effective means of charging semi-literate people with a sense of national and social purpose." The question for the United States was whether these dictators, or heroic leaders, "can be reconciled to the theory and practice of democracy." His answer was that they could. Given the right conditions and a government "genuinely desirous of moving in a democratic direction" and willing to "concentrate on developing appropriate institutions," such as education, free press, honest public servants, and the supremacy of law, "heroic leadership can lead towards democracy." It was, therefore, necessary for the United States to develop programs that encouraged these institutional developments while supporting the leaders who maintained order during the transition to modernity.[11]

Schlesinger toured South America in February 1961 and reported that the chief obstacles to modernization were the landholding oligarchy, who benefited from the current economic structures and backwardness, and Castro and the communists, who sought to take advantage of the growing demands for change. The United States needed to promote a "*middle-class revolution* where the processes of economic modernization carry the new urban middle class into power and produce, along with it, such necessities of modern technical society as constitutional government, honest public administration, a responsible party system, a rational land system, an efficient system of taxation, mass education, social mobility, etc." Wearing his historian's hat, Schlesinger argued that middle-class revolutions "arise typically out of a combination of technological change, entrepreneurial initiative (often set off by foreign capital) and statist doctrine." The best current example in Latin America, he found, was Betancourt and his efforts in Venezuela. While the middle class was increasing in size and influence, "an increase reflected in the swing away from dictatorship . . . and the increasing demand for stable free government," the continuation of this trend could not be taken for granted or left to chance. The landed classes still held most of the power, and the "democratic parties . . . have thus far failed to deliver the goods to the satisfaction of the younger and more impatient members of the middle and working classes." For the United States, the "pressing need in Latin America is to promote the middle-class revolution as speedily as possible. The corollary is that, *if the possessing classes of Latin America make the middle-class revolution impossible, they will make a 'workers and peasants' revolution inevitable*; that is, if they destroy a Betancourt, they will guarantee a Castro or a Peron." [12]

To hasten the middle-class revolution, Schlesinger advised Kennedy that the United States had "to make it absolutely clear that we regard dictatorship and the suppression of popular rights as ultimately incompatible with the principles of the hemisphere." He did not want to see "an anti-dictatorship crusade" and acknowledged that there was "no doubt we will continue to have short-run dealings with dictators." Still, "no one in the hemisphere should be under any illusion how the US feels about dictatorships in the long-run. We should give every dictator a sense of impermanence." Moreover, "we should give our positive and particular support to governments which seem likely to bring about the sort of middle-class revolution we regard as favorable to our own interests— countries where social reform and economic development promise to be attained through democratic means. Full backing for the Betancourt government of Venezuela, for example, might be the best possible way of convincing aspiring Latin Americans that the democratic road to national fulfillment is both more reliable and more agreeable than the Castro road." [13]

This new direction had to be supported by substantial capital assistance from the United States with the emphasis on economic development instead of the policy of financial stabilization favored by the Eisenhower administration and the International Monetary Fund (IMF). "The IMF argument, of course, is that stabilization will ultimately bring about development by attracting foreign capital." Schlesinger flatly stated that this policy had failed to produce economic growth and "has probably retarded the middle-class revolution." Loans, capital outlays, and technical assistance needed to focus on promoting industrialization and land reform. Such a program "would enable the US to lend strength to the tendencies already emerging in Latin America toward modernity—that is, toward middle-class, educated, mobile, industrialized, urban, technically proficient society." In addition, it would demonstrate that U.S. opposition to "Castro is *not* a rejection of social revolution; it is a rejection of a leader for having *betrayed* social revolution."[14]

On 13 March 1961, Kennedy announced the Alliance for Progress, the boldest initiative ever undertaken by the United States to promote economic growth and political democracy in Latin America. "We propose," Kennedy declared, "to complete the revolution of the Americas, to build a hemisphere where all men can hope for a suitable standard of living, and all can live out their lives in freedom and dignity. To achieve this goal political freedom must accompany material progress." The president concluded that the program would "once again transform the American continent into a vast crucible of revolutionary ideas and efforts . . . an example to all the world that liberty and progress walk hand in hand."[15] The United States would create stability and combat communism through an enlightened program of capital investment, economic growth, educational reform, and the promotion of democracy. Poverty, oppression, and the lack of economic and political opportunity were the breeding ground for unrest and communist subversion and just as great a danger as Castro. Authoritarian governments needed to be replaced by viable democratic states so as to isolate communist insurgents and indigenous left-wing parties.

The Alliance was formalized in August with the signing of the Charter of Punta del Este by the United States and the nations of Latin America. The plan called for the investment of $100 billion over the next ten years. The United States was to provide $20 billion as well as technicians, economists, and advisers to ensure that the money was properly used. The administration aimed for an annual 5.5 percent growth rate in Latin America's economy. This would allow for peaceful, evolutionary change and negate the need for radical, revolutionary upheaval. As a strong and stable middle class and political center developed, the need for dictators would be lessened while the political left would be isolated. The charter reflected these ambitious and idealistic goals. The first purpose of the Alliance for Progress was the cooperation of all states to "achieve maximum levels of well-being, with equal opportunities for all, in democratic societies adapted to their own needs and desires." The accompanying declaration to the charter declared that people "working through the institutions of representative democracy can best satisfy man's aspirations, including those for work, home and land, health and schools. No system can guarantee true progress unless it affirms the dignity of the individual which is the foundation of our civilization."[16] Change had to come or, as Kennedy stated the next year, "those who make peaceful revolution impossible will make violent revolution inevitable."[17]

Modernization theory and economic development apparently resolved the dilemma of which strategy to emphasize the most, containing Castro and communism or promoting democracy. The Kennedy administration believed that with the right programs, efforts, and guidance of Latin America, it could do both simultaneously. Indeed, under modernization theory the projects were seen as closely intertwined and dependent on each other. Economic growth would foster stability, a middle-class revolution, and democratic institutions that would replace the power of the landholding elite and the dictators they relied on while isolating Castro and the communists. What could not be planned for was the quick pace of changes and heightened demands—the revolution of rising expectations—that would place the course of events outside the control of American reformers and, despite the administration's initial intentions, force Kennedy and his advisers to choose between social revolution or stability.

The Search for New Leaders

At the outset, Kennedy's new approach seemed to work well. Following the recommendations of his advisers, the president publicly aligned himself with democratic leaders in Latin America, particularly Rómulo Betancourt of Venezuela. Betancourt represented, Kennedy said, "all that we admire in a political leader." The Venezuelan leader's efforts to spread democracy "in the entire area of the Caribbean" were held up as "a symbol of what we wish for our own country and for our sister republics."[18] Administration officials saw Betancourt as "a tough, good-humored man . . . of strength, authority and inextinguishable vitality," who demonstrated that the best way to combat Castro was through democratic reform.[19] Invoking a domino theory for Latin America, administration officials believed that if Venezuela became communist, "a general explosion all the way north to Guatemala seems probable." Betancourt was viewed as the most "forward-looking, socially-minded" leader in South America. His symbolic importance to the United States was heightened by the political attacks on him from both the right and the left. Trujillo's three attempts to overthrow or assassinate Betancourt provided the Venezuelan with the stature as a fighter for democracy unsurpassed in Latin America. At the same time, Betancourt's government crushed a procommunist revolt.[20] The presidential election of 1962 and the peaceful transition of power in Venezuela were hailed as a triumph for democracy and Kennedy's policy.

When the military overthrew the government in Peru in 1962, the Kennedy administration acted decisively. Relations were broken, aid suspended, and pressure applied to force a return to constitutional government. Kennedy stated that the United States was "anxious to see a return to constitutional forms in Peru. . . . We feel that this hemisphere can only be secure and free with democratic governments." Within a year, new presidential elections were held and the military returned to the barracks.[21] It was in the Dominican Republic, however, that the new policy toward right-wing dictators was immediately applied and received its most difficult test.

From the outset, the Kennedy administration believed that "obviously Castro is a more far-reaching threat to us than Trujillo—though our indecision about Trujillo compromises our moral position." It was, therefore, "imperative that the new administration immediately demonstrate America's . . . disapproval of Trujillo's continuing dictatorship and take the lead in procuring additional sanctions. Any other course will alienate more important South American countries, and undermine our efforts against Castro."[22] The State Department reported that owing to "his savage repressive methods Trujillo has deservedly acquired the reputation as the most distasteful dictator in the Americas."[23] Kennedy and his national security adviser McGeorge Bundy rejected the venerable diplomat Robert Murphy's advice to repair relations with Trujillo. Murphy criticized opposition to Trujillo as inconsistent with past policy and support of dictators in other regions and recommended that Kennedy "walk back the cat and initiate a policy of guidance" toward democratic reforms. Bundy advised Kennedy that such an action would gravely compromise the Alliance for Progress "in the eyes of Latin Americans."[24]

As the State Department noted, "The paramount interest of the U.S. is to prevent Castro-Communist or other unfriendly elements from taking control and to insure that Trujillo is succeeded by a friendly, democratic government."[25] The assassination of Trujillo in May 1961 provided Kennedy a perfect opportunity to implement his new policy of opposition to dictatorships and the promotion of democracy. Initially, however, the administration moved with caution. Most senior officials believed that "there is no group currently capable of undertaking the task of government" and creating a successful middle-class revolution. American officials needed time to select and train groups for that work.[26] They advocated supporting the government of Jacquín Balaguer until elections could be arranged. Balaguer had been the figurehead president under Trujillo and now, with the support of the military under the command of Trujillo's son Ramfis, controlled the Dominican Republic. Balaguer and the younger Trujillo provided assurances that they would move toward a more moderate and democratic government. In June, Attorney General Robert Kennedy summarized the position of most senior White House officials when he argued that the United States "should give the current regime a chance to do what they promised to do; that it is worth our while to wait out the situation."[27]

Deputy Assistant Secretary of State for Inter-American Affairs Arturo Morales-Carrión, however, argued for supporting the democratic opposition. He noted that it would take time and assistance for these groups to create an effective government, but that was the only road to success. "Naturally they are not too well disciplined at the moment. They have lived under tyranny for thirty years." Still, he continued, "we must understand them and their position and their hopes. Otherwise we will lose all chance of bringing democracy to the Dominican Republic."[28]

For the next month, the administration debated which course of action to follow "to prevent Castro/Communism from developing or taking control of the Dominican Republic and to promote the establishment there of a friendly government as democratic as possible."[29] The State Department found that "Balaguer has given indication of good intentions with respect to liberalizing Dominican politics, but he has not yet thoroughly proved those good intentions and the past record indicates the need for considerable skepticism." The department thought that over time Balaguer would lose support and that his ability to rule would erode as his political base was "subject to attrition and . . . become[s] progressively disorganized." In those circumstances, the most likely scenario would be a takeover by the left and the establishment of a government in the Dominican Republic similar to the "Castro government of Cuba." The United States, therefore, had to work with the democratic elements, the Partido Revolucionario Dominicano (PRD), to create a stable democratic society. Balaguer should be forced to join a "de facto alliance" with the PRD or persuaded "to abdicate in favor of the PRD." It would be a mistake to back Balaguer without specific assurances, and it "should be made clear to Balaguer that we are not going to back him in any circumstances simply because there is a threat that the Dominican Republic may be Cubanized. Indeed, a failure on Balaguer's part to provide real reform is the best possible assurance that this threat will become a fact." The only other course of action, the department believed, was direct American intervention to block a takeover by the left.[30]

A special National Intelligence Estimate, prepared by the CIA in conjunction with members of the State and Defense Departments, offered a different analysis of the political situation in Santo Domingo. The intelligence community concluded that Balaguer would be able to maintain order and block any communist advances until elections could be held in 1962. Given the divisions within the democratic opposition groups, the CIA was skeptical of the PRD's ability to rule effectively and prevent the left from gaining power. It found "that there is no more than an even chance" of a successful transition to a representative political system at the moment, and the "evident danger is that, unless the anti-Communist opposition bestirs itself," the communists "may capture the leadership of popular dissidence." The CIA recommended, therefore, that the United States support the Balaguer government during the period of relaxation of political controls and development of democratic political activity in the Dominican Republic until it was sure the left could be contained.[31]

Kennedy sided with those who advocated supporting Balaguer. He cabled John Hill, the U.S. consul in the Dominican Republic, that he was "encouraged by measures President Balaguer had taken towards establishment representative democracy [in] DR and orderly exercise [of] political rights by all non-Communist elements." Kennedy noted with "particular satisfaction President Balaguer's stated determination [to] prevent pro-Communist and pro-Castro activities, pointing out danger [to] DR, US and Hemisphere if Castroists should establish themselves in DR." The president emphasized to Hill that he was to remind Balaguer that the "development of solidly based representative democracy provides [the] only alternative to either repression, which would eventually bring on revolt, or uncontrollable disorder and violence which would open way for exploitation by Castro/Communist elements."[32]

In August 1961, Kennedy outlined his reasons for supporting the current regime. "Balaguer is our only tool," the president stated. "The anti-communist liberals aren't strong enough. We must use our influence to take Balaguer along the road to democracy." He saw the issue as one of finding the right leader, not the process of establishing democratic systems and institutions: "The whole key in all those countries is the emergence of a leader—a liberal figure who can command popular support as against the military and who will carry out social and economic reform."

Unfortunately, Kennedy stated, "No such figure has emerged. We don't know who he will be." Stability was essential until that person could be found. Kennedy warned that in the Dominican Republic, "the great danger in the next six months is a take-over by the army, which could lead straight to Castro." Under those circumstances, he saw no alternative to backing Balaguer and getting all of the opposition groups to accept this until the proper leader could be found. "We must get a modus vivendi," the president insisted, "among all the forces preparing to commit themselves to democracy, instead of letting them tear themselves apart and let in the far right or far left. The eventual problem is to find someone who will symbolize the future of the island."[33]

Kennedy may have seen progress in the Dominican Republic under Balaguer, but the PRD did not, and it refused to support Balaguer until Ramfis Trujillo was removed. Hill reported that Trujillo was working to consolidate his power and exclude the democratic opposition from power. Balaguer and Trujillo could succeed, but the "economic and social conditions and residual political hatreds and economic distortions of Trujilla [sic] era argue against any expectation long-term stability."[34] The State Department worried that the continued deadlock could produce a military coup that would drive the "currently non-Communist opposition . . . to reject moderate leaders and tactics . . . and carry out their threat to seek alliance with Castro-Communists." Such occurrences "would almost certainly provoke an eventual explosion that would give the Castro-Communists ideal conditions for gaining strength and assuming power." The United States, the department informed Kennedy, should continue to support Balaguer's government but urge him to disassociate himself from Trujillo so as to guarantee continued reform and support from moderate forces.[35] By September, the fear of a coup escalated. The department argued that the current regime was transitory and that "the demand for the Trujillos to leave has become an obsession." The continued support of a government aligned with Trujillo was "*seriously jeopardizing . . . long-term interests in the Dominican Republic*."[36]

To assess the situation further, Kennedy dispatched John Bartlow Martin to the Dominican Republic to analyze the political situation and report to him. Martin returned at the end of September with a 115-page study that questioned the possibility of building a democracy in the Dominican Republic and reluctantly concluded that the United States had to continue to work with Balaguer and Ramfis Trujillo. Martin noted that the "Dominican Republic is a disheartening tragic shattered country." Trujillo's rule had destroyed the people's confidence in government, which meant that "there is little or nothing here on which to build a viable democracy." Under these circumstances, the United States needed Balaguer, "but in view of his record we must never really trust him. We should accept him with grave hidden reservations, and not get stuck with his 'democratization' window dressing. In fact, I'd prefer the word 'democracy' was never used again down there." Martin recommended continuing to work with Balaguer and Trujillo because it would "ensure stability, at least for awhile," until a "workable base can be built for a democratic constitutional government." All negotiations should take place "with the fleet just over the horizon."[37]

Kennedy concurred with Martin, but events in the Dominican Republic forced him to follow the State Department's recommendations. The Dominican middle class and democratic opposition continued to refuse to support Balaguer as long as his government included Ramfis Trujillo. In November 1961, in an effort to prevent their final ouster, the Trujillo family attempted to seize power. Kennedy, standing by his pledge to block any return of the Trujillo dictatorship, sent naval vessels with eighteen hundred marines to the waters off the coast of the Dominican Republic. In the face of strong domestic opposition and a threatened American intervention, the Trujillos fled the island. In the subsequent unrest, Balaguer was forced out of power and a Council of State, headed by Rafael Bonnelly and supported by the United States, took control. Instead of marines, the administration now sent Martin back to the Dominican Republic as the new ambassador along with a host of economists, engineers, military advisers, and social scientists to assist Santo Domingo in its preparations for elections and self-government. Despite Bonnelly's former service as Trujillo's secretary of interior and police, Martin found him to be a "decent, sensible, patriotic, and upright" man. The Dominican Republic was to become a showcase of enlightened development supported by the United States.[38]

Over the next year and a half, the United States sent $84 million in aid to the government in Santo Domingo. Despite these efforts, unrest continued. To ensure order, Martin urged Bonnelly to crack down on the opposition and the military to step up its efforts to harass and arrest suspected opposition leaders. Martin acknowledged that such methods were the antithesis of democratic reform, but he believed them necessary to support a "faltering Caribbean government that the Castro/Communists sought to overthrow."[39] In December 1962, elections were finally held. Juan Bosch, the leader of the PRD, who campaigned on a program of land reform and increased wages, won over 60 percent of the vote in the nation's first free election for president.

The administration claimed the elections demonstrated the effectiveness of its programs and its commitment to progressive reform in Latin America and marked a new day for the Dominican Republic. Bosch visited the United States in January 1963 and held a highly publicized meeting with Kennedy. The president told Bosch that "if the Dominican Republic experiment were to fail, the Communists would have gained a big victory" and promised continued economic assistance.[40] The first two years of Kennedy's Latin American policy convinced the administration that it was making significant progress in countering Castro and promoting democratic reform. In Vietnam, however, nothing appeared to be working as Kennedy encountered grave difficulties in working with the Diem regime.

Coup in Saigon

When Kennedy took office, the American effort at creating a viable, independent, and noncommunist South Vietnam was in trouble. The formation of the National Liberation Front in 1960 and the resumption of fighting exposed the weaknesses of the Diem regime and its lack of widespread support among the peasants of South Vietnam. Despite massive infusions of American military and economic aid that ranked South Vietnam fifth worldwide in total aid received, Diem was continuing to alienate most of the population while the South Vietnamese Army (ARVN) was proving unable or unwilling effectively to combat NLF guerrillas. The Kennedy administration had to find some method to overcome the fact that the Saigon government was an unpopular American creation rather than a solid Vietnamese structure. Moreover, in the wake of the debacle at the Bay of Pigs and the failure to oust Castro from power, Kennedy needed to prove his determination to fight the Cold War and retain the credibility of American commitments overseas.

Speaking to the American Society of Newspaper Editors on 20 April 1961, Kennedy made clear the connection between events in Cuba and Vietnam and his commitment to action. "We dare not fail to see the insidious nature of this new and deeper struggle," he warned the nation. "We dare not fail to grasp the new concepts, the new tools, the new sense of urgency we will need to combat it—whether in Cuba or South Vietnam." The message was the same: "The complacent, the self-indulgent, the soft societies are about to be swept away with the debris of history.

Only the strong, only the industrious, only the determined, only the courageous, only the visionary who determine the real nature of our struggle can possibly survive." Kennedy was prepared for the challenge and to use any methods necessary for victory.[41] As the president told the reporter James Reston, if Nikita Khrushchev believed that he had "no guts . . . we won't get anywhere with him. So we have to act." That meant taking the initiative in Vietnam. "We have a problem in trying to make our power credible," Kennedy stated, "and Vietnam looks like the place."[42]

Democratic societies, Kennedy believed, stood at a disadvantage in struggles with their adversaries. What was needed in Vietnam was unity and discipline to defeat the NLF. In that context, reform and adherence to democratic methods would have to yield to the discipline necessary to win the military battle. Political and social issues could wait until after the enemy was defeated. Using a frontier analogy, General Maxwell Taylor, a close adviser to Kennedy and later ambassador to South Vietnam, argued that "it is very hard to plant the corn outside the stockade when the Indians are still around. We have to get the Indians further away" before reform can begin.[43] Economic development programs may have been the answer in Latin America and ultimately in Vietnam, but with a hot war in progress it was necessary first to control the battlefield before embarking on dramatic reforms.

The American commitment to Vietnam had to be deepened because the struggle was too central to American national interests to leave to the Vietnamese. To demonstrate his commitment, Kennedy sent Vice President Johnson to Vietnam to meet with Diem and to assure him of American support. While in Vietnam, Johnson praised Diem as the Winston Churchill of South Vietnam. When asked by a reporter if he sincerely meant that, Johnson replied, "Shit, Diem's the only boy we got out there."[44] Johnson's report to Kennedy left little room for doubt as to the importance he placed on Vietnam. "The battle against Communism must be joined in Southeast Asia with strength and determination to achieve success there," Johnson wrote, "or the United States, inevitably, must surrender the Pacific and take up our defenses on our own shores." At this point, American forces were not required. People who had only recently freed themselves from colonialism "would not look with favor upon governments which invited or accepted the return this soon of Western troops." He did not, however, think extensive aid programs, military missions and advisers, and civilian technicians would create the same problem. What Vietnam required, Johnson stressed, was "the attention of our very best talents—under the very closest Washington direction—on matters economic, military and political." The vice president declared that "the basic decision in Southeast Asia is here. We must decide whether to help these countries to the best of our ability or throw in the towel in the area and pull back our defenses to San Francisco and a 'Fortress America' concept." There was no doubt that Johnson and Kennedy wanted to move forward promptly. Johnson found Diem to be "a complex figure beset by many problems." He had many good qualities, "but he is remote from the people, is surrounded by persons less admirable and capable than he." The government in Saigon was not, for Johnson, the key to the situation. That rested in Washington, D.C., and the administration's willingness to act. "The country can be saved—if we move quickly and wisely," Johnson reported. "We must have coordination of purpose in our country team, diplomatic and military. The most important thing is imaginative, creative, American management of our military aid program."[45]

Following the advice of Johnson and his other top advisers, Kennedy dramatically heightened the U.S. effort and presence in Vietnam. From 1961 to 1963 the president increased the number of American military advisers from five hundred to over sixteen thousand, initiated the Strategic Hamlet program, provided more sophisticated military equipment to ARVN, and placed a greater emphasis on counterinsurgency measures and training by the Green Berets. None of these efforts proved sufficient to turn the tide of the military battle or increase the effectiveness or popularity of the Diem regime. Indeed, by the summer of 1963, many American officials were deciding that if the war and the preservation of South Vietnam were left in the hands of Diem, the United States would suffer a tremendous defeat.

The year 1963 began with the stunning defeat of ARVN forces in the battle of Ap Bac, where the South Vietnamese military held all the advantages but still managed to snatch defeat from the jaws of victory. An NLF battalion that was surrounded by a superior number of ARVN troops supported by tanks, artillery, and airpower managed to escape because South Vietnamese commanders were unwilling to fully engage the battle.[46] By the summer, discontent with Diem's rule exploded into protests by noncommunist students and Buddhists. The most dramatic of these protests were a series of self-immolations by Buddhist monks. Diem and his brother Ngo Dinh Nhu, who headed the secret police, responded with attacks against their political enemies, massive arrests, and the closing of Buddhist pagodas. Nhu's wife likened the self-immolations to barbecues and stated that she would welcome more. Diem stubbornly refused to criticize her actions or distance himself from his brother and his brutal tactics. It was clear that Diem was unwilling to heed American advice for reform and greater tolerance.

Diem's repressive measures and the callous actions of his family were eliciting criticism in the United States of American policy and support of Diem. When Senator Frank Church (D.-Idaho) introduced a resolution calling for a cessation of all aid to South Vietnam if the persecution of Buddhists was not ended and reforms undertaken, he received secret support from the administration. The State Department sought to use the resolution as part of a plan to "persuade Diem and Nhu separately that the Nhus should leave the country for an extended period."[47] Bundy called Church and told him to "'Keep it up,' that they thought that was kind of hopeful pressure."[48] Secretary of State Dean Rusk instructed the new American ambassador to Saigon, Henry Cabot Lodge, to use the "Congressional storm warning" in his efforts to persuade Diem to yield.[49]

Yet there were few alternatives to Diem. Outside of the military, all other noncommunist groups were willing to negotiate a settlement with the NLF to end the war, a position the United States rejected. When it appeared that Diem himself had contacted the NLF through his brother and was willing to consider a neutral South Vietnam, he too became suspect.[50] Having supported Diem and his repressive government for almost a decade, Washington found that there was no political center and that it held far less leverage with Diem than it thought. That left only the military to impose order, hold the society together, and prosecute the war. After the failure of numerous efforts to convince Diem to change his course, broaden the composition of his government, and fire his brother, the Kennedy administration signaled the South Vietnamese generals that it would support a coup. The fault, according to administration officials, lay completely with Diem and not American policy. Ambassador Lodge informed Washington that the Diem government was "essentially a medieval, Oriental despotism of the classic family type" that understood "few, if any, of the arts of popular government."[51] The United States, Lodge commented, "can get along with corrupt dictators who manage to stay out of the newspapers. But an inefficient Hitlerism, the leaders of which make fantastic statements to the press, is the hardest thing on earth for the U.S. Government to support."[52] A coup was necessary to complete the U.S. effort to bring "this medieval country into the 20th century." Considerable progress had been made in "military and economic ways but to gain victory we must also bring them into the 20th century politically and that can only be done by either a thoroughgoing change in the behavior of the present government or by another government."[53]

The talk of a coup in early September, however, fizzled as the generals squabbled among themselves and worried about betrayal to Nhu's secret police. To obtain a better understanding of the crisis in Saigon, Kennedy sent Defense Secretary Robert McNamara and Maxwell Taylor to Saigon at the end of September to evaluate the military situation and Diem's rule. McNamara and Taylor reported that military progress was being made, but that it could all be lost because of the political crisis in Saigon. "Further repressive actions by Diem and Nhu," they told the president, "could change the present favorable military trends" and ultimately cause the loss of South Vietnam. There was, however, no easy answer to the problem. Their recommendation was that the United States apply selective pressure while continuing to "work with the Diem government but not support it." McNamara and Taylor, however, held out little hope that Diem would change his ways. "It is not clear that pressures exerted by the U.S. will move Diem and Nhu toward moderation," they informed Kennedy. "Indeed, pressures may increase their obduracy. But unless such pressures are exerted, they are almost certain to continue past patterns of behavior." They did not, however, recommend a coup because it was unclear who could replace Diem. Instead, American "policy should be to seek urgently to identify and build contacts with an alternative leadership if and when it appears." Again, signals were sent to the South Vietnamese military that if they hoped to salvage the war, they needed to act. The McNamara-Taylor report concluded that if the political crisis began to have a significantly negative effect on the fighting of the war, the United States would have to review its support. "Any long-term reduction of aid cannot but have an eventual adverse effect on the military campaign since both the military and economic programs have been consciously designed and justified in terms of their contribution to the war." The form of the government was not the issue. "Although we are deeply concerned by repressive practices, effective performance in the conduct of the war should be the determining factor in our relations with the GVN [Government of Vietnam]."[54]

Kennedy emphatically agreed with the last point during a National Security Council meeting that endorsed the McNamara-Taylor report as the basis for future U.S. policy. The United States, the president stated, had to "find an effective means of changing the political atmosphere in Saigon" by cutting some aid so as to improve the long-term military outlook. These actions were based on the "harm which Diem's political actions are causing to the effort against the Viet Cong rather than on our moral opposition to the kind of government Diem is running."[55] Soon after the announcement that the suspension of some forms of aid would continue, plotting for a coup resumed in Saigon. Rusk captured the reluctant support these efforts received from American officials who still worried that there was no one better to replace Diem: "If we say we are not for a coup, then the coup-minded leaders will turn against us and the war effort will drop off rapidly."[56]

On 1 November 1963, the South Vietnamese military moved against the Diem government. Diem and Nhu surrendered in exchange for safe passage out of the country. Once arrested, however, both were killed. Three weeks later, Kennedy was assassinated in Dallas and the problems of Vietnam fell onto the shoulders of Lyndon Johnson. The new president would continue the elusive pursuit of the right leader to rescue the military effort in Vietnam. Comments concerning reform and winning the hearts and minds of the South Vietnamese notwithstanding, the main purpose of the government in Saigon was to fight the war against the NLF and North Vietnam. As Johnson stated upon becoming president, "I am not going to lose Vietnam. I am not going to be the President who saw Southeast Asia go the way China went."[57] It was now the South Vietnamese military's job to do what Diem could not: stabilize the political situation in Saigon and win the war. Democratic freedoms and representative government were at best distractions and at worst impediments to the fight against communism in Southeast Asia.

An Apologia for Coups

Impatience with the difficulties of promoting democracy and reform also began to appear in Latin American policy by 1962. As political unrest mounted and American policy confronted the economic and social complexity of Latin America, policymakers emphasized the creation and maintenance of stability rather than the establishment and support of democratic institutions and rule. The rethinking of the administration's policy was first evident in the response to the military takeover in Argentina in 1962. By the next year, as the administration confronted the continued unrest in the Dominican Republic, Kennedy was in full retreat from his opposition to right-wing dictators and military governments.

When Kennedy took office in 1961, Argentina was seen as one of the leading democratic nations in South America and a model for progressive reform throughout the hemisphere. President Frondizi, who first took office in 1958, was credited with reestablishing democratic government and protecting civil liberties that had disappeared under the rule of Juan Perón. The State Department praised him for "carrying out a courageous program of stabilization and economic recovery which, although problems remain, is producing favorable results." It was a tribute to Frondizi's leadership that Argentina was "endeavoring to rise above nationalism, neutrality, sensitivity, egocentricity, and fancied rivalry with the United States for hemispheric leadership."[58]

Two related problems, however, worried American officials. First, the costs of Frondizi's economic stabilization program fell most heavily on Argentina's workers. With elections scheduled for March 1962, Frondizi was attempting to curry favor and votes from labor by establishing new programs. These efforts were "opposed by the politically active Argentine military." Frondizi's ability to bear up under the pressure of broadening his political base on the one hand and the strong military pressure on the other would "be crucial for the success of his overall program." In a prediction that was soon proved wrong, the State Department believed that Frondizi's power was secure and that the "odds run strongly against the overthrow of his Government by force, although he had become increasingly vulnerable to pressure by the military."[59]

The second problem was Argentina's policy toward Cuba. One aspect of Frondizi's efforts to gain labor votes was his unwillingness to join with the United States in criticizing Castro and endorsing OAS-sponsored sanctions against Cuba. Argentina, to the dismay of American officials, saw the disputes between Washington and Havana as a problem that "involves only the United States and Cuba." The administration sought to change this attitude because it believed that "Argentina's full collaboration is needed in the common effort to resist the encroachments of international Communism."[60] The lever to be used was Argentina's request for over $1 billion in development loans and other forms of aid.[61] Kennedy wrote Frondizi that the "penetration of this hemisphere by international communism has endangered the security of the American nations." He urged the Argentine president to support the U.S. efforts to isolate Cuba so that a "consensus might be achieved in favor of the imposition of sanctions" against Cuba.[62]

Argentina was soon, however, engulfed in a political crisis surrounding the March elections. Peronist candidates gained control of at least seven of Argentina's provinces and increased their representation in the Chamber of Deputies. Frondizi, fearing their growing power, tried to block certain Peronist candidates from taking office. The military, worried about Frondizi's ability to control the Peronists, saw this as an opportunity to seize power. As American ambassador Robert McClintock reported, the military was "incensed at what they regard as a gigantic miscalculation by Frondizi" and might just ask themselves, "'Why not go the whole hog?' 'Why not throw out Frondizi?'" Claiming that Frondizi had endangered the nation by creating a political crisis through his actions and that they were protecting the constitution of Argentina, the military ousted the president on 29 March.[63]

The Kennedy administration was divided over how to respond to the Argentine military's actions. Arthur Schlesinger wanted the president to uphold his policy of opposition to military takeovers, announce that the United States would not recognize the new government, and insist on a return to constitutional government. Under Secretary of State George Ball supported this view. Secretary of State Dean Rusk and Assistant Secretary of State for Inter-American Affairs Edwin Martin supported recognizing the new military government. Martin stated that the United States needed to "turn our attention to the need for a government in Argentina which can govern effectively and vigorously and with some degree of popular support."[64]

The military installed José Guido, the president of the Senate, as the new president, and Argentina's Supreme Court recognized him as the legal successor. Martin argued that while it was "clear that the army removed President Frondizi from the scene," the Argentine court's action meant that Guido "can be considered as the legal successor to the presidency."[65] There was, however, no doubt that the military was in charge. McClintock reported that the military officers held the "power of veto and suggestion over the civilian government." In his summary of events, the ambassador wrote that the military took over because of the "inability of President Frondizi . . . to follow a consistent policy of telling the truth which aroused many elements of the population against him and particularly the military who thought that he was either a front man for Peronism or, worse, a Judas who would eventually betray the country to Communism." McClintock portrayed the Argentine public as apathetic and saw the only hope for Argentina in his belief that "most of the Argentine military are sincere in their patriotism and in their desire to make way for a truly democratic state." The generals were friendly to-

ward the United States, staunchly anticommunist, and "should be regarded as an asset by the United States (if rightly used) and not as a liability as some people in Washington seem to believe."[66]

The military government did not disappoint its supporters in the administration. Argentina broke relations with Cuba and agreed to U.S.-
sponsored sanctions. Military rule was seen as essential until the non-
communist parties in Argentina could learn to work together. Currently,
they "provide only unsteady foundations for civilian government."[67] In
the end, despite his dislike of military coups, Kennedy agreed to recognize the new government. According to Schlesinger, he did so because
he "had a realist's concern not to place himself in positions from which
he could neither advance nor retreat." For the administration, the "prudent policy seemed to be to accept the constitutional argument, however
tenuous."[68] The overriding concern was with Castro and communism.
The desire for hemispheric unity and stability led to the abandonment
of Kennedy's opposition to right-wing dictatorships and the promotion
of democracy.

On 25 September 1963, a military coup in the Dominican Republic
ousted Bosch. This time there was no intervention by the Kennedy administration or any attempt to restore Bosch to power. From the outset,
Bosch had posed a dilemma for American leaders. They sincerely wanted
a democratic government in the Dominican Republic and hoped that
Bosch could establish a stable and effective government that would, with
U.S. assistance, begin to solve the long-standing and difficult problems
in his nation. Bosch had formed close relations with other leading reformers in Latin America, particularly Betancourt and former Costa Ri-
can president José Figueres, and was seen by most people as a liberal
nationalist. Yet in Washington doubts persisted about Bosch's true political leanings and whether he was procommunist, and there was great
concern that his rule would eventually lead to a communist takeover
of the Dominican Republic. Bosch was a frequent critic of the "'imperialistic errors' committed in the past by American business firms in
Latin America," sought extensive redistribution of land, and was known
for his idiosyncrasies and opportunism. The CIA concluded that because there was insufficient evidence to reach a definitive answer, "the
possibility that he was secretly pro-Communist or a party member could
not be ruled out." Ambassador John Martin had few doubts. He found
that "dealing with Bosch can be most difficult. He is devious, inclined
by nature to dissemble and hide his real motives."[69] The ambassador
believed Bosch was a "divider, a splitter, a schemer, a destroyer," who

made the successful development of democracy in the Dominican Republic almost impossible.[70]

By June 1963, extensive concern was being expressed about Bosch's "tolerance of communist activities in the Dominican Republic." The State Department believed his decision to allow communists to return to Santo Domingo and operate freely was "a dangerous risk, since the security forces of the Dominican Republic are not in a position to maintain proper surveillance over communist activities." Ambassador Martin reported that Bosch "made a deal with the left before the elections" not to attack them if they supported his candidacy and refrained from violence and that he "is living up to it."[71] The CIA concluded that there was "genuine concern regarding Bosch's remarkably tolerant attitude toward Communist activities." Although Bosch "understands that the security of his regime depends ultimately upon continued US support," he is more concerned about a reactionary coup than an attack by the left. He apparently considers that "his tolerance demonstrates . . . the democratic character of his rule," and he "welcomes any assistance in discrediting the traditional society and any potential support in resisting a possible military coup." His policies, therefore, could lead to a serious problem in the future. "If Bosch should fail to satisfy the expectations of the Dominican masses, or if he should be overthrown by a reactionary coup, the Communists would have an opportunity to seize the leadership of the popular revolutionary movement."[72] Given these concerns, and in conjunction with reversals in Vietnam and continued unrest in Latin America, the Kennedy administration began to rethink its policy toward right-wing dictators.

Kennedy met with Ambassador Martin immediately after Bosch was ousted from power. He said to Martin, "I take it we don't want Bosch back." Martin replied no. When Kennedy asked why not, Martin replied, "Because he isn't a President." The White House dismissed Bosch as a mere "literary figure." The problem of how to respond to Bosch's ouster was compounded by a military coup on 3 October in Honduras. Secretary of State Rusk announced that the United States was cutting off all economic and military aid to both the Dominican Republic and Honduras. These steps appeared to be a continuation of the policy of opposing all new military governments in the hemisphere, but they were not. Kennedy refused to state categorically that the United States would not recognize these governments, and Rusk's statement noted only that under existing conditions there could not be normal relations, leaving the door open to a change later.[73]

Caught in the midst of the crisis in Saigon and the South Vietnam-ese military's planning to overthrow Diem, supporting democracy in the Dominican Republic was no longer a high priority. The emphasis was on controlling subversive activities. The Department of State saw the Dominican Republic as one of the five countries in Latin America where communists had the greatest potential for success. Bosch was faulted for failing to make "appreciable progress toward [a] solution of the country's political and economic difficulties." He was, therefore, held responsible for his demise. "Although Bosch began with a strong popu-lar mandate," the CIA concluded that "he did not consolidate his elec-toral victory by decisive and constructive action." He alienated the upper class and large landowners with his reforms and the military by "his re-fusal to adopt a strong anti-Communist posture." Although there was no easy solution to the economic difficulties that faced the Dominican Re-public, at least the military junta "has taken a strongly anti-Communist and anti-Castroist position and has acted to curb Communist and other extreme leftist activities."[74] In December 1963, the Johnson adminis-tration recognized the military regime.

The relaxation of the Kennedy administration's opposition to author-itarian governments was indicated by Assistant Secretary of State for Inter-American Affairs Edwin Martin in a 6 October 1963 article in the *New York Herald Tribune*. Martin began by providing the time-honored public assurances of U.S. support for democracy and opposition to the overthrow of constitutional governments which was most recently re-affirmed under the Charter of Punta del Este. But the guiding principles of policy had to be how the United States "can assist the peoples of other sovereign nations to develop stable political institutions" rather than "theoretical notions of the manner in which men should and do operate in a complex world." The most important considerations were a "gen-uine concern with an overturn of the established order, fear of left-wing extremism, [and] frustration with incompetence in an era of great and ris-ing expectations." These were all "formidable obstacles to stable, con-stitutional government—especially in countries where the traditional method of transferring political power has been by revolution or coup d'etat."[75]

The necessary ingredient for stability was a respect for the benefits of political legitimacy that depended on an "educated middle class with a stake in the country, and hence in peace and order and democracy." In many nations, such a group did not yet exist. During the transition to a modern state only the military could fill this void. "To tip the balance even more in favor of established civilian governments, we also must assist the military to assume the more constructive peacetime role of maintaining internal security." Martin recognized that "military coups thwart the will of the people, destroy political stability and the growth of the tradition of respect for democratic constitutions, and nurture Communist opposition to their tyranny." But what else, short of unilateral military intervention, could the United States rely on to maintain order? The governments had to be accepted as necessary short-term solutions in certain nations given the problems of development. In these instances, the United States should not oppose military governments but work with them and use its "leverage to keep these new regimes as liberal and considerate of the welfare of the people as possible" and press for new elections as soon as conditions would permit. In the recent military seizures of power, Martin found there to be "a novel and notable absence of reprisals against the leaders of the ousted regimes. The firing squads or prison guards, so characteristic of earlier political upheavals in Latin America, have been eschewed." For this the United States could rightfully take much credit because of influences "brought to bear through all means open to us, to produce moderation and a prompt return to constitutional and democratic regimes." In his conclusion, Martin stated that he feared he would be criticized for writing "an apologia for coups." Rather, he argued, what he presented was not an apology but a realistic assessment of the role of the military and an understanding of the "Anglo-Saxon notion that democracy is a living thing which must have time and soil and sunlight in which to grow." He believed it was unfortunate but true that the time and conditions necessary for the growth of democracy in Latin America depended on the military protecting "traditional order."[76]

Kennedy was asked on 9 October if Martin's statement represented a reversal of his policy on dictatorships. The president responded that there was no change; he was still opposed to military coups and committed to democratic governments and the Alliance for Progress. "Dictatorships," he stated, "are the seedbeds from which communism ultimately springs up." But Kennedy refused to renounce Martin's article or repudiate his arguments. He was able to straddle the fence by claiming that Martin was "merely attempting to explain some of the problems in Latin America, why coups take place, and what problems they present us with."[77]

Martin's article, however, represented much more than the president allowed for in his press conference, as was made evident two days later in confidential testimony by State Department officials to the Senate Foreign Relations Committee. The committee was concerned about the recent coups in the Dominican Republic and Honduras and the apparent shift in United States policy. Did Martin's article mean the administration would no longer oppose military governments and employ sanctions to force a return to constitutional rule? Was the United States now ready to provide support to such regimes? Senator Wayne Morse charged that the administration was only paying lip service to the policy of opposing military coups and that the president's statement did not add up to much "by way of being definitive in nature." Two constitutional governments that had recently been overthrown in the Dominican Republic and Honduras were currently in exile. If the administration wanted to back up its statements, Morse declared, and "if [it] want[ed] to throw a diplomatic bomb that would leave no room for doubt as to our intention to explode support to military juntas," it would recognize the two governments in exile. Morse told Under Secretary of State George Ball that he did not think the administration was "selling [its] bill of goods that you are against military juntas when you let two constitutional governments in exile go down the drain."[78]

Ball responded that the maintenance of constitutional government remained "a prime objective of policy." He then turned to the readily available argument of nonintervention to defend the administration's actions. "There is always a problem," Ball noted, "in situations of this kind as to the extent to which we interfere on a unilateral basis without the full support of the other American states in what is an internal situation." Ball insisted that the administration was taking actions against the new governments and that he was confident that in the Dominican Republic "we will be able to bring about the necessary steps toward a restoration of constitutional government." Sterling Cottrell, deputy assistant secretary of state for inter-American affairs, added that Morse's argument was over methods and not principles or intentions. "We recognize that this ancient pattern of coup replacing coup and dictatorship replacing dictatorship, has a very stultifying effect on every one of those countries." The administration, he asserted, was still committed to breaking this pattern but believed it was best done by focusing "on our main objective, the restoration of representational government, without focusing on the individuals involved." In other words, the United States should cooperate with the military governments rather than defending the governments in exile.

Morse disagreed that the debate was only about tactics. If governments driven into exile ceased to be recognized, there was little to deter coups. "I just don't think that the military coups can be allowed any longer to follow this course of action and think when they overthrow the government the government is dead." Ball noted that no one was happy with the increasing military takeovers. The problem was that Latin America was "a condition and not a theory. What we are faced with is that in more countries than not, there are weak governments, that there are governments which are trying to govern under great pressure from a variety of interests, some from the left, some from the right, and that they are not very brave or bold when it comes to taking positions on matters that affect other nations within the system."

Ball argued, therefore, that the United States could not afford to turn its back on the governments that replaced these weak and ineffective democracies: "The consequences of diminishing our assistance to these countries, in effect the rejection of the idea of trying to work with them, a substantial reduction in the kind of resources that we have available to encourage the trends in the right direction would . . . hold dangers for us that are very considerable indeed." The military forces, Ball thought, were often the best option available. The United States had to "work with materials which are in most cases imperfect, trying to make the best out of a situation which is anything but simple or easy." Thus, given this lesser-of-two-evils approach, it required "that resources be available for this and that we do the best we can." The United States could still assert strong leadership but had to take care not to bump up against the historical aversion to "American interference in their internal affairs . . . which can have a negative effect and can play into the very powers and pressures we are trying to resist." U.S. pressure on the military governments would be exploited by the antidemocratic forces, and recognition of a government in exile would make that government appear as "an agent or stooge of the United States," selected by Washington to do its bidding. The best course was to work with the dictators while "insisting on the principles of constitutionality which do not at all preclude the restoration of a government by an election" but did not make it contingent for cooperation. Ball believed this approach placed the United States "in a very much better position so far as the impact on the psychology of the people that we are trying to work with is concerned."

Other senators joined Ball in supporting the change in policy. George Smathers of Florida warned that it was dangerous to tie policy too tightly to a position of always supporting constitutional governments and opposing military coups. A military overthrow of Cheddi Jagan in British

Guiana, who was duly elected, would be welcome. "He had turned the resources and propaganda of his country against us." A set policy of opposition to coups would lock the administration into a position "where you couldn't give them any aid, the new crowd," even though they were friendly to the United States. He argued that the military in Peru blocked the left from taking power and turned "the country in the direction of democracy, and with certain limitations we could finally bring about a democratic system which would be friendly to us." Senator Frank Lausche of Ohio added that the fall of Bosch in the Dominican Republic was no loss. It was a situation, he claimed, in which the "Communists are breaking through . . . and the businessman and the peasant and the professional man and the religious man uniformly begin to complain." Yet "Bosch, a sentimentalist, a romanticist, a poet, completely devoid of realistic knowledge that is necessary sometimes in government, does nothing about it." The issue, Lausche believed, was whether the United States should allow the "Communists to penetrate and take over or is firmness of approach going to be needed." Lausche found Ball correct when he argued that the "objective of procuring a situation where constitutional selection of officials will be made without saying it must be Bosch is a far better approach."

Ball reiterated his optimism about the Dominican Republic, based on his assessment of the ruling junta as "men of reasonably good character," returning to a constitutional government. But there was a problem. The people had lived "for so many decades under . . . authoritarian rule that they really have had no experience in the adult lifetime of most of the active people in the Dominican Republic . . . with constitutional government." He found it "only normal" that they would "make mistakes." In a vast understatement, Ball noted that the situation "will continue uneasy for a long time to come, even though constitutional government may be resumed." Flexibility was the new rationale for supporting dictatorships. Thus policy had already changed when President Kennedy was assassinated in November 1963 and Johnson became president.

The Mann Doctrine

Lyndon Johnson was always skeptical about the Alliance for Progress and Kennedy's policy toward Latin America. CIA director John McCone noted after his first meeting with Johnson in November 1963 to discuss foreign policy that he "received . . . the first 'President Johnson tone' for action as contrasted with the 'Kennedy tone.' Johnson definitely feels that we place too much emphasis on social reforms; he has very little tolerance with our spending so much time being 'do-gooders.'"[79] Johnson saw and understood the tremendous upheaval the Alliance was fueling and sought to provide greater stability before it was too late. Johnson asked Thomas Mann to reorient Latin American policy. A fellow Texan and longtime State Department expert on Latin America, Mann was made director of the Alliance, appointed as a special assistant to the president, and promoted to assistant secretary of state for inter-American affairs.

Mann shared Johnson's skepticism concerning the Alliance's ability to create peaceful revolutions. He believed that massive aid programs only created false hopes. Mann recalled that he saw himself as a "realist and pragmatist." His disagreement with Kennedy's Alliance for Progress stemmed from "a difference of opinion whether we should, in effect, espouse revolution without defining what kind of revolution we're talking about. I think in the Latin American mind, one who talks about revolution is understood to be saying that he favors violence in the streets and disorders. I thought we should favor orderly evolution and be careful of what we said and orient our program so that that kind would be made clear." Moreover, Mann had a positive view of the military in Latin America. They "considered themselves the guardians of the independence and order of the hemisphere. Most people would say that this makes them ultraconservative." Mann disagreed. He saw them "on the whole, [as] a pretty decent group of people."[80]

Policy soon reflected these attitudes. Military funds received priority over other forms of assistance, and Johnson, while maintaining a rhetorical commitment to the Alliance for Progress, allowed the amount of money allocated to decline steadily.[81] In conjunction with the third anniversary of Kennedy's call for the Alliance for Progress, the Johnson administration convened a meeting of all American diplomatic representatives to Latin America in Washington, D.C. In a private speech to all ambassadors on 18 March 1964, Mann outlined the reversal of policy from the early days of the Kennedy administration. He never once mentioned the Alliance for Progress. Instead of actively opposing rightist and military dictatorships through nonrecognition and the cessation of aid, which he declared involved Washington in the internal affairs of those nations, the United States would base its recognition policy and support of Latin American governments on a case-by-case basis. The determining factors would be what Mann termed the four basic fundamentals of American policy: the fostering of economic growth, the protection of the $9 billion in United States investments, nonintervention in the internal affairs of the Latin American republics, and opposition to the spread of communism. Under these terms, economic growth was not to be tied to social reform, and there was no need to demonstrate a preference for democratic governments over authoritarian regimes. When asked by John Bell, ambassador to Guatemala, whether this new policy meant that there would no longer be "good guys or bad guys" in the determination of American policy, Mann said that was correct.[82]

Mann's comments were reported the next day in the *New York Times* by Tad Szulc. The administration made little effort to deny the new policy. Gordon Chase reported to Bundy that the *Times* report was "fairly accurate. . . . Apparently, somebody took notes and ran out and gave them to Tad Szulc." Chase assumed that the policy had not changed, "at least publicly," and wondered what could be done to "beat down this unfortunate story." Bundy noted it was an issue for Mann to handle himself.[83] The State Department issued a statement the next day proclaiming that the U.S. "devotion to the principles of democracy is a historical fact." The issue, however, was not the U.S. attitude toward democracy but its policy toward dictatorships. On that point, the department spokesperson, Richard Phillips, would state only that decisions would be "guided by the national interest and the circumstances peculiar to each situation as it arises." Communist governments fell under a separate category and were always to be opposed.[84]

Unfavorable press coverage of the shift in policy continued for the next week, prompting Mann to request permission to respond by making some speeches on the topic of Latin American policy. Bundy recommended to Johnson that he approve the speeches after review by the White House "so that it can be clear that these are official U.S. statements." There was a risk that if "these speeches aren't skillfully done, they will be turned against us by people who should be our friends." Mann assumed "that all our trouble comes from a few far-left-wingers." Bundy concurred that "a lot of it does," as demonstrated by Szulc, but "a lot comes also from honest misunderstanding." It was important to fight back because it was necessary to hang onto the support of "men like [Luís] Munoz and Betancourt, and the sensible press." White House review would allow Bundy to watch over the drafts and "make sure that they do the job Tom has in mind but with a minimum danger of a boomerang effect." Bundy signed his memo to the president, "Special Ambassador to the *New York Times* and *Washington Post*." Johnson agreed to the national security adviser's idea.[85]

The speech that finally emerged was delivered by Mann on 7 June 1964 as the commencement address at Notre Dame University. Bill Moyers wrote Bundy that he "admire[d] Tom for trying to introduce *reason* into the debate on The U.S. and Representative Democracy in Latin America," and found that his "arguments are sound." He remained concerned, however, that the speech "is likely to be interpreted as a labored attempt to justify what has already been interpreted as Tom's 'hard line.'"[86] Moyers was apparently unaware that explaining the new "hard line" was the purpose of the speech. The title of Mann's talk was "The Democratic Ideal in Our Policy toward Latin America," but he devoted the longest section to defending the support of military governments. While he declared that it was "our firm policy to discourage any who conspire to overthrow constitutionally elected governments," Mann insisted that the United States should not place itself "in a doctrinaire straightjacket of automatic application of sanctions to every unconstitutional regime in the hemisphere with the obvious intention of dictating internal political developments in other countries." Rather, "each case must be looked at in the light of its own facts." It was "understandable that all of us become impatient with the rate of progress" toward democracy in the hemisphere. In many nations "democracy seems at times to take two steps forward only to temporarily be pushed back a step." He asserted, however, that the cause of freedom in nations ruled by military dictators remained alive. By contrast, he found that in Cuba the "light of democracy has temporarily been extinguished." To illustrate his point, Mann argued that if the United States was "unconditionally committed to the support of all constitutional governments under all circumstances, we would have been obliged to do everything within our power to bring about the overthrow of Castillo [Armas] and to restore a Marxist-Leninist to power" in Guatemala.[87]

The announcement of the Mann Doctrine prompted Supreme Court justice Arthur Goldberg to send Johnson a quote from John Stuart Mill on interventions. Goldberg was sure the president would agree "that this statement is particularly appropriate at the present time and to our present occasions." Mill stated: "The doctrine of non-intervention, to be a legitimate principle of morality, must be accepted by all governments. The despots must consent and be bound by it as well as the free states. Unless they do, the profession of it by the free countries comes to this miserable issue, that the wrong side may help the wrong, but the right side must not help the right. Intervention to enforce non-intervention is always rightful, almost moral, if not always prudent. Though it be a mistake to give freedom to a people who do not value the boon, it cannot but be right to insist that if they do value it, they shall not be hindered from the pursuit of it by foreign coercion."[88] As he attempted to explain his policy in Vietnam, Johnson would often express these same ideas, albeit in different language, in the next year.

A Fine Fellow in Brazil

The Mann Doctrine was immediately applied to the military overthrow of the government in Brazil. United States relations with Brazil had steadily declined since the end of World War II. By 1961, they were marked by mistrust and a growing concern in Washington over Brazil's increasing independence in the Cold War and reform efforts at home. Indeed, the more representative the Brazilian government became, as constitutional democracy took root and workers and peasants organized and participated in politics, the worse relations with the United States became. Because Brazil was the largest nation in South America in size, population, and potential for economic growth, it demanded American attention. The Kennedy administration sought to make it a cornerstone of the Alliance for Progress. The Bureau of Inter-American Affairs of the State Department believed that it was "extremely important that the United States take the initiative to quickly establish good relations with the new Brazilian administration" by extending economic assistance and other forms of aid.[89] The administration initially thought that the new Brazilian president, Jânio Quadros, who took office the same month as Kennedy, would closely align Brazil with U.S. efforts to generate economic growth and reform in Latin America while isolating Castro. This confidence was based in large part on Quadros's apparent willingness to implement an austerity program supported by the International Monetary Fund to combat Brazil's growing economic problems and to reverse the trend toward economic nationalism in his country. Quadros's favorable comments about Cuba caused some concern, but American officials saw them as election-year efforts to gain support on the left. As one NSC staff member argued, Brazil should be built up "as a counter to Cuba in Latin America" because of its great potential. Although "Quadros may be difficult to deal with . . . deal with him we must, or lose a great opportunity to thwart Castroism in the area."[90]

Quadros, however, had his own agenda. He sought to establish a policy independent of the United States and set out to develop a foreign policy based on the principles of "development, disarmament, and decolonization." Brazil, Quadros believed, needed to establish closer relations with the other nations of the developing world. Its international concerns were economic, and rather than looking to the East or the West in the Cold War, Brazil's policy should be that of the South. Finally, Quadros believed Brazil had to stand for nonintervention and self-determination for all nations. This meant supporting Castro and opposing any efforts to impose sanctions against Cuba. To demonstrate that Brazil would not be dictated to by the United States, Quadros reestablished relations with the Soviet Union, presented Brazil's highest medal to Che Guevara, and invited Yugoslavia's communist leader Tito to visit his country.[91]

Unrest and division continued in Brazil as American diplomats nervously watched to see what steps the government would take in response to offers of economic aid. It was apparent to the embassy in Rio de Janeiro that conservatives and the military in Brazil distrusted Quadros and were working to undermine his authority. Unexpectedly, Quadros resigned from office right after the signing of the Charter of Punta del Este in August 1961. The CIA believed that the president's move was made "in the expectation of provoking a strong manifestation of popular support, in response to which he would return to office in a better position against his opponents." If so, the plan backfired. There was no popular upsurge to return Quadros to office, and an effort by the military to block Vice President João Goulart from assuming the presidency failed.[92] Kennedy agreed with the advice of the American embassy in Rio that the United States refrain from issuing a statement supporting constitutional process versus a military solution because in the "present situation in Brazil it would constitute clear endorsement Goulart cause which would be deeply resented by those of our friends who support effort of military to exclude Goulart from Presidency on ground his known Communist sympathies."[93]

Goulart set out an agenda of land reform, restrictions on the annual profits that could be taken out of the country, and the extension of democratic rights and the legalization of the Communist Party. American officials treated his coming to power as a crisis. The embassy defended the military's efforts to prevent Goulart from taking office. "Although ostensibly acting in contravention of constitution," the armed forces "were beyond doubt sincerely motivated by desire preserve ultimate democratic values." In contrast, Goulart's political past "could scarcely be less promising from US point of view." It would be necessary to see if he could "live down his fellow-traveling past and establish amicable basis for continuing US-Brazilian relations."[94] The CIA characterized Goulart as an opportunist who "has a long history of working with Communists in an effort to increase his political strength." His early actions appeared to favor communists in Brazil, and it was possible "that we may be witnessing the early stages of an attempted slow-motion coup in which Goulart, wittingly or unwittingly, is paving the way for effective Communist infiltration designed as a prelude to an eventual takeover."[95] The new American ambassador to Brazil, Lincoln Gordon, reported in October that "there can be no doubt as to Goulart's past record of service to Communist cause in Brazil or his continuing hospitality to Communists and their friends in present administration."[96] It was widely believed in Washington that "the Communists will benefit by the tolerance not only of Goulart but of many other Brazilian political leaders."[97]

In 1962, the administration experienced a brief period of hope that relations with Goulart would prove workable. The Brazilian president was invited to visit the United States in April, and American officials hoped to "persuade Goulart that cooperation with us is in his and Brazil's best interest." Brazil was the most important nation in Latin America and the nation "in which are centered all the economic, social and strategic problems to which the Alliance for Progress is a response." It was critical for the United States, therefore, that Goulart "clearly understand the directions of our policy in Latin America and elsewhere and what we hope to accomplish."[98] Gordon reported that Goulart's administration "has succeeded in establishing status of relative confidence which seemed almost impossible a few months ago." The ambassador found Goulart to be following a moderate economic course, and the outlook for Brazil was more optimistic than "the Embassy had reason to anticipate several months ago. Goulart has proven himself clever politician able and willing [to] win over long-term opposition on basis moderate, responsible-sounding objectives while still claiming loyalty to his popular political base."[99] Schlesinger recommended that Kennedy use the visit to reaffirm his position that the United States not only welcomed "New Frontier governments in Brazil and elsewhere in Latin America but regard[ed] such governments as indispensable to the success of the Alliance." The contest in Latin America was not between the status quo and communism but "between democratic revolution and Communist revolution."[100]

In two conversations, Kennedy and Goulart discussed U.S. policy in the hemisphere, the labor movement in Latin America, American investments in Brazil, and Goulart's efforts to promote development while controlling inflation. On all accounts, the two leaders appeared to be in accord, and American officials were particularly pleased by Goulart's criticisms of Castro and Cuba. Kennedy assured Goulart that the United States would assist him in his efforts to control inflation and would "continue to support President Goulart and his government." The president said he realized "that Brazil has had internal difficulties, and that it is a complex matter to maintain the proper balance between stability and deflation on the one hand and growth and development on the other." [101]

Yet within three months, the negative assessments and fears of Goulart had returned. The resignation of Brazil's prime minister and cabinet in June, the State Department reported to Kennedy, "resulted in a renewal of the struggle, initiated in the August 1961 crisis, between Leftist forces supporting President Goulart and the Moderates and Conservatives who control Congress." Goulart was seeking greater power, and the "far Left 'compact' group of the Labor Party is exercising an inordinate influence, Communist and fellow-traveling support is welcome, even courted, and there has been an increase of Communist sympathizers in the ranks of Cabinet aides." These developments had "revived dormant fears of Goulart's intentions to maneuver a Left-wing takeover, not only among civilian centrists but more important in military circles." Goulart's discussions of democratic reforms "superficially resembling Alliance for Progress policies" was little more than demagoguery. "Goulart's understanding of economic or broader policy problems seems virtually nil." Brazil's economic crisis was growing progressively worse, and Goulart was apparently "willing to bring the country to the verge of anarchy." His actions, whether intentional or not, were opening "the way for a Leftist though probably not orthodox Communist takeover." The main group restraining Goulart from a complete revolutionary change was the armed forces. The State Department concluded, however, that "there is a danger . . . that the President may be able to neutralize his military opposition through a series of command changes and legally emasculate the capability of this bulwark against a Leftist takeover in Brazil." [102]

The Kennedy administration decided in December 1962 to confront Goulart in hopes of influencing him "toward a more moderate and more constructive political course, including much heavier reliance on center forces in the country willing to collaborate with him if he acts responsibly." In addition, to counter Goulart, contacts with the military were increased and planning begun for the overthrow of the government. The administration sought to continue "to encourage Brazilian moderate democratic elements in Congress, armed forces and elsewhere who advocate democratic and foreign policies we can support." The military was "obviously the key element . . . as ultimate political censors and guardians of constitutional system."[103] Ambassador Gordon advised the State Department that good relations with the military were essential and that greater aid "would increase the influence they have on shaping of regime and would also increase their awareness they could count on us in emergency." The ambassador realized that the measures he was proposing would aid the military in carrying out a coup and would, therefore, act "as precedent . . . with other countries." He believed, however, "that size and importance of Brazil, extreme criticality of situation and importance of exerting maximum influence to prevent major turn toward bloc make it necessary to formulate our policies toward Brazil on their own merits."[104] The CIA had reached the conclusion that Goulart was a man "whose inclinations and associations are populist and leftist," and it feared that he would be unable to withstand the pressures from the left. There was a real "danger that he will become a captive of the left" or attempt to establish his own left-wing regime.[105]

Military aid and the shipment of military supplies were increased throughout 1962 and 1963, but all other assistance to the central government was ended in June 1963. Alliance for Progress funds were instead sent directly to individual states in Brazil led by governors Washington saw as anti-Goulart and pro–United States. Termed the "island-of-administrative sanity" policy, the purpose was to increase tensions within Brazil, destabilize Goulart's government, and force Goulart to change course or openly rely on the left. The latter choice might prompt the military to act.[106]

Gordon reported in August 1963 that Goulart was increasingly relying "on mass demagogy . . . in open class warfare." His advisers ranged from "irresponsible adolescent opportunists through fellow travelers to probable communists," and no moderate voices remained to balance policy.[107] A 1963 National Intelligence Estimate summarized U.S. concerns. "Under Goulart," the report concluded, "Communists and their sympathizers have achieved a strong position from which to carry on a continuing expansion of influence over Brazilian policy." All efforts at moderating his course of action had failed. Even if American aid were "provided Brazil in the quantities needed, we believe there is a good chance that the course of Brazilian politics will continue moving toward leftist solutions for its internal difficulties." The "profound political and economic instability of the country and the strong positions being won by Communists, extreme leftists, and ultranationalists will tend to push the country toward more radical departures in domestic and foreign policies. This could lead ultimately to the establishment of an extreme leftist regime with a strongly anti-US character."[108] In the cautious language the State Department used for discussing support of a military coup, the United States now had to "promote and strengthen in all sectors of Brazilian life democratically-oriented forces which can restrain undemocratic or anti-democratic excesses by Goulart or his extreme leftist or ultranationalist supporters . . . and facilitate the most favorable possible succession in the event that a crisis of regime leads to Goulart's removal."[109]

In January 1964, the Johnson administration drew up "A Contingency Plan for Brazil" that examined the various possible directions the Brazilian political situation might turn. While the paper's introduction contained the disclaimers that the study "should not be construed as predicting that the Goulart Regime . . . will be overthrown" or that "it is the policy of the U.S. Government to attempt to bring about the overthrow of the Goulart Regime," an overthrow of the government by the military was welcomed. In fact, the State Department believed that was the only viable contingency. "Any change in the existing constitutional democratic regime," the report stated, "is highly unlikely if such a change is opposed by the bulk of the armed forces." The paper was, therefore, more of a preparation for a coup that U.S. officials supported than a serious examination of differing possibilities and a caution that the United States should not be caught associating with any plotting lest that "be used as a pretext by Goulart to strengthen his own powers." Four possibilities were discussed: an "Extreme Leftist Revolt," a "Democratic Revolt against Excesses of Regime," the "Removal of Goulart by Constructive Forces," and a "Gradual Extreme Leftist Takeover." A revolt by the left was dismissed as the "least likely" scenario of those presented, because of military opposition, and was quickly passed over. A democratic revolt was possible, but it implied "the possibility of civil war." In such a case the United States would "carefully abstain from giving support to Goulart" and seek ways to aid the democratic forces. Any efforts toward this path should be discouraged by U.S. officials, and "planning and preparation against this contingency should be undertaken." A gradual takeover by the extreme left was a danger that it would be "extremely difficult" to counter effectively, but it was a real possibility. Only forces from within could prevent this growing danger under Goulart's rule. The administration concluded, therefore, that it had to support the removal of Goulart by constructive forces, that is, the military, to return "more moderate and democratic elements in Brazil" to power. "No problem would be raised for U.S. policy in the event of a constitutionally contrived change, with Goulart 'persuaded' to withdraw." This could include "an interim military takeover." In that circumstance, the United States "should take a constructive friendly attitude . . . being prepared to give quick support and assistance to the new regime as soon as it is sufficiently committed to a return to democratic processes."[110]

In March 1964, two weeks before the military coup in Brazil, American officials met in Washington. Gordon used this opportunity to discuss what course of action the United States should follow after the military removed Goulart. He reported that "the only thing worse than the economic situation is the political situation." He argued that "a communist takeover is conceivable" and spoke in alarmist terms of the urgency for action before Goulart established a left-wing regime. Gordon disagreed with those who saw the issues as merely domestic matters that concerned only Brazilians or believed the United States should take a hands-off approach to Brazil "until the Brazilians behave." Following such suggestions "would be tragic because it does not take into account the fact that Brazil is a multiple society and that there are many segments who are with us and whom we should not ignore." Specifically, Gordon meant the military. "Our relations with the Brazilian military are good. This is very important." Brazil's generals needed to be assured of the American position.[111]

All the difficulties in relations between Washington and Rio were laid at the feet of Goulart. He was blamed for the economic crisis that beset Brazil and for "creating a situation of basic political instability and polarization of the political extremes." In this situation, increased military aid was recommended and approved by President Johnson. "The military," the Department of State believed, "has traditionally been, and continues to be, a decisive voice for moderation, constitutionalism and democracy in Brazil." The generals, who administration officials knew were plotting a coup against the constitutional president of their country, were described as "both constitutionally-minded and friendly to United States objectives." In the event of unrest and disorder, "it would be of utmost importance to the United States that the military have both the means and the training to control violence and prevent communist exploitation of the situation."[112]

Goulart's worst sins were his agricultural reforms, efforts to increase the power of workers and peasants, and economic nationalism. Goulart was criticized for blaming "Brazil's financial woes on the unfavorable terms of trade and . . . expand[ing] the government's role in the economy as a remedy. Thus, for example, he established a state monopoly on crude oil imports and advocated similar monopoly on foreign exchange transactions and the coffee trade." His actions "brought a decline in business confidence and slowed economic growth." These actions were fueled by his "increasingly nationalistic and 'independent'" foreign policy and his belief that Brazil was "entitled to great power status." He maintained relations with Cuba and all of the Eastern bloc countries except East Germany and was developing trade with China. Finally, he was "unable or unwilling to take the necessary self-help measures which would have permitted the Alliance to play an effective role."[113] Thomas Mann's speech at this meeting, discussed above, provided Gordon with the go-ahead to make what he saw as the necessary assurances to the Brazilian military.

The coup began on 31 March 1964 and was immediately supported by the Johnson administration. A U.S. carrier task force was secretly dispatched toward Brazil in case the Brazilian military needed assistance. None was necessary. Goulart quickly fled the capital, and the military was in full control within two days. The CIA reported on 1 April that the ousting of Goulart came as the result of the "political uncertainty, critical economic problems, and increasing Communist influence" in the government. Goulart's "ineptness . . . demagogic maneuvering in favor of leftist extremists . . . were both cause and occasion for his ouster." The administration believed that the most immediate and important benefits the military government would provide were economic. "The change in government will create a greatly improved climate for private investment, which had dropped off sharply due to Goulart's statist policies." Amazingly, the agency concluded that "Brazil's democratic development has probably been strengthened in the long run" by the coup. The logic for this position was found in the bipolar worldview of the Cold War. The CIA concluded that the military's motive for overturning the constitutional government "was to a large extent a reaction against the growing Communist influence in Brazil." Any move that blocked what the United States saw as a possible communist takeover was by definition a long-run defense of democracy.[114]

The first discussion in the National Security Council of the coup focused on whether any pockets of resistance remained and the question of how the generals would seek to legitimize their actions. Secretary Rusk commented that "it was more important to the Brazilians than to us to achieve a legitimate transfer of power. The domestic situation in Brazil would be improved if a new government could be legitimized quickly." When Johnson asked why the Brazilian Congress could not just make the president of the Congress, Ranieri Mazzilli, the legal president pro tem to provide the cover of legitimacy, Rusk responded that "Ambassador Gordon was using the resources available to him to encourage Brazilian legislators to do just this." Ball pointed out that there would be no problem for the United States in recognizing the new government. Meanwhile, until final word was received, the naval task force was to proceed toward Brazil until it was certain the military had matters fully in hand.[115]

The next day, 3 April, Thomas Mann called the president to say that "I hope you're as happy about Brazil as I am." Johnson replied, "I am." Mann continued by calling the coup "the most important thing that's happened in the hemisphere in three years."[116] Later that day the National Security Council met again along with congressional leaders. Brazil was the first item on the agenda. Rusk defended the coup and American support of it by recalling for the members of the NSC and Congress the difficulties the United States had faced in dealing with Goulart. He placed the blame for the coup squarely on Goulart's shoulders and insisted that the "U.S. did not engineer the revolt. It was an entirely indigenous effort." Goulart had forced the military to act by turning Brazil toward communism. "Despite our efforts," Rusk declared, "to persuade Goulart to follow a democratic reform program, and despite our efforts to support the Brazilian economy by making large loans, Goulart had moved toward the creation of an authoritarian regime politically far to the left." With that explanation as background, Rusk went on to say that the "current revolt in Brazil was not the traditional 'golpe' of the Latin American variety but rather a combination of governors, government officials and military leaders." These were the factions the administration saw as the constructive forces in contrast to the extreme democratic ones in Brazil, "who had joined together to oust Goulart when they became convinced that he was leading Brazil to economic and political disaster." Thus the establishment of a military regime deserved the full support of the United States. For Rusk and other top officials, the proper interpretation of events in Brazil was that the military had not engineered a coup, or a "traditional 'golpe,'" but a countercoup against Goulart's moving Brazil to communism. "The military leaders in Brazil," Rusk asserted, "have long visualized themselves as guardians of the democratic process."[117] Ambassador Gordon claimed that "Goulart had chosen to . . . carry out a coup of his own. In that sense, the revolution was a countercoup."[118] Afterward, the administration frequently referred to the military's seizure of power as an anticommunist revolution.[119] No one on the National Security Council or among the congressional representatives questioned this odd defense of democracy through the overthrowing of the constitutional president. Rather, they concurred with Rusk's and Gordon's interpretations of the event.

The new government faced major problems of inflation and foreign loan payments. The administration was confident, however, that the military was ready to "turn its attention to the major problems of Brazil." Rusk exclaimed that "we now have fresh hope that Brazil can face up to its current problems." Johnson pledged that he would "provide the economic help which the new Brazilian government will need" and assured the congressional representatives that he was "doing everything possible to get on top of the problem of helping the new government." Whereas previously aid for land reform and other structural changes in Brazil's economy were withheld, now monies for inflation control and payment of international debts would be readily available.[120] In a draft statement that was never released, the State Department praised the Brazilian military for once again, "as at critical times in the past," providing "a stabilizing influence" and demonstrating their commitment "to the maintenance of constitutional government in their country so that Brazil [could] resume its process of modernization."[121]

The Brazilian military leaders acted quickly to consolidate their control of power. On 9 April, the Military Ministers issued a decree, the "Institutional Act," to free them from constitutional restrictions and, as the title suggests, institutionalize their revolt. The State Department's director of intelligence and research reported to Rusk that the act's language "is hardly compatible with constitutional forms." It declared that the military's right to rule stemmed from an "authentic revolution," and it "does not attempt to legitimize itself through the Congress . . . it is Congress which receives from this Institutional Act . . . its own legitimacy."[122] The Military Ministers selected General Humberto Castello Branco, one of the principal leaders of the coup, to head the military government.

Most American officials did not know Castello Branco before the coup. The administration, however, would quickly hail his selection and rule. Johnson informed Bundy that he wanted a warm message sent to Castello Branco on his inauguration. When Bundy expressed some hesitation because the Brazilian government was jailing opponents and noted that the message would be published, Johnson responded: "I know it. But I don't give a damn. I think that there's some people that need to be locked up here and there too. I haven't got any crusade on 'em but I wish they'd locked up some before they took Cuba."[123] Gordon reported that the "most striking single characteristic about new cabinet of Castello Branco . . . is high level of competence which ministers bring to posts." Gordon portrayed them as "strongly democratic in philosophy and pro-western in orientation." All are "staunchly anti-communist, [and] considered to be strong leaders who will tolerate no indiscipline."[124] Castello Branco's plan to control inflation through austerity measures, economic development, and political reform was welcomed in Washington. The State Department praised his "good faith" efforts "to solve the many problems left behind by a deposed regime which was taking the country toward economic chaos and encouraging a rapid drift toward communism." Castello Branco's assurances of his "dedication to the reinstitution and further strengthening of democratic processes in Brazil" were taken at face value.[125]

Gordon's initial impressions of Castello Branco were "extremely favorable." He portrayed the general as a man of "calm resolve to get on with problems of clean-up, administrative rebuilding, and positive program" to overcome the damage done during the Goulart years.[126] Mann reported to the White House that Castello Branco's government had eliminated communist infiltration of Brazil and brought order "to the economy which was on the verge of collapse." He further claimed that the "frustration of communist objectives in Brazil was the single most important victory for freedom in the hemisphere in recent years."[127] After returning from Brazil, William Rogers of the State Department reported that Castello Branco was "a man of dignity, knowledge, and courage."[128] White House officials were equally enthusiastic. Johnson authorized $50 million in emergency aid and sent Rostow to Brazil in August 1964 to assess further needs. Rostow concluded that the general was "a remarkable Latin American chief of state."[129] The same month, Bundy wrote that "Branco does seem to be turning into quite a fine fellow."[130]

At Mann's suggestion, Johnson wrote Castello Branco a long letter professing his admiration for "the initial efforts of [his] government to reverse the serious economic deterioration which confronted you when you took office" and promising continued American support.[131] Bundy told Johnson that the letter was longer than the president preferred, but "Brazilians . . . are a people who measure interest by length."[132] In addition to the initial $50 million, $150 million was sent in December, and over $80 million in loans from private U.S. banks were extended to assist Brazil in refinancing its foreign debt. In 1964–66, Brazil received almost 50 percent of all Agency for International Development (AID) funds allocated, and from 1964 to 1970 only South Vietnam and India received more American assistance.[133]

When some former Kennedy officials questioned American support for the Brazilian generals and suggested that Kennedy would have taken a different course of action, McGeorge Bundy was quick to defend the Johnson administration. He wrote Kennedy's former press secretary Pierre Salinger that policy toward Brazil was "based on the recommendations of Linc Gordon, George Ball, and Dean Rusk—all Kennedy men—and that the fact of the matter was that Tom Mann had been in favor of a slightly slower and cooler expression of support." When Arthur Schlesinger Jr. wondered what the reasons were for "a change from the Kennedy policy of supporting democratic governments back to the Eisenhower-Dulles policy of backing military regimes on the right," Bundy argued that there was no change. He informed Schlesinger that policy "was determined almost entirely by the recommendations of Lincoln Gordon, whose commitment to democratic values and to the policies of President Kennedy himself can hardly be doubted." Given Kennedy's own comments that the United States could not renounce dictatorships until it was sure a nation would not go communist, Bundy was correct in his claim that there was no departure in the objectives of American policy. The administration believed that supporting the generals was the best means to achieve American goals in Brazil.[134]

Rusk asked George Ball to respond to media critics who questioned the support of the military regime and raised concerns about violations of civil liberties in Brazil. Ball argued that most of the arrests took place in the first few days after the revolution and, though there had been some excesses, the trials were taking place under an orderly and legal procedure. There were "no star chambers or railroading." On an ABC special report on Brazil, Ball defended the actions of the military as representing the "preponderant will of various sectors of Brazilian life." There was general agreement, he asserted, "that the deposing of Goulart was born out of a widespread and deep concern in Brazil that orderly democratic processes were seriously threatened, that those who were a party to this subversion of democracy had to be checked." Goulart's continuation in office would have "brought even more serious, perhaps permanent, political and economic damage to Brazil." Ignoring the Institutional Act, Ball claimed that the military intended to "reenforce" the constitutional system and that Castello Branco intended to hold the scheduled elections in 1965 and would "turn the government over to his duly elected successor." Most important, economic confidence was returning in Brazil. Ball described Castello Branco and his advisers as "able, technically competent" men who were committed to "restore order out of economic chaos, to bring about needed reforms, to revive economic growth."[135]

In July 1964, the first summary of recent events in Brazil was filled with praise for the "Brazilian revolution which brought Goulart's downfall [and] marked a serious setback for Soviet interests." Brazil's severing of relations with Cuba and efforts to strengthen the economic boycott of the island destroyed Castro's hope of "breaking out of isolation in the hemisphere." Moscow and Havana had welcomed Goulart's "denunciations of alleged US economic imperialism and were encouraged over prospects that Brazil would have drawn further away from the US" and hoped to continue to use his "assertive nationalism" as a vehicle to bring communism to Brazil through nonviolent tactics. "The Brazilian revolution dashed these hopes." Domestically, Castello Branco had "thus far provided firm, responsible, executive leadership, and his regime is making a promising start toward the alleviation of some of Brazil's severe economic and social problems." He was characterized as "developing a cautious, systematic, and forceful style of governing" that reflected his "basically centrist" views. The CIA acknowledged that the military's economic policies were creating widespread resentment and that the government "faces the challenge of producing results that will ease the social and political pressures before they become unmanageable." In addition, the postponement of the elections set for October 1965 and extension of Castello Branco's term as president until 1967 demonstrated that the military intended to hold onto power as long as it deemed necessary. Rather than causing concern, this change was viewed positively as a means to improve "the government's prospects of achieving its goals." A prolonged term without elections allowed Castello Branco "the opportunity to press on with his program without the handicaps of an early political campaign." If more time was needed "to achieve adequate progress toward restoring economic stability and easing social pressures," or if political unrest increased, Castello Branco "might then feel compelled to adopt, with military support, authoritarian methods to achieve his goals."[136]

Castello Branco's decision not to return to constitutional order and the military's decision to hold onto power, which would last into the 1980s, did not change U.S. policy. In year-end evaluations, both the State Department and the Central Intelligence Agency provided justifications for Castello Branco's "retreat . . . on constitutionalism." Summarizing American relations and assistance to Latin American militaries, Mann singled out Brazil for praise. "Generally," Mann noted, "the military have been friendly to the United States, anti-communist, and conservative, preferring stability but increasingly supporting orderly economic and social reform and progress." At times, it had been necessary for them to intervene "in normal political processes, sometimes out of the ultimate necessity to prevent internal chaos and extremism, as in the recent case of Brazil."[137] Castello Branco had initially decided that "qualified constitutionalism" was the best vehicle for the military to use rather than "an outright military regime." Time was needed for implementation of his government's harsh economic measures. "Unfortunately, the regime's measures have borne no obvious fruit so far as the Brazilian population at large is concerned." Becoming "increasingly aware of a growing popular discontent with its stabilization measures and of its ability . . . to do much about relieving this discontent without jeopardizing its overall economic program" and fearing that "the regime's arduous efforts to promote national recovery could easily be undone by a successor government," the CIA concluded that Castello Branco and the military had become apprehensive of being able to give up power. Finding it difficult to balance military unity and stabilization with constitutionalism, "the regime is unlikely to endanger its progress toward economic recovery by retreating on its stabilization policy." It would, therefore, probably again "retreat first on constitutionalism."[138]

McGeorge Bundy, in a January 1965 assessment of U.S. foreign policy for President Johnson, counted Mann's policies and the turn of events in Brazil as prime reasons why "1964 was a consistently good year in Latin America." The concentration of authority in Mann's hands "increased U.S. effectiveness on every front—diplomatic, economic, and political." The national security adviser concluded that in Brazil, "a responsible and progressive new government had begun an important program of economic and social reform—and the threat of a crumbling toward Communism has been removed."[139]

The CIA's one-year evaluation of events in Brazil justified continued military rule in Brazil. The abandonment of the constitutional system was necessary to prevent "a return to the chaotic politics that prevailed in Brazil" before the overthrow of Goulart.[140] Bill Moyers wrote Johnson at the end of 1965 that Brazil had "reversed the downward plunge" of its economy by making "major strides in curbing inflation," balancing the budget, and meeting foreign debt obligations. Castello Branco, "in order to preserve his general objective of a moderate government devoted to economic and social progress," took on more power and accepted measures "which have generally been regarded as a departure from democratic procedures." Again, this was done to preserve his program, maintain order, and prevent a return to chaos. Moyers concluded that along with the rest of Latin America, the trend was "in the right direction" (surely no pun intended) even if "we have a long way to go until revolutions and coups are a rare phenomenon." But Brazil and others "face the necessity of maintaining or undertaking unpopular economic and social measures to get on with the important business of development and reform."[141]

American Intervention

Events in the Dominican Republic and Vietnam were not, from Johnson's point of view, heading in the right direction. But unlike in Brazil, few options were left to improve the situation. In each nation, the civilian governments, which Washington had found weak and ineffectual, had already been replaced by military dictators. Yet the authoritarian regimes were failing to maintain order in the Dominican Republic or successfully counter the communists' military efforts in Vietnam. American policy since the 1920s had rejected direct intervention and "big stick" diplomacy in unstable areas of the Third World in favor of working through indigenous right-wing forces to maintain stability and order. Having no other local forces to turn to, Johnson increased military aid and the number of American forces in Vietnam, but to no avail. The logic of containment and the American reliance on right-wing dictators to preserve order and block communism were facing a crisis. When all else had failed before, direct American intervention had at least ensured stability even if it generated criticism and failed to solve all problems. Why would this policy not work again? In 1965, when the military dictatorships in the Dominican Republic and Vietnam failed to establish stability and quiet demands for change, Johnson turned to American force to protect the anticommunist governments and impose order.

The military coup that ousted Bosch from power and established a ruling triumvirate headed by Reid Cabral failed to solve any of the problems in the Dominican Republic. The nation remained, the intelligence community concluded in January 1964, "one of the Latin American countries least prepared for representative government." The Trujillo dictatorship had so "warped the political and economic framework of the country" that the Dominican people "doubt that they can accomplish anything by themselves." The Johnson administration conducted its policy on the basis of this analysis. The economic prospects for the nation were bleak, the administration believed, but for the "immediate future at least, the leftists pose no serious threat to seize control," and the government should be able to maintain order. The situation would bear watching, however, because the "leftists' strongest card is the instability of the present regime and the magnitude of the problems that face it." If no improvements were made in the long run, "the present limited threat of insurgency could increase sharply."[142]

This negative assessment remained unchanged for the remainder of the year. In an April 1964 survey of Latin America, the CIA concluded that "the prospects are gloomy for the early restoration of representative government in the Dominican Republic and also for launching fundamental socio-economic reforms." The only positive remained the government's ability to control any leftist activity. The main concern of the Cabral regime was self-preservation and order.[143] The administration's policy, therefore, remained "to support the present group and to keep the situation from deteriorating into chaos." If the situation worsened, it could mean the return of a "Trujillo-style dictatorship." Gordon Chase of the National Security Council staff reported to Bundy that "it is clear that the D.R. is not ready for elections yet, and if they were held today, the results would probably be disastrous; inter alia, no one is prepared to govern the country. We are not pushing hard on this issue, preferring to wait until the present situation shakes out some more."[144]

The effectiveness of the Reid Cabral regime continued to decline. Bundy reported to the president that the "triumvirate is shaky, lacks popular support." In the face of increasing economic problems, it had to rely on the military to stay in power. The United States had few alternatives but to continue its support. "The moderate opposition is deeply divided and there is no national consensus on what form a solution to the country's continuing political crisis should take." If Cabral should fail, the military would probably establish "a dictatorial regime under military dominance."[145]

On 24 April 1965, a rebellion broke out in the Dominican Republic in an effort to return Bosch to power. The Dominican military was divided between supporting Cabral's government or Bosch. By 28 April, the rebels appeared to have the upper hand, and loyalists to Cabral informed the American embassy that the government could not guarantee protection to American citizens. That night, Johnson sent the first five hundred of an eventual force of twenty-three thousand marines to Santo Domingo.[146] Ambassador W. Tapley Bennett reported that "all indications point to the fact that if present efforts of forces loyal to the government fail, power will be assumed by groups clearly identified with the Communist party." He recommended that the United States "intervene to prevent another Cuba from arising out of the ashes of this uncontrollable situation."[147] The initial explanation that force was used to protect American lives was quickly expanded to include the argument that the action was necessary to block a communist takeover of the Dominican Republic.

Presidential adviser Jack Valenti informed Johnson on 30 April that "*one fact is sure*: If the Castro-types take over the Dominican Republic, it will be the worst domestic political disaster any Administration could suffer." It was important to act quickly and lay out the argument that the choice is "Castro in Dominican Republic or U.S. intervention." The case must be made public and supported by "*indisputable evidence* that Castro-types are in charge" of the revolt.[148] The director of the United States Information Agency, Carl Rowan, concurred. He informed Johnson that a concerted effort needed to be made to justify American actions on the basis of protecting the "short-range and long-range well-being of the people of the Dominican Republic and *the rest* of Latin America." Rowan emphasized that "in order to do this meaningfully . . . I believe we must exploit as shrewdly as possible, without overdoing it, the Communist and Castroite leadership of the rebels."[149]

Johnson publicly stated that day that "people trained outside the Dominican Republic are seeking to gain control."[150] The president's rhetoric quickly inflated the events in the Dominican Republic to another challenge by the Soviet Union to the free world. "We have resisted Communism all over the world," Johnson said to his advisers, in "Vietnam, Lebanon, Greece—why are we disregarding our doorstep?"[151]

Speaking to a prime-time Sunday evening audience on 4 May, Johnson informed the nation that his timely actions had prevented another Cuba in the hemisphere. He claimed that this was a time "when great principles are tested in an ordeal of conflict and danger." The United States must not come up short. "Communist leaders, many of them trained in Cuba," sought to take advantage of the disorder in the Dominican Republic to gain power. "What began as a popular democratic revolution, committed to democracy and social justice, very shortly moved and was taken over and really seized and placed into the hands of a band of Communist conspirators." Intervention was justified, therefore, because "the American nations, cannot, must not, and will not permit the establishment of another Communist government in the Western Hemisphere." With his attention as much on events in Vietnam as the Dominican Republic and in an effort to link his actions to those of Truman, Eisenhower, and Kennedy, Johnson closed his address by declaring that he wanted all to know that "as long as I am President of this country, we are going to defend ourselves. . . . We will honor our treaties. We will keep our commitments."[152]

The State Department immediately assembled a paper titled "Communist Participation in the Current Dominican Rebellion" and made its findings available to reporters and other officials. Over the next week, the department released more information supporting the case of a communist threat in the Dominican Republic.[153] Critics offered a different view. They claimed that the administration sought to maintain in power a corrupt and repressive regime rather than allow Bosch to return and resume his efforts to reform Dominican society. American reporters in Santo Domingo, particularly Tad Szulc of the *New York Times*, rejected the administration's claim of a communist-controlled revolt and discredited the lists offered by the State Department as proof of a coordinated communist effort. Juan Bosch, however, offered the most damning critique. "This was a democratic revolution," the legitimate president of the Dominican Republic declared, "smashed by the leading democracy of the world."[154]

Administration officials were not deterred. Mann defended the intervention in terms of "our own peace and security." The United States could not permit another Castro on the island of Hispaniola. As to the question of blocking the legitimate ruler of the Dominican Republic and thwarting the will of the Dominican people, Mann noted that the critics were convinced "that Bosch was the choice of the people and that this was a good revolution that was coming about." The administration believed, however, that Bosch, "while at one time popular, had lost a lot of his popularity as a result of the way he handled himself when he was President." Mann claimed that he was a "very bad administrator, more of a poet than a politician," and asserted that Balaguer would defeat Bosch in a free election.[155]

Given that assumption, Mann argued that the American intervention was designed to allow the Dominican people to reject Bosch and not to impose any particular government. Yet Johnson was so determined that a proper order be established in the wake of American forces that he dispatched his national security adviser McGeorge Bundy to Santo Domingo to head the American effort to establish a stable and friendly regime in that unfortunate city. At the same time, the president secured an agreement from the OAS to form an inter-American peace force to replace U.S. troops. In the end, the United States established a government headed once again by Balaguer that promised to protect the Dominican Republic from communism and ensure American interests.

Johnson, who, according to George Ball, acted as his own desk officer during the Dominican crisis, remained convinced that his actions thwarted a communist effort to gain another beachhead in the Western Hemisphere.[156] Three days after sending troops, Johnson asked Bundy if there was any linkage between communist efforts in the Dominican Republic and the war in Vietnam. Bundy turned the question over to Ray Cline of the CIA for an answer. Cline responded that there was no evidence of a direct link. The communist role in the Dominican Republic was "one of exploitation, not initiation." Furthermore, because the situation in the Dominican Republic did not threaten to expand into a wider conflict, it was not the "sort of tactic which Moscow or Peiping would have calculated might significantly ease the pressure in Vietnam." There were, however, other connections that weighed in the favor of the United States. Cline believed that communist leaders would respond by "revising upward, somewhat, their estimates of U.S. willingness (a) to use force against threatened Communist advances, and (b) to override the sensitivities of world opinion in the process."[157]

It is not surprising that Johnson connected the situations in Vietnam and the Dominican Republic. His question not only fit the standard American interpretation of monolithic communism and revolution directed from Moscow but also reflected the immediate problems that confronted Johnson in his efforts to prevent the collapse of the Saigon government. More than four decades of policy had conditioned American leaders to believe that they could establish order and security in nations around the world if they could just find the right leader to take charge and use U.S. assistance properly. Now, confronted by the possibility in Vietnam that this was not true, Johnson was facing the decision of whether to take over the war from the Vietnamese to ensure the continuation of the American-backed regime in Saigon or witness the collapse of South Vietnam.

During Johnson's first fourteen months as president, there were over a half dozen changes in the government in Saigon. The political chaos was matched by a military decline as well. Bundy wrote the president on 27 January 1965 that he and Secretary of Defense Robert McNamara were "now pretty well convinced that our current policy can lead only to disastrous defeat." The policy of providing massive aid, military assistance, and advice while waiting "for a stable government" had proven to be a failure. "There is no real hope of success in this area unless and until our own policy and priorities change." Bundy argued that the "underlying difficulties in Saigon arise from the spreading conviction there that the future is without hope for anti-Communists." America's friends were discouraged by a lack of action on Washington's part in the face of the known advances being made by the NLF in the countryside. Bundy and McNamara concluded that the United States had to abandon its "essentially passive role which can only lead to eventual defeat and an invitation to get out in humiliating circumstances." Two alternative policies were outlined for Johnson. The first, which Bundy and McNamara favored, was the use of American "military power . . . to force a change of Communist policy." The second was to seek a negotiated settlement to salvage what could be preserved with no additional military risks. This amounted to defeat under a different guise.[158] Johnson's response was unequivocal: "Stable government or no stable government, we'll do what we have to do—we will move strongly. I'm prepared to do that."[159]

The first step was the authorization of Operation Rolling Thunder, a sustained bombing campaign against North Vietnam. Begun in February 1965, Rolling Thunder was designed to demonstrate the power of the United States and its commitment to the defense of South Vietnam. In theory, this action would destroy the North's capacity to resist while demonstrating to Hanoi that the costs of continued fighting outweighed any potential gain. North Vietnam would then abandon the NLF and negotiate a settlement on American terms. The bombing had another purpose as well: to strengthen the government in Saigon by proving the willingness of the United States to fight for its survival. Most senior officials, however, never believed that the bombing campaign was the final answer to the problems of maintaining a noncommunist government in South Vietnam. It did, however, buy the administration time while it debated the decision to send American troops to Vietnam.[160]

Facing a situation where a continuation of the status quo meant defeat, Johnson inched ever closer to escalating the war by sending in American troops. In March, the first marine units landed in Danang to protect American air bases. More followed in April, and the first army units arrived in May. French and South Vietnamese forces might have failed, but American leaders were certain that the United States, the world's richest and most powerful nation, could force its will on a poor, peasant nation. The "successful" operation in the Dominican Republic served to fuel the optimists who believed American military forces could quickly defeat the NLF. The "loss" of South Vietnam was politically unthinkable and presumably unnecessary given American might. On 28 July 1965, Johnson announced an open-ended escalation of American forces in Vietnam.

To Washington's great surprise, the NLF and the North Vietnamese did not crumble under the weight of American firepower and met every United States escalation with one of their own. The best the United States could attain was a bloody and frustrating stalemate. The U.S. failure to maintain a noncommunist government in Saigon stemmed from the shortcomings of the South Vietnamese government. The central problem Washington ignored was the lack of any broad-based support for the Saigon regime, no matter which strongman was in charge. U.S. policymakers expected the Vietnamese to understand the war on the same terms Washington did, as an effort to block the expansion of communism. The majority of the Vietnamese, however, believed that the NLF and Ho Chi Minh represented Vietnamese nationalism and independence. Thus they were willing to endure enormous casualties, suffering, and destruction to continue to inflict losses on American forces and avoid defeat. The war fully exposed the reality that the government of South Vietnam was merely an American facade and began a public debate that would eventually include a discussion concerning American policy toward right-wing dictators.

Dictators and the World

The second effort to implement a policy of opposition to right-wing dictatorships proved to be as brief as the first after World War II. Just as the Truman administration soon abandoned its efforts to oust Perón and Franco, so too did Kennedy and Johnson quickly retreat from idealism to the relative safety of the familiar American-defined anticommunist stability and world order. When forced to choose between stability or nationalist reform movements, the Kennedy and Johnson administrations abandoned their efforts to support change in Latin America and opted again for imposed order based on anticommunism and the protection of American interests. This time, however, the switch back to supporting right-wing dictators was accompanied by American intervention in the Dominican Republic and war in Vietnam to maintain unpopular and corrupt military dictatorships. Unlike Truman's reversal, Kennedy's and Johnson's was met by public criticism.

Prominent among these critics were Senators William Fulbright and Frank Church, who questioned the American willingness to support unpopular dictatorships and automatically oppose revolutionary movements around the world. They saw Johnson's use of the military as symptomatic of the problems of American foreign policy and the logical outcome of defending right-wing dictators. Fulbright, after taking note of the various different versions of events offered by Lyndon Johnson in the days and weeks after the Dominican intervention, decided to investigate to see if there had indeed been a communist threat in Santo Domingo. Using his position as chair of the Senate Foreign Relations Committee to its full advantage, Fulbright conducted a series of hearings throughout the summer in which he questioned top administrative officials concerning all aspects of the American intervention and occupation of the Dominican Republic.

Fulbright concluded that the administration had exaggerated the communist threat and the danger to American lives as a means to block the return of Juan Bosch to power. In a September 1965 speech, Fulbright charged that the administration had intervened only to prevent the PRD from coming to power. The protection of American lives was a pretext for the establishment and protection of an anticommunist regime. "In their apprehension lest the Dominican Republic become another Cuba," Fulbright declared, "some of our officials seem to have forgotten that virtually all reform movements attract some Communist support." This break from the administration would soon make Fulbright the leading figure in the Senate in the debate over the Vietnam War and the direction of American foreign policy.[161]

Church titled an article in the *New York Times Magazine*, "How Many Dominican Republics and Vietnams Can We Take On?" In the twenty years since World War II, nationalist revolutions had exploded all over the world. Faced with that reality, "no nation—not even our own—possesses an arsenal so large, or a treasury so rich, as to damp down the fires of smoldering revolution throughout the whole awakening world." The United States had to "escape the trap of becoming so preoccupied with Communism . . . that we dissipate our strength in a vain attempt to enforce a global guarantee against it." Church rejected the notion that there was any danger from Russia or China in Vietnam or the Dominican Republic. "As an international force under one directorate . . . Communism is a bust. China and Russia are bitter enemies." The communist world, he concluded, "bears no resemblance to a monolithic mass." The United States should "exercise a prudent restraint and develop a foreign policy more closely tied to a sober assessment of our own national interests." Supporting right-wing dictators placed the United States on the wrong side of the changes sweeping the world and damaged the long-term interests of the nation and its relations with the Third World. There were many who now questioned "our efforts in behalf of so many tottering governments afflicted by decadence and despotism and frequently despised by their own people." The nation was embarking on a war in Vietnam and intervening again in Latin America because it had "downgrade[d] freedom by equating it with the absence of Communism; we upgrade a host of dictatorial regimes by dignifying them with membership in what we like to call the 'Free World.'"[162]

Secretary of State Dean Rusk provided the standard responses to these criticisms. In 1964, he instructed Church at a closed session of the Senate Foreign Relations Committee that he had to keep the "two different revolutions separate." The first was the "revolution of modernization, economic and social development, education and all these things, the rising expectations, that kind of thing." He asserted that until 1960, South Vietnam was "in the full stream of that revolution." The other revolution was "the Communist world revolution . . . the dynamic force that concerns us all." Ho was attempting to destroy the South because it was exposing the shortcomings of his own revolution. "We have reason to believe from intelligence sources," Rusk argued, "that progress with that revolution in South Vietnam was one of the reasons why North Vietnam decided in 1959 and 1960 that they had to do something about it, that they were being outstripped by the south." Church challenged Rusk's assertions that the Vietnam War represented outside aggression and argued that Ho was primarily a nationalist. The war was more about independence and unity, he claimed, than communism. There was no reason a revolution could not be both nationalist and led by communists.[163]

Rusk and Church renewed the debate in 1966, this time in public. As questions concerning the American involvement in Vietnam mounted, the SFRC held a series of hearings in January 1966 to raise questions about the war and the direction of American foreign policy. Senator Church had requested that public hearings be held to allow the committee to question a broad range of people with different opinions about the war and open up a "whole philosophical argument as it affects American foreign policy generally, which has led us into Vietnam."[164] Only a full, painful, open debate could turn American policy around. Church began his questioning of Rusk by asserting that revolutions were the order of the day and that the United States could expect to see many other challenges to the status quo to redress long-standing ills and to oust many of the tyrants that the United States had supported for so long. The fundamental question was what American policy would be in response to the revolutionary nationalism that appeared so prevalent in the world. From Rusk's explanations and American policy in the Dominican Republic and Vietnam, Church concluded: "I gather that wherever a revolution occurs against an established government, and that revolution, as most will doubtlessly be, will be infiltrated with Communists, that the United States regards it in its interest to prevent the success of Communist uprising." Church found such a policy "self-defeating" and urged a more conciliatory and understanding approach to cope with the "phenomena of revolt in the underdeveloped world." Rusk responded that he found a "fundamental difference between the kind of revolution which the Communists call their wars of national liberation, and the kind of revolution which is congenial to our own experience." The secretary of state declared that "there is nothing liberal about that revolution that they are trying to push from Peiping. . . . It has nothing in common with the great American revolutionary condition." Church retorted that he could not recall "many revolutions that have been fought in splendid isolation. There were as many Frenchmen at Yorktown when Cornwallis surrendered as there were American Continentals. . . . It seems to me that the Communists have not changed the rules of revolution by meddling in them."[165]

Church had no doubt that the impact of the committee's hearings was profound. "Once it became apparent to the American people," Church concluded, "that there were members of this Committee, who obviously were good, loyal Americans, knowledgeable in public affairs and informed on foreign policy, who disagreed with the war . . . and who strongly opposed the widening of the war, then the general resistance to the war and the debate itself over the war began to spread in the country. But if we had not gone out from behind closed doors, this never would have happened."[166]

These nascent criticisms of American foreign policy provided legitimacy to the critics of American support of right-wing dictators and the postwar consensus on containment and presidential domination of American foreign policy that provided the rationale for aiding authoritarian regimes. No longer would the debates and decisions be left to the private deliberations of the executive branch. The Vietnam War sparked a decade-long challenge to the fundamental tenets of American policy that culminated in the Senate Select Committee Hearings on Covert Activities and Assassinations and President Jimmy Carter's reversal of American support for right-wing dictators in favor of a policy based on human rights.[167] The Vietnam War, therefore, marks the end of the policy examined in this book. There was no immediate shift in policy or complete reversal of course. But after 1965, American support for right-wing dictators would be criticized and contested in Congress and by various grass-roots organizations and political groups.

Critics such as Church strongly believed that the United States had an important role to play in international affairs. Church, however, believed it should be guided by the sentiment and warnings first expressed in 1821 by John Quincy Adams that the United States should not go abroad "in search of monsters to destroy"; the country was better served by the "countenance of her voice, and by the benignant sympathy of her example." If it continued to support right-wing regimes and intervene around the globe, it might "become the dictatress of the world," but it "would no longer be the ruler of her own spirit."[168]

EPILOGUE
Carter, Kirkpatrick, and Right-Wing Dictators

After 1965, American policy toward right-wing dictators became a contested issue. The Vietnam War served to undercut much of the logic and rationale used to justify American support of right-wing dictatorships. America's longest war and the battles over executive power that emerged at its conclusion provided an opportune time for a reevaluation of the policies that led to that protracted, painful, and divisive conflict. Support of authoritarian regimes was not completely abandoned by any means, as Richard Nixon's policy toward Chile demonstrated. Policymakers, however, were now forced to take into account sustained criticisms of American support of dictatorships and at times congressional restrictions on the freedom of the executive branch to act. For many, Vietnam and the postwar revelations of American covert action in the Third World provided convincing evidence that the old policy of support for dictators was flawed and, more important, doomed to backfire. Critics called for the United States to reorient its moral compass and to find methods other than covert activity and support of brutal dictators to advance American interests in the world. Though no complete swing of the policy pendulum occurred, new views were heard and different approaches implemented, most notably

President Jimmy Carter's emphasis on human rights. The election of Ronald Reagan, however, returned the policy to one of support of various dictators throughout the world. A brief outline of these debates, one that is illustrative rather than exhaustive, demonstrates the divisions that emerged after the Vietnam War and provides the basis for an evaluation of American policy toward right-wing dictatorships from the 1920s to the 1960s and 1970s.

Chile and the Church Committee

At the same time the Johnson administration was supporting the April 1964 military takeover in Brazil, policymakers worried about the political future of Chile. Socialist leader Salvadore Allende's plans for nationalizing important industries in Chile, particularly mining and communications that were dominated by U.S. corporations, frightened American officials. As Allende gained ground on the Christian Democratic candidate Eduardo Frei in the 1964 presidential campaign, the United States actively intervened to ensure Frei's victory. American officials saw Allende as a communist who threatened American interests in Chile and throughout the hemisphere. The CIA reported in April that "of all the Latin American nations, Chile offers the Communists their best prospects for entering and potentially dominating a government through the electoral process." Allende had been a strong runner-up in 1958, and his election would pose a threat to "US private investment of more that $750 million."[1] Gordon Chase reported to McGeorge Bundy in March that Allende was an "extreme leftist" and that if "Allende wins and stays in power, we are in trouble. For example, he will probably nationalize the copper mines." Because the "U.S. has big stakes in copper and manufacturing of all kinds," it was important that "we should simply do what we can to get people to back Frei."[2] At the end of the next month, Chase again alerted Bundy to the electoral dangers in Chile: "A Communist election victory in September 1964 . . . is intolerable for national security and domestic political reasons."[3] Bundy described the upcoming election as a potential "crisis" but was optimistic that it would be properly managed.[4] The United States, through both its aid programs and covert CIA funding, spent $20 million to ensure that the Chilean people backed Frei.[5]

Six years later, however, American opposition could not prevent Allende from being elected president in a three-way race. The American ambassador to Chile, Edward Korry, lamented that it was a "sad fact that

Chile has taken the path to communism with only a little more than a third (36 percent) of the nation approving this choice." Nixon ordered his national security adviser Henry Kissinger to block Allende from taking power. Kissinger believed that "Allende's election was a challenge to our national interest." It would be difficult to "reconcile ourselves to a second communist state in the Western hemisphere." Allende would provide a base for anti-American attacks, support for Castro, and eventually an alliance with the Soviet Union. The national security adviser worried about a domino theory in South America because "Chile bordered Argentina, Peru, and Bolivia, all plagued by radical movements."[6] Nixon ordered the CIA to "leave no stone unturned . . . to block Allende's confirmation." He promised $10 million for the operation and asked CIA director Richard Helms to "make the economy scream."[7]

Although Nixon was unable to prevent Allende's confirmation as president by Chile's Congress, he was able to help destabilize Chile through U.S. economic warfare and covert activity. The Nixon administration undertook "vigorous efforts . . . to assure that other governments in Latin America understand fully that the United States opposes the consolidation of a Communist state in Chile hostile to the interests of the United States." Specifically, the administration sought to exclude any further U.S. financial assistance to Chile and to "bring a maximum feasible influence to bear in international financial institutions to limit credit or other financing assistance to Chile." In addition, at least $8 million was spent on covert activities to support Allende's political opposition and anti-Allende plotting.[8] The military attacked in September 1973, and Allende is officially reported to have committed suicide during the coup that brought General Augusto Pinochet to power. Many, however, believed he was killed. The exact role the United States played in the coup is still debated. What is certain is that Nixon welcomed the overthrow of Allende and extended immediate support to Pinochet despite the brutal killings, torture, and imprisonment of his political opposition. Nixon, Kissinger, and Gerald Ford all believed that supporting Pinochet was necessary to protect American interests, provide order, and combat communism.

A series of discussions in July 1975 of policy toward Chile by Ford's National Security Council made it clear that the administration saw Pinochet's rule as necessary to block communism in South America, provide stability in Chile, and protect American investments. Both Ford and Kissinger "expressed support and sympathy for [Chile's] efforts to rebuild the nation" and worked to obtain foreign economic aid for Pinochet's regime and the approval of a rescheduling of Chile's debt by America's European allies. The major problem was the "strong criticism of this policy from the Congress," where human rights advocates forced a temporary halt to military sales and credits.[9] In preparation for National Security Adviser Brent Scowcroft's meeting with a member of the Chilean junta, Admiral José Toribio Merino, the NSC noted the importance of Chile's economy to the United States and the necessity, over congressional opposition, to continue to supply American military aid to ensure stability in the region. The military government in Santiago was "more self-confident that at any time since it came to power," largely because of American support, an improving economy, and the "coming to power of a number of conservative military governments in neighboring areas." The Ford administration valued the "friendship and traditionally close ties with Chile" and hoped "that they might be strengthened in the future." To these ends, the National Security Council was grateful for Chile's expressed intention to take positive steps in the area of human rights. It would improve the administration's "ability to be responsive to the legitimate defense and development needs" of Chile.[10] The next year Scowcroft wrote Ford that U.S. relations with Latin America were better than at any time in the recent past. He believed this improvement resulted from the resumption of an active American role in hemispheric affairs and the "process of maturation" by the nations to the south.[11]

These documents also reveal a new factor in American policy toward right-wing dictatorships: the worry about criticisms and the restrictions on aid placed by the Congress. Outside of the administration, many people refused to accept American support for such a government. The establishment of the Senate Select Committee on Intelligence (Church Committee) guaranteed that American policy toward Chile would be controversial. The formation of the Church Committee stemmed from a series of revelations concerning the CIA in the fall of 1974. The *Progressive* published an explosive story in November that charged that former CIA director Richard Helms had lied to Senator Church's subcommittee investigating the role of American multinationals in efforts to destabilize Chile.[12] An angry Church vowed that he would hold hearings, and he publicly clashed with President Ford over the incident. When Ford defended the CIA's actions and argued that the Soviet Union spent "more money than we do for the same kind of purpose," Church shot back the next day, "I thought there was a difference, and the difference is what it's all about."[13]

The Ford administration attempted to thwart a congressional probe by setting up a commission headed by Vice President Nelson Rockefeller. In the wake of Vietnam and Watergate, though, an executive investigation was not to be trusted, and the Senate voted overwhelmingly to establish the Select Committee on Intelligence Activities. Senator Church was named chair.[14] Earlier, Church's foreign relations subcommittee on multinationals discovered that the head of International Telephone and Telegraph and the CIA had discussed in 1970 means for blocking Allende's election and subsequently explored ways of disrupting and overturning his regime. The news of the September 1973 military coup against Allende reached Church during Kissinger's confirmation hearings for secretary of state. On the back of the note his aide handed him, Church wrote: "The military will inherit the earth!"[15]

Church decided that Chile would be the case study that the committee would use in its examination of covert activities. This choice reflected his view that Chile "contained all of the elements . . . that are normally associated with covert operations. . . . Second . . . it contained the most dramatic examples of abuse conflicting with our professed principles as a Nation and interfering with the right of the Chilean people to choose their own government by peaceful means in accordance with their own constitutional processes."[16] Ford and Kissinger attempted to deny the Church Committee the necessary documents to conduct its investigation. Although Church assured the president that the committee would respect legitimate secrecy concerns,[17] Ford believed that the committee's actions could jeopardize American security and credibility, and he warned Church that "we are a great power and it is important that we be perceived as such." Intelligence, he said, needs to be "to a certain extent . . . cloaked in mystery and held in awe."[18]

Ford wrote Church at the end of October 1975 to urge the committee not to make public its findings on assassinations and covert actions. The president asserted that any public disclosure of allegations on the overthrow of foreign governments would "result in serious harm to the national interest." Church's response revealed the fundamental differences between the administration and its critics. In the senator's view, "the national interest is better served by letting the American people know the truth and complete story. A basic tenet of our democracy is that the people must be told of the mistakes of their government so that they may have the opportunity to correct them." In addition, other nations would admire the United States "for keeping faith with our democratic ideals [more] that they will condemn us for the misconduct itself."[19]

The administration's efforts to control information and documents were not surprising, but the claims of damage to national security masked the larger issue at stake: American policy toward the Third World and dictatorships. The Church Committee investigations revealed the pattern and extent of American support of right-wing dictators, often through U.S. involvement in the overthrow of constitutional governments. As the report on Chile made clear, U.S. policy was still based on the logic and rationale developed during the 1920s and carried forward throughout the Cold War. Church believed American opposition to Allende was groundless, and he dismissed the claim that Chile was a danger to U.S. national security. Nixon, Kissinger, and Ford, however, were still operating by the old verities that supporting right-wing dictators provided stability, promoted anticommunism, and ensured protection of American economic interests. Kissinger stated, "I have yet to meet somebody who firmly believes that if Allende wins, there is likely to be another free election in Chile." Democracy, however, was not the issue. Allende's threat was economic and the challenge to American dominance of the Western Hemisphere. Rather than test Allende's commitment to democracy, the administration helped subvert the democratic process by supporting a coup. Kissinger was sure that Allende would "establish over a period of years some sort of communist government. In that case, we would have one not on an island . . . but in a major Latin American country. . . . So I don't think we should delude ourselves on an Allende takeover and [the fact that] Chile would not present massive problems for us." [20]

The work of the Church Committee, in conjunction with other criticisms of American policy, was, however, having an impact. When Kissinger employed similar arguments to generate support for American intervention in the Angolan civil war, Congress blocked the Ford administration's efforts. The situation was well tailored to raise the hackles of veteran Cold Warriors. The Soviet Union and Cuba supported the largest and most powerful faction, the Popular Movement for the Liberation of Angola (MPLA). Ford and Kissinger increased covert aid to Portugal in 1975 to $32 million and, after Angola gained its independence in November 1975, sought to prevent an MPLA victory. Nathaniel Davis, the State Department officer in charge of African affairs, resigned in protest, sparking concern among members of Congress who worried that the administration was starting down a slippery slope of escalation reminiscent of support for Diem in Vietnam. [21]

In December 1975, the Senate voted against military expenditures in Angola. Ford complained that the Soviets had to be countered and wondered how the Senate could "take the position that the Soviet Union can act with impunity many thousands of miles away . . . while we refuse any assistance to the majority of the local people who ask only for military equipment to defend themselves." In a meeting with Republican congressional leaders following a trip to China, Indonesia, and the Philippines, Ford and Kissinger stressed that those nations and others wanted an active American policy and that it was necessary for the United States to demonstrate its power to maintain their confidence.[22] A failure to act "would inevitably lead our friends and supporters to conclusions about our steadfastness and resolve."[23]

The administration was particularly concerned with assuring the Shah of Iran and President Suharto of Indonesia of continued U.S. support. Both leaders were seen as vital for maintaining stability in key Third World areas, blocking communist advances, and providing the United States access to vital raw materials. Kissinger told Ford that the Shah was a man of "extraordinary ability and knowledge," who was concerned about "how much he can count on the U.S. to provide the world leadership, strength, and initiatives, which he has seen as crucial in the period since World War II." The Shah had to be reassured "of our firm determination to continue to play a positive, active role in world affairs despite the recent setbacks in some areas" and that Congress was not moving the nation to isolationism.[24] Suharto was seen as the "most stabilizing element in Southeast Asia." His "strongly anti-communist government is deeply concerned with the problem of living with a communist Indochina." It was essential to let him know that the United States would continue to "meet our commitments and continue supporting our friends in Southeast Asia."[25]

Ford claimed that Congress "had lost its nerve" in denying him the funds to intervene in Angola.[26] Opponents responded that Angola was locked in a civil war in which the United States had no role. Moreover, the MPLA was no more a Soviet puppet than the National Liberation Front had been in Vietnam. To intervene would only lead to an escalating commitment that would eventually discredit the United States. The policy pendulum was moving away from an unquestioned support of any right-wing dictator clothed in anticommunist garb. Church summarized the position of many critics of American policy in an early 1976 talk titled "The Erosion of Principle in American Foreign Policy: A Call for a New Morality." It was the bicentennial year, and Church began by quoting James Madison, who had said that "our country, if it does justice to itself, will be the workshop of the Civilized World." Church believed that "an objective close to the hearts of our founders was to place the United States at the helm of moral leadership in the world." Yet that notion had fallen by the wayside, replaced by the support of brutal dictators, CIA-orchestrated coups in democratic nations, failed efforts to overthrow Castro and others, and assassination plots by three administrations against foreign leaders. For all of its efforts, the country found itself involved in a divisive, immoral war in Vietnam and allied to nations that mock "the professed ideals of the United States." Church asked, "If we have gained little" from these policies, "what then have we lost? I suggest we have lost—or grievously impaired—the good name of the United States from which we once drew a unique capacity to exercise matchless moral leadership." The damage affected both domestic and foreign affairs. It stemmed from an "arrogance of power" that led the United States into Vietnam and allowed Nixon to declare "like Caesar peering into the colonies from distant Rome" that the government of Chile was "unacceptable to the President of the United States." Church concluded that the "remedy is clear. American foreign policy must be made to conform once more to our historic ideals, the . . . fundamental belief in freedom and popular government." [27]

Carter and Human Rights

The Vietnam War, the Church Committee's findings, and other challenges to the legacy of the "imperial presidency" and American support of right-wing dictatorships brought forth alternative views about America's role in the world and made possible Jimmy Carter's emphasis on human rights. In his inaugural address, Carter echoed Church when he called upon the American people to "take on those moral duties which, when assumed, seem inevitably to be in our own best interests" and to let the "recent mistakes bring a resurgent commitment to the basic principles of our Nation." The best means to defend freedom and advance the national interests, Carter asserted, "is to demonstrate here that our democratic system is worthy of emulation. . . . We will not behave in foreign places so as to violate our rules and standards here at home." [28]

On 22 May 1977, Carter outlined his new policy in his commencement address at Notre Dame University. He declared that "I believe we can have a foreign policy that is democratic, that is based on fundamental values, and that uses power and influence . . . for humane purposes. We can also have a foreign policy that the American people both support and, for a change, know about and understand." The president was convinced that democracy was the wave of the future and that the continued support of repressive dictatorships was not only against American ideals but also against the nation's self-interest. "Democracy's great recent successes—in India, Portugal, Spain, Greece—show that our confidence in this system is not misplaced. Being confident of our own future, we are now free of that inordinate fear of communism which once led us to embrace any dictator who joined us in that fear. I'm glad that that's being changed."[29]

Carter succinctly summarized the criticisms of supporting right-wing dictators. "For too many years," the president announced, "we've been willing to adopt the flawed and erroneous principles and tactics of our adversaries, sometimes abandoning our own values for theirs. We've fought fire with fire, never thinking that fire is better quenched with water. This approach," he noted, "failed, with Vietnam the best example of its intellectual and moral poverty." The United States, he believed, had to return to its belief in self-determination and faith in democracy. It took the Vietnam War to demonstrate the fallacy of the old policy and to get the United States off the self-defeating path of collaborating with dictators. Instead of supporting right-wing dictators, Carter called for a policy based on a commitment to "human rights as a fundamental tenet of our foreign policy." The president wanted the "world to know that our Nation stands for more than financial prosperity." The nation must be drawn together and its policy guided by "a belief in human freedom." The old policy was, according to Carter, based on an inaccurate reading of history and the development of democracy. Strength and stability were not the prerequisites of freedom: "The great democracies are not free because we are strong and prosperous." Rather, Carter concluded, "I believe we are strong and influential and prosperous because we are free." Following a foreign policy based on human rights did not dictate a policy conducted by "rigid moral maxims." But it did demand a belief in the power of ideas and a toleration of change and diversity internationally. American policy was to be based on "a larger view of global change" rather than the bipolar Cold War prism.[30]

Carter was aware of the limits of moral suasion, and he did not believe that change would come quickly. Moreover, he realized that he would have to continue to support certain allies despite their record on human rights. As Carter noted, he was "determined to combine support for our more authoritarian allies and friends with the effective promotion of human rights with their countries." He hoped for reform from below to prevent revolution from above. "By inducing them to change

their repressive policies," Carter believed, "we would be enhancing freedom and democracy, and helping to remove the reasons for revolution
that often erupt among those who suffer from persecution." This would,
he hoped, allow for the replacement of right-wing dictators by democratic rather than leftist regimes.[31]

Advocates of the old policy of supporting right-wing dictators blamed
Carter in 1979 for the overthrow of two of America's staunchest allies,
Somoza in Nicaragua to the leftist Sandinistas and the Shah of Iran to
the religious fundamentalists headed by the Ayatollah Khomeini, despite
Carter's continued support of both Somoza and the Shah. Only when it
was clear that their governments would be overturned did Carter attempt to establish moderate centrist governments to promote change
and forestall the more radical alternatives. In each case, these last-ditch
efforts failed because no political center existed. Reminiscent of the effort to prevent Castro from coming to power in Cuba, these actions were
too little, too late. The United States found itself confronted with governments that were hostile to American policies and, in the case of Nicaragua, friendly with its enemies in Cuba and the Soviet Union. Nonetheless, Carter's critics blamed his advocacy of human rights, rather than
the widespread popular discontent in Nicaragua and Iran, for the overthrow of Somoza and the Shah.

The most vocal critic was Georgetown University professor and future Reagan administration ambassador to the United Nations Jeane
Kirkpatrick. She created a stir in 1979 with the publication of her article
"Dictatorships and Double Standards" in *Commentary*. Together with a
second piece published in January 1981, "U.S. Security and Latin America," her work constituted the most comprehensive public defense of the
policy of supporting authoritarian regimes. Kirkpatrick argued that in
the 1970s the United States witnessed a decline in power and prestige
resulting from its failure in Vietnam and a "posture of continuous self-
abasement and apology vis-à-vis the Third World."[32] In particular, she
blamed Carter's policy of human rights and criticism of longtime allies.
Kirkpatrick contended that the United States need not apologize for its
support of "moderate autocrats." Such a policy was in the national interest and not incompatible with the defense of freedom. Using Nicaragua
and Iran as her primary examples, Kirkpatrick argued that autocratic governments were to be expected in these nations and that the rule of the Somoza family and the Shah of Iran was not as negative as their opponents
claimed. For example, in discussing the Somozas, Kirkpatrick claimed
that their government "was moderately competent in encouraging eco-

nomic development, moderately oppressive, and moderately corrupt."[33] Moreover, Kirkpatrick emphasized that each government was a strong bulwark against communism and a good, loyal strategic ally of the United States.

Central to her argument was the concept that there was a fundamental difference between right-wing and communist dictatorships, or what she called authoritarian and totalitarian regimes. The crucial distinction, according to Kirkpatrick, was that "traditional autocrats," such as Somoza and the Shah, "leave in place existing allocations of wealth, power, status, and other resources," and "they do not disturb the habitual rhythms of work and leisure, habitual places of residence, habitual patterns of family and personal relations. Because the miseries of traditional life are familiar, they are bearable to ordinary people who . . . acquire the skills and attitudes necessary for survival in the miserable roles they are destined to fill." The almost exact opposite was true, she claimed, for life under communist rule. Left-wing regimes established totalitarian states that "create" the type of "social inequities, brutality, and poverty" that traditional autocrats merely "tolerate."[34]

Kirkpatrick claimed that because right-wing dictators left traditional patterns in place, "given time, propitious economic, social, and political circumstances, talented leaders, and a strong indigenous demand for representative government," their nations could evolve from autocratic societies into democracies.[35] Totalitarian communist states could not. Indeed, by their very nature, communist nations shut off any of these avenues toward development and, therefore, any democratic change. Hence right-wing dictatorships were a necessary and inevitable stage of government for Third World nations, and support by Washington not only was in the interest of the United States but served to protect liberalism and promote democracy. The United States was helping to provide the necessary stability and economic modernization these states needed for the development of democratic institutions.

Though Kirkpatrick's arguments generated much discussion and her views were adopted by the Reagan administration as a starting point for its policies toward right-wing dictators, they held little that was new. She was only publicly stating what had been the basis for policy decisions for much of the century. Moreover, the collapse of communism in Eastern Europe in 1989, the reunification of Germany, and the disintegration of the Soviet Union demonstrated that this reasoning remained as faulty as it was during the 1920s when it was first being developed.

CONCLUSION

From the end of World War I to the 1960s, American policy-makers supported authoritarian regimes that promised stability, anticommunism, and economic trade and investment opportunities for the United States. Although this policy violated the stated ideals of the United States, American leaders believed it served the national interest. The justifications used in support of the policy were remarkably similar throughout the decades. Non–Western European people were seen as incapable of handling the difficult demands of democratic rule. Their natural inferiority, American officials believed, made them susceptible to radical ideas and solutions to their persistent problems and, therefore, in need of a strong leader who would maintain order and implement the economic policies necessary for their nations to mature. Right-wing dictators, policymakers contended, were the antidotes to the ills of political and social disorder and the conduits of modernization. They would prevent unstable areas from falling to communism while allowing time for nations to develop a middle class and democratic institutions. In addition, these dictators protected foreign investments, provided a favorable atmosphere for American trade, and after 1945 sided with the United States in the Cold War. The policy appeared to provide numerous immediate benefits as the United States gained friendly, albeit brutal, allies who supposedly provided stability, support for American policies, and access to their markets and raw materials.

The consistent support of right-wing dictators raises the question of continuity regarding American foreign policy during the twentieth century and challenges the "triumphalist" school that has emerged since the end of the Cold War. Much of the scholarship on U.S. foreign policy treats the post-1945 period as a distinct era. Although there is no doubt that the conflict with the Soviet Union and the globalization of the Cold War were the signal events of the post–World War II period and that they brought forth an expanded American involvement in world affairs and unprecedented military commitments and spending, it does not necessarily follow that these events meant a sharp break with the traditions and policies of the past or that the emergence of the Cold War marked a totally new departure for the United States. The self-imposed obligations of a great power had been developing since the expansion of the 1890s and the interventions of the preceding decades. As this book makes clear, in American policy toward right-wing dictatorships, the Cold War represented a continuation and an intensification of policies developed during the first half of the century that placed the fear of Bolshevism, socialism, and the spread of disorder at the center of policymakers' concerns. The Cold War demanded new approaches and tactics, and a powerful Soviet state gave these matters more urgency, but the ideological basis and fundamental assumptions of American policy remained remarkably consistent. The context for policymaking and the challenges American leaders faced had changed, but the primary goals and objectives of stability, economic expansion, and security remained.

Policymakers of the 1940s and 1950s formed their ideas about the world during the early stages of American imperialism and World War I. The dual influences of Theodore Roosevelt's imperialism and Woodrow Wilson's liberal internationalism shaped the thinking of America's Cold Warriors. The conviction that the United States was destined for world leadership and justified in using its military and economic power abroad did not emerge solely in response to Soviet power. The logic of containment and American Cold War policies were updated versions of the internationalists' outlook that motivated administrations from William McKinley's to Franklin Roosevelt's. In their response to the creation of the Soviet Union, the Chinese revolution, and the rise of revolutionary nationalism around the world, American leaders found few reasons to challenge and change the fundamental objectives of American foreign policy or their thinking about the world.

Yet, in the wake of the end of the Cold War, the view that the United States was victorious, in large part, because of its values and steadfast adherence to the promotion of liberalism and democracy has gained wide currency. Op-ed pages, popular magazines, and the best-seller list were populated in the early 1990s by proponents of the view that the U.S. victory in the Cold War was a testament to the correctness of the nation's forty-five-year policy of containment and a validation of the superiority of its values: democracy, free enterprise, and liberal internationalism. While much of the euphoria, which led to claims such as Francis Fukuyama's that the U.S. triumph in the Cold War marked the "end of history,"[1] has receded in the face of the wars in the former Yugoslavia, the former Soviet Union, and Africa, continued unrest in Latin America, and the economic crisis looming over much of Asia, many scholars are using the end of the Cold War as a new prism with which to view and applaud American policy. The best account of this triumphalist interpretation is Tony Smith's *America's Mission*.

Smith contends that the American commitment to promoting democracy abroad was "the central ambition of American foreign policy during the twentieth century" and that this effort greatly contributed to the surge of liberal democracies in the early 1990s. What Smith terms a policy of "liberal democratic internationalism" reflected American idealism and an understanding that "to promote democracy abroad" was the best "way of enhancing the national security." Moreover, Smith claims that it was the best policy for confronting "the chief political problem of the twentieth century," the "problem of taming nationalism politically by founding a stable form of mass-based state capable of participating in world affairs peacefully."[2]

In support of his argument, Smith covers all of the twentieth century and includes an impressive number of cases and a detailed analysis of American policy from the colonization of the Philippines at the beginning of the century to the response to revolution in Central America during the 1980s. Unlike many critics who have viewed neo-Wilsonian pronouncements concerning liberal democratic internationalism as rhetorical covers for the expansion of American economic influence and power, Smith takes these statements at face value and sees the pursuit of Wilsonian objectives as an effective, practical policy that has furthered the development of liberalism in the world. United States leadership and the promotion of democracy and liberal capitalist institutions internationally, from "McKinley's taking of the Philippines and Puerto Rico in 1898; Woodrow Wilson's interventions in Central America and the Caribbean . . . and his subsequent intention 'to make the world safe for democracy' . . . Franklin Roosevelt's concern for democracy in postwar Europe and Harry Truman's determination to democratize Germany and Japan during their occupation," to "John Kennedy's ambitions in the Alliance for Progress in Latin America; Jimmy Carter's 'human rights campaign'; [and] Ronald Reagan's 'democratic revolution'" promised prosperity and stability and "were the product of an American conviction that if democracy were to spread, America's place in the world would be more secure."[3]

The book has two purposes, which create the fundamental problem with Smith's analysis. The first is to "recount the history of the various American efforts to foster democracy abroad and to evaluate the results of these attempts in terms of their own ambitions." On this score there is much to commend in Smith's work. He provides detailed discussions of failed efforts, such as in the Philippines and the Dominican Republic, as well as successes in Germany and Japan. The second purpose "is to ask how American foreign policy has contributed to the surge in the number, strength, and prestige of liberal democratic governments worldwide at the end of the twentieth century."[4] This concern comes to override his historical narrative and provides the basis for his main thesis. Here, his argument hinges on the actions of Ronald Reagan. According to Smith, "No administration since Wilson's has been as vigorous or as consistent in its dedication to the promotion of democracy abroad as that of Ronald Reagan." His policies of constructive engagement and the Reagan Doctrine, Smith contends, meant that "by 1992 democracy stood unchallenged as the only form of mass politics that offered itself as a model worldwide."[5] If this is the case, then all that led to it must have been preparation, and Smith's historical analysis gives way to policy prescriptions.

Smith's emphasis on the continuities in American policymaking is welcome, but his main concern is to use his history to demonstrate that American foreign policy would best be served by making the promotion of democracy central for protecting the national interest. Smith is convinced that this is the best policy to follow, and his examination of various case studies, particularly the failures to follow this course of action, leaves little reason to argue with his position. But what would be the best theoretical policy to follow does not mean that it was the policy of the United States or the central ambition of its leaders. In his effort to influence current policymaking by demonstrating that it was the pursuit of democracy which led to victory in the Cold War, Smith has to ignore his own evidence about the shortcomings and failures of the policy to promote democracy and dismiss large amounts of the history of American foreign policy that do not support his claim. It is telling that the book completely ignores the 1920s and provides only general overviews of the Eisenhower and Nixon administrations.

American support of right-wing dictators demonstrates that the promotion of democracy was not a consistent, central goal of American policy throughout the century. From helping Mussolini to maintain power in Italy, establishing the Somoza dynasty in Nicaragua, and supporting military rulers throughout Latin America, to the use of covert activities to place rulers such as the Shah of Iran in power and the creation of Diem's South Vietnam, American officials consciously and purposefully supported nondemocratic rulers and forces in the pursuit of expanded trade and investments, anticommunism, and stability. Whatever the reasons for the end of communist rule in Eastern Europe and the collapse of the Soviet Union and the credit the United States does or does not deserve for these developments, the long history of supporting right-wing dictators cannot be erased or ignored. The means of policymaking matter. American support of authoritarian regimes was central to U.S. foreign policy since World War I, influenced its response to the rise of Nazi Germany, helped shape the Cold War, influenced various regions of the world, and continues to play a role in policymaking today and many other nations' perceptions of and reactions to the United States.

U.S. support for right-wing dictatorships was always morally questionable. Because American leaders used moral arguments and appeals to gain public support for their Cold War policies, those policies can be fairly judged on moral terms. The United States has to accept varying degrees of responsibility for aiding in the oppression of people around the world by supplying economic assistance, military goods, and political legitimacy to a large number of despots. This oppression took multiple forms in terms of the denial of human rights, political repression of opposition voices, supporting economic policies that kept people in poverty, and providing the means for governments to use violence against their own people. Worse, the United States often was responsible for the very existence of many of these governments and undermined genuine efforts at reform, self-determination, and democratic change around the world.

Moreover, beyond undermining the avowed rectitude of American officials, the policy was a failure as an effort to advance American interests in the world. It rarely served the national interest and at times, as the Vietnam War and the Watergate crisis best demonstrate, caused significant damage to the nation. The support of various dictators often provided short-term benefits that became long-term problems. Saddam Hussein in Iraq and Suharto in Indonesia provide only the latest examples of this problem. The United States has always had far less leverage with the various dictators it has supported than American leaders believed, and policy often became captive to their personal agendas. A policy designed to produce stability and order, block communists and radical nationalists from power, and protect American economic interests often failed on all accounts. Right-wing dictators more often than not created political polarization in their nations that led to long-term instability and an anti-American sentiment that fostered radical nationalist movements and brought to power, in Cuba, Vietnam, Nicaragua, and Iran, among other nations, the exact forms of governments the United States originally sought to prevent.

The end of the Cold War and the establishment of new governments in Eastern Europe and the former Soviet Union challenge many of the ideas previously used to justify American support of right-wing dictators. If anticommunism no longer provides a unifying theme for American policy, some evidence still suggests that the ideological, economic, and racial arguments used to rationalize American support for authoritarian regimes continue to shape policy toward certain nations. The gathering of world leaders in New York City for the fiftieth anniversary of the founding of the United Nations brought to light the persistence of the positive views of right-wing dictators held by many American officials. President Bill Clinton made sure that he never came face-to-face with Fidel Castro, yet President Suharto of Indonesia was hosted at a White House meeting that was attended by all of the top diplomatic and military officials in the administration. Although Suharto continued to rule by force and the corruption and repression of his regime were well known, the *New York Times* reported that there was not an empty seat in the cabinet room for the meeting with Suharto. Clinton "made the requisite complaints about Indonesia's repressive tactics in East Timor . . . and moved right on to business, getting Mr. Suharto's support for market-opening progress during the annual Asian Pacific Economic Cooperation meeting." As one senior administration official stated, "He's our kind of guy."[6] Three years later, Suharto was driven from power by the Indonesian people.

Notes

ABBREVIATIONS

AWF   Papers as President of the United States, 1953–61 (Ann
              Whitman Files), Dwight D. Eisenhower Papers, Dwight D.
              Eisenhower Presidential Library
BLP   Breckinridge Long Papers, Library of Congress
CEHP   Charles Evans Hughes Papers, Library of Congress
CF   Confidential File (followed in citations by the abbreviation for
              the relevant presidential library)
CFR   Council on Foreign Relations, New York
CHP   Cordell Hull Papers (microfilm edition), Library of Congress
CIA   Central Intelligence Agency
CO   Country Files (followed in citations by the abbreviation for the
              relevant presidential library)
DDE   Dwight D. Eisenhower
DDEL   Dwight D. Eisenhower Presidential Library
DH Series Dulles-Herter Series, Dwight D. Eisenhower Presidential
              Library
FBKP   Frank B. Kellogg Papers (microfilm edition), Minnesota
              Historical Society
FCP   Frank Church Papers, Boise State University Library
FDRL   Franklin D. Roosevelt Presidential Library

FRUS	*Foreign Relations of the United States*
GRFL	Gerald R. Ford Presidential Library
HHL	Herbert Hoover Presidential Library
HLSD	Henry L. Stimson Diaries (microfilm edition), Sterling Library, Yale University
HLSP	Henry L. Stimson Papers (microfilm edition), Sterling Library, Yale University
HSTL	Harry S. Truman Presidential Library
JFDP	John Foster Dulles Papers, Dwight D. Eisenhower Presidential Library
JFKL	John F. Kennedy Presidential Library
JPMP	Jay Pierrepont Moffat Papers, Houghton Library, Harvard University
LBJL	Lyndon B. Johnson Presidential Library
M527	Record Group 59, Microcopy 527
M529	Record Group 59, Microcopy 529
NIE	National Intelligence Estimate (followed in citations by the abbreviation for the relevant presidential library)
NSAM	National Security Action Memorandum (followed in citations by the abbreviation for the relevant presidential library)
NSC	National Security Council (followed in citations by the abbreviation for the relevant presidential library)
NSF	National Security Files (followed in citations by the abbreviation for the relevant presidential library)
NSF:CO	National Security Files: Country (followed in citations by the abbreviation for the relevant presidential library)
NSF:NIE	National Security Files: National Intelligence Estimates (followed in citations by the abbreviation for the relevant presidential library
NSF:NSAM	National Security Files: National Security Action Memorandum (followed in citations by the abbreviation for the relevant presidential library)
OF	Official File (followed in citations by the abbreviation for the relevant presidential library)
OSANSA	Office of the Special Assistant for National Security Affairs (followed in citations by the abbreviation for the relevant presidential library)
OSS	Office of Staff Secretary (followed in citations by the abbreviation for the relevant presidential library)
POF	President's Office Files (followed in citations by the abbreviation for the relevant presidential library)
PPF	President's Personal File
PSF	President's Secretary's File (followed in citations by the abbreviation for the relevant presidential library)
RG38	Record Group 38: Office of Naval Intelligence, National Archives

RG59   Record Group 59: Records of the Department of State, National
        Archives
RWCP   Richard Washburn Child Papers, Library of Congress
TWLP   Thomas W. Lamont Papers, Baker Library, Harvard University
WGHP   Warren G. Harding Papers (microfilm edition), Ohio Historical
        Society
WHCF   White House Central File (followed in citations by the
        abbreviation for the relevant presidential library)
WHO   White House Office (followed in citations by the abbreviation for
        the relevant presidential library)
WPP   William Phillips Papers, Houghton Library, Harvard University
WWP   Woodrow Wilson Papers (microfilm edition), Library of Congress

INTRODUCTION

1. Robert Pastor and archivists at the Franklin D. Roosevelt Presidential Library, Hyde Park, New York, have searched for the origins of this statement but have been unable to find one. See Pastor, *Condemned to Repetition*, 3. The first time it appeared was in *Time*, 15 November 1948, 43. A 17 March 1960 *CBS Reports* broadcast, "Trujillo: Portrait of a Dictator," asserted that Roosevelt was referring to Rafael Trujillo of the Dominican Republic when he allegedly made the statement.

2. Adler and Paterson sparked a brief debate on this question with their article "Red Fascism"; see also Smith, "Authoritarianism and American Policy Makers in Two World Wars"; and Maddux, "Red Fascism, Brown Bolshevism." I use the terms *right-wing dictatorships* and *authoritarian regimes* interchangeably throughout the text.

Adler and Paterson argue that many "Americans took the unhistorical and illogical view that Russia in the 1940s would behave as Germany had in the previous decade" because of a popular analogy that merged Nazi Germany and Soviet Russia as similar totalitarian states ("Red Fascism," 1061). Their purpose was to demonstrate how the analogy of Red Fascism misled policymakers concerning Soviet policy and played a part in the development of the Cold War. Smith observed in response that the comparison between Hitler and Stalin "actually had its origins far earlier" than World War II. Rather, "its immediate roots lie in the First World War, when American officials proclaimed the concept of an evil authoritarian or statist menace and bracketed together autocratic Germany, militaristic Japan (to a lesser degree), and Bolshevik Russia." Smith, therefore, found continuity in the similar attitudes of policymakers during the 1930s in comparing Nazi Germany, Japan, and the Soviet Union and concludes that for American leaders "authoritarianism, whether on the 'right' or the 'left,' represented the antithesis of American values and constituted a menace to the . . . interests of the United States" ("Authoritarianism and American Policy Makers in Two World Wars," 303–4, 310).

Yet the question was not so clear-cut as American efforts at appeasement of Nazi Germany indicate. As Smith notes, Franklin Roosevelt "distinguished between those [authoritarian governments] that threatened peace and those that apparently did not" (ibid., 313). Moreover, Robert Skotheim has argued in his examination of the development of the American idea of totalitarianism during the interwar years that Americans often adopted a "pragmatic rationale" for defending dictatorships they favored. Moral judgments were invoked only when the government opposed a regime. My research confirms Skotheim's observation. See Skotheim, "The Idea of Totalitarianism," in Skotheim and McGiffert, eds., *American Social Thought*, 349.

Friendly Tyrants, edited by Daniel Pipes and Adam Garfinkle, contains twenty-three essays on American policy toward anticommunist authoritarian states. Funded by the Foreign Policy Research Institute and published in 1991, the volume attempts to discover whether any patterns existed in American policy toward right-wing dictators and whether "knowledge of such patterns could be put to practical use in managing current troubles and preventing future ones" (ix). The book does not provide a historical overview of American policy toward right-wing dictators. Indeed, only three of the essays examine crises before the 1970s, and most are based on public records. Support for dictators is taken as a given. The focus of the studies is on crisis management and the question "how does one gauge when an authoritarian regime may be susceptible to an overthrow that will damage U.S. interests?" (4). A second volume, Garfinkle et al., *The Devil and Uncle Sam*, is a guide for policymakers to use in managing the problem of friendly tyrants. The authors conclude that on the whole, "U.S. foreign policy has been reasonably effective in achieving a proper balance of realism and idealism, and that balance has stood us in good stead most of the time" (17). This book questions that conclusion.

Tony Smith's *America's Mission* examines U.S. efforts in the twentieth century to promote democratic governments as a means of protecting the national interest. He contends that the American commitment to promoting democracy was not merely rhetorical but marks the "central ambition of American foreign policy during the twentieth century" (3). See the conclusion for a further discussion.

3. Quoted in Schlesinger, *Thousand Days*, 769.

4. The extent to which anticommunism played a role in American foreign policy during the interwar years is examined in Little, "Antibolshevism and American Foreign Policy"; Weil, *Pretty Good Club*; Costigliola, *Awkward Dominion*, 87–93; Jones, ed., *U.S. Diplomats in Europe*; Hunt, *Ideology and U.S. Foreign Policy*, 135–50; and Buckingham, *America Sees Red*, 31–48.

5. In 1848 Secretary of State James Buchanan, summarizing American policy, stated: "We do not go behind the existing Government to involve ourselves in the question of legitimacy. It is sufficient for us to know that a government exists, capable of maintaining itself; and then its recognition on our part inevitably follows" (quoted in Smith, *America's Mission*, 68).

1. Hughes, *Pathway of Peace*, 3–19.
2. The stabilization thesis has dominated most of the recent writing on New Era foreign policy. See, for example, Costigliola, *Awkward Dominion*; Hogan, *Informal Entente*; Leffler, *Elusive Quest*; Parrini, *Heir to Empire*.
3. Quoted in Pusey, *Charles Evans Hughes*, 2:579.
4. Hughes, *Pathway of Peace*, 53.
5. Ibid., 250–66.
6. Link, ed., *Papers of Woodrow Wilson*, 15:545–49.
7. Cronon, ed., *Cabinet Diaries of Josephus Daniels*, 5–7.
8. *FRUS* 1913, 7.
9. Link, ed., *Papers of Woodrow Wilson*, 35:246–52.
10. Gardner, *Safe for Democracy*, 62 (emphasis in the original).
11. Hunt, *Ideology and U.S. Foreign Policy*, 109.
12. Gardner, ed., *Wilson and Revolutions*, 66.
13. Gardner, *Safe for Democracy*, 6.
14. Ibid., 1.
15. *FRUS: The Lansing Papers*, 2:343–45.
16. Filene, *American Views of Soviet Russia*, 26–28; Foglesong, *America's Secret War against Bolshevism*.
17. Gardner, ed., *Wilson and Revolutions*, 49, 53.
18. Filene, *American Views of Soviet Russia*, 43–46.
19. Hunt, *Ideology and U.S. Foreign Policy*, 114.
20. Gardner, ed., *Wilson and Revolutions*, 139–40.
21. Hughes, Speech to the Union League Club, 26 March 1919, CEHP.
22. Hughes, "The Republic after the War," 17 January 1919, CEHP.
23. Hughes, Speech to the Union League Club, 26 March 1919, CEHP.
24. Hughes, Campaign Speech, Box 189, CEHP.
25. Quoted in Williams, *Tragedy of American Diplomacy*, 130.
26. Hughes, *Pathway of Peace*, 9–10.
27. Quoted in Glad, *Charles Evans Hughes and the Illusions of Innocence*, 91.
28. Cohen, *Empire without Tears*, 16.
29. Hughes, *Pathway of Peace*, 250–66.
30. Hughes to Harding, 10 May 1922, WGHP.
31. Quoted in Woodward, "Postwar Reconstruction and International Order," 13.
32. Quoted in Downes, *Rise of Warren Gamaliel Harding*, 258, 260, 269.
33. Ibid., 315–19, 321.
34. On Hoover's views, see Hogan, *Informal Entente*, 1–12, 38–42; Brandes, *Herbert Hoover and Economic Diplomacy*; Melvyn P. Leffler, "Herbert Hoover, the 'New Era,' and American Foreign Policy, 1921–1929," in Hawley, ed., *Herbert Hoover as Secretary of Commerce*, 148–82; Wilson, *Herbert Hoover*, 79–92, 168–96.
35. Leffler, "Herbert Hoover, the 'New Era,' and American Foreign Policy, 1921–1929," in Hawley, ed., *Herbert Hoover as Secretary of Commerce*, 152–53.

36. Quoted in Costigliola, *Awkward Dominion*, 41.

37. Hoover to Wilson, 28 March 1919, WWP, Series 5B, Reel 398.

38. Costigliola, *Awkward Dominion*, 40, 43. See also Hoover to Wilson, 20 December 1918, in O'Brien, ed., *Two Peacemakers in Paris*, 21–23.

39. Hoover to Wilson, 28 March 1919, WWP, Series 5B, Reel 398.

40. Hoover, *Ordeal of Woodrow Wilson*, 136.

41. Burner, *Herbert Hoover*, 123–24; Costigliola, *Awkward Dominion*, 52–53.

42. Hoover to Wilson, 28 March 1919, WWP, Series 5B, Reel 398.

43. Ibid., emphasis added. See also Hoover memorandum on Bolshevism, 25 April 1919, in O'Brien, ed., *Two Peacemakers in Paris*, 135–41, where he restates these same positions.

44. Hoover, *American Individualism*, 68–69.

45. Ibid., 1–4, 18, 36.

46. Ibid., 70–71, emphasis added.

47. Horsman, *Race and Manifest Destiny*. See also Johannsen, *To the Halls of Montezuma*; Hofstader, *Social Darwinism in American Thought*; Weston, *Racism in U.S. Imperialism*; Hunt, *Ideology and U.S. Foreign Policy*; Drinnon, *Facing West*.

48. Hunt, *Ideology and U.S. Foreign Policy*, 78–79.

49. Ibid., 52. See also Healy, *Drive to Hegemony*, 58–76. Healy demonstrates that as the United States embarked on its quest to dominate the Caribbean basin, "many of the nation's people and policy makers already harbored a set of shared assumptions which would condition their future actions in the area" (58).

50. Hofstader, *Social Darwinism in American Thought*, 172.

51. Hunt, *Ideology and U.S. Foreign Policy*, 81.

52. Welch, *Response to Imperialism*, 15.

53. Weston, *Racism in U.S. Imperialism*, 99.

54. Welch, *Response to Imperialism*, 59.

55. Weston, *Racism in U.S. Imperialism*, 35, 39.

56. *FRUS* 1901, xxxii.

57. Ibid.

58. Lael, *Arrogant Diplomacy*, 11.

59. Welch, *Response to Imperialism*, 104.

60. Quoted in Hofstader, *Social Darwinism in American Thought*, 175.

61. Weston, *Racism in U.S. Imperialism*, 19.

62. Welch, *Response to Imperialism*, 72.

63. *FRUS* 1898, 755–60.

64. Hunt, *Ideology and U.S. Foreign Policy*, 62.

65. Weston, *Racism in U.S. Imperialism*, 159. As former secretary of state John W. Foster said in opposing annexation, "With the negro problem in our Southern States pressing upon us for solution . . . do we desire to aggravate the situation by adding a million more of the despised race to our voting population" (159–60).

66. Quoted in LaFeber, *Panama Canal*, 54.

67. Quoted in Blum, *Republican Roosevelt*, 127.

68. *FRUS* 1904, xli.

69. Burton, *Theodore Roosevelt*, 106.
70. Quoted in Healy, *Drive to Hegemony*, 176.
71. Schmidt, *Maverick Marine*, 75, 76.
72. Schmidt, *United States Occupation of Haiti*, 63.
73. Quoted in Healy, *Drive to Hegemony*, 64–65.
74. Schmidt, *Maverick Marine*, 59.
75. Stampp, *Era of Reconstruction*, 4–8; Foner, *Reconstruction*, xix–xx.
76. Stampp, *Era of Reconstruction*, 22.
77. Foner, *Reconstruction*, xxi–xxii.
78. Quoted in Novick, *That Noble Dream*, 76.
79. *FRUS* 1904, xlvi–xlvii.
80. Ibid.
81. Healy, *Drive to Hegemony*, 62–63.
82. Quoted in LaFeber, *Inevitable Revolutions*, 36–37.
83. Hughes, *Our Relations to the Nations of the Western Hemisphere*, 8.
84. Castle Diary, 7 July 1923, 16 January 1925.
85. Schulzinger, *Making of the Diplomatic Mind*, 91.
86. Ibid., 95, 90–94.
87. Ibid., 130–31.
88. For a discussion of Wilson's policy on Fiume, see Schmitz, *The United States and Fascist Italy*, chap. 1.
89. Wilson, *Messages and Papers of Woodrow Wilson*, 2:659–62.
90. Auchincloss Diary, 10 May 1918, Box 2, Folder 20, Auchincloss Papers.
91. Memorandum, E. L. Bogart to William R. Castle, 18 July 1919, 865.00/63, RG59 M527.
92. The American embassy and consulates in Italy kept the State Department well informed on the violence in Italy. For examples of these reports, see Embassy Weekly Report, 4 June 1921, 865.00/876; Consul Geneo to Department, 17 May 1921, 865.99/856; Consul Piedmont to Department, 24 May 1921, 865.00/857; Embassy to Department, 14 and 21 June 1921, 865.99/877 and 865.99/890. For reports that the fascists instigated most battles, see Consul Venice to Department, 7 July 1921, 865.00/908; Embassy to Department, 19 and 25 July 1921, 865.00/919 and 865.00/925, all in RG59 M527. See also Maier, *Recasting Bourgeois Europe*, 109–34, 322–50; Seton-Watson, *Italy from Liberalism to Fascism*, 561–629; Lyttelton, *Seizure of Power*, 15–76; Mack Smith, *Mussolini*, 40–51.
93. Seton-Watson, *Italy from Liberalism to Fascism*, 580.
94. A table of American prearmistice and postarmistice loans appears in Bemis, *Diplomatic History of the United States*, 713.
95. Robert Underwood Johnson to Charles Evans Hughes, 7 March 1921, 865.00/1125; 22 March 1921, 865.00/1126; 12 April 1921, 865.00/1127, all in RG59 M527.
96. Telegram, Johnson to Secretary of State, 22 July 1920, 865.00/567, RG59 M527.
97. For example, see Embassy Weekly, 8 February 1921, 865.00/758, RG59 M527.

98. Embassy Weekly to Hughes, 14 June 1921, 865.00/877, RG59 M527.

99. Embassy Weekly to Hughes, 21 June 1921, 856.00/890, RG59 M527.

100. Embassy Weekly to Hughes, 19 July 1921, 865.00/919, RG59 M527.

101. Giolitti to Rossi, 30 April 1921, 711.65/5, RG59 M529.

102. See De Santi, "United States Relations with Italy under Mussolini," 26.

103. Child to Hughes, 30 August 1921, 711.65/-, RG59 M529.

104. Child to Hughes, 10 October 1921, 711.65/8, RG59 M529.

105. Child to Harding, 5 September, 11 October 1921; Harding to Child, 24 September, 7 November 1921, Executive File 638, WGHP.

106. Harding to Child, 17 June, 24 July 1922, ibid.

107. Memorandum, Gunther to Child, 28 July 1922, forwarded to the Department by Ambassador Child, 28 July 1922, 865.00/1145, RG59 M527.

108. "Fascism," 12 August 1922, Report prepared for the Ambassador by the Embassy Military Attaché, 865.00/1151, RG59 M527.

109. Ibid.

110. Child to Harding, 17 August 1922, Executive File 638, WGHP.

111. Child to Hughes, 9 October 1922, 865.00/1162; Child to Hughes, 26 October 1922, 865.00/1164, both in RG59 M527.

112. Richard W. Child to H. Walter Child, 31 October 1922, Box 2, RWCP.

113. Telegram, Child to Hughes, 1 November 1922, 865.00/1170, RG59 M527.

114. Telegram, Child to Hughes, 30 October 1922, 865.00/1167, RG59 M527 (emphasis in the original).

115. Child to Hughes, 30 October 1922, 865.00/1167, RG59 M527.

116. Embassy Weekly to Department, 4 November 1922, 865.00/1180, RG59 M527.

117. Harding to Child, 2 November 1922, Executive File 638, WGHP.

118. Embassy Weekly to Department, 4 November 1922, 865.00/1180, RG59 M527.

119. Mussolini to Hughes, 31 October 1922, 865.002/67, RG59. Mussolini's telegram was published in the *New York Times*, 1 November 1922, 1.

120. Hughes to Mussolini, 2 November 1922, 865.002/67, RG59.

121. Child to Harding, 16 November 1922, Executive File 638, WGHP.

122. The Italian ambassador is quoted in Embassy Weekly, 14 July 1923, 865.00/1241, RG59 M527. The Italian embassy in Washington had made similar observations in November 1922. See Berutti, "Italo-American Diplomatic Relations," 7.

123. Telegram, Child to Hughes, 30 October 1922, 865.00/1167; telegram, Child to Hughes, 1 November 1922, 856.00/1170, both in RG59 M527.

124. Embassy Weekly to Department, 4 November 1922, 865.00/1180; Embassy Weekly to Department, 11 November 1922, 865.00/1184; see also Child to Hughes, 1 May 1923, 865.00/1227, all in RG59 M527.

125. Child to Hughes, 1 May 1923, 865.00/1227, RG59 M527; see also Gunther to Hughes, 18 November 1922, 865.00/1187, RG59 M527.

126. Gunther to Hughes, 18 November 1922, 856.00/1187; 26 November 1922, 865.00/1190, 20 December 1922, 865.00/1199, all in RG59 M527.

127. Mellon, quoted in the *New York Times*, 13 October 1926, 25; 26 June 1925,

19; United States World War Foreign Debt Commission, *Combined Annual Reports of the World War Foreign Debt Commission*.

128. Castle Diary, 11 January 1924.
129. Lamont to Dwight Morrow, 23 May 1923, 113–14, TWLP.
130. Lamont to R. C. Leffingwell, 20 April 1925, 103–11, TWLP.
131. Quoted in Jordan, "America's Mussolini," 82–83.
132. Ralph Easley to Lamont, 27 November 1925, 149–37, TWLP.
133. *Nation*, 18 April 1923, 459.
134. See Ambassador Fletcher's report of 16 June 1924, 865.00/1323, and Fletcher to Hughes, 23 June 1924, 865.00/1325, for information, quotation, and background, both in RG59 M527. See also Seldes, *Sawdust Caesar*, 147–75; Lyttelton, *Seizure of Power*, 237–68.
135. Telegram, Fletcher to Hughes, 20 June 1924, 865.00/1315, RG59 M527.
136. Fletcher to Hughes, 23 June 1924, 865.00/1325, RG59 M527.
137. Memorandum, Western European Division, State Department, 3 October 1924, 865.00/1356, RG59 M527.
138. Castle Diary, 12, 15 November 1924.
139. Ibid., 15 November 1924.
140. Telegram, Fletcher to Department, 29 December 1924, 865.00/1383, with Castle's memorandum attached, RG59 M527.
141. Embassy Weekly to Department, 3 January 1925, 865.00/1398, RG59 M527.
142. Embassy Weekly to Department, 21 February 1925, 865.00/1416, RG59 M527.
143. Fletcher to Kellogg, 13 July 1925, 865.00/1455, RG59 M527.
144. Nitti to Kellogg, 17 August 1925, 865.00/1466, with attached memorandum, Castle to Kellogg, 2 September 1925, RG59 M527.
145. Kellogg to Fletcher, 10 July 1926, Reel 21, FBKP.
146. See Schmitz, *The United States and Fascist Italy*, for a complete discussion of these points. The total amount loaned is cited in De Santi, "United States Relations with Italy under Mussolini," 100; investment figures are from U.S. Department of Commerce, Bureau of Foreign and Domestic Commerce, *A New Estimate of American Investments Abroad*, 10–15, and Lary et al., *The United States in the World Economy*, 100–105.
147. Castle Diary, 25 September 1926.
148. Elihu Root to the Council on Foreign Relations, Records of Meetings, 14 December 1926, CFR.

CHAPTER TWO

1. Quoted in Pusey, *Charles Evans Hughes*, 2:531.
2. Hughes, *Our Relations to the Nations of the Western Hemisphere*, 4, 50.
3. Schulzinger, *Making of the Diplomatic Mind*, 95–97.
4. Stimson, "The United States and the Other American Republics."
5. Quoted in LaFeber, *Inevitable Revolutions*, 64.

6. Rippy, "Dictatorship and Democracy in Latin America."

7. Kamman, *Search for Stability*; Millett, *Guardians of the Dynasty*; Crawley, *Nicaragua in Perspective*; Bacevich, "American Electoral Mission in Nicaragua."

8. Langley, *The United States and the Caribbean*, 107–8.

9. Hughes, *Our Relations to the Nations of the Western Hemisphere*, 46, 50.

10. Stimson, "The United States and the Other American Republics."

11. Memorandum of Conversation between Hughes and Lamont, 26 September 1921, Box 195, TWLP.

12. Hughes, *Our Relations to the Nations of the Western Hemisphere*, 45–46. For a complete analysis of the United States response to economic nationalism in Latin America, see Krenn, *U.S. Policy toward Economic Nationalism in Latin America*.

13. Quoted in Krenn, *U.S. Policy toward Economic Nationalism in Latin America*, 44, 58, 62.

14. See Horn, "U.S. Diplomacy and 'The Specter of Bolshevism' in Mexico," 37.

15. Quoted in Hodgson, *The Colonel*, 108.

16. Kamman, *Search for Stability*, 19–68.

17. McCoy, *Calvin Coolidge*, 352.

18. Memorandum by Under Secretary of State Robert Olds, 2 January 1927, 817.00/4350, RG59.

19. Calvin Coolidge, "Conditions in Nicaragua," 10 January 1927, in *FRUS* 1927, 3:288–98.

20. Eder to Hoover, 8 January 1927, "American Interests in Nicaragua," Commerce Papers, Nicaragua, Box 449, HHL.

21. Frank B. Kellogg, "Bolshevik Aims and Policies in Mexico and Latin America," 12 January 1927, Reel 34, FBKP; see also *New York Times*, 13 January 1927, 1.

22. Kamman, *Search for Stability*, 96. An excellent summary of the press reaction to Kellogg's appearance in front of the Senate Foreign Relations Committee is found in "Mexico and Nicaragua," 14 January 1927, Commerce Papers, Mexico, HHL; see also Kellogg to Stimson, 30 April 1927, 817.00/4736, RG59, for the influence of public opinion on American policy. On Borah and the other Peace Progressives, see Johnson, *Peace Progressives and American Foreign Relations*.

23. Stimson, *American Policy in Nicaragua*, 6–10.

24. Stimson, "Memorandum of Conference with Mr. Root, July 6, 1927, Re Nicaragua," HLSP.

25. Stimson, *American Policy in Nicaragua*, 18, 59–61; see also Stimson to Kellogg, 20 April 1927, 817.00/4714, RG59.

26. Stimson Diary, 23 April 1927, HLSD.

27. *FRUS* 1927, 3:331–32.

28. Stimson, *American Policy in Nicaragua*, 65–77; Memorandum of conversation with the president and Robert Olds, 7 April 1927, HLSD; for conversation with Moncada, see *FRUS* 1927, 3:337–42; Stimson Diary, 21 May 1927, HLSD.

29. Stimson Diary, 3 May 1927, HLSD.

30. Ibid., 15 May 1927.
31. Stimson and Bundy, *On Active Service*, 115; Stimson, *American Policy in Nicaragua*, 114–15.
32. Hodgson, *The Colonel*, 117.
33. Stimson, *American Policy in Nicaragua*, 85.
34. Stimson and Bundy, *On Active Service*, 183.
35. Eberhardt to Kellogg, 20 July 1927, Box 211, HLSP.
36. Quoted in Hodgson, *The Colonel*, 119.
37. Boeker, ed., *Henry L. Stimson's American Policy in Nicaragua*, 233–35.
38. McCoy to Kellogg, 12 September 1927, 817.00/5028, RG59; Bacevich, "American Electoral Mission in Nicaragua," 246–50, 253.
39. Walter, *Regime of Anastasio Somoza*, 18.
40. *FRUS* 1929, 3:574.
41. Stimson and Bundy, *On Active Service*, 182.
42. Millett, *Guardians of the Dynasty*, 110–11, 128–30.
43. Hanna to White, 28 October 1932, 817.1051/701 1/2, RG59.
44. Millett, *Guardians of the Dynasty*, 139.
45. LaFeber, *Inevitable Revolutions*, 68.
46. *FRUS* 1936, 5:844–46.
47. Montgomery, *Revolution in El Salvador*, 42; see also Dunkerley, *Long War*.
48. Montgomery, *Revolution in El Salvador*, 42–46.
49. LaFeber, *Inevitable Revolutions*, 71.
50. Quoted in Montgomery, *Revolution in El Salvador*, 46–47.
51. Findling, *Close Neighbors, Distant Friends*, 80; Dunkerley, *Long War*, 22; see also Wilson, "Crisis of National Integration in El Salvador."
52. Anderson, *Matanza*, 7.
53. Robbins to Secretary of State, 2 March 1929, 816.00/742, RG59.
54. Caffery to Kellogg, 2 February 1928, 816.00/703, RG59.
55. Caffery to Kellogg, 1 March 1928, 816.00/707, RG59; see also 14 February 1928, 816.00/708, RG59.
56. Dickson to Kellogg, 5 September 1928, 816.00/731, and 10 September 1928, 816.00/732, RG59.
57. Stimson, "The United States and the Other American Republics."
58. Dickson to Kellogg, 17 October 1928, 816.00/736, RG59.
59. Robbins to Stimson, 27 April 1929, 816.00/746, RG59.
60. Robbins to Stimson, 7 June 1929, 816.00/748, RG59.
61. Robbins to Stimson, 4 October 1929, 816.00/754, RG59.
62. Arnson, *El Salvador*, 13; Dunkerley, *Long War*, 22.
63. Schott to Stimson, 30 March 1930, 816.00B/11, RG59.
64. Schott to Stimson, 14 August 1930, 816.00B/15, RG59.
65. Schott to Stimson, 1 August 1930, 816.00B/14, RG59.
66. Harris to Secretary of War, 22 December 1931, 816.00/828, RG59.
67. Cruse, "Central America: Political," 24 September 1931, 813.00/1257, RG59; Stimson Diary, 4 December 1931, HLSD.
68. Anderson, *Matanza*, 40–63.
69. Robbins to Stimson, 27 March 1931, 816.00/801, RG59.

70. Finley to Stimson, 8 July 1931, 816.00/807, RG59; see also 20 May 1931, 816.00B/38, 27 May 1931, 816.00B/39, and 3 October 1931, 816.00B/42, RG59.

71. For examples of this reporting, see Finley to Stimson, 13 July 1931, 816.00/806, 11 September 1931, 816.00/813, and 21 October 1931, 816.00/815, RG59.

72. Arnson, *El Salvador*, 12.

73. Anderson, *Matanza*, 49–63.

74. Stimson Diary, 4 December 1931, HLSD; see also Grieb, "The United States and the Rise of General Maximiliano Hernández Martínez," for a day-by-day account of the decision on recognition. Grieb's article is narrowly focused on the question of recognition and the 1923 treaty. He does not discuss the *matanza*, nor does he attempt to place American policy in a broader context.

75. Stimson to Curtis, 4 December 1931, 816.00Revolutions/11, RG59.

76. *FRUS* 1931, 2:177–85, 195–96.

77. Stimson Diary, 9 December 1931, HLSD; see also Stimson to Curtis, 7 December 1931, 816.00Revolutions/31, RG59.

78. Stimson to Curtis, 11 December 1931, 816.01/17A, RG59; see also 7 December 1931, 816.00Revolutions/31, RG59.

79. Stimson Diary, 11 December 1931, HLSD; *FRUS* 1931, 2:201.

80. *FRUS* 1931, 2:206, 203.

81. Caffery to Stimson, 1 January 1932, 816.01Caffery Mission/14, RG59.

82. *FRUS* 1931, 2:210–12.

83. Stimson Diary, 8 January 1932, HLSD.

84. *FRUS* 1932, 5:613.

85. McCafferty to Stimson, 20 January 1932, 816.00B/44, RG59.

86. Anderson, *Matanza*, 21; see also 84 and 145.

87. Ibid., 136.

88. Bonner, *Weakness and Deceit*, 23.

89. See Anderson, *Matanza*, 134.

90. McCafferty to Stimson, 23 January 1932, 816.00Revolutions/60 and 816.00 Revolutions/62, RG59.

91. *FRUS* 1932, 5:618–19.

92. Ibid., 615.

93. Stimson Diary, 25 January 1932, HLSD.

94. De Lambert to Wilson, "Growth of Communism in El Salvador," 26 January 1932, 816.00B/55, RG59; for the view of the Eastern European Division, see the summary, "The Communist Movement in Salvador, 1920–1931," Division of Eastern European Affairs, 9 March 1932, 816.00B/56, RG59.

95. Department of State Press Releases, 30 January 1932; *New York Times*, 26 January 1932, 1; see also Hackett, "Communist Uprising in El Salvador," 843–44.

96. Department of State, "Review of Accomplishments," Vol. 1, p. 75, President's Cabinet Offices, Box 49, HHL (emphasis added).

97. Stimson Diary, 25 January 1932, HLSD.

98. *FRUS* 1932, 5:574–75.

99. Ibid., 619–20.

100. Ibid., 579–80; see also 577–79.

101. Ibid., 581, 584–86.

102. Thomson, "Caribbean Situation," 148. An agreement was reached in May 1933 for resumption of interest payments.

103. *FRUS 1932*, 5:584–86.

104. Ibid., 593–94, 602–3.

105. Wilson to White, 11 June 1932, 816.00/877, RG59.

106. Department of State, "Review of Accomplishments," Vol. 1, p. 40, President's Cabinet Offices, Box 49, HHL.

107. *FRUS 1934*, 5:218–19, 255–56.

108. In Nixon, ed., *Franklin D. Roosevelt and Foreign Affairs*, 1:20.

109. Dozer, *Are We Good Neighbors?*, 17.

110. "Uncle Sam as Good Neighbor," *New Republic* 77 (1933): 240.

111. Nixon, ed., *Franklin D. Roosevelt and Foreign Affairs*, 1:560.

112. Maney, *Roosevelt Presence*, 110.

113. Ibid., 18.

114. Freidel, *Franklin D. Roosevelt*, 71.

115. Stimson Diary, "Memorandum of Conversation with Franklin D. Roosevelt," 9 January 1933; "Memorandum of Conversation between Mr. Stimson and the President, Franklin D. Roosevelt," 28 March 1933, HLSD.

116. Welles, "Is America Imperialistic?"; Inman, "Imperialistic America."

117. Herring, "Downfall of Machado," 14–15.

118. Stimson Diary, "Memorandum of Conversation with Franklin D. Roosevelt," 9 January 1933, HLSD.

119. Herring, "Downfall of Machado," 20.

120. Welles, "Relations between the United States and Cuba"; Graff, "Strategy of Involvement," 62–64.

121. Welles to Hull, 14 May 1933, 837.00/3513, RG59.

122. *FRUS 1933*, 5:290.

123. Ibid., 323–27; see also 330–43.

124. Graff, "Strategy of Involvement," 74–77.

125. *FRUS 1933*, 5:334–35, 340–45.

126. Aguilar, *Cuba 1933*, 150.

127. Welles to Hull, 20, 24 August 1933, PSF, Box 40, FDRL.

128. Aguilar, *Cuba 1933*, 175.

129. *FRUS 1933*, 5:381–86.

130. Welles to Hull, 17 September 1933, 837.00/3908, RG59.

131. Quoted in Pérez, *Cuba under the Platt Amendment*, 323–24.

132. Bowers, "Hull, Russian Subversion in Cuba, and Recognition of the U.S.S.R.," 548–50.

133. *FRUS 1933*, 5:403–4.

134. Ibid., 469–73, 477.

135. Quoted in Gellman, *Roosevelt and Batista*, 67.

136. *FRUS 1933*, 5:406, 535–36.

137. Green, *Containment of Latin America*, 17.

138. Paterson, *Contesting Castro*, 16.

139. Matthews to Hull, 26 February 1934, 837.00B/118, RG59.

140. Caffery to Hull, 2 April 1934, 837.00/4964, RG59.

141. Gellman, *Roosevelt and Batista*, 99.

142. Caffery to Hull, 4 May 1934, 837.00/5055, RG59.

143. Caffery to Hull, 5 September 1934, 837.00/5424, RG59.

144. "Observations on Coming Cuban Elections," Division of Latin American Affairs, Memorandum, 19 December 1935, 837.00/6938, RG59.

145. Barry, "Cuba Boils Again—With Two Dictators," 17.

146. Herring, "Another Chance in Cuba," 656–60.

147. Barry, "Batista—Ruler of Cuba," 48–51, 73.

148. Wright to Hull, 15 January 1938, 837.00/8226, RG59.

149. Messersmith to Hull, 12 July 1940, 711.37/342, RG59.

150. Roosevelt's toast, 8 December 1942, "At the State Dinner for President Fulgencio Batista of Cuba," PSF, Box 40, FDRL.

151. Spruhs to Watson, 29 April 1939, PSF: Diplomatic, Box 62, FDRL.

CHAPTER THREE

1. Roosevelt to Earle, 22 December 1933, in Roosevelt, ed., *F.D.R.*, 1:379–80.

2. See Schulzinger, *Making of the Diplomatic Mind*; Weil, *Pretty Good Club*; DeSantis, *Diplomacy of Silence*; Jones, ed., *U.S. Diplomats in Europe*; and Little, "Antibolshevism and American Foreign Policy."

3. Weil, *Pretty Good Club*, 22.

4. DeSantis, *Diplomacy of Silence*, 8–9.

5. Jones, ed., *U.S. Diplomats in Europe*, xvii, xxii.

6. Wyman, *Paper Walls*, and *Abandonment of the Jews*.

7. Weil, *Pretty Good Club*, 56.

8. Stimson and Bundy, *On Active Service*, 268–70.

9. Schmitz, *The United States and Fascist Italy*, 135–52.

10. Roosevelt to Long, 16 June 1933, Box 105, BLP.

11. Roosevelt to Lawrence, 27 July 1933, PPF 101, FDRL.

12. Roosevelt to Long, 11 September 1933, Box 104, BLP.

13. *FRUS* 1933, 2:209.

14. See Burke, *Ambassador Frederic Sackett and the Collapse of the Weimar Republic*.

15. *FRUS* 1933, 2:193–98; see also 216–20.

16. Ibid., 328–30.

17. Ibid, 186.

18. Offner, *American Appeasement*, 58.

19. State Department, 16 February 1937, "Memorandum for the Honorable Norman H. Davis: A Contribution to a Peace Settlement," Box 24, Davis Papers.

20. Quoted in MacDonald, *The United States, Britain and Appeasement*, 8.

21. Long to Roosevelt, 19 April 1935, PSF: Italy: Breckinridge Long, FDRL.

22. William Phillips Diary, 14 August 1934, WPP.
23. "Italy," State Department Information Series No. 67, 4 February 1935, 865.00/1713, RG59.
24. Roosevelt to Long, 9 March 1935, Box 114, BLP.
25. Long to Roosevelt, 5 April 1935, PSF: Breckinridge Long, FDRL.
26. Nixon, ed., *Franklin D. Roosevelt and Foreign Affairs*, 3:12–14.
27. Rosenman, ed., *Public Papers and Addresses of Franklin D. Roosevelt*, 4:442–43.
28. Roosevelt to Straus, 13 February 1936, PSF: Diplomatic, Box 42, FDRL.
29. Hull, *Memoirs*, 1:421.
30. For examples, see *FRUS* 1934, 2:754–57; Long to Roosevelt, 15, 21 February, 5, 19 April, 29 November 1935; Roosevelt to Long, 8 May 1935, all in PSF: Breckinridge Long, FDRL; Long to Hull, 6 March 1935, 765.84/216, 24 September 1935, 765.84/1342, 18 October 1935, 765.84/2245, all in RG59.
31. Harris, *The United States and the Italo-Ethiopian Crisis*, 31.
32. Millsap, "Mussolini and the United States," 8–9.
33. Moffat to Dunn, 3 January 1936, Moffat to Castle, 28 February 1936, vol. 10, JPMP.
34. Phillips, *Ventures in Diplomacy*, 168.
35. Roosevelt to Hull, 4 October 1935, Official File 547A, FDRL.
36. Quoted in Sherwood, *Roosevelt and Hopkins*, 79.
37. Jablon, *Crossroads of Decision*, 108–9; Harris, *The United States and the Italo-Ethiopian Crisis*, 67–68; Burns, *Roosevelt*, 257.
38. Harris, *The United States and the Italo-Ethiopian Crisis*, 97–113.
39. *FRUS* 1935, 1:826–33.
40. Laughlin to Stimson, 5 May 1931, 852.00/1843, RG59.
41. Little, *Malevolent Neutrality*, 69–70, 11.
42. Park, *Latin American Underdevelopment*, 13–15.
43. Laughlin to Stimson, 16 April 1931, 852.00/1818, RG59.
44. Laughlin to Stimson, 10 March 1930, 852.00/1782, and 28 February 1931, 852.00/1811, RG59.
45. Laughlin to Stimson, 5 May 1931, 852.00/1843, RG59; see also Laughlin to Stimson, 19 May 1931, 852.00/1846 1//2, RG59.
46. For examples, see Laughlin to Stimson, 25 January 1932, 852.00/1891, 27 January 1932, 852.00/1927, and Dawson to Department of State, 13 January 1932, 852.00/1926, RG59.
47. Phillips Diary, August 1935, WPP.
48. Quoted in Little, *Malevolent Neutrality*, 201.
49. Bowers to Hull, 19 February 1936, 852.00/2140, and 18 March 1936, 852.00/2147, RG59.
50. Quoted in Little, *Malevolent Neutrality*, 195.
51. Bowers to Hull, 21 April 1936, 852.00/2157, RG59.
52. Quoted in Little, *Malevolent Neutrality*, 201; see also Lane to Hull, 29 July 1936, 852.00/2308, RG59.
53. Morgan Report, "United States Policy during the Spanish Civil War, July 1936–April 1939," Reel 49, CHP.

54. Dunn, undated memorandum attached to Bowers to Hull, 3 June 1936, 852.00/2170, RG59.
55. Quoted in Little, *Malevolent Neutrality*, 263.
56. Phillips Diary, 3 August 1936, WPP; Phillips probably meant anarchists when he wrote "radicalists."
57. Ibid., 4 August 1936.
58. Quoted in Little, *Malevolent Neutrality*, 257.
59. Wendelin to Hull, 12 August 1936, 852.00/2980, RG59; Bowers to Hull, 6 October 1936, Reel 13, CHP.
60. *FRUS* 1937, 1:346–47, 352–53.
61. Moffat Diary, 10 September 1937, JPMP.
62. There is no study of U.S.-Greek relations during the 1930s. Lawrence Wittner notes in his work on America's post–World War II policy toward Greece, *American Intervention in Greece*, that "American relations with Greece predated the establishment of the United States, but acquired significance for U.S. policymakers only with the onset of World War II" (1). My analysis seeks to modify this claim. As Louis P. Cassimatis has demonstrated in his study of U.S.-Greek relations during the 1920s, *American Influence in Greece*, Greece was important to the Near East policy of the United States during the interwar years, and "it was American relief, technical knowledge, and investment capital," in the wake of the disastrous Asia Minor war in 1922, "which contributed in no small measure to the rehabilitation of the country" (x).
63. The discussion of Greek politics is drawn from Clogg, *Short History of Modern Greece*, 105–32; Cliadakis, "Political and Diplomatic Background to the Metaxas Dictatorship"; Sherrard and Campbell, *Modern Greece*, 144–66; and Kousoulas, *Modern Greece*, 136–93.
64. Clogg, *Short History of Modern Greece*, 128.
65. Cliadakis, "Political and Diplomatic Background to the Metaxas Dictatorship," 119.
66. See Iatrides, *Ambassador MacVeagh Reports*, 37.
67. See, for example, MacVeagh to Hull, 14 December 1933, 868.00/728, 18 July 1934, 868.00/742, 11 September 1934, 868.00/746, 18 October 1934, 868.00/751, and 15 January 1935, 868.00/757, all in RG59.
68. MacVeagh to Hull, 18 October 1934, 868.00/751, RG59.
69. MacVeagh to Hull, 15 January 1935, 868.00/757, RG59.
70. MacVeagh to Hull, 11 September 1934, 868.00/746, RG59.
71. MacVeagh to Hull, 13 March 1935, 868.00/815, RG59.
72. MacVeagh to Hull, 17 March 1935, 868.00/822, RG59.
73. MacVeagh to Hull, 2 April 1935, 868.00/834, RG59.
74. MacVeagh to Hull, 18 March 1935, 868.00/824, RG59.
75. MacVeagh to Hull, 24 April 1935, 868.00/851, 24 April 1935, 868.00/852, 24 March 1935, 868.00/827, and 6 May 1935, 868.00/847, all in RG59.
76. MacVeagh to Hull, 10 June 1935, 868.00/865, RG59; Cliadakis, "Political and Diplomatic Background to the Metaxas Dictatorship," 118–20.
77. Cliadakis, "Political and Diplomatic Background to the Metaxas Dictatorship," 120.

78. The British analysis was similar to MacVeagh's. London feared that "anarchy" in Greece was leading to a growing opportunity for the spread of communism into Greece. The issue for Britain, according to John Koliopoulos, was whether Greece "was to become a constitutional monarchy, or fall into anarchy and 'Communism,' which would endanger British interests there" (*Greece and the British Connection*, 18–25).
79. MacVeagh to Hull, 24 September 1935, 868.00/910, RG59.
80. Ibid.
81. MacVeagh to Hull, 14 October 1935, 868.00/917, RG59; MacVeagh to Roosevelt, 15 October 1935, PSF: Greece, FDRL.
82. Howland, "Greece and the Greeks," 458, 463. See also Howland, "Greece and Her Refugees."
83. Miller, "A New Era in Greece," 656.
84. Loukes, "Greece's Benevolent Despotism," 92.
85. MacVeagh to Hull, 30 October 1935, 868.00/913, RG59.
86. MacVeagh to Hull, 9 November 1935, 868.00/934, RG59.
87. MacVeagh to Hull, 18 November 1935, 868.00/924, and 21 November 1935, 868.00/939, RG59. King George II, a relative of the British royal family, had been in exile in London.
88. MacVeagh to Roosevelt, 28 November 1935, PSF: Greece, FDRL.
89. MacVeagh to Roosevelt, 29 February 1936, PSF: Greece, FDRL; see also MacVeagh to Hull, 10 March 1936, 868.00/964, RG59.
90. MacVeagh to Hull, 2 May 1936, 868.00/974, RG59.
91. Iatrides, *Ambassador MacVeagh Reports*, 82.
92. MacVeagh to Hull, 29 May 1936, 868.00/976, RG59.
93. Ibid.
94. Murray to MacVeagh, 13 June 1936, 868.00/978, RG59.
95. Koliopoulos, *Greece and the British Connection*, 41.
96. MacVeagh to Hull, 13 June 1936, 868.00/979, RG59.
97. MacVeagh to Hull, 3 July 1936, 868.00/982, RG59.
98. Shantz to Hull, 5 August 1936, 868.00/983, RG59.
99. Shantz to Hull, 8 August 1936, 868.00/988, RG59.
100. Shantz to Hull, 22 August 1936, 868.00/989, RG59.
101. Murray to Phillips, Memorandum, Division of Near Eastern Affairs, 5 August 1936, 868.00/987, RG59.
102. MacVeagh to Hull, 19 September 1936, 868.00/995, RG59.
103. Cliadakis, "Political and Diplomatic Background to the Metaxas Dictatorship," 129–34.
104. MacVeagh to Hull, 19 September 1936, 868.00/995, RG59.
105. Iatrides, *Ambassador MacVeagh Reports*, 105.
106. MacVeagh to Hull, 5 February 1937, 868.00/1005, RG59; see also MacVeagh to Hull, 17 October 1936, 868.00/997, RG59, and MacVeagh to Roosevelt, 9 November 1936, 17 February 1937, PSF: Greece, FDRL.
107. Quoted in Koliopoulos, *Greece and the British Connection*, 8.
108. Ibid., 106–7.
109. Quoted in DeSantis, *Diplomacy of Silence*, 65.

110. MacVeagh to Roosevelt, 20 May 1938, PSF: Greece, FDRL.
111. On American appeasement and Germany, see Offner, *American Appeasement*, and "Appeasement Revisited"; MacDonald, *The United States, Britain and Appeasement*; Hearden, *Roosevelt Confronts Hitler*; Schmitz and Challener, eds., *Appeasement in Europe*; and Hans-Jurgen Schroder, "The Ambiguities of Appeasement: Great Britain, the United States and Germany, 1937–39," in Mommsen and Kettenacker, eds., *The Fascist Challenge and the Policy of Appeasement*.
112. State Department, 16 February 1937, "Memorandum for the Honorable Norman H. Davis: Contribution to a Peace Settlement," Box 24, Davis Papers. This analysis, compiled in preparation for Davis's visit to England, is thirty pages long.
113. For Hull's views on trade and war, see Hull, *Memoirs*, esp. 1:75–81, 100–101, 235–45, 438–39, 518–19, and 572–73.
114. Nixon, ed., *Franklin D. Roosevelt and Foreign Affairs*, 3:186–87.
115. Memorandum by Moffat, Chief European Division, Department of State, 21 January 1938, 611.6231/1002 1//2, RG59.
116. State Department, 16 February 1937, "Memorandum for the Honorable Norman H. Davis: Contribution to a Peace Settlement," Box 24, Davis Papers.
117. Schewe, ed., *Franklin D. Roosevelt and Foreign Affairs* vol. 1, document 11.
118. Phillips to Roosevelt, 22 April 1937, WPP.
119. Ibid.
120. Wilson, *Diplomat between Wars*, 323.
121. Quoted in DeSantis, *Diplomacy of Silence*, 71.
122. "Italy: Political Estimate," 30 June 1937, 865.00/1745, RG59.
123. Quoted in MacDonald, *The United States, Britain and Appeasement*, 31.
124. Graff, "Strategy of Involvement," 168.
125. Schewe, ed., *Roosevelt and Foreign Affairs*, vol. 2, document 402.
126. Roosevelt, ed., *F.D.R.*, 1:656.
127. Roosevelt to Phillips, 13 May 1937, WPP.
128. *FRUS* 1937, 1:665–70.
129. Hooker, ed., *Moffat Papers*, 183.
130. *FRUS* 1937, 2:24–26.
131. Quoted in MacDonald, *The United States, Britain and Appeasement*, 38, 87–88.
132. Welles, *Time for Decision*, 50, 65.
133. Hull, *Memoirs*, 1:546–49.
134. *FRUS* 1938, 1:115–20.
135. Ibid., 118–20.
136. Ibid., 120–22.
137. Quoted in MacDonald, *The United States, Britain and Appeasement*, 71.
138. Phillips Diary, 4 April 1938, WPP.
139. *FRUS* 1938, 1:147–48.
140. Roosevelt, ed., *F.D.R.*, 2:810–11.
141. Phillips, *Ventures in Diplomacy*, 221.

142. Quoted in MacDonald, *The United States, Britain and Appeasement*, 88.
143. Berle and Jacobs, eds., *Navigating the Rapids*, 184–85.
144. Phillips, *Ventures in Diplomacy*, 222; see also Phillips to Hull, 7, 21 October 1938, RG38.
145. Schewe, ed., *Franklin D. Roosevelt and Foreign Affairs*, vol. 7, document 1309.
146. Moffat Diary, 30 September 1938, JPMP.
147. Address, Sumner Welles, 3 October 1938, copy in Berle Papers. See also Graff, "Strategy of Involvement," 242.
148. Quoted in Blum, ed., *From the Morganthau Diaries*, 524.
149. Roosevelt to Stephen T. Early, 10 January 1939, PPF:5763, FDRL.
150. Phillips, Oral History, Columbia University.
151. Memorandum by Roosevelt, 19 March 1939, PSF: Italy, Phillips, FDRL. This memorandum was drawn up by the president for his own use during his meeting with Ambassador Colonna.
152. *FRUS* 1939, 2:620–22.

CHAPTER FOUR

1. Division of American Republics, "Ambassador Braden's Proposed Policy Respecting Dictatorships and Disreputable Governments in the Other American Republics," October 1945, Records of Deputy Assistant Secretaries of State for Inter-American Affairs, 1945–56, Box 2, RG59. Quotations in the following eight paragraphs are from this source.
2. Division of American Republics, "Policy toward Dictatorships and Disreputable Governments," 24 January 1946, ibid.
3. On wartime relations with Argentina, see Woods, *Roosevelt Foreign Policy Establishment*.
4. Stettinius to Roosevelt, 1944, "Our Policy toward Argentina," PSF: Argentina, Box 23, FDRL; see also memorandum, 2 January 1945, "United States Policy toward Argentina," ibid.
5. Quoted in Woods, *Roosevelt Foreign Policy Establishment*, 192; see also Green, *Containment of Latin America*, 237–54.
6. For Acheson's comment, see Smith, *Last Years of the Monroe Doctrine*, 57.
7. Braden to Secretary of State, 31 May 1945, PSF: Subject File, Box 188, HSTL.
8. *Time*, 5 November 1945, "Democracy's Bull," 45–47; Tulchin, *Argentina and the United States*, 88–96; Woods, *Roosevelt Foreign Policy Establishment*, 205–9.
9. *FRUS* 1945, 9:406–10.
10. Ibid., 190–96.
11. Byrnes to Truman, 8 February 1946 Memorandum, "Argentine Complicity with the Enemy," PSF: Subject File, Box 170, Argentina no. 2, HSTL. The Blue Book is attached.
12. Tulchin, *Argentina and the United States*, 94; Rabe, *Eisenhower and Latin America*, 14.

13. Tulchin, *Argentina and the United States*, 94.

14. Messersmith to Byrnes, 15 June 1946, and Messersmith to Truman, 15 June 1946, PSF: Subject File, Box 170, HSTL.

15. Messersmith to Byrnes, 15 June 1946, and Messersmith to Truman, 15 June 1946, PSF: Subject File, Box 170, HSTL.

16. Truman to Acheson, 22 July 1946; Braden's July 1946 "Memorandum on the Argentine Situation" is attached, PSF: Subject File, Box 170, HSTL.

17. Messersmith to Byrnes, 15 August 1946; for other examples, see Messersmith to Truman, 16 August 1946; Messersmith to Byrnes, 28 August 1946; Messersmith to Truman, 9 October 1946; Messersmith to Byrnes, 12 October 1946; Messersmith to Truman, 23 October 1946; and Messersmith to Byrnes, 30 October 1946, all in PSF: Subject File, Box 170, HSTL. On the conflict between the two men, see Trask, "Spruille Braden versus George Messersmith."

18. Messersmith to Truman, 16 August 1946, with copy of Messersmith to Byrnes, 16 August 1946; Messersmith to Acheson, 16 August 1946; Acheson to Messersmith, 29 August 1946; Truman to Messersmith, 6 September 1946, all in PSF: Subject File, Box 170, HSTL.

19. Trask, "Spruille Braden versus George Messersmith," 83–84; *Time*, 2 December 1946, "Career Man's Mission," 22–24.

20. *Public Papers of the Presidents: Truman, 1947*, 167–70.

21. Quoted in Leffler, *Specter of Communism*, 52.

22. Kennan, *Memoirs, 1925–1950*, 271–97, 547–59.

23. For a summary of these concerns, see NSC, "Review of the World Situation as It Relates to the Security of the United States," 12 September 1947, Records of the National Security Council, Box 1, HSTL.

24. Adler and Paterson, "Red Fascism," 1061.

25. *FRUS* 1946, 7:840–42.

26. Hamby, *Man of the People*, 353–54.

27. Acheson, *Present at the Creation*, 219.

28. *Public Papers of the Presidents: Truman, 1947*, 176–80.

29. *FRUS* 1947, 1:725–26.

30. Quoted in Trask, "Spruille Braden versus George Messersmith," 85.

31. Ibid., 85–86.

32. *Public Papers of the Presidents: Truman, 1947*, 261.

33. *FRUS* 1947, 8:109.

34. Bruce to Truman, 7 November 1947, and Truman to Bruce, 12 November 1947, PSF: Subject File, Box 170, HSTL.

35. 6 October 1953 Dictation, Post-Presidential File: Memoirs File, Box 4, HSTL.

36. *FRUS* 1950, 2:696–701.

37. Miller, "American Policy in the Western Hemisphere," 25 April 1950, Records of Meetings, CFR.

38. Records of the Deputy Assistant Secretaries of State for Inter-American Affairs, 1945–56, Box 6, Folder: Policy Statements, RG59. Halle's report is attached to Woodward to Barber, Memorandum, 29 July 1949, ibid.

39. *Department of State Bulletin*, 2 January 1949, 30.

40. Records of the Deputy Assistant Secretaries of State for Inter-American Affairs, 1945–56, "Support for Democracy in Latin America," 14 January 1949, Folder: Policy-Position Papers, Box 6, RG59.

41. *FRUS* 1948, 9:141–52.

42. National Security Council Documents, 3d Supplement, CIA, "Review of the World Situation," CIA 12-48, 16 December 1948, Reel 1.

43. CFR, Study Group on Inter-American Affairs, "General Observations on Inter-American Relationships," 10 February 1949, Miller Papers, Box 3, HSTL.

44. *FRUS* 1950, 2:589–92.

45. Records of the Assistant Secretary of State for Latin American Affairs, Miller Papers, 29 August 1949, Box 10, RG59.

46. Quoted in Smith, *Last Years of the Monroe Doctrine*, 63.

47. Records of the Assistant Secretary of State for Latin American Affairs, Miller Papers, 29 August 1949, Box 10, RG59; for a similar analysis that fall, see State Department, Office of Intelligence, Research Report 4780, 1 October 1949, "Political Developments and Trends in the Other American Republics in the Twentieth Century," RG59.

48. Hamby, *Man of the People*, 364–65. See also Hunt, *Ideology and U.S. Foreign Policy*, 163.

49. Smith, *Last Years of the Monroe Doctrine*, 67.

50. *FRUS* 1950, 2:589.

51. Acheson, *Present at the Creation*, 257–58.

52. Quoted in Krenn, "Their Proper Share," 71.

53. Regional Conference of United States Chiefs of Mission, 6–9 March 1950, Records of the Assistant Secretary of State for Latin American Affairs, Miller Papers, Box 5, RG59.

54. Ibid.

55. *FRUS* 1950, 1:234–92.

56. For other discussions of this document, see Smith, *Last Years of the Monroe Doctrine*, 65–73, and "Legacy of Monroe's Doctrine"; and Trask, "George F. Kennan's Report on Latin America (1950)."

57. *FRUS* 1950, 2:598–624.

58. Ibid.

59. Ibid.

60. Ibid., 624; see also Halle to Armstrong (n.d.) and Woodward to Barber, "Area Policy Statement," 29 July 1949, Records of the Deputy Assistant Secretaries of State for Inter-American Affairs, 1945–56, Box 6, RG59.

61. Y, "On a Certain Impatience with Latin America."

62. Miller, "Non-Intervention and Collective Responsibility in the Americas," *Department of State Bulletin*, 15 May 1950, 768–70.

63. Y, "On a Certain Impatience with Latin America," 565–79.

64. Records of the Deputy Assistant Secretaries of State for Inter-American Affairs, 1945–56, Division of Inter-American Affairs to Secretary of State, January 1947, "Policy Matters of Less Immediate Character," Box 6, RG59.

65. Byrnes to Truman, 5 March 1946, PSF: Subject File: Foreign Affairs, Box 183, HSTL.

66. Records of the Deputy Assistant Secretaries of State for Inter-American Affairs, 1945–56, Division of Inter-American Affairs to Secretary of State, January 1947, "Policy Matters of Less Immediate Character," Box 6, RG59.

67. Byrnes to Truman, 23 November 1945, March 1946, PSF: Subject File, Foreign Affairs, Box 176, HSTL.

68. On the Dominican Republic and Trujillo's visits, see *FRUS* 1952–54, 4: 927–38.

69. Reid to Wise and Reveley, 14 October 1949, Records of the Office of Middle American Affairs: Costa Rica and Nicaragua, Box 1, RG59.

70. Waynick to Acheson, 18 January, 31 March 1950, 717.00/1-1850 and 3-3150, RG59.

71. Miller to Whelan, 31 July 1951, Records of the Assistant Secretary of State for Latin American Affairs, Miller Papers, Box 8, RG59.

72. "Study Group Reports, Inter-American Affairs," 7 February 1949, Records of Groups, CFR.

73. Acheson to Truman, 1 May 1952, "Visit of General Anastasio Somoza President of Nicaragua," PSF: Subject File, Foreign Affairs, Box 183, HSTL; see also Miller to Acheson, 28 April 1952, Records of the Assistant Secretary of State for Latin American Affairs, Miller Papers, Box 8, RG59.

74. "Second Meeting of Discussion Group on Political Unrest in Latin America," 18 November 1952, Records of Groups, CFR.

75. Quoted in Hayes, *Wartime Mission in Spain*, 87–91.

76. Hayes to Roosevelt, 26 June, 9 November 1944, PSF: Box 50, "Spain: 1940–45," FDRL.

77. Hayes, "Memorandum on the Spanish Situation with Special Reference to Relations between Spain and the United States," February 1945, PSF: Box 50, "Spain 1940–45," FDRL.

78. Ibid.

79. Roosevelt to Armour, 10 March 1945, PSF: Box 50, "Spain 1940–45," FDRL.

80. Ibid.

81. Hamby, *Man of the People*, 329; *FRUS: The Conference of Berlin (Potsdam)*, 2:1171–76.

82. *FRUS: The Conference of Berlin (Potsdam)*, 2:1509–10; see also 621–30.

83. Acheson to Truman, 22 September 1945; Truman to Acheson, 25 September 1945, and attachments, WHCF: CF State Department Correspondence, Box 37, HSTL; the letter appeared in the *New York Times* on 27 September 1945, 1.

84. "Position of the United States, the United Kingdom and France on Relations with the Spanish Government," 4 March 1946, Council on Foreign Relations, *Documents on American Foreign Relations*, vol. 8, 1945–46, 888.

85. United States Department of State, *The Spanish Government and the Axis*.

86. Council on Foreign Relations, *Documents on American Foreign Relations*, vol. 8, 1945–46, 890–91.

87. Cortada, *Two Nations over Time*, 217–18.

88. NSC Report, "Base Rights in Greenland, Iceland, and the Azores," 25 November 1947, PSF: NSC Files Meetings, Box 203, HSTL.

89. CIA, "Portugal," 13 October 1949, PSF: Intelligence File, Box 261, HSTL.

90. Princeton Seminars, 14 March 1954, Acheson Papers, HSTL.

91. Acheson, *Present at the Creation*, 627–28.

92. Princeton Seminars, 14 March 1954, Acheson Papers, HSTL.

93. NSC, "Report of U.S. Policy toward Spain," 17 December 1947; Souers to Truman, 10 January 1948, PSF: NSC Files, Box 203, HSTL.

94. CIA, "The Political Future of Spain," 5 December 1947, PSF: Intelligence File, Box 254, HSTL.

95. "Statement by the Secretary of State on Spain," 18 January 1950, WHCF: CF State Department Correspondence, Box 41 HSTL; Clifford to Truman, 9 January 1950, Souers to Clifford, 6 January 1950, and Elsey to Clifford, 9 January 1950, Files of Clark Clifford, Box 6, HSTL.

96. Bissell to Truman, 14 November 1950, Subject File, Box 64, Elsey Papers, HSTL; Griffis to Truman, 24 November 1950, Miller Papers, Box 2, HSTL; Leffler, *Preponderance of Power*, 417; Whitaker, *Spain and Defense of the West*, 37; "Statement of Policy Proposed by the National Security Council on Spain," 7 June 1951, NSC 72/5, PSF: NSC Files, Box 213, HSTL.

97. Minutes of the 82d Meeting of the NSC, 1 February 1951, NSC 72/4, PSF: NSC Files, Box 211, HSTL; Souers to Truman, 2 February 1951, PSF: NSC Files, Box 220, HSTL.

98. Minutes of the 82d Meeting of the NSC, 1 February 1951, NSC 72/2, PSF: NSC Files, Box 211, HSTL.

99. NSC, "Progress Report on United States Policy toward Spain (NSC 72/4)," 5 June 1951; "Report to the National Security Council on United States Policy toward Spain," 7 June 1951, PSF: NSC Files, Box 213, HSTL; "NSC Progress Report on the Implementation of United States Policy toward Spain," 7 September 1951, PSF: NSC Files, Box 214, HSTL. See also NIE, "Spain's Potentialities in Western Defense," 30 July 1951, PSF: Intelligence File, Box 253, HSTL.

100. The discussions of this issue are in the Lloyd Papers, Box 1, "Franco Letter," HSTL.

101. Quoted in Hamby, *Man of the People*, 572; see also 517–18 and Statement by Griffis, 8 February 1952, OF, Box 1587, HSTL.

102. Truman to Franco, 23 July 1952, Lloyd Papers, Box 1, "Franco Letter," HSTL.

103. Cortada, *Two Nations over Time*, 230–32.

104. Roosevelt to Hull, 24 January 1944, in Williams et al., *America in Vietnam*, 30.

105. See Gardner, *Approaching Vietnam*, 21–53.

106. Rosenman, ed., *Public Papers and Addresses of Franklin D. Roosevelt*, 5:556–65.

107. *FRUS* 1945, 1:121–24.

108. Ibid., 6:307.

109. Memorandum for the President, Division of Far East Affairs, 21 April 1945, "American Policy with Respect to Indochina," in Porter, ed., *Vietnam*, 22.

110. Patti, *Why Viet Nam?*, 382.

111. *FRUS* 1947, 6:95–97.

112. Quoted in Williams et al., *America in Vietnam*, 95.

113. Ibid., 90–92.

114. *FRUS* 1949, 7:29–30.

115. *FRUS* 1950, 6:711–15.

116. Quoted in Patti, *Why Viet Nam?*, 389.

117. *FRUS* 1950, 6:878–79.

118. *FRUS* 1952–54, 13, pt. 1:124–29.

119. Mann to Murphy, 11 December 1952, "Latin America and U.S. Policy," PSF: Foreign Affairs File, Box 182, HSTL; see also NSC, "Current Policies of the Government of the United States Relating to the National Security," November 1952, PSF: Subject File NSC, Box 194, HSTL; and CIA, "Conditions and Trends in Latin America Affecting US Security," 12 December 1952, PSF: Intelligence File, Box 254, HSTL.

120. Mann to Murphy, 11 December 1952, "Latin America and U.S. Policy," PSF: Foreign Affairs File, Box 182, HSTL.

121. Ibid.

122. Ibid.

123. Ibid.

124. Ibid.

125. LaFeber, *Inevitable Revolutions*, 97.

126. See, for example, Acheson, "Waging Peace in the Americas," *Department of State Bulletin*, 26 September 1949, 462–66; Rabe, *Eisenhower and Latin America*, 18–19.

127. *FRUS* 1950, 2:628–35.

128. LaFeber, *Inevitable Revolutions*, 111–12; Rabe, "Inter-American Military Cooperation"; Green, *Containment of Latin America*, 255–90.

129. U.S. Congress, *Executive Sessions*, 1951, 3:348–56.

130. Ibid.

CHAPTER FIVE

1. Eisenhower, *Mandate for Change*, 3.

2. An excellent example of these views can be found in 410th Meeting of the NSC, 18 June 1959, AWF, NSC Series, DDEL.

3. Quoted in Rabe, *Eisenhower and Latin America*, 27; Eisenhower to Dulles, 8 August 1953, AWF, DH Series, Box 1, DDEL.

4. Quoted in Hunt, *Ideology and U.S. Foreign Policy*, 164; on Eisenhower and Arabs, see 410th Meeting of the NSC, 18 June 1959, AWF, NSC Series, DDEL.

5. 132d Meeting of the NSC, 18 February 1953, AWF, NSC Series, DDEL; Dulles to Eisenhower, 26 February 1953, Telephone Series, Box 10, JFDP.

6. Quoted in Hunt, *Ideology and U.S. Foreign Policy*, 166.

7. Eisenhower to Smith, 7 August 1953, AWF, DH Series, Box 1, DDEL.

8. Lodge to Eisenhower, 28 March 1956, AWF, DH Series, Box 6, DDEL (emphasis in the original); Eisenhower to Dulles, 30 March 1956, Memorandum Series, Box 4, JFDP.
9. Eisenhower to Patterson, unsent letter, 15 June 1953, AWF, DDE Diaries, Box 3, DDEL.
10. U.S. Congress, *Executive Sessions*, 1953, 5:387.
11. 177th Meeting of the NSC, 12 December 1953, AWF, NSC Series, DDEL.
12. 150th Meeting of the NSC, 25 June 1953, AWF, NSC Series, DDEL.
13. *FRUS* 1952–54, 4:1602.
14. Ibid., 150–53.
15. Ibid., 86.
16. Ibid., 397.
17. Quoted in Berle and Jacobs, eds., *Navigating the Rapids*, 653–54.
18. 237th Meeting of the NSC, 17 February 1955, AWF, NSC Series, DDEL.
19. NSC 5412, "National Security Council Directive on Covert Operations," March 1954, WHO, OSANSA, Box 10, DDEL.
20. Ambrose, *Eisenhower*, 226–27.
21. Quoted in U.S. Congress, Senate, *Final Report*, Senate Select Committee to Study Governmental Operations with Respect to Intelligence Activities; Anne Karalekas, "History of the Central Intelligence Agency," Supplementary Detailed Staff Reports on Foreign and Military Intelligence, Vol. 4, 94th Cong., 2d sess., 52–53; Leary, ed., *Central Intelligence Agency*, 144.
22. Quoted in Smith, *America's Mission*, 189–90.
23. Yergin, *The Prize*, 452–58.
24. Acheson, *Present at the Creation*, 501; *FRUS* 1952–54, 10:92–173, 241–300; Hamby, *Man of the People*, 571–72.
25. Quoted in Yergin, *The Prize*, 467.
26. Acheson, *Present at the Creation*, 501.
27. 132d Meeting of the NSC, 19 February 1953; 134th Meeting of the NSC, 25 February 1953, AWF, NSC Series, DDEL.
28. 135th Meeting of the NSC, 4 March 1953, AWF, NSC Series, DDEL.
29. Smith to Eisenhower, 23 May 1953, AWF, DH Series, Box 1, DDEL.
30. On the coup, see *FRUS* 1952–54, 10:752–60; Heiss, *Empire and Nationhood*; Roosevelt, *Countercoup*; Rubin, *Paved with Good Intentions*, 78–89; and Bill, *The Eagle and the Lion*, 86–97, for descriptions of the events.
31. *FRUS* 1952–54, 10:756–65.
32. 160th Meeting of the NSC, 27 August 1953, AWF, NSC Series, DDEL.
33. *FRUS* 1952–54, 10:766–68, 775–77; *Department of State Bulletin*, 14 September 1953, 349–50.
34. "United States Policy toward Iran," December 1953, WHO, OSANSA, Box 8, DDEL. A final expanded version was adopted on 2 January 1954; see *FRUS* 1952–54, 10:865–89.
35. 177th Meeting of the NSC, 24 December 1953, AWF, NSC Series, DDEL.
36. *FRUS* 1952–54, 10:855–64.
37. On the negotiations and settlement, see Yergin, *The Prize*, 470–78.
38. Bill, *The Eagle and the Lion*, 114–15.

39. Henderson to Dulles, 9 August 1954, AWF, DH Series, Box 4, DDEL.

40. Dulles to Eisenhower, "Background Information on the Visit of the Shah of Iran," 28 June 1958, AWF, International Series, Box 32, DDEL.

41. Memorandum of Conversation, "Lebanon and the Middle East," 1 July 1958, Eisenhower, Dulles, and Shah of Iran, AWF, International Series, Box 32, DDEL.

42. 410th Meeting of the NSC, 18 June 1959, AWF, NSC Series, DDEL.

43. See Immerman, *CIA in Guatemala*; Gleijeses, *Shattered Hope*; Schlesinger and Kinzer, *Bitter Fruit*; Cook, *Declassified Eisenhower*, 218–92; LaFeber, *Inevitable Revolutions*, 113–27; Rabe, *Eisenhower and Latin America*, 42–63; and Smith, *Last Years of the Monroe Doctrine*, 73–88.

44. Mann, "The Democratic Ideal in Our Policy toward Latin America," 7 June 1964, NSF:CO, Box 2, LBJL.

45. Immerman, *CIA in Guatemala*, 61–82.

46. Quoted in Rabe, *Eisenhower and Latin America*, 47.

47. 132d Meeting of the NSC, 18 February 1953, AWF, NSC Series, DDEL.

48. *FRUS 1952–54*, 4:1–10; 137th Meeting of the NSC, 18 March 1953, AWF, NSC Series, DDEL; Annex to NSC 144, 6 March 1953, WHO, OSANSA, Box 4, DDEL. For the 1952 State Department report, see Mann to Murphy, 11 December 1952, "Latin America and U.S. Policy," PSF: Foreign Affairs File, Box 152, HSTL.

49. Annex to NSC 144, 6 March 1953, WHO, OSANSA, Box 4, DDEL.

50. Smith to Eisenhower, 15 January 1954, AWF, International Series, Box 24, DDEL.

51. *FRUS 1952–54*, 4:1061–71.

52. Ibid., 1091–95.

53. U.S. Congress, *Executive Sessions*, 1954, 6:15.

54. John Foster Dulles, "International Communism in Guatemala," *Department of State Bulletin*, 12 July 1954, 43–45.

55. *Public Papers of the Presidents: Eisenhower, 1954*, 731.

56. Quoted in Rabe, *Eisenhower and Latin America*, 60–61.

57. Immerman, *CIA in Guatemala*, 198–200.

58. 240th Meeting of the NSC, 10 March 1955, AWF, NSC Series, DDEL.

59. Rabe, *Eisenhower and Latin America*, 62.

60. Hoover to Eisenhower, 4 November 1955, "Visit of President Carlos Castillo Armas," AWF, International Series, Guatemala (6), Box 26, DDEL; Immerman, *CIA in Guatemala*, 180.

61. Briefing Memorandum, 1958, AWF, International Series, Guatemala (5), Box 26, DDEL; see also 355th Meeting of the NSC, 13 February 1958, AWF, NSC Series, DDEL.

62. Ydígoras to Eisenhower, 23 August 1960; Herter to Eisenhower, 10 September 1960; Eisenhower to Ydígoras, 12 September 1960, AWF, International Series, Guatemala (2), Box 26, DDEL.

63. U.S. Congress, *Executive Sessions*, 1953, 5:139–40.

64. *Public Papers of the Presidents: Eisenhower, 1953*, 4.

65. Ibid., 258.

66. Ibid., *1954*, 382–83.
67. U.S. Congress, *Executive Sessions*, 1953, 5:386–88.
68. Ibid., 1954, 6:23–24.
69. Ibid., 114–15.
70. Ibid.
71. Ibid.
72. Ibid., 142–45.
73. 177th Meeting of the NSC, 24 December 1953, AWF, NSC Series, DDEL.
74. *FRUS* 1952–54, 13, pt. 1:1250–65.
75. U.S. Congress, *Executive Sessions*, 1954, 6:267–77.
76. Ibid., 642–43.
77. Eisenhower, *Mandate for Change*, 372.
78. Quoted in Gardner, *Approaching Vietnam*, 270.
79. Ibid., 258.
80. Quoted in George McT. Kahin, "Gambling on Diem," in McMahon, ed.,
    Major Problems, 150.
81. Quoted in Young, *Vietnam Wars*, 46.
82. Karnow, *In Our Image*, 346–55.
83. *FRUS* 1952–54, 13, pt. 2:1608–9.
84. Dulles to Eisenhower, 18 August 1954; Dulles to Mendès-France, 16 Au-
    gust 1954, AWF, DH Series, Box 4, DDEL.
85. *FRUS* 1952–54, 13, pt. 2:2085–86.
86. Ibid., 1954–56.
87. 218th Meeting of the NSC, 22 October 1954, AWF, NSC Series, DDEL;
    FRUS 1952–54, 13, pt. 1:1250–65.
88. Quoted in Gardner, *Approaching Vietnam*, 350–51.
89. Young, *Vietnam Wars*, 52–53.
90. U.S. Congress, *Executive Sessions*, 1955, 7:6.
91. Ibid., 1956, 8:160; see also 249th Meeting of the NSC, 19 May 1955, AWF,
    NSC Series, DDEL.
92. Quoted in Baritz, *Backfire*, 96; Olson, *Mansfield and Vietnam*, 74.
93. Quoted in Fitzgerald, *Fire in the Lake*, 114.
94. Quoted in Olson, *Mansfield and Vietnam*, 76.
95. Quoted in Young, *Vietnam Wars*, 58.
96. Rubottom to Dulles, 26 December 1957, and Eisenhower to Dulles, 31 De-
    cember 1957, AWF, DH Series, Box 9, DDEL.
97. *FRUS* 1958–60, 5:226–27, 236–38; see also U.S. Congress, *Executive Ses-
    sions*, 1958, 10:201–55.
98. John Foster Dulles to Allen Dulles, 19 June 1958, Telephone Series, Box 8,
    JFDP.
99. CIA, Memorandum for the Secretary of State, 27 May 1958, Memorandum
    Series, Box 8, JFDP.
100. *FRUS* 1958–60, 5:238–39.
101. 366th Meeting of the NSC, 22 May 1958, AWF, NSC Series, DDEL.
102. Ibid.
103. Ibid.

104. Ibid.

105. Rabe, *Eisenhower and Latin America*, 104.

106. Henry Holland to John Foster Dulles, 28 September 1956, Telephone Series, Box 5, JFDP.

107. U.S. Congress, *Executive Sessions*, 1958, 10:201.

108. *FRUS* 1958–60, 5:238–39.

109. 366th Meeting of the NSC, 22 May 1958, AWF, NSC Series, DDEL.

110. Dulles to Nixon, 19 May 1958, Telephone Series, Box 8, JFDP; for Senate criticisms, see U.S. Congress, *Executive Sessions*, 1958, 10:201–83.

111. Dulles, Memorandum of Conversation with the President, 18 May 1958, Memorandum Series, Box 6, JFDP.

112. 366th Meeting of the NSC, 22 May 1958, AWF, NSC Series, DDEL.

113. Quoted in Rabe, *Eisenhower and Latin America*, 105.

114. *New York Times*, 4 January 1959, 12; see also Rippy, "Dictatorship and Democracy in Latin America," 99–104.

115. 407th Meeting of the NSC, 21 May 1959, AWF, NSC Series, DDEL.

116. Rabe, *Eisenhower and Latin America*, 140–52.

117. Paterson, *Contesting Castro*, 35–36.

118. Quoted in Smith, *Last Years of the Monroe Doctrine*, 94.

119. *FRUS* 1952–54, 4:871–72; Paterson, *Contesting Castro*, 17.

120. See Hunt, *Ideology and U.S. Foreign Policy*; Johnson, *Latin America in Caricature*.

121. U.S. Congress, *Executive Sessions*, 1956, 8:511, 247–48.

122. Paterson, *Contesting Castro*, 25–26.

123. Quoted ibid., 120.

124. *FRUS* 1958–60, 6:21–22; on public opinion and the difficulties the Eisenhower administration faced in continuing to support Batista, see Paterson, *Contesting Castro*, esp. 69–108.

125. *FRUS* 1958–60, 6:77–78; see also *FRUS* 1955–57, 6:865–76, and Paterson, *Contesting Castro*, 109–21.

126. 362d Meeting of the NSC, 14 April 1958, AWF, NSC Series, DDEL.

127. U.S. Congress, *Executive Sessions*, 1959, 11:124–26; *FRUS* 1958–60, 5:80.

128. U.S. Congress, *Executive Sessions*, 1959, 11:207–8.

129. Herter to Eisenhower, 23 April 1959, AWF, DH Series, Box 11, DDEL.

130. *Public Papers of the Presidents: Eisenhower, 1959*, 751.

131. Herter to Eisenhower, 5 November 1959, WHO, OSS, Box 4, DDEL.

132. Memorandum of Conference with the President, 26 January 1960, WHO, OSS, Box 4, DDEL.

133. "A Program of Covert Action against the Castro Regime," 17 March 1960, WHO, OSS, Box 4, DDEL.

134. *FRUS* 1958–60, 5:26–31.

135. Ibid., 79–91; see also 91–116.

136. Ibid., 391–92.

137. "Political Implications of Afro-Asian Military Takeovers," May 1959, Policy Subseries, NSC Series, Box 19, OSANSA, DDEL; "Briefing Note for the

NSC Meeting 18 June 1959," 27 May 1959, with "Summary of Conclusion: Political Implications of Afro-Asian Military Takeovers," 410th Meeting of the NSC, 18 June 1959, AWF, NSC Series, DDEL.

138. "Political Implications of Afro-Asian Military Takeovers," May 1959, Policy Subseries, NSC Series, Box 19, OSANSA, DDEL

139. Ibid.

140. Ibid.

141. Ibid.

142. 410th Meeting of the NSC, 18 June 1959, AWF, NSC Series, DDEL. Quotations in the following six paragraphs are from this source.

143. 450th Meeting of the NSC, 7 July 1960, AWF, NSC Series, DDEL.

144. *FRUS* 1958–60, 5:91–116.

145. Quoted in Rabe, *Eisenhower and Latin America*, 107.

146. State Department Memorandum, "President's Good Will Trip to South America," 16 February 1960, CF, Box 56, DDEL; see also *FRUS* 1958–60, Microfiche Supplement, 5:DR-1.

147. *FRUS* 1958–60, Microfiche Supplement, 5:DR-7.

148. Ibid., DR-9.

149. 432d Meeting of the NSC, 14 January 1960, AWF, NSC Series, DDEL.

150. Memorandum of Conversation between Eisenhower and Herter, 15 February 1960, AWF, DDE Diaries, Box 47, DDEL.

151. Clark to Eisenhower, 21 March 1960, AWF, DH Series, DDEL; see also the discussion of efforts by Senator George Smathers and William Pawley in Dillon to Eisenhower, "United States–Dominican Relations and Their Impact at Home and in Latin America," 12 May 1960, AWF, DH Series, Box 13, DDEL, and Memorandum of Conversation, "U.S.-Dominican Relations," 16 May 1960, WHO, OSS, Box 4, DDEL.

152. *FRUS* 1958–60, Microfiche Supplement, 5:DR-15.

153. 441st Meeting of the NSC, 14 April 1960, AWF, NSC Series, DDEL.

154. Herter to Eisenhower, "Possible Action to Prevent Castroist Takeover of Dominican Republic," 14 April 1960, AWF, DH Series, Box 12, DDEL; see also *FRUS* 1958–60, Microfiche Supplement, 5:DR-20.

155. 453d Meeting of the NSC, 25 July 1960, AWF, NSC Series, DDEL.

156. Rabe, *Eisenhower and Latin America*, 158–59.

157. Memorandum of Conversation, 13 October 1960, AWF, DDE Diaries, Box 53, DDEL.

158. *FRUS* 1958–60, Microfiche Supplement, 5:DR-29.

159. Quoted in Rabe, *Eisenhower and Latin America*, 148.

CHAPTER SIX

1. *Public Papers of the Presidents: Kennedy, 1961,* 1–3.

2. Schlesinger, *Thousand Days,* 769.

3. "Report to the President-Elect of the Task Force on Immediate Latin

American Problems," Adolf Berle, Robert Alexander, Arturo Morales-Carrion, Lincoln Gordon, Theodore Moscoso, Arthur P. Whitaker, 4 January 1961, Kennedy Pre-Presidential Papers, Box 1074, JFKL.

4. Ibid.

5. Ibid.

6. Quoted in Schlesinger, *Thousand Days*, 766.

7. See Park, *Latin American Underdevelopment*, 167–203, for an excellent summary of this material.

8. Rostow, *Stages of Economic Growth*, 2, 166.

9. Rostow, "Guerilla Warfare in the Underdeveloped Areas," *Department of State Bulletin*, 7 August 1961, 234–37.

10. Rostow to Kennedy, 2 March 1961, NSF, Box 215, JFKL.

11. Schlesinger, "On Heroic Leadership."

12. Schlesinger to Kennedy, 10 March 1961, NSF, Box 215, JFKL (emphasis in the original).

13. Ibid.

14. Ibid. (emphasis in the original).

15. *Public Papers of the Presidents: Kennedy, 1961*, 170–75.

16. The Charter of Punta del Este and accompanying Declaration are in *Department of State Bulletin*, 11 September 1961, 462–69.

17. *Public Papers of the Presidents: Kennedy, 1962*, 223.

18. Quoted in Schlesinger, *Thousand Days*, 768–69.

19. Schlesinger to Bundy and Rostow, 15 March 1961, NSF, Box 215, JFKL.

20. "Report to the President-Elect of the Task Force on Immediate Latin American Problems," 4 January 1961, Kennedy Pre-Presidential Papers, Box 1074, JFKL.

21. Schlesinger, *Thousand Days*, 785–87.

22. "Report to the President-Elect of the Task Force on Immediate Latin American Problems," 4 January 1961, Kennedy Pre-Presidential Papers, Box 1074, JFKL.

23. Rusk to Kennedy, 15 February 1961, NSF:CO, Box 66, JFKL.

24. Murphy to Bundy, 16 April 1961; Bundy to Kennedy, 2 May 1961, NSF:CO, Box 66, JFKL.

25. Memorandum from the Cuban Task Force of the National Security Council to Bundy, "The Current Situation in and Contingency Plans for the Dominican Republic," 15 May 1961, NSF:CO, Box 66, JFKL.

26. "Report to the President-Elect of the Task Force on Immediate Latin American Problems," 4 January 1961, Kennedy Pre-Presidential Papers, Box 1074, JFKL.

27. Goodwin to Bundy, 8 June 1961, NSF:CO, Box 66, JFKL.

28. Schlesinger, *Thousand Days*, 770.

29. "Courses of Action in the Dominican Republic," 17 July 1961, NSF:CO, Box 66, JFKL.

30. "The Dominican Republic," 12 July 1961, POF, Box 115A, JFKL.

31. NIE, "The Dominican Situation," 25 July 1961, NSF:NIE, Box 8 and 9, LBJL.

32. Rusk to Kennedy, 19 July 1961; Rusk to Hill, 21 July 1961, NSF:CO, Box 66, JFKL.
33. Schlesinger, *Thousand Days*, 769–71.
34. Hill to Rusk, 27 July 1961, NSF:CO, Box 66, JFKL.
35. Rusk to Kennedy, August 1961, NSF:CO, Box 66, JFKL.
36. Hilsman to Acting Secretary of State, 20 September 1961, NSF:CO, Box 66, JFKL (emphasis in the original).
37. "Martin Report on the Dominican Republic," POF, Box 115A, JFKL; see also Goodwin to Kennedy, 3 October 1961, NSF:CO, Box 66, JFKL.
38. Martin, *Overtaken by Events*, 81–83, 89.
39. Ibid., 100; NSAM No. 153, 15 May 1962, NSF, Box 336, JFKL.
40. "Conversation between the President and Dr. Juan Bosch, President-Elect of the Dominican Republic," 10 January 1963, NSF:CO, Box 66, JFKL.
41. *Public Papers of the Presidents: Kennedy, 1961*, 304–6.
42. Quoted in Gardner, *Pay Any Price*, 47.
43. Quoted in Drinnon, *Facing West*, 369.
44. Karnow, *Vietnam*, 214.
45. Johnson to Kennedy, 23 May 1961, NSF: Bundy Files, Box 18 and 19, LBJL.
46. Sheehan, *Bright Shining Lie*, 203–65.
47. "A Plan to Achieve U.S. Objectives in South Vietnam," 16 September 1963, Box 4, Hilsman Papers, JFKL.
48. Gibbons, *U.S. Government and the Vietnam War*, 167.
49. Rusk to Lodge, 6 September 1963, POF, Box 128A, JFKL; "A Plan to Achieve U.S. Objectives in South Vietnam," 16 September 1963, Box 4, Hilsman Papers, JFKL.
50. Kahin, *Intervention*.
51. Quoted in Gardner, *Pay Any Price*, 81.
52. Quoted in Blair, *Lodge in Vietnam*, vi.
53. Quoted in Gardner, *Pay Any Price*, 85.
54. McNamara and Taylor to Kennedy, "Report of McNamara-Taylor Mission to South Vietnam," 2 October 1963, NSF, Box 314, JFKL.
55. Summary Record of National Security Council Meeting, 2 October 1963, NSF, Box 314, JFKL.
56. Gardner, *Pay Any Price*, 83–85.
57. Ibid., 87.
58. "Argentine Relations with the United States and the West," 20 September 1961, NSF:CO, Box 8, JFKL.
59. "Argentine Political Situation," 20 September 1961, NSF:CO, Box 8, JFKL.
60. "Argentine Relations with the United States and the West," 20 September 1961, NSF:CO, Box 8, JFKL.
61. Rusk to Kennedy, 26 September 1961, POF, Box 111, JFKL.
62. Kennedy to Frondizi, 10 January 1962, POF, Box 111, JFKL.
63. *FRUS* 1961–63, 12:363–68.
64. Schlesinger to Kennedy, "Attitude toward the Argentine Situation," 30 March 1962, NSF:CO, Box 6, JFKL; *FRUS* 1961–63, 12:366–73.
65. Rusk to McClintock, 9 April 1962, NSF:CO, Box 6, JFKL.

66. *FRUS* 1961–63, 12:385–88.
67. Ibid., 402–5.
68. Schlesinger, *Thousand Days*, 785.
69. CIA, "Dominican Republic's President-elect Juan Bosch," 2 January 1963, NSF:CO, Box 66, JFKL.
70. Martin, *Overtaken by Events*, 329.
71. Brubeck to Bundy, "President Juan Bosch of the Dominican Republic," 4 June 1963; see also CIA Current Intelligence Memorandum, 4 June 1963, both in NSF:CO, Box 66, JFKL.
72. CIA, "President Juan Bosch and Internal Security in the Dominican Republic," 14 June 1963, NSF:CO, Box 66, JFKL.
73. Martin, *Overtaken by Events*, 601; Schlesinger, *Thousand Days*, 773; *Department of State Bulletin*, 21 October 1963, 624.
74. Chase to Bundy, 12 May 1964, NSF:CO, Box 1, LBJL; NIE, "Instability and the Insurgency Threat in the Dominican Republic," 17 January 1964, NSF: NIE, Box 8 and 9, LBJL.
75. Martin, "U.S. Policy Regarding Military Governments in Latin America," *Department of State Bulletin*, 4 November 1963, 698–700.
76. Ibid.
77. *Public Papers of the Presidents: Kennedy, 1963,* 770–71.
78. U.S. Congress, *Executive Sessions,* 1963, 15:833–48. Quotations in the remainder of this section are from this source.
79. Memorandum, "South Vietnam Situation," 25 November 1963, President, 1963–69: Meeting Notes File, Box 1, LBJL.
80. Mann, Oral History, LBJL.
81. LaFeber, *Inevitable Revolutions,* 158.
82. *New York Times,* 19 March 1964, 1.
83. Chase to Bundy, 19 March 1964, NSF:CO, Box 1, LBJL.
84. *New York Times,* 20 March 1964, 1.
85. Bundy to Johnson, 25 March 1964, NSF: Memos to the President, Bundy, Box 1, LBJL.
86. Moyers to Bundy, 5 June 1964, NSF:CO, Box 1, LBJL (emphasis in the original).
87. Mann, "The Democratic Ideal in Our Policy toward Latin America," 5 June 1964, NSF:CO, Box 2, LBJL.
88. Goldberg to Johnson, 9 July 1964, WHCF: Subject File CO, Box 9, LBJL.
89. "Establishing Relations with New Brazilian Administration," 1 February 1961, NSF:CO, Box 12, JFKL; Weis, *Cold Warriors and Coups d'Etat,* 137–46.
90. Belk to Bundy, 26 January 1961, NSF:CO, Box 12, JFKL.
91. Quadros, "Brazil's New Foreign Policy"; Leacock, *Requiem for Revolution,* 18–33.
92. CIA to White House, 25 August 1961, POF, Box 112, JFKL; Dulles Memorandum, "The Situation in Brazil," 28 August 1961, POF, Box 112, JFKL; Weis, *Cold Warriors and Coups d'Etat,* 146–49.
93. Embassy Rio to White House, 1 September 1961, NSF:CO, Box 12, JFKL.
94. Bond to Rusk, 7 September 1961, NSF:CO, Box 12, JFKL.

95. "Communist Inroads in the Brazilian Government," 27 September 1961, NSF:CO, Box 12, JFKL.
96. Gordon to Rusk, 11 October 1961, NSF:CO, Box 12, JFKL.
97. *FRUS* 1961–63, 12:453.
98. Battle to Bundy, "Visit to the United States of President Goulart of Brazil," 23 March 1962, NSF:CO, Box 12, JFKL.
99. Gordon to Rusk, 27 March 1962, NSF:CO, Box 12, JFKL.
100. Schlesinger to Kennedy, 31 March 1963, NSF:CO, Box 12, JFKL.
101. "Conversation between President Goulart and President Kennedy," 3 April 1962; Memorandum of Conversation, "US-Brazilian Relations," 4 April 1962, both in NSF:CO Box 12, JFKL.
102. Brubeck to Bundy, "Background on Current Situation in Brazil," 30 July 1962; see also Brubeck to Bundy, "Current Situation Report Brazil," 6 September 1962; Hilsman to Rusk, "President Goulart and Recent Political Developments in Brazil," 2 October 1962; and American Embassy Rio de Janeiro to Rusk, 23 November 1962, all in NSF:CO, Box 13, JFKL.
103. NSC, "U.S. Short Term Policy toward Brazil," 11 December 1962, NSF:CO, Box 13, JFKL; Gordon to Rusk, 14 January 1963, NSF:CO, Box 13A, JFKL; on the U.S. role in the overthrow of Goulart, see Parker, *Brazil and the Quiet Intervention*; Black, *United States Penetration of Brazil*; Leacock, *Requiem for Revolution*; and Weis, *Cold Warriors and Coups d'Etat*.
104. Gordon to Rusk, 14 January 1963; see also Gordon to Rusk, 8 February 1963, both in NSF:CO, Box 13A, JFKL.
105. NIE, 10 July 1963, NSF:NIE, Box 8 and 9, LBJL.
106. Weis, *Cold Warriors and Coups d'Etat*, 156–62.
107. Gordon to Rusk, 17 August 1963, NSF:CO, Box 14, JFKL.
108. NIE, 10 July 1963, NSF:NIE, Box 8 and 9, LBJL.
109. "Approved Short Term Policy—Brazil," 11 October 1963, NSF:CO, Box 14, JFKL.
110. Read to Bundy, 6 January 1964, NSF:CO, Box 9, LBJL; see also McCone to Johnson, 8 January 1964, "Latin American Situation Report," NSF:CO, Box 1, LBJL.
111. Chase to Bundy, "Chiefs of Mission Conference," 19 March 1964, NSF:CO, Box 1, LBJL.
112. Department of State, Memorandum for the President, 19 March 1964, NSF:NSAM Box 4, LBJL.
113. CIA, "Survey of Latin America," 1 April 1964, NSF:CO, Box 1, LBJL; the report was originally prepared for the Chiefs of Mission Conference in March and was updated to account for the coup in Brazil. See Cline to Bundy, 17 April 1964, NSF:CO, Box 1, LBJL.
114. CIA, "Survey of Latin America," 1 April 1964, NSF:CO, Box 1, LBJL.
115. NSC Meeting No. 525, 2 April 1964, NSF: NSC Meetings File, Box 1, LBJL.
116. Beschloss, ed., *Taking Charge*, 306.
117. NSC Meeting No. 526, 3 April 1964, NSF: NSC Meetings File, Box 1, LBJL.

118. Quoted in Black, "Lincoln Gordon and Brazil's Military Counter-revolution," in Ronning and Vannucci, eds., *Ambassadors in Foreign Policy*, 106.

119. For examples, see Bundy to Johnson, 9 July 1964, NSF:CO, Box 2, LBJL; CIA, "Summary," 29 July 1964, NSF:CO, Box 10, LBJL; and CIA, "The Role of the Military in the Brazilian Government," 26 March 1965, NSF:CO, Box 10, LBJL.

120. NSC Meeting No. 526, 3 April 1964, NSF: NSC Meetings File, Box 1, LBJL.

121. Draft Departmental Statement, 3 April 1964, NSF:CO, Box 10, LBJL.

122. Hughes to Rusk, "Brazilian Military Ministers Decree 'Institutional Act,'" 10 April 1964, NSF:CO, Box 10, LBJL.

123. Beschloss, ed., *Taking Charge*, 318.

124. Gordon to Rusk, 15 April 1965, NSF:CO, Box 10, LBJL.

125. Mann to Valenti, 17 June 1964, WHCF: Subject File CO, Box 9, LBJL.

126. Gordon to Rusk, 10 June 1964, NSF:CO, Box 10, LBJL.

127. Mann to Busby, 17 August 1964, NSF:CO, Box 2, LBJL.

128. Chase to Bundy, 25 August 1964, NSF:CO, Box 2, LBJL.

129. Rostow to Mann, 7 September 1964, NSF:CO, Box 10, LBJL.

130. Bundy to Humphrey, 31 August 1964, NSF:CO, Box 2, LBJL.

131. *Public Papers of the Presidents: Johnson, 1963–64*, 2:1047–48.

132. Bundy to Johnson, 24 August 1964, NSF: Special Head of State Correspondence File, Box 5, LBJL.

133. State Department, "Political-Economic Conditions in Brazil," August 1965, NSF:CO, Box 9, LBJL; Weis, *Cold Warriors and Coups d'Etat*, 168.

134. Bundy to Johnson, 26 May 1964, Bundy to Schlesinger, 12 May 1964, and Schlesinger to State Department, 23 April 1964, NSF: Memos to the President, Bundy, Box 1, LBJL.

135. Chase to Bundy, 4 May 1964, NSF:CO, Box 10, LBJL; Greenfield to Chase, 5 May 1964, NSF:CO, Box 10, LBJL.

136. CIA, "Summary," 29 July 1964, NSF:CO, Box 10, LBJL.

137. Mann to Martin, 1 January 1965, NSF:CO, Box 2, LBJL.

138. CIA, "Policies of the Castello Branco Regime in Brazil," 31 December 1964, NSF:CO, Box 10, LBJL.

139. Bundy to Johnson, 2 January 1965, NSF: Memos to the President, Bundy, Box 2, LBJL.

140. CIA, "The Role of the Military in the Brazilian Government," 26 March 1965, NSF:CO, Box 10, LBJL; see also NIE, "Prospects for Brazil," 12 May 1965, NSF:NIE, Box 8 and 9, LBJL.

141. Moyers to Johnson, "Latin America: Year-end Round-up," December 1965, NSF: Name File, Box 7, LBJL.

142. NIE, "Instability and the Insurgency Threat in the Dominican Republic," 17 January 1964, NSF:NIE, Box 8 and 9, LBJL.

143. CIA, "Survey of Latin America," 1 April 1964, NSF:CO, Box 1, LBJL.

144. Chase to Bundy, 27 April 1964, NSF:CO, Box 1, LBJL.

145. Bundy to Johnson, 9 July 1964, NSF:CO, Box 2, LBJL.

146. *Public Papers of the Presidents: Johnson, 1965*, 1:461.

147. Quoted in Johnson, *Vantage Point*, 197.

148. Valenti to Johnson, 30 April 1965, WHCF: Subject File, Box 10, LBJL (emphasis in the original).

149. Rowan to Johnson, 1 May 1965, NSF:CO, Box 39, LBJL (emphasis in the original).

150. *Public Papers of the Presidents: Johnson, 1965*, 1:465.

151. Quoted in Smith, *Last Years of the Monroe Doctrine*, 128.

152. *Public Papers of the Presidents: Johnson, 1965*, 1:469–74.

153. MacArthur to Marcy, 7 May 1965, with enclosure, Series 8.1/Box 4/Folder 149, FCP; see also CIA, "The Communist Role in the Dominican Revolt," 7 May 1965, NSF:CO, Boxes 48 and 49, LBJL.

154. Gardner, *Pay Any Price*, 210.

155. Mann, Oral History, LBJL.

156. Ball, Oral History, LBJL.

157. Cline to Bundy, "Are the Vietnam and Dominican Crises Linked?," 3 May 1965, NSF:CO, Box 39, LBJL.

158. Bundy to Johnson, "Basic Policy in Vietnam," 27 January 1965, NSF: Memos to the President, Bundy, Box 2, LBJL.

159. Gardner, *Pay Any Price*, 167.

160. Young, *Vietnam Wars*, 135–42.

161. Woods, *Fulbright*, 381–92.

162. Church, "How Many Dominican Republics and Vietnams Can We Take On?," *New York Times Magazine*, 28 November 1965, 44–45, 177–78.

163. U.S. Congress, *Executive Sessions, 1964*, 16:195–96.

164. Ibid., 17:939–53.

165. Fulbright, ed., *Vietnam Hearings*, 52–54.

166. Church, Oral History, LBJL.

167. Schmitz and Fousekis, "Frank Church, the Senate, and the Emergence of Dissent on the Vietnam War"; Schmitz, "Senator Frank Church, the Ford Administration, and the Challenges of Post-Vietnam Foreign Policy."

168. Quoted in Fulbright, ed., *Vietnam Hearings*, 115.

EPILOGUE

1. CIA, "Survey of Latin America," 1 April 1964, NSF:CO, Box 1, LBJL.

2. Chase to Bundy, Memorandum, 19 March 1964, NSF:CO, Box 1, LBJL.

3. Chase to Bundy, Memorandum, 30 April 1964, NSF:CO, Box 1, LBJL.

4. Bundy to Humphrey, Memorandum, 31 August 1964, NSF:CO, Box 2, LBJL.

5. Hersh, *Price of Power*, 260.

6. Kissinger, *White House Years*, 653–57.

7. Powers, *Man Who Kept the Secrets*, 235.

8. Hersh, *Price of Power*, 294–95.

9. Low to Scowcroft, Memorandum, 1 July 1975, NSC:Kissinger-Scowcroft Files, GRFL.

10. Brownell to Scowcroft, Memorandum, 9 July 1975, CO: Latin America, GRFL.
11. Scowcroft to Ford, 17 July 1996, CO: Latin America, GRFL.
12. Miller, "Criminal Negligence."
13. Ashby and Gramer, *Fighting the Odds*, 469–70.
14. See Schmitz, "Senator Frank Church, the Ford Administration, and the Challenges of Post-Vietnam Foreign Policy," for a more detailed discussion of the clashes between Congress and the Ford administration.
15. Note, Kissinger Confirmation, 10 September 1973, 10.6/3/21, Church Papers.
16. U.S. Congress, *Hearings on Covert Action*, 63–64.
17. Johnson, *Season of Inquiry*, 30.
18. Memorandum, 5 March 1975, Box 7, Friedersdorf Files, GRFL.
19. Ford to Church, 31 October 1975, and Church to Ford, 4 November 1975, 10.6/1/21, Church Papers.
20. U.S. Congress, *Covert Action in Chile*, 9.
21. Davis, "The Angola Decision of 1974," 109–24.
22. Minutes, GOP Leadership Meeting, 10 December 1975, Box 2, Wolthuis Files, GRFL.
23. Ford, *Time to Heal*, 358–59.
24. Kissinger to Ford, May 1975, "Strategy for Your Discussions with the Shah of Iran"; Briefing Memorandum for Kissinger, 9 May 1975, both in Box 3, Savage Files, GRFL.
25. Kissinger Memorandum, 5 July 1975; Ingersoll to Ford, 1 July 1975, both in Box A6, VIP Visits: Indonesia, Kissinger-Scowcroft Files, GRFL.
26. Ford, *Time to Heal*, 359.
27. Church, "The Erosion of Principle in American Foreign Policy," 10.6/1/17, Church Papers.
28. *Public Papers of the Presidents: Carter*, 1977, 1–4.
29. Ibid., 954–62.
30. Ibid.
31. Carter, *Keeping Faith*, 143.
32. Kirkpatrick, "Dictatorships and Double Standards," 45.
33. Kirkpatrick, "U.S. Security and Latin America," 35.
34. Kirkpatrick, "Dictatorships and Double Standards," 44.
35. Ibid., 37.

CONCLUSION

1. Fukuyama, *The End of History and the Last Man*.
2. Smith, *America's Mission*, 3–4, xiv.
3. Ibid., xiii.
4. Ibid.
5. Ibid., 304, 267.
6. *New York Times*, 31 October 1995, 3.

Bibliography

PRIMARY SOURCES

Archives

Boise State University Library, Boise, Idaho
  Frank Church Papers
Columbia University Library, New York, New York
  Oral History Transcript of William Phillips
Council on Foreign Relations, New York, New York
  Records of Groups
  Records of Meetings
Dwight D. Eisenhower Presidential Library, Abilene, Kansas
  John Foster Dulles Papers, 1952–59
  Dwight D. Eisenhower Papers
    Diaries
    Papers as President of the United States, 1953–61
      (Ann Whitman Files)
    White House Central Files, 1953–61
  Christian Herter Papers
  U.S. President's Committee to Study the U.S. Military Assistance Program
    (Draper Committee), 1958–59

White House Office
- Office of the Special Assistant for National Security Affairs, 1952–61
- Office of the Staff Secretary, 1952–61

Gerald R. Ford Presidential Library, Ann Arbor, Michigan
- Gerald Ford Papers
    - Friedersdorf Files
    - Kissinger-Scowcroft Files
    - Savage Files
    - White House Central Files
    - Wolthuis Files

Harvard University, Cambridge, Massachusetts
- Baker Library: Thomas W. Lamont Papers
- Houghton Library:
    - William R. Castle Diary
    - Jay Pierrepont Moffat Papers
    - William Phillips Papers

Herbert Hoover Presidential Library, West Branch, Iowa
- William R. Castle Jr. Papers
- Herbert C. Hoover Commerce Papers
- Herbert C. Hoover Presidential Papers
- Hugh Wilson Papers

Lyndon B. Johnson Presidential Library, Austin, Texas
- Lyndon B. Johnson Presidential Papers
    - National Security File, 1963–69
    - White House Central Files, 1963–69
- Oral History Transcripts of
    - George Ball
    - Frank Church
    - Thomas Mann

John F. Kennedy Presidential Library, Boston, Massachusetts
- Roger Hilsman Papers
- John F. Kennedy Pre-Presidential Papers, 1946–60
- John F. Kennedy Presidential Papers, 1961–63
    - National Security Files
    - President's Office Files
    - White House Central Files

Library of Congress, Washington, D.C.
- Richard Washburn Child Papers
- Calvin Coolidge Papers (microfilm edition)
- Norman H. Davis Papers
- Henry P. Fletcher Papers
- Charles Evans Hughes Papers
- Cordell Hull Papers (microfilm edition)
- Breckinridge Long Papers
- Woodrow Wilson Papers (microfilm edition)

Minnesota Historical Society, Division of Archives and Manuscripts,
    Minneapolis, Minnesota
    Frank B. Kellogg Papers (microfilm edition)
National Archives, College Park, Maryland
    Record Group 38: Office of Naval Intelligence
    Record Group 59: Records of the Department of State
    Records of the Assistant Secretary of State for Inter-American Affairs,
        1949–53
    Records of the Deputy Assistant Secretaries of State for Inter-American
        Affairs, 1945–56
    Records of the Office of Intelligence
    Records of the Office of Middle American Affairs: Records Relating to
        Costa Rica and Nicaragua, 1951–55
Ohio Historical Society, Columbus, Ohio
    Warren G. Harding Papers (microfilm edition)
Princeton University, Princeton, New Jersey
    Firestone Library: Otto Kahn Papers
    Mudd Library: Arthur Krock Papers
Franklin D. Roosevelt Presidential Library, Hyde Park, New York
    Adolf A. Berle Papers (microfilm edition)
    Henry L. Morgenthau Papers (microfilm edition)
    Franklin D. Roosevelt Papers
        Official File
        President's Personal File
        President's Secretary's File
Sterling Library, Yale University, New Haven, Connecticut
    Gordon Auchincloss Papers
    Henry L. Stimson Diaries (microfilm edition)
    Henry L. Stimson Papers (microfilm edition)
Harry S. Truman Presidential Library, Independence, Missouri
    Dean Acheson Papers
    Clark M. Clifford Files
    David D. Lloyd Papers
    Frank McNaughton Papers
    Edward Miller Papers
    Records of National Security Council
    Harry S. Truman Papers
        Confidential File
        General File
        Official File
        President's Personal File
        President's Secretary's Files, 1945–53
        White House Central Files
    Oral History Transcripts of
        Dean Acheson

John M. Cabot
José Figueres Ferrer
John Wesley Jones
Thomas Mann

Public Documents and Government Publications

Berle, Beatrice B., and Travis Beal Jacobs, eds. *Navigating the Rapids, 1918–1971: From the Papers of Adolf A. Berle*. New York: Harcourt Brace Jovanovich, 1973.

Blum, John Morton, ed. *From the Morgenthau Diaries: Years of Crisis, 1928–1938*. Boston: Houghton Mifflin, 1959.

Bullitt, Orville H., ed. *For the President, Personal and Secret: Correspondence between Franklin D. Roosevelt and William C. Bullitt*. Boston: Houghton Mifflin, 1972.

Congressional Record. Washington, D.C.: U.S. Government Printing Office.

Council on Foreign Relations. *Documents on American Foreign Relations*. New York: Council on Foreign Relations.

Cronon, E. David, ed. *The Cabinet Diaries of Josephus Daniels, 1913–1921*. Lincoln: University of Nebraska Press, 1963.

Fulbright, J. William, ed. *The Vietnam Hearings*. New York: Random House, 1966.

Hooker, Nancy Harvison, ed. *The Moffat Papers: Selections from the Diplomatic Journals of Jay Pierrepont Moffat, 1919–1943*. Cambridge, Mass.: Harvard University Press, 1956.

Hoover, Herbert. *American Individualism*. Garden City, N.Y.: Doubleday, Page, 1922.

Hughes, Charles Evans. *Our Relations to the Nations of the Western Hemisphere*. Princeton: Princeton University Press, 1928.

———. *The Pathway of Peace: Representative Addresses Delivered during His Term as Secretary of State (1921–1925)*. New York: Harper, 1925.

Ickes, Harold. *The Secret Diary of Harold Ickes*. 3 vols. New York: Simon and Schuster, 1953–54.

Kimball, Warren F., ed. *Churchill and Roosevelt: The Complete Correspondence*. 3 vols. Princeton: Princeton University Press, 1984.

Lary, H., et al. *The United States in the World Economy*. Department of Commerce Economic Series no. 23. Washington, D.C.: U.S. Government Printing Office, 1943.

Leary, William, ed. *The Central Intelligence Agency: History and Documents*. Tuscaloosa: University of Alabama Press, 1984.

Link, Arthur S., ed. *The Papers of Woodrow Wilson*. 69 vols. Princeton: Princeton University Press, 1966–94.

National Security Council. *Documents* (microfilm edition). University Publications of America.

Nixon, Edgar B., ed. *Franklin D. Roosevelt and Foreign Affairs*. 3 vols. Cambridge, Mass.: Belknap Press of Harvard University Press, 1969.

O'Brien, Francis W., ed. *Two Peacemakers in Paris: The Hoover-Wilson Post-Armistice Letters, 1918–1920*. College Station: Texas A&M University Press, 1978.

Porter, Gareth, ed. *Vietnam: A History in Documents*. New York: New American Library, 1981.

Public Papers of the Presidents. Washington, D.C.: U.S. Government Printing Office, 1956–.

Roosevelt, Elliot, ed. *F.D.R.: His Personal Letters, 1938–1945*. 2 vols. New York: Duell, Sloan and Pearce, 1950.

Rosenman, Samuel, ed. *The Public Papers and Addresses of Franklin D. Roosevelt*. 13 vols. New York: Random House, 1938–50.

Schewe, Donald B., ed. *Franklin D. Roosevelt and Foreign Affairs*. 11 vols. New York: Garland Press, 1979.

Stimson, Henry L. "The United States and the Other American Republics." Address before the Council on Foreign Relations, 6 February 1931. Washington, D.C.: U.S. Government Printing Office, 1931.

United States Congress. *Covert Action in Chile, 1963–1973*. 94th Cong., 2d sess., 18 December 1975.

———. *Executive Sessions of the Senate Foreign Relations Committee (Historical Series)*. Washington, D.C.: U.S. Government Printing Office.

———. Senate Select Committee to Study Governmental Operations with Respect to Intelligence Activities. *Hearings on Covert Action*. Vol. 5, 94th Cong., 2d sess., 18 December 1975.

United States. Department of Commerce. *Annual Report, 1915–1921*. Washington, D.C.: U.S. Government Printing Office, 1916–22.

———. *Foreign Commerce and Navigation of the United States, 1921–1940*. Washington, D.C.: U.S. Government Printing Office, 1922–42.

———. Bureau of Foreign and Domestic Commerce. *A New Estimate of American Investment Abroad*. Trade Information Bulletin no. 767. Washington, D.C.: U.S. Government Printing Office, 1931.

United States. Department of State. *Foreign Relations of the United States*. Washington, D.C.: U.S. Government Printing Office.

———. *Foreign Relations of the United States: The Conference of Berlin (Potsdam)*. Washington, D.C.: U.S. Government Printing Office, 1960.

———. *Foreign Relations of the United States: The Lansing Papers, 1914–1920*. 2 vols. Washington D.C.: U.S. Government Printing Office, 1939–40.

———. *Foreign Relations of the United States: Paris Peace Conference*. 13 vols. Washington, D.C.: U.S. Government Printing Office, 1942–47.

———. *The Spanish Government and the Axis*. Washington, D.C.: U.S. Government Printing Office, 1946.

———. *The United States and Nicaragua: A Survey of the Relations from 1909 to 1932*. Latin American Series 6. Washington, D.C.: U.S. Government Printing Office, 1932.

United States. *Department of State Bulletin*. Washington, D.C.: U.S. Government Printing Office.

United States World War Foreign Debt Commission. *Combined Annual Reports of the World War Foreign Debt Commission*. Washington, D.C.: U.S. Government Printing Office, 1927.

Welles, Sumner. *Relations between the United States and Cuba*. Department of State, Latin American Series 7. Washington, D.C.: U.S. Government Printing Office, 1934.

Williams, William Appleman, et al. *America in Vietnam: A Documentary History*. Garden City, N.Y.: Anchor Press/Doubleday, 1985.

Wilson, Woodrow. *The Messages and Papers of Woodrow Wilson*. 2 vols. New York: Harper and Bros., 1924.

Autobiographies and Memoirs

Acheson, Dean. *Present at the Creation: My Years in the State Department*. New York: Norton, 1969.

Bowers, Claude. *My Mission to Spain: Watching the Rehearsal for World War II*. New York: Simon and Schuster, 1954.

Carter, Jimmy. *Keeping Faith: Memoirs of a President*. New York: Bantam Books, 1982.

Child, Richard. *A Diplomat Looks at Europe*. New York: Duffield, 1925.

Davis, Nathaniel. "The Angola Decision of 1974: A Personal Memoir." *Foreign Affairs* 57 (Fall 1978): 109–24.

Ford, Gerald R. *A Time to Heal*. New York: Harper & Row, 1979.

Eisenhower, Dwight D. *Mandate for Change, 1953–1956*. Garden City, N.Y.: Doubleday, 1963.

———. *Waging Peace, 1956–1961*. Garden City, N.Y.: Doubleday, 1963.

Hayes, Carlton. *Wartime Mission in Spain, 1942–1945*. New York: Da Capo Press, 1976.

Hoover, Herbert. *Memoirs: The Cabinet and the Presidency*. New York: Macmillan, 1952.

Hull, Cordell. *The Memoirs of Cordell Hull*. 2 vols. New York: Macmillan, 1948.

Johnson, Lyndon B. *The Vantage Point: Perspectives of the Presidency, 1963–1969*. New York: Holt, Rinehart and Winston, 1971.

Kennan, George F. *Memoirs*. 2 vols. Boston: Little, Brown, 1967–72.

Kissinger, Henry. *White House Years*. Boston: Little, Brown, 1979.

Martin, John Bartlow. *Overtaken by Events: The Dominican Crisis from the Fall of Trujillo to the Civil War*. Garden City, N.Y.: Doubleday, 1966.

Phillips, William. *Ventures in Diplomacy*. Boston: Beacon Press, 1952.

Roosevelt, Kermit. *Countercoup: The Struggle for the Control of Iran*. New York: McGraw-Hill, 1979.

Stimson, Henry L. *American Policy in Nicaragua*. New York: Scribner's and Sons, 1927.

Stimson, Henry L., and McGeorge Bundy. *On Active Service in Peace and War*. New York: Harper and Brothers, 1947.

Welles, Sumner. *Seven Decisions That Shaped History*. New York: Harper and Brothers, 1950.

———. *The Time for Decision*. New York: Harper and Brothers, 1950.

Wilson, Hugh R. *Diplomat between Wars*. New York: Longmans, Green, 1941.

Newspaper

New York Times

SECONDARY SOURCES

Adas, Michael. *Machines as the Measure of Men: Science, Technology, and Ideologies of Western Dominance*. Ithaca: Cornell University Press, 1989.

Adler, Les, and Thomas Paterson. "Red Fascism: The Merger of Nazi Germany and Soviet Russia in the American Image of Totalitarianism, 1930s–1950s." *American Historical Review* 75 (April 1970): 1046–64.

Aguilar, Luis E. *Cuba 1933: Prologue to Revolution*. Ithaca: Cornell University Press, 1972.

Ambrose, Stephen E. *Eisenhower: The President*. New York: Simon and Schuster, 1984.

Anderson, David L. *Trapped by Success: The Eisenhower Administration and Vietnam, 1953–1961*. New York: Columbia University Press, 1991.

Anderson, Thomas P. *Matanza: El Salvador's Communist Revolt of 1932*. Lincoln: University of Nebraska Press, 1971.

Arnson, Cynthia. *El Salvador: A Revolution Confronts the United States*. Washington, D.C.: Institute for Policy Studies, 1982.

Ashby, LeRoy, and Rod Gramer. *Fighting the Odds: The Life of Senator Frank Church*. Pullman: Washington State University Press, 1994.

Bacevich, Andrew J., Jr. "The American Electoral Mission in Nicaragua, 1927–28." *Diplomatic History* 4 (1980): 241–61.

Bailey, Samuel L. *The United States and the Development of South America, 1945–1975*. New York: New Viewpoints, 1976.

Baritz, Loren. *Backfire: A History of How American Culture Led Us into Vietnam and Made Us Fight the Way We Did*. New York: Morrow, 1985.

Barnet, Richard J. *Intervention and Revolution: The United States in the Third World*. New York: New American Library, 1972.

Barry, Richard. "Batista—Ruler of Cuba." *Review of Reviews*, June 1935, 48–51, 73.

———. "Cuba Boils Again—With Two Dictators." *Literary Digest*, 20 October 1934, 17.

Bemis, Samuel F. *A Diplomatic History of the United States*. 5th ed. New York: Holt, 1955.

Berutti, John. "Italo-American Diplomatic Relations, 1922–1928." Ph.D. dissertation, Stanford University, 1960.

Beschloss, Michael R., ed. *Taking Charge: The Johnson White House Tapes, 1963–1964*. New York: Simon and Schuster, 1997.

Bill, James A. *The Eagle and the Lion: The Tragedy of American-Iranian Relations*. New Haven: Yale University Press, 1988.

Black, Jan Knippers. *United States Penetration of Brazil*. Philadelphia: University of Pennsylvania Press, 1977.

Blair, Anne E. *Lodge in Vietnam: A Patriot Abroad.* New Haven: Yale University Press, 1995.

Blum, John M. *The Republican Roosevelt.* Cambridge, Mass.: Harvard University Press, 1954.

Boeker, Paul H., ed. *Henry L. Stimson's American Policy in Nicaragua: The Lasting Legacy.* New York: Markus Wiener, 1991.

Bonner, Raymond. *Weakness and Deceit: U.S. Policy and El Salvador.* New York: Times Books, 1984.

Bowers, Robert. "Hull, Russian Subversion in Cuba, and Recognition of the U.S.S.R." *Journal of American History* 53 (December 1966): 542–54.

Brandes, Joseph. *Herbert Hoover and Economic Diplomacy: Department of Commerce Policy, 1921–1928.* Pittsburgh: University of Pittsburgh Press, 1962.

Buckingham, Peter. *America Sees Red.* Claremont, Calif.: Regina Books, 1988.

Burke, Bernard V. *Ambassador Frederic Sackett and the Collapse of the Weimar Republic, 1930–1933.* Stanford: Stanford University Press, 1964.

Burner, David. *Herbert Hoover: A Public Life.* New York: Knopf, 1979.

Burns, James MacGregor. *Roosevelt: The Lion and the Fox.* New York: Harcourt Brace Jovanovich, 1956.

Burton, David Henry. *Theodore Roosevelt: Confident Imperialist.* Philadelphia: University of Pennsylvania Press, 1969.

Cassimatis, Louis P. *American Influence in Greece, 1917–1929.* Kent: Kent State University Press, 1988.

CBS Reports. "Trujillo: Portrait of a Dictator." 17 March 1960.

Cliadakis, Harry. "The Political and Diplomatic Background to the Metaxas Dictatorship, 1935–36." *Journal of Contemporary History* 14 (1979): 117–38.

Clogg, Richard. *A Short History of Modern Greece.* New York: Cambridge University Press, 1979.

Cohen, Warren I. *Empire without Tears: America's Foreign Relations, 1921–1933.* New York: Knopf, 1987.

Cook, Blanche Wiesen. *The Declassified Eisenhower: A Divided Legacy.* Garden City, N.Y.: Doubleday, 1981.

Cortada, James W. *Two Nations over Time: Spain and the United States, 1776–1977.* Westport, Conn.: Greenwood Press, 1978.

Cosmetatos, S. P. P. "General Metaxas and the New Greek Regime." *Nineteenth Century* 121 (April 1937): 564–71.

Costigliola, Frank. *Awkward Dominion: American Political, Economic, and Cultural Relations with Europe, 1919–1933.* Ithaca: Cornell University Press, 1984.

Crawley, Eduardo. *Nicaragua in Perspective.* New York: St. Martin's Press, 1984.

Cumings, Bruce. *The Origins of the Korean War: Liberation and the Emergence of Separate Regimes, 1945–1947.* Princeton: Princeton University Press, 1981.

———. *The Origins of the Korean War: The Roaring of the Cataract, 1947–1950.* Princeton: Princeton University Press, 1990.

————, ed. *Child of Conflict: The Korean-American Relationship, 1943–1953*. Seattle: University of Washington Press, 1983.

De Santi, Louis A. "United States Relations with Italy under Mussolini, 1922–1941." Ph.D. dissertation, Columbia University, 1951.

DeSantis, Hugh. *The Diplomacy of Silence: The American Foreign Service, the Soviet Union, and the Cold War, 1933–1947*. Chicago: University of Chicago Press, 1980.

Diggins, John P. *Mussolini and Fascism*. Princeton: Princeton University Press, 1972.

Downes, Randolph C. *The Rise of Warren Gamaliel Harding, 1865–1920*. Columbus: Ohio State University Press, 1970.

Dozer, Donald. *Are We Good Neighbors?* Gainesville: University of Florida Press, 1959.

Drinnon, Richard. *Facing West: The Metaphysics of Indian-Hating and Empire-Building*. Minneapolis: University of Minnesota Press, 1980.

Dunkerley, Jones. *The Long War: Dictatorship and Revolution in El Salvador*. London: Junction Books, 1982.

Eisenberg, Carolyn. *Drawing the Line: The American Decision to Divide Germany, 1944–1949*. New York: Cambridge University Press, 1996.

Filene, Peter G., ed. *American Views of Soviet Russia, 1917–1965*. Homewood, Ill.: Dorsey Press, 1968.

Findling, John E. *Close Neighbors, Distant Friends: United States–Central American Relations*. New York: Greenwood Press, 1987.

Fitzgerald, Frances. *Fire in the Lake: The Vietnamese and the Americans in Vietnam*. Boston: Little, Brown, 1972.

Foglesong, David S. *America's Secret War against Bolshevism: U.S. Intervention in the Russian Civil War, 1917–1920*. Chapel Hill: University of North Carolina Press, 1995.

Foner, Eric. *Reconstruction: America's Unfinished Revolution, 1863–1877*. New York: Harper & Row, 1988.

Freidel, Frank. *Franklin D. Roosevelt: Ordeal*. Boston: Little, Brown, 1954.

Fukuyama, Francis. *The End of History and the Last Man*. New York: Free Press, 1992.

Gardner, Lloyd C. *Approaching Vietnam: From World War II through Dienbienphu, 1941–1954*. New York: Norton, 1988.

————. *Pay Any Price: Lyndon Johnson and the Wars for Vietnam*. Chicago: I. R. Dee, 1995.

————. *Safe for Democracy: The Anglo-American Response to Revolution, 1913–1923*. New York: Oxford University Press, 1984.

————, ed. *Wilson and Revolutions, 1913–1921*. Washington, D.C.: University Press of America, 1982.

Garfinkle, Adam, et al. *The Devil and Uncle Sam: A User's Guide to the Friendly Tyrants Dilemma*. New Brunswick: Transaction, 1992.

Gellman, Irwin F. *Roosevelt and Batista: Good Neighbor Diplomacy in Cuba, 1933–1945*. Albuquerque: University of New Mexico Press, 1973.

Gibbons, William Conrad. *The U.S. Government and the Vietnam War:*

Executive and Legislative Roles and Relationships, Part II, 1961–1964. Princeton: Princeton University Press, 1986.

Glad, Betty. *Charles Evans Hughes and the Illusions of Innocence.* Urbana: University of Illinois Press, 1966.

Gleijeses, Piero. *Shattered Hope: The Guatemalan Revolution and the United States, 1944–1954.* Princeton: Princeton University Press, 1991.

Graff, Frank Warren. "The Strategy of Involvement: A Diplomatic Biography of Sumner Welles, 1933–1943." Ph.D. dissertation, University of Michigan, 1971.

Green, David. *The Containment of Latin America: A History of the Myths and Realities of the Good Neighbor Policy.* Chicago: Quadrangle Books, 1971.

Grieb, Kenneth J. "The United States and the Rise of General Maximiliano Hernández Martínez." *Journal of Latin American Studies* 3 (November 1971): 151–72.

Hackett, Charles W. "Communist Uprising in El Salvador." *Current History,* March 1932, 843.

Hamby, Alonzo L. *Man of the People: A Life of Harry S. Truman.* New York: Oxford University Press, 1995.

Harris, Brice, Jr. *The United States and the Italo-Ethiopian Crisis.* Stanford: Stanford University Press, 1964.

Hawley, Ellis W., ed. *Herbert Hoover as Secretary of Commerce: Studies in New Era Thought and Practice.* Iowa City: University of Iowa Press, 1981.

Healy, David. *Drive to Hegemony: The United States in the Caribbean, 1898–1917.* Madison: University of Wisconsin Press, 1988.

Hearden, Patrick J. *Roosevelt Confronts Hitler: America's Entry into World War II.* DeKalb: Northern Illinois University Press, 1987.

Heiss, Mary Ann. *Empire and Nationhood: The United States, Great Britain, and Iranian Oil, 1950–1954.* New York: Columbia University Press, 1997.

Herring, George C. *America's Longest War: The United States and Vietnam, 1950–1975.* Philadelphia: Temple University Press, 1986.

Herring, Hubert. "Another Chance in Cuba." *Current History,* March 1934, 656–60.

———. "The Downfall of Machado." *Current History,* October 1933, 14–24.

Hersh, Seymour M. *The Price of Power: Kissinger in the Nixon White House.* New York: Summit Books, 1983.

Hodgson, Godfrey. *The Colonel: The Life and Wars of Henry Stimson, 1867–1950.* New York: Knopf, 1990.

Hofstader, Richard. *Social Darwinism in American Thought.* Boston: Beacon Press, 1992.

Hogan, Michael J. *Informal Entente: The Private Structure of Cooperation in Anglo-American Economic Diplomacy, 1918–1928.* Columbia: University of Missouri Press, 1977.

Hoover, Herbert. *The Ordeal of Woodrow Wilson.* New York: McGraw-Hill, 1958.

Horn, James J. "U.S. Diplomacy and 'The Specter of Bolshevism' in Mexico (1924–1927)." *Americas* 32 (July 1975): 31–45.

Horsman, Reginald. *Race and Manifest Destiny: The Origins of American Racial Anglo-Saxonism*. Cambridge, Mass.: Harvard University Press, 1981.

Howland, Charles P. "Greece and Her Refugees." *Foreign Affairs* 4 (July 1926): 613–23.

———. "Greece and the Greeks." *Foreign Affairs* 4 (April 1926): 454–64.

Hunt, Michael H. *Ideology and U.S. Foreign Policy*. New Haven: Yale University Press, 1987.

Iatrides, John O., ed. *Ambassador MacVeagh Reports: Greece, 1933–1947*. Princeton: Princeton University Press, 1980.

Immerman, Richard H. *The CIA in Guatemala: The Foreign Policy of Intervention*. Austin: University of Texas Press, 1982.

Inman, Samuel. "Imperialistic America." *Atlantic Monthly*, July 1924, 107–16.

Jablon, Howard. *Crossroads of Decision: The State Department and Foreign Policy, 1933–1937*. Lexington: University Press of Kentucky, 1983.

Johannsen, Robert W. *To the Halls of Montezuma: The Mexican War in the American Imagination*. New York: Oxford University Press, 1985.

Johnson, John J. *Latin America in Caricature*. Austin: University of Texas Press, 1980.

Johnson, Loch. *A Season of Inquiry: The Senate Intelligence Investigation*. Lexington: University Press of Kentucky, 1985.

Johnson, Robert David. *The Peace Progressives and American Foreign Relations*. Cambridge, Mass.: Harvard University Press, 1995.

Jones, Kenneth Paul, ed. *U.S. Diplomats in Europe, 1919–1941*. Oxford: ABC-Clio, 1983.

Jordan, Laylon W. "America's Mussolini: The United States and Italy, 1919–1936." Ph.D. dissertation, University of Virginia, 1972.

Kahin, George McT. *Intervention: How America Became Involved in Vietnam*. New York: Knopf, 1986.

Kaltchas, Nicholas S. "Post-War Politics in Greece." *Foreign Policy Reports* 12 (1 September 1936): 146–60.

Kamman, William. *A Search for Stability: U.S. Diplomacy toward Nicaragua, 1925–1933*. Notre Dame: University of Notre Dame Press, 1968.

Karnow, Stanley. *In Our Image: America's Empire in the Philippines*. New York: Random House, 1989.

———. *Vietnam: A History*. New York: Viking Press, 1983.

Kirkpatrick, Jeane. "Dictatorships and Double Standards." *Commentary*, November 1979, 34–45.

———. "U.S. Security and Latin America." *Commentary*, January 1981, 29–40.

Knock, Thomas. *To End All Wars: Woodrow Wilson and the Quest for a New World Order*. New York: Oxford University Press, 1992.

Koliopoulos, Giannes. *Greece and the British Connection, 1935–1941*. New York: Clarendon Press, 1977.

Kousoulas, Dimitrios George. *Modern Greece: Profile of a Nation*. New York: Scribner, 1974.

Krenn, Michael L. *The Chains of Interdependence: U.S. Policy toward Central America, 1945–1954*. Armonk, N.Y.: M. E. Sharpe, 1996.

———. "Their Proper Share: The Changing Role of Racism in U.S. Foreign Policy since World War One." *Nature, Society, and Thought* 4 (1991): 57–79.

———. *U.S. Policy toward Economic Nationalism in Latin America, 1917–1929.* Wilmington, Del: Scholarly Resources, 1990.

Kwitny, Jonathan. *Endless Enemies: The Making of an Unfriendly World.* New York: Congdon and Weed, 1984.

Lael, Richard L. *Arrogant Diplomacy: U.S. Policy toward Columbia, 1903–1922.* Wilmington, Del: Scholarly Resources, 1987.

LaFeber, Walter. *Inevitable Revolutions: The United States in Central America.* New York: Norton, 1983.

———. *The Panama Canal: The Crisis in Historical Perspective.* New York: Oxford University Press, 1978.

Langley, Lester D. *The United States and the Caribbean in the Twentieth Century.* Rev. ed. Athens: University of Georgia Press, 1985.

Leacock, Ruth. *Requiem for Revolution: The United States and Brazil, 1961–1969.* Kent, Ohio: Kent State University Press, 1990.

Leffler, Melvyn P. *The Elusive Quest: America's Pursuit of European Stability and French Security, 1919–1933.* Chapel Hill: University of North Carolina Press, 1979.

———. *A Preponderance of Power: National Security, the Truman Administration, and the Cold War.* Stanford: Stanford University Press, 1992.

———. *The Specter of Communism: The United States and the Origins of the Cold War.* New York: Hill and Wang, 1994.

Levin, N. Gordon, Jr. *Woodrow Wilson and World Politics: America's Response to War and Revolution.* New York: Oxford University Press, 1968.

Link, Arthur S., ed. *Woodrow Wilson and a Revolutionary World, 1913–1921.* Chapel Hill: University of North Carolina Press, 1982.

Little, Douglas. "Antibolshevism and American Foreign Policy, 1919–1939: The Diplomacy of Self-Delusion." *American Quarterly* 35 (Fall 1983): 376–90.

———. *Malevolent Neutrality: The U.S., Great Britain, and the Origins of the Spanish Civil War.* Ithaca: Cornell University Press, 1985.

Loukes, Christ. "Greece's Benevolent Despotism." *Current History*, March 1937, 90–95.

Lyttelton, Adrian. *The Seizure of Power: Fascism in Italy, 1919–1929.* New York: Scribner, 1973.

MacDonald, C. A. *Korea, the War before Vietnam.* New York: Free Press, 1987.

———. *The United States, Britain, and Appeasement, 1936–1939.* New York: St. Martin's Press, 1981.

Mack Smith, Dennis. *Mussolini.* New York: Knopf, 1982.

Maddox, Thomas R. "Red Fascism, Brown Bolshevism: The American Image of Totalitarianism in the 1930s." *Historian* 40 (November 1977): 85–103.

Maier, Charles S. *Recasting Bourgeois Europe: Stabilization in France, Germany, and Italy in the Decade after World War I.* Princeton: Princeton University Press, 1975.

Maney, Patrick J. *The Roosevelt Presence: A Biography of Franklin Delano Roosevelt*. New York: Twayne, 1992.

Mayer, Arno J. *Politics and Diplomacy of Peacemaking: Containment and Counterrevolution at Versailles, 1918–1919*. New York: Knopf, 1967.

———. *Wilson vs. Lenin: Political Origins of the New Diplomacy, 1917–1918*. Cleveland: World, 1964.

McCoy, Donald R. *Calvin Coolidge: The Quiet President*. New York: Macmillan, 1967.

McMahon, Robert J. *Colonialism and Cold War: The United States and the Struggle for Indonesian Independence, 1945–1949*. Ithaca: Cornell University Press, 1981.

———, ed. *Major Problems in the History of the Vietnam War*. Lexington, Mass.: D. C. Heath, 1990.

Miller, Judith. "Criminal Negligence: Congress, Chile, and the CIA." *Progressive*, November 1974, 15–19.

Miller, William. "A New Era in Greece." *Foreign Affairs* 15 (July 1936): 654–61.

Millett, Richard. *Guardians of the Dynasty*. Maryknoll, N.Y.: Orbis Books, 1977.

Millsap, Mary P. "Mussolini and the United States: Italo-American Relations, 1935–1941." Ph.D. dissertation, University of California, Los Angeles, 1972.

Mommsen, Wolfgang, and Lother Kettenacker, eds. *The Fascist Challenge and the Policy of Appeasement*. Boston: G. Allen and Unwin, 1983.

Montgomery, Tommie S. *Revolution in El Salvador: Origins and Evolution*. Boulder: Westview Press, 1982.

Murray, Robert K. *The Harding Era: Warren G. Harding and His Administration*. Minneapolis: University of Minnesota Press, 1969.

———. *Red Scare: A Study in National Hysteria, 1919–1920*. Minneapolis: University of Minnesota Press, 1955.

Novick, Peter. *That Noble Dream: The "Objectivity Question" and the American Historical Profession*. New York: Cambridge University Press, 1988.

Offner, Arnold A. *American Appeasement: U.S. Foreign Policy and Germany, 1933–1938*. New York: Norton, 1976.

———. "Appeasement Revisited: The United States, Great Britain, and Germany, 1933–1940." *Journal of American History* 64 (September 1977): 373–93.

Ogg, Frederic A. "Greece Again Under a King." *Current History*, January 1936, 430.

Olson, Gregory Allen. *Mansfield and Vietnam: A Study in Rhetorical Adaptation*. East Lansing: Michigan State University Press, 1995.

Pach, Chester J. *Arming the Free World: The Origins of the United States Military Assistance Program, 1945–1950*. Chapel Hill: University of North Carolina Press, 1991.

Park, James William. *Latin American Underdevelopment: A History of Perspectives in the United States, 1870–1965*. Baton Rouge: Louisiana State University Press, 1995.

Parker, Phyllis R. *Brazil and the Quiet Intervention, 1964.* Austin: University of
Texas Press, 1979.

Parrini, Carl P. *Heir to Empire: United States Economic Diplomacy, 1916–1923.*
Pittsburgh: University of Pittsburgh Press, 1969.

Pastor, Robert. *Condemned to Repetition: The United States and Nicaragua.*
Princeton: Princeton University Press, 1987.

Paterson, Thomas G. *Contesting Castro: The United States and the Triumph of the
Cuban Revolution.* New York: Oxford University Press, 1994.

———. *Kennedy's Quest for Victory: American Foreign Policy, 1961–1963.* New
York: Oxford University Press, 1989.

———. *Meeting the Communist Threat: Truman to Reagan.* New York: Oxford
University Press, 1988.

Patti, Archimedes L. A. *Why Viet Nam?: Prelude to America's Albatross.*
Berkeley: University of California Press, 1980.

Pérez, Louis, Jr. *Cuba under the Platt Amendment, 1902–1934.* Pittsburgh:
University of Pittsburgh Press, 1986.

Pipes, Daniel, and Adam Garfinkle, eds. *Friendly Tyrants: An American
Dilemma.* New York: St. Martin's Press, 1991.

Powers, Thomas. *The Man Who Kept the Secrets: Richard Helms and the CIA.*
New York: Knopf, 1979.

Pusey, Merlo J. *Charles Evans Hughes.* 2 vols. New York: Macmillan, 1951.

Quadros, Jânio. "Brazil's New Foreign Policy." *Foreign Affairs* 40
(October 1961): 19–27.

Rabe, Stephen G. *Eisenhower and Latin America: The Foreign Policy of
Anticommunism.* Chapel Hill: University of North Carolina Press, 1988.

———. "Inter-American Military Cooperation, 1944–1951." *World Affairs* 137
(Fall 1974): 132–49.

Rippy, J. Fred. "Dictatorship and Democracy in Latin America." *Inter-American
Economic Affairs* 14 (1960): 99–104.

Ronning, Neale C., and Albert P. Vannucci, eds. *Ambassadors in Foreign Policy:
The Influence of Individuals on U.S.-Latin American Policy.* New York:
Praeger, 1987.

Rosenberg, Emily S. *Spreading the American Dream: American Economic and
Cultural Expansion, 1890–1945.* New York: Hill and Wang, 1982.

Rostow, W. W. *The Stages of Economic Growth: A Non-Communist Manifesto.*
3d ed. New York: Cambridge University Press, 1991.

Rubin, Barry M. *Paved with Good Intentions: The American Experience and Iran.*
New York: Oxford University Press, 1980.

Salisbury, Richard V. *Anti-Imperialism and International Cooperation in Central
America.* Wilmington, Del.: Scholarly Resources, 1989.

Schlesinger, Arthur M., Jr. "On Heroic Leadership and the Dilemma of
Strong Men and Weak Peoples." *Encounter* 15 (December 1960): 3–11.

———. *A Thousand Days: John F. Kennedy in the White House.* Boston:
Houghton Mifflin, 1965.

Schlesinger, Stephen C., and Stephen Kinzer. *Bitter Fruit: The Untold Story* of the American Coup in Guatemala. Garden City, N.Y.: Doubleday, 1982.

Schmidt, Hans. *Maverick Marine: General Smedley D. Butler and the Contradictions of American Military History.* Lexington: University Press of Kentucky, 1987.

———. *The United States Occupation of Haiti, 1915–1934.* New Brunswick: Rutgers University Press, 1971.

Schmitz, David. "Senator Frank Church, the Ford Administration, and the Challenges of Post-Vietnam Foreign Policy." *Peace and Change* 21 (Fall 1996): 438–63.

———. *The United States and Fascist Italy, 1922–1940.* Chapel Hill: University of North Carolina Press, 1988.

Schmitz, David, and Richard D. Challener, eds. *Appeasement in Europe: A Reassessment of U.S. Policies.* New York: Greenwood Press, 1990.

Schmitz, David, and Natalie Fousekis. "Frank Church, the Senate, and the Emergence of Dissent on the Vietnam War." *Pacific Historical Review* 63 (November 1994): 561–81.

Schulzinger, Robert D. *The Making of the Diplomatic Mind: The Training, Outlook, and Style of the United States Foreign Service Officers, 1908–1931.* Middletown, Conn.: Wesleyan University Press, 1975.

Seldes, George. *Sawdust Caesar: The Untold Story of Mussolini and Fascism.* New York: Harper and Brothers, 1935.

Seton-Watson, Christopher. *Italy from Liberalism to Fascism, 1870–1925.* New York: Barnes and Noble, 1967.

Sheehan, Neil. *A Bright Shining Lie: John Paul Vann and America in Vietnam.* New York: Random House, 1988.

Sherrard, Philip, and John Kennedy Campbell. *Modern Greece.* New York: Praeger, 1968.

Sherwood, Robert E. *Roosevelt and Hopkins: An Intimate History.* New York: Harper and Brothers, 1948.

Skotheim, Robert A. *Totalitarianism and American Social Thought.* New York: Holt, Rinehart and Winston, 1971.

Skotheim, Robert A., and Michael McGiffert, eds. *American Social Thought.* Vol. 2. Reading, Mass.: Addison-Wesley, 1972.

Slotkin, Richard. *The Fatal Environment: The Myth of the Frontier in the Age of Industrialization, 1800–1890.* Middletown, Conn.: Wesleyan University Press, 1986.

———. *Gunfighter Nation: The Myth of the Frontier in Twentieth-Century America.* New York: Maxwell Macmillan International, 1992.

———. *Regeneration through Violence: The Mythology of the American Frontier, 1600–1860.* Middletown, Conn.: Wesleyan University Press, 1973.

Smith, Daniel M. "Authoritarianism and American Policy Makers in Two World Wars." *Pacific Historical Review* 43 (August 1974): 303–23.

Smith, Gaddis. *The Last Years of the Monroe Doctrine, 1945–1993.* New York: Hill and Wang, 1994.

————. "The Legacy of Monroe's Doctrine." *New York Times Magazine*, 9 September 1984, 46, 124–28.

Smith, Robert F. *The United States and Cuba: Business and Diplomacy, 1917–1960*. New York: Bookman Associates, 1961.

Smith, Tony. *America's Mission: The United States and the Worldwide Struggle for Democracy in the 20th Century*. Princeton: Princeton University Press, 1994.

Stampp, Kenneth M. *The Era of Reconstruction, 1865–1877*. New York: Knopf, 1965.

Stueck, William W. *The Road to Confrontation: American Policy toward China and Korea, 1947–1950*. Chapel Hill: University of North Carolina Press, 1981.

Thomson, Charles A. "The Caribbean Situation: Nicaragua and Salvador." *Foreign Policy Reports* 9 (30 August 1933): 142–48.

Time. "Career Man's Mission." 48, pt. 2 (2 December 1946): 22–24.

Time. "Democracy's Bull." 46, pt. 2 (5 November 1945): 42–47.

Time. "I'm the Champ." 52, pt. 2 (15 November 1948): 38–43.

Trask, Roger R. "George F. Kennan's Report on Latin America (1950)." *Diplomatic History* 2 (Summer 1978): 307–11.

————. "Spruille Braden versus George Messersmith: World War II, the Cold War, and Argentine Policy, 1945–1947." *Journal of Interamerican Studies and World Affairs* 26 (February 1984): 69–95.

Tucker, Nancy B. *Patterns in the Dust: Chinese-American Relations and the Recognition Controversy, 1949–1950*. New York: Columbia University Press, 1983.

Tulchin, Joseph S. *Argentina and the United States: A Conflicted Relationship*. Boston: Twayne, 1990.

Walter, Knut. *The Regime of Anastasio Somoza, 1936–1956*. Chapel Hill: University of North Carolina Press, 1993.

Weil, Martin. *A Pretty Good Club: The Founding Fathers of the U.S. Foreign Service*. New York: Norton, 1978.

Weis, W. Michael. *Cold Warriors and Coups d'Etat: Brazilian-American Relations, 1945–1964*. Albuquerque: University of New Mexico, 1993.

Welch, Richard E. *Response to Imperialism: The United States and the Philippine-American War, 1899–1902*. Chapel Hill: University of North Carolina Press, 1979.

————. *Response to Revolution: The United States and the Cuban Revolution, 1959–1961*. Chapel Hill: University of North Carolina Press, 1985.

Welles, Sumner. "Is America Imperialistic?" *Atlantic Monthly*, September 1924, 412–23.

Weston, Rubin F. *Racism in U.S. Imperialism: The Influence of Racial Assumptions on U.S. Foreign Policy, 1893–1946*. Columbia: University of South Carolina Press, 1972.

Whitaker, Arthur Preston. *Spain and Defense of the West: Ally and Liability*. New York: Harper, 1961.

Williams, William Appleman. *The Tragedy of American Diplomacy*. New York: Dell, 1962.

Wilson, Everett A. "The Crisis of National Integration in El Salvador, 1919–1935." Ph.D. dissertation, Stanford University, 1970.

Wilson, Joan Hoff. *Herbert Hoover, Forgotten Progressive*. Boston: Little, Brown, 1975.

Wittner, Lawrence S. *American Intervention in Greece, 1943–1949*. New York: Columbia University Press, 1982.

Woods, Randall Bennett. *Fulbright: A Biography*. New York: Oxford University Press, 1995.

———. *The Roosevelt Foreign Policy Establishment and the "Good Neighbor": The United States and Argentina, 1941–1945*. Lawrence: Regents Press of Kansas, 1979.

Woodward, Nelson E. "Postwar Reconstruction and International Order: A Study of the Diplomacy of Charles Evans Hughes, 1921–1925." Ph.D. dissertation, University of Wisconsin, 1970.

Wyman, David S. *The Abandonment of the Jews: America and the Holocaust, 1941–1945*. New York: Pantheon Books, 1984.

———. *Paper Walls: America and the Refugee Crisis, 1938–1941*. New York: Pantheon Books, 1968.

Y [Louis Halle]. "On a Certain Impatience with Latin America." *Foreign Affairs* 28 (July 1950): 565–79.

Yergin, Daniel. *The Prize: The Epic Quest for Oil, Money, and Power*. New York: Simon and Schuster, 1991.

Young, Marilyn Blatt. *The Vietnam Wars, 1945–1990*. New York: Harper Collins, 1991.

Index

gua, 50, 51, 57; and El Salvador, 58, 70, 72; and Great Depression, 87; and Foreign Service, 88–89; and Spanish Republic, 98–101; and Greece, 102, 106, 108, 110–12

Bonnelly, Rafael, 249

Bonner, Raymond, 67

Borah, William, 52

Bosch, Juan, 249–50, 258–60, 264, 282–83, 285

Bowers, Claude, 99–100, 130

Braden, Spruille, 127–38, 143–44, 149, 232; and Somoza, 157

Bradenism, 212–23

Bradley, Omar, 166

Brazil: Johnson's support for military overthrow, 7, 268–82; and strategic materials, 173

Brenner Pass, 92

Bruce, James, 143

Bullitt, William, 99, 100

Bundy, McGeorge, 245, 253, 266, 277–79, 281, 283, 287, 294; and trip to Dominican Republic, 285–86

Burgess, John, 27

Burke, Arleigh, 224

Burma, 199

Butler, Smedley Darlington, 26

Byrnes, James, 134, 135, 138, 155

Caballero, Largo, 99, 100

Cabral, Reid, 282–83

Caetani, Don Gelasio, 37

Caffery, Jefferson, 65–66, 79, 215; and Batista, 80–81

Calles, Plutarco Elias, 50

Cambodia, 199

Caribbean, 25; and resources, 28; and imperialism, 47; conflict in, 185

Carter, Jimmy, 292, 294, 300–301

Castello Branco, Humberto, 277–82

Castillo Armas, Carlos, 196; and stability, 197

Castle, William R., 29, 39; and Mussolini, 41, 43

Castro, Fidel, 4; and Cuban revolution, 7, 181, 215–21, 256

Central America, 25; and resources, 28; and Stimson, 47; and Bolshevism, 50; and coffee, 58–59, 67; and Washington Treaty, 64, 71–72

Central Intelligence Agency. *See* CIA

Cespedes, Carlos Manuel de, 78–79, 83

Chamberlain, Neville, 119–22

Chamorro, Emiliano, 50

Chase, Gordon, 266, 283, 294

Chiang Kai-shek, 184

Child, Richard, 32–35; and democracy vs. fascism in Italy, 35–38

Chile, 8, 130, 174, 293, 294–98; and strategic materials, 173

China, 55, 85, 140; communist victory in, 150; and Vietnam, 168, 172; and civil war, 178–79; and territorial integrity, 205

Church, Frank, 228, 253, 296–98, 299–300; criticism of U.S. support of right-wing dictators, 289–92

Church Committee, 296–98

Churchill, Winston, Iron Curtain speech of, 140

CIA (Central Intelligence Agency), 146; on benevolent dictatorships, 163; and Spain, 165; and Eisenhower, 180; menu of covert operations, 186–87; and Iran, 189; and anti-Mossadegh coup, 190; and Guatemala and Cuba, 193; and Fuentes, 197; and Chile, 294–98

Civil War (U.S.), 45, 159–60

Clark, Edwin, 230

Clifford, Clark, 141

Cline, Ray, 286

Clinton, Bill, 309

Colby, Bainbridge, 14–15

Cold War, 7, 124, 126, 139, 142, 143, 148, 180; and maintaining order, 156; and shifting allegiances, 158, 164; logic and strategy of, 168; and Vietnam, 168; and foreign aid,

175; and Eisenhower, 181–82; and
  covert operations, 187
Collective security, 139
Collins, Lawton, 207
Colombia, 24
Colonialism, 125, 127, 140; in Latin
  America, 147–48, 151, 203; in
  Southeast Asia, 168, 170; as anti-
  communist, 171; post–World
  War II, 179; and U.S. support,
  193
Colonna, Ascanio, 123
Communism, 5, 51, 87; postwar
  threat, 5; policy of nonrecognition,
  6; threat of overthrow of democratic governments, 7, 181; in Italy,
  32, 42; in Nicaragua, 51–54, 57; in
  El Salvador, 57, 61–62, 67–69; and
  de Lambert, 68; and *matanza*, 68;
  and Mexico, 68–69; in Cuba, 75,
  78–82; and Great Depression, 87;
  and 1930s, 88–90; and confiscatory
  policy of Spain, 98–100; and arms
  sales, 101; in Greece, 102, 105–7;
  blamed for oppression in Greece,
  110–12; as result of World War I,
  114; as greater threat than Nazism,
  118; irony of policy, 123; and Cold
  War, 124; and Argentina, 138;
  postwar, 140; and Truman Doctrine, 141; and Venezuela, 146; and
  dictatorships, 148; in Latin America, 149, 151; best defense against,
  150; in China, 150; distinguishing
  communist from noncommunist,
  150; and OAS, 153–54; in Spain,
  163, 165; in Vietnam, 170, 171,
  198; conditions favorable to, 173,
  174; vs. nationalism, 175; threat
  to resources, trade, 176, 191, 199;
  agent theory of, 182; and Eisenhower, 183–232 passim; in Iran,
  187–93; in Guatemala, 194; vs.
  United Fruit Company, 195; and
  Guatemalan revolt, 197; in Southeast Asia, 204

Connally, Tom, 134, 143, 165
Containment, 140, 142; vs. democ-
  racy, 144; in Vietnam, 169; in
  Europe, 178
Coolidge, Calvin, 49, 55; and inter-
  vention in Nicaragua, 50–51; and
  Latin America, 153
Costa Rica, 71, 74
Cottrell, Sterling, 262
Council on Foreign Relations, 44–45,
  146, 156
Covert operations: justification of,
  186–87; in Iran, 190; Bay of Pigs,
  193; as only option in Guatemala,
  196
Crichfield, George W., 26
Cuba, 6, 47–48, 127, 214–21, 256;
  Cuban revolution, 7; and Wilson,
  12; and McKinley, 24–25; and
  Theodore Roosevelt, 24–26; and
  FDR and Welles, 75–76; Machado
  and the army, 77–78; U.S. loans,
  78; and Grau, 78–79; and non-
  intervention, 84; and Guatemala,
  197
Cudahy, John, 119
Curtis, Charles, 64–65
Czechoslovakia: Czech Legion, 14;
  Czech crisis, 121

Daniels, Josephus, 11
Darlan, Jean, 123, 158
Davis, Nathaniel, 298–99
Davis, Norman, 91; development
  of appeasement policy, 114; and
  Welles plan, 119
Dawes Plan, 88
Defense Department, and covert
  operations, 186
Democracy, 150; expediency vs.
  ideology, 5; and newly independ-
  ent nations, 5, 146–47; democratic
  governments, 7; and Harding,
  17–18, 35; and Hoover, 20–21; in
  Italy, 35, 39; and "normalcy," 36;
  in El Salvador, 64; and U.S. sup-

port, 66; shift toward authoritarian rule, 86, 127; fear of instability, 87; destruction of in Greece, 107; and fascism, 116, 122; triumph of, 125–26; redefinition, 130; and standard of living, 131; and bipolar worldview, 141, 144; history of, 147; imposition of, 148; vs. authoritarian regimes, 152, 153; under tyranny, 152; evolution vs. revolution, 153; as "political maturity," 153, 156, 181; as anticommunist, 154; and Portugal, 164; and Vietnam, 170; lack of as problem or solution, 173; and history of freedom, 181; as weak and ineffective, 185; and gradualism, 187; in Guatemala, 193

Diaz, Adolfo, 50–53

Dickson, Samuel, 60

Dictators: and modernization, 5; and polarization, 6; redefinition, 108; and FDR, 122; waning of after World War II, 126; and anticommunism, 131; as part of free world, 142; in Peru and Venezuela, 145; and social conditions, 145; as necessary step toward democracy, 146–47; distinguishing traditions of, 148; fostering democracy, 150; as moral embarrassment, 153; vs. democracy, 153; tolerance of, 154, 155, 164; vs. totalitarianism, 156; benevolent, 163; and Salazar, 164; military, 173; relative hazards of, 174; arming of, 176; and Eisenhower's strategy, 180; self-defined, 185. See also Right-wing dictatorships, support of

Diem. See Ngo Dinh Diem

Dienbienphu, 197, 203; as blessing, 205

Dillon, Douglas, 205, 226

Disarmament, 119

Disreputable governments, 127, 128, 132, 155

Division of American Republics (U.S. State Department), 127, 131, 144

Division of Eastern European Affairs (U.S. State Department), 68, 88

Division of Latin American Affairs (U.S. State Department), 46, 62, 75, 81–82, 156

Division of Mexican Affairs (U.S. State Department), 50

Division of Western European Affairs (U.S. State Department), 89

Dodd, William, 101

Dominican Republic, 4, 7, 177, 289; and Wilson, 12; and Theodore Roosevelt, 25; financial supervision, 47; and intervention, 154, 155; and Eisenhower, 181, 213, 227–33; and Kennedy, 236, 245–50, 255, 258–60; and Johnson, 264, 282–86; revolt in 1965, 285–86

Domino theory, 141, 199, 202

Doolittle, James, 187

Dulles, Allen, 210, 217, 229

Dulles, John Foster, 179; on trusting dictators, 185; and gradualism, 187; and CIA and Iran, 189; on Guatemala, 194, 196; on Vietnam, 199–208; and Latin America, 209–14; and Cuba, 214–21

Dunn, James, 100; on Mussolini as peacemaker, 117

Early, Stephen, 122

Easley, Ralph, 40

Eberhardt, Charles, 54

Economic appeasement, 113–17, 121; FDR's doubts about, 118; and Versailles Treaty, 118–19, 121; and international economy, 119; and Munich, 122

Economic assistance, 132; in Iran, 191

Economic development, 5; in Latin America, 29, 175; in fascist Italy, 38–39; in Mexico, 49; in Cuba, 76,

81–83; as tool against expansionist Germany, 91; and Somoza, 157

Economic nationalism, 194

Economic recovery, 10; and Italy, 44, 97; in Cuba, 76; and New Deal, 85–86; and disarmament, 118; global, 139; postwar, 140; and Spain, 166; and France in Vietnam, 170

Eden, Anthony, 120; and coup against Mossadegh, 188, 190

Egypt, 141, 184

Eisenhower, Dwight, 4; and authoritarian rulers, 7; Eisenhower-Dulles years, 173, 178–233 passim; and Truman's "policy of neglect," 179; and anticommunist dictators, 180, 185; promoting freedom and democracy abroad, 181; and racism, 182; humanitarian dilemma, 183; and Iran and Guatemala, 185; and Arbenz as communist dupe, 194; denial of Arbenz overthrow, 196; and Vietnam, 198–208; and domino theory, 199; and Latin America, 209–14; and Cuba, 214–21; and Dominican Republic, 227–33; and military takeovers, 227–33

Eisenhower, Milton, 183, 213–14

El Salvador, 47–48, 57–72; and Hoover administration, 57–58; and elimination of communal lands, 58; and U.S. loans, 58, 65, 70; and coffee, 59–60, 67; first free elections, 63–66; warships dispatched to, 68

Elsey, George, 141

Emerson, Ralph Waldo, 82

Ethiopia, 93, 94–96, 116; and Chamberlain, 120

Europe, 8, 9, 10, 164; cooperation against Bolsheviks, 16; as threat to U.S. interests, 17; and Harding, 18; and FDR, 85–86; three ideological options in, 87; and Mus-solini, 90; economic cures, 92; war as cure, 92; and Greece, 102, 113; achieving peace in, 113; importance relative to Africa, 116; and Truman, 134; and Argentina, 137; and economic recovery, 140; and Southeast Asia, 168, 170; and foreign aid, 175

Exceptionalism, 152

Export-Import Bank, 130, 166

Falange Party (Spain), 157, 160–63

Farinacci, Roberto, 41

Farrell, Edelmiro, 132–33

Fascism, 6; and Italy, 11, 31–45, 87–88; in Europe, 85–124 passim; and aid to Franco, 86, 157–58, 161; moderates and extremists, 89, 97; vs. Nazism, 90–91, 158; and Metaxas, 102, and communism in Greece, 107, 142; compatibility with liberalism, 91, 114; corruption by Hitler, 122–23; defeat of, 125; vs. traditional authoritarianism, 127; in Argentina, 132–35; and anticommunism, 142; in Latin America, 147; as cause of World War II, 157; and Stalin, 161

Figueres, José, 258

Filipelli, Filippo, 40

Finley, Harold D., 64

Fiume, 30–33

Fletcher, Henry, 40–43

Ford, Gerald, 295–99

Foreign aid, 175, 176

Foreign Office (Great Britain), 96, 110, 119, 120

Foreign policy, U.S.: philosophical support for democracy and human rights abroad, 3; support for right-wing dictators, 3, 44, 72, 282, 288–92, 293–94, 304–5, 313–14 (n. 2); stated principles and ideals, 4, 5, 165; ideological support, 4, 102, 144–45; emphasis on order, 6; critics of, 6, 52, 145; equating dictators with freedom, 7; toward Latin America, 7, 12, 47, 209–24, 237–44; challenges to, 8; and Vietnam, 8, 198–208, 250–55, 286–88; and racism, 22; toward Bolshevik regime, 14, 47; and intervention in Nicaragua, 51; protecting U.S. investments abroad, 52, 75, 175; basis for change, 68; and Cuba, 75, 83, 214–21; central contradiction revealed, 86; effects of fixation on communism, 87; three ideological visions, 87; and Germany, 87–88; FDR's Armistice Day speech (1935), 94; no reevaluation of, 97; neutrality in Spain, 97–98; new policy toward Spain, 100–101, 164–65; rationale in Greece, 105; appeasement, 114; and Mussolini's influence on Hitler, 116; FDR's revisions, 123; opposition to dictators, 126; Braden proposal, 127–38 passim; bipolar worldview, 141–42; and Truman, 143–44, 155; the need to appear tough, 149; pragmatism, 150; and popular attitudes, 152; nonsupport of dictators, 155; and strategic interests, 165–66, 194; inherited, 169; hazards of supporting reform, 174; encouraging dictatorships, 176; and military funding, 176; and Eisenhower, 178, 180; post-Castro reforms, 181; abandoning fair play, 187; and Guatemala as example of weak democracy, 193; and NSC, 194; and military takeovers, 221–27; and Dominican Republic, 227–33, 245–50, 258–60, 282–86; and Brazil, 268–82; and Chile, 294–98; and Angola, 298–99; continuity of, 305–6, 307

Foreign Service, 88
Four Freedoms, 124, 125
Fourth of August Regime, 110
France, 88, 92, 94, 96, 97, 98, 105, 159; and arms race, 118; and Welles plan, 119–21; Vichy, 123; and communism, 140, 141, 172; and North Africa, 158; and Franco, 166, 167; and Southeast Asia, 167–74, 198, 203; as paradigm of democratic tradition, 171; and Middle East, 179; recurring crises, 184; and Vietnam, 198, 199, 200; financial aid to, 199

Franco, Francisco, 6, 86, 126, 130, 203; and Spanish Civil War, 97, 100; "not a fascist," 101; recognition of, 101–2; fascist aid to, 116; and refurbished image, 157–68 passim; and Stalin, 161; appearing less dictatorial, 163; as anticommunist, 165; and Truman, 167

Free world, 7, 167; defense of, 172, 198; imperfect members of, 173; and dictators, 176; and CIA operations, 186; psychology of, 191

Frei, Eduardo, 294
French Revolution, 100
Frondizi, Arturo, 209, 211, 256–58
Fukuyama, Francis, 306
Fulbright, J. William, 200–201, 228, 289

Gardner, Lloyd, 13
Garay, Fidel, 70
Gary, Elbert, 40
Geneva Conference (1954), 198, 203, 207
Geneva Conference on Southeast Asia, 198
George II (king of Greece), 102, 107; and Great Britain, 112
Germany, 7, 14, 15, 86, 87–124 passim, 157–59, 164; onset of World War II, 88; as anticommunist force, 90; and League of Nations, 91; foreign policy of, 92; and Franco, 97, 101, 158; pressure on Greece, 112; strength in 1930s, 114; need for natural resources,

Herring, Hubert, 76, 82

Herter, Christian: and Cuba, 218–21; and Dominican Republic, 228–33

Hevia, Carlos, 80, 83

Hill, John, 247

Hitler, Adolf, 6, 86, 89, 91, 130; American optimism about, 90; and Versailles Treaty, 90; and Mussolini, 92–93, 101, 114, 120; as result of World War I, 114; and annexation of Austria, 120–21; and FDR, 122–23; and Franco, 157–58, 161–62

Hoare-Laval peace plan, 96

Ho Chi Minh, 169, 170–71, 172, 199, 288; and elections, 204

Holland, 169

Honduras, 25, 71, 130

Hoover, Herbert, 4, 11, 17, 54; and Wilson, 19–20; *American Individualism*, 20–21; and Thomas Jefferson, 20–21; and El Salvador, 57; position on Far East and Nicaragua, 65; review of accomplishments, 69

Hopkins, Harry, 96

Howland, Charles P., 106

Hughes, Charles Evans, 9, 73, 100; and U.S. prosperity and European economy, 10; vs. Wilson, 15–16; and revolution, 16; and Mexico, 17; and racism, 28–29; and Italy America Society, 31; and Child, 33; and Mussolini, 37, 44–45; Latin American policy, 46

Hughes Doctrine, 64

Huk rebellion, 205

Hull, Cordell, 80, 83, 169; and Nicaragua, 56; and Cuba, 76–77; and prewar fears, 94; "moral embargo," 96–97; on Ethiopia, 97; on cause of war, 115; blocking Welles plan, 119;

Humanitarian problems, 183

Human rights policy, 292, 294, 300–302

Humphrey, George, 185, 202

Humphrey, Hubert, 202

Hungary, 15, 19

Hunt, Michael, 22

Hussein, Saddam, 309

Iatrides, John, 112

Iceland, 167

Imperialism, 46–47, 51, 52, 75, 97, 126, 136; and democracy, 148; and Franco, 158; Dutch, 169; European, and war in Pacific, 169; attacks upon, 179

Independence, in Southeast Asia, 168, 203; readiness for, 169; French to grant to Vietnam, 199, 200

India, 191

Indians, 148, 149, 151, 182

Indochina, 169, 183, 199; danger of collapse, 198, 199

Indonesia, 199

Inman, Samuel, 75

Instability, 147, 148; of democratic governments, 172; causes of in Latin America, 173; postcolonial, 174

Inter-American Council, Caracas Conference, 196

Inter-American system, 144–47, 156; in Guatemala, 196

International Chamber of Commerce, 40

"International Communism," 180; and CIA, 186; and Vietnam, 197

International law, 10, 16

Intervention, 154, 177; and covert activity, 187

Iran, 5, 6, 7, 177, 184, 198, 205, 208; Shah of, 8, 188; and Greece, 141; and nationalism, 179; and oil, 179, 186, 188, 189, 190, 191; and Eisenhower's policies, 187–93; and communism, 188–91

Israel, 179

Italo-Ethiopian War, 93, 94–96; barrier of removed, 117

Italy, 11, 30–45, 47, 86, 89–90,
157–59, 164; Italy America Society, 31; and fascism, 31–35, 87–88,
122; and Facta ministry, 35; and
economic recovery, 38–39, 118;
war debts to United States, 44;
and self-governance, 45; and
understanding Germany, 89; and
Ethiopia, 94–96; and Franco, 97,
101, 157, 160; pressure on Greece,
112; spirit of, 116; and natural
resources, 117; Chamberlain's de
jure recognition of, 120; Badoglio
government, 123; defeat of, 125;
and communism, 140, 141; and
Portugal, 163
Ivanissevich, Oscar, 143

Jagan, Cheddi, 263–64
Japan, 7, 55, 85, 128, 157–58, 170;
and Chamberlain, 120; defeat of,
125; reversal of policy toward, 164;
and Eisenhower, 180; and trade,
199
Jefferson, Thomas, 20–21
Jim Crow laws, 27
Jiménez, Marcos Pérez, 146, 147, 184
Johnson, Lyndon, 4, 233, 236–37;
and military interventions in 1965,
7; and Brazil, 237; and Vietnam,
237, 251–52, 255, 282, 286–88;
and Dominican Republic, 237,
260, 282–86; and Alliance for
Progress, 264–65; and right-wing
dictators, 264–68; and Brazil, 268,
273–82; and military intervention
in Dominican Republic, 284; and
military intervention in Vietnam,
287–88
Johnson, Nelson T., 29
Johnson, Robert, 31–32

Kahn, Otto, 40
Kelley, Robert, 68, 88
Kellogg, Frank B., 43, 54; and Mexico, 49, 51; and Borah's critique, 52

Kennan, George, 140, 141, 149,
150–51, 152
Kennedy, John F., 4; and Castro,
Trujillo, and democracy, 4; and
Alliance for Progress, 7; and Diem,
205; and Vietnam, 205, 208,
232–33, 235, 250–55; and Cuba,
234–35, 250; and right-wing
dictators, 235–44, 260–64; and
Dominican Republic, 236, 245–50,
258–60; and Latin America, 237–
44; and Venezuela, 244–45; and
Peru, 246; and Argentina, 255–58;
and Brazil, 268–73
"Kerensky interlude," 98, 100
Khomeini, Ayatollah Ruholla
Mussaui, 302
Kirkpatrick, Jeane, 302; critique of
human rights policy, 302–3
Kissinger, Henry, 295, 297
Kohler, Foy, 113
Kondylis, George, 103, 105–6
Korea, 198, 203; crisis in, 175; stalemate in, 178; and Iranian oil, 188
Korean War, 166, 167, 183
Korry, Edward, 294–95
Kun, Bela, 19

Labour Party (Great Britain), 63
Lambert, R. M. de, 68
Lamont, Thomas, 31, 40
Land reform, in Guatemala, 185,
193, 195
Lane, Arthur Bliss, 56
Lansdale, Edward Geary, 206
Lansing, Robert, 12, 14
Laos, 199
Larreta, Eduardo Rodríguez, 135
Larreta doctrine, 135, 136
Latin America, 7, 149; and democracy, 5, 148, 152; and Wilson, 6,
12; and racism, 26, 29, 149, 153;
and imperialism, 46–47; dictators
in 1933, 48; Good Neighbor Policy, 73–75, 84, 85; post–World
War II, 126–28, 145; and Braden,

nomic autarky, 115; and Argentina, 134, 135, 136, 143; and dictatorships, 148

Neutrality: of Argentina, 133; of Spain, 157, 158–59, 166–67; of Portugal, 163

Neutrality Act, 94, 96,

New Deal, 85

New Era diplomacy, 11

New Guinea, 169

New Zealand, 199

Ngo Dinh Diem, 7, 198, 205, 206–8, 252, 254–55, 308

Ngo Dinh Nhu, 252, 254–55

Nhu. *See* Ngo Dinh Nhu

Nicaragua, 5, 6, 25–26, 47–57, 71–72, 74, 84, 154–55, 226, 302–3; and resources, 28; financial supervision of, 47; civil war in, 50; and United States, Mexico, and Panama, 50–51; and U.S. intervention, 51, 154; and communism, 52, 156, 176; and Stimson and Diaz, 53; and Sandino, 53–54; and Somoza, 53–54, 157; and Zelaya, 156

Nitti, Francisco, 43

Nixon, Richard, 8, 178, 180, 234, 298, 300; on South Korea, 184; and Shah of Iran, 191; and Guatemala, 197; and Asian tour, 202; and Cuba, 206; and trip to Latin America, 209–12; and Castro, 231; and Chile, 293, 294–98

Nonintervention policy, 73, 76–79, 83–84, 144–45; in Spain, 97, 101, 162; and Braden, 130, 135; and dictatorships, 148; and OAS, 153–54; clarification of, 174–75; and local control, 194

Nonrecognition policy, 57; and Stimson, 64–65; and coup against Martínez, 66–67; and Grau, 79; and Franco, 101–2; and Italy in Ethiopia, 116, 120; and Argentina, 132–34, 137; and Venezuela, 146; history of, 151–52

North Atlantic Treaty Organization. *See* NATO

NSC, 163, 165–67; and Iran, 189, 190. *See also* NSC policy papers

NSC policy papers: NSC-68, 150, 166; NSC 5432/1, 185; NSC 5412, 186; NSC 5402, 191; NSC 144/1, 194, 196

Obregón, Alvaro, government of, 49

Olds, Robert, 50–51, 55

Order and stability, 10; and economy, 10, 21; and Mussolini, 11, 43, 89; and Wilson, 12; and Hoover, 20, 65; and Theodore Roosevelt, 25, 28; and Hughes, 48; and FDR, 48, 86; and Central America, 51, and Nicaragua, 57, 157; and El Salvador, 58, 59–60, 71; and Stimson, 65; and Martínez's *matanza*, 72; and Good Neighbor Policy, 73–74; and imperialism, 75; and Cuba, 83; and Hitler and Mussolini vs. Russia, 92–93; in interwar years, 93; in Greece, 105; rationalization for in Greece, 110–12; in Latin America, 147; and Cold War, 155; and Spain, 165, 167; and financial and military assistance, 168, 176; in Vietnam, 169, 170, 172; vs. communism, 174; and economic takeoff, 175; protecting freedom, 176; and dictators, 185; in Iran, 190, 191; and resources, 191

Organization of American States (OAS), 153–54

Orlando, Vittorio, 30

Pact of Madrid, 168

Pakistan, 191

Panama, 24, 50, 68

Panama Canal, 50

Partido Communista de El Salvador, 61, 67

Paterson, Robert, 143

Patti, Archimedes, 170

48, 86; and nonrecognition policy as regards El Salvador, 57; and anticommunism, 178–79

Resources: in Mexico, 49; and Nazi Germany, 92; and economic appeasement, 119, 123; in Venezuela, 146; for war, 151; in Vietnam, 170; and communist menace, 176; in Iran, 187–91; in Latin America, 194

Reston, James, 251

Revolution, 9, 93; in Mexico, 4; in Russia, 4, 15, 91; in China, 4, 140; and U.S. intervention, 12, 46; local causes of, 12, 75, 142; in Bavaria, 15; in Hungary, 15, 17; and Hughes, 15, 49; in Europe, 16; and Hoover, 20–21; in Italy, 31–45; in Latin America, 48–49, 194; and Coolidge, 50; prohibition by treaty, 52; in Nicaragua, 53; in El Salvador, 57, 65; in Cuba, 84, 180; of 1848, 94; and FDR, 88, 94; French, 100; Soviet movement, 101; in Greece, 112; as result of wars, 114; in Argentina, 135; in evolution to democracy, 146–47, 153, 176–77; in Portugal, 163; postcolonial, 174; relative hazards of, 174; in Middle East, 194

Revolutionary nationalism, 182

Rhee, Syngman, 184, 202, 204, 208

Rhineland, 91

Rhodes, James Ford, 27

Right-wing dictatorships
—defined, 5
—support of: in defense of freedom, 5; after World War I, 6; and economic recovery, 10; and post–World War I Italy, 11; in Central America, 47–48; in 1930s, 48, 86; and Diaz in Nicaragua, 53; and Martínez, 57–58; Republican rationale for, 58; Martínez, 72; in Cuba, 83; and change during World War II, 86; and Great

Depression, 87; accommodation of, 97; and Spain, 101; in Greece, 102, 108, 109; compatibility with Liberalism, 114, 145; questioned, 122; and Truman's policies, 124–77 passim; moral arguments concerning, 142, 144–45, 185; and anticommunism, 144; distinguishing dictatorial traditions, 148, 156; fully developed policy, 149; post–World War II, 161; and Southeast Asia, 168, 171, 198; problematic aspects of, 172; and Eisenhower, 180, 227–33; and Cuban revolution, 181; creates strange bedfellows, 184; as only alternative to military intervention, 185; and Vietnam, 198; and Kennedy, 260–64; and Johnson, 264–68

Rio de Janeiro conference on military assistance, 136, 138, 143

Robbins, Warren D., 59, 60; and Araujo, 64

Rockefeller, Nelson, 127, 297; and Argentina, 133, 134; on dictators and democracy, 185

Rogers, William, 278

Rolling Thunder, 287

Roman Catholic Church, 98

Romero Bosque, Pío, 59, 60–61

Roosevelt, Franklin Delano, 3, 77, 305; and Hitler, 6; and Latin American dictators, 48, 153; and El Salvador, 57, 71–72; and Somoza, 57, 84; and Good Neighbor Policy, 73, 129; worldview of, 73–74; and Mexico, 74; and Cuba and Stimson, 76; and Batista, 81, 82, 83, 84; and fascism in Europe, 84–124 passim; policy toward Germany and European fascism, 86–87; policy reversal, 87; and Republicans, 89; and Mussolini, 89–90, 121–22; on Ethiopia and outbreak of war, 93–97; regret over appeasement, 101; and Metaxas, 102; and Greece, 107; German policy, 113–24; and economic appeasement, 115, 121–22; and peace through trade, 117; and Welles's idea for peace, 118; and interpretation of fascism, 118, 161; and Chamberlain, 118–22; and Hitler, 122; and Argentina, 132–33; and Somoza, 156; and Franco, 158, 160–61; and Southeast Asia, 168, 169; and racism, 169

Roosevelt, Theodore, 16, 53, 305; and Root, 22, 25, 28, 53; and racism, 22–29; and Philippines, 25–28; and Booker T. Washington, 27; and self-government, 45, 52

Root, Elihu, 22, 25, 28–29, 44–45

Root Doctrine, 44–45

Rossi, Cesare, 40–42

"Rossi Memorial," 42

Rostow, Walt Whitman, 239–41, 278; and modernization, 240

Rowan, Carl, 284

Rubottom, Roy, 209, 218

Ruhr, 88

Rusk, Dean, 253, 255, 257, 259, 275–77, 279, 290–91

Sacasa, Juan, 50, 53, 56

Sackett, Frederic, 90

Salazar, Antonio Oliveira, 163–64; on free government in Latin America, 185

Salinger, Pierre, 279

Salonica, 109

Sandino, Augusto, 53–56

San Salvador, 47, 61, 62

Schacht, Hjalmar Horace Greeley, 91

Schlesinger, Arthur, Jr., 241–43, 257–58, 270, 279; tour of South America, 241–42

Schott, W. W., 61–62

Schurman Commission, 22

Scowcroft, Brent, 296

Self-determination, 10; and Hughes, 16; and Giolitti, 33; and Root, 45;

and Central America, 47–48; and Somoza, 57; post–World War II, 125; and American values, 139; vs. containment, 144; and Vietnam, 170, 199

Senate Foreign Relations Committee, 176, 183, 218, 262, 290–91; and Latin American communism, 195–96; and change in Vietnam, 199–200; and Geneva Accords, 203–4

"Sergeants' Revolution," 78

Shah of Iran, 8, 188, 299, 302, 308; as alternative to communism, 189; and U.S. aid, 190, 191

Shantz, Harold, 110–11

Sheffield, James, 49

Sherman, Forrest, 167

Smathers, George, 263

Smith, Earl, 216

Smith, Tony, 306–8, 314 (n. 2)

Smith, Walter Bedell, 183, 206; on Bao Dai, 200

Social Darwinism, 22

Socialism, 21, 32; in Italy, 34–35, 40–45; in Mexico, 49–50; in El Salvador, 64; in Spain, 99–101

Somoza García, Anastasio, 3, 48, 50, 73, 83–84, 302–3, 308; and Stimson, 53, and Guardia Nacional, 55–56; and murder of Sandino, 56; after World War II, 126; and U.S. policy, 154–55; as anticommunist, 155–57; and Eisenhower administration, 184; and stability, 197

Sonsonate, 67

Sophoulis, Themistocles, 112

South America: and trade with United States, 173; and forces of unrest, 184

Southeast Asia, 168, 170, 172; and domino theory, 179, 202; Geneva Conference on, 198; blocking communism in, 203

South Vietnam, 186, 206. See also Vietnam

self-government, 199; and Bao Dai, 200; and strongman, 201; partition of, 203–8; and Buddhist crisis, 252–55
Vietnam War, 286–92

Wal-Wal, 94
War Department, 143
Washington, Booker T., 27
Washington Treaty (1923), 49, 58, 64, 65, 70; Martínez abandons, 71; and Central America, 71
Waterlow, Sydney, 105, 110, 112–13
Waynick, Capus, 156
Welles, Sumner, 71–72, 123; and FDR, 73–76; and Cuba, 76–79, 81; and appeasement, 114, 122; on Versailles Treaty, 117–18; peace plan of, 118–19; and Chamberlain, 118–20; end of Welles plan, 120
Western Hemisphere, 144, 147
Weston, Rubin F., 25
White, Francis, 29
Wilhelmina (queen of Holland), 169
Wilson, Edwin, 71
Wilson, Hugh R., 121; on Italy in Ethiopia, 117
Wilson, Woodrow, 73, 85, 305; and policy of self-determination, 6, 12; and League of Nations, 9; and

Hughes, 10; and Populists, 11; and Mexico, 12–13, 49, 74; and Bolsheviks, 13–15; and Hoover, 19; and Anglo-Saxonism, 24; and Mussolini, 38, 42; and Latin America, 153
Winning of the West, The 24
Wood, Leonard, 24
World War I, 5, 58, 85, 93; and international disorder, 6; and Italy, 34; and Foreign Service, 88; disillusionment over, 114, 117, 118
World War II, 4, 6, 9, 89, 101, 154; and support for Batista and Somoza, 83–84; and change in U.S. foreign policy, 86–87, 142, 145; and Germany, 97; origins of U.S. involvement in, 123–24; implications of victory in, 125; and racism, 148; and Franco, 157–58, 162; and Portugal, 163; effects of, 179
Wright, J. Butler, 83

Ydígoras Fuentes, Miguel, 197; and communist threat from Cuba, 198
Young Plan, 88
Yugoslavia, 31

Zelaya, José Santos, 156